CAPITAL BUDGETING TECHNIQUES

TECHNIQUES

Second Edition

F. M. Wilkes

University of Birmingham

A Wiley–Interscience Publication

JOHN WILEY & SONS

Chichester · New York · Brisbane · Toronto · Singapore

Library of Congress Cataloging in Publication Data:
Wilkes, F. M.
  Capital budgeting techniques.

  Includes bibliographical references and index.
  1. Capital budget.   2. Capital investments.   I. Title.
HG4028.C4W52   1983   658.1'54   83–5885
ISBN 0 471 90184 9

British Library Cataloguing in Publication Data:
Wilkes, F. M.
  Capital budgeting techniques.—2nd ed.
  1. Capital budget
  I. Title
  658.1'54   HG4028.C4

ISBN 0 471 90184 9

Phototypeset by MCS Ltd., Salisbury, Wilts.
Printed by Page Brothers Ltd., Norwich.

'War fever ran high in the New England town . . .'

This edition is dedicated with gratitude to those whose life experience leads to recognition of these words.

FMW

Preface

As the title makes clear, this book is concerned with techniques that may be applied in the making of capital budgeting decisions. It is concerned with the methods available to determine the best use of funds in investment, and is not a textbook in general financial management. *Capital Budgeting Techniques* collects together the various devices and procedures of investment appraisal, develops them, applies them in various circumstances and draws comparisons. While most existing textbooks give brief presentations of some of the methods and allude to others, none gives a comprehensive technical coverage.

The style of approach adopted here is intended to be straightforward and pragmatic. The methods of operational research are drawn upon and novel and recent applications of OR methods in investment appraisal are presented. When possible, an environment of 'effective certainty' is presumed. By this we mean that either (a) the micro-environment in which the investment decision is set has stochastic components which are sufficiently small to be disregarded, or else (b) the investor initially treats the environment *as if* it were certain (for example by using point estimates of data). Under (b) it is not intended that the risk component be ignored, but rather that it is treated in a judgemental fashion or by use of post-optimality (sensitivity) analysis. Case (b) would represent the operating approach of the investor. This in accord with the observation that few businesses and very few, if any, private individual investors actually use formalized models in which risk is explicitly incorporated.

We do not dwell excessively on the theoretical utilitarian background to capital budgeting, and few of the techniques presented in detail require the assumption of a hypothetical perfect market in equilibrium. Such methods are described *en passant*. Rather we choose to take the world as it is; massively and permanently 'imperfect'—in which the use of discounting and programming methods is clearly established.

In preparing the second edition of this work I have eliminated certain gratuitous technicalities, compressed the network and transportation chapters and pruned the range of financial planning models. This has released spaced for a considerably extended treatment of risk and uncertainty in an unsophisticated fashion. This area is now covered in the 19 sections of Chapters 8, 9 and 10. Chapters 1 and 2 introduce the basic methods, apply them in certain well-known contexts and consider some complications that arise. Chapter 3 introduces linear programming in an investment context and Chapter 4 shows the use of methods in capital rationing and financial planning. Many investment problems require integrality, and examples and appropriate techniques are presented in Chapter 5. Chapter 6 gives a composite presentation of distribution and network methods in capital budgeting. Chapter 7 shows how the methods of non-linear and dynamic programming may find application in the capital budgeting context.

I should like to express my thanks to my editor, James Cameron, and his staff at John Wiley (UK) for their encouragement and assistance in the production of this book. I should also like to thank the world's leading expert in scrawl deciphering and pristine mathematical typing, Marilyn Mansell, without whose efforts none of this would have come to light.

Contents

CHAPTER 1

Basic Techniques of Appraisal

Overview
After the introduction to discounting, the basic discounted cash flow methods of investment appraisal are described. More advanced techniques of applying yield-based decision rules are considered. Problems relating to input information are outlined. In conclusion the various types of annuity are considered.

1.1 The Mechanics of Discounting

The making of an investment will require money to be outlaid at some times (usually including the present) while the 'returns' to the investment will be received at other times. Financially, the investment produces a set of changes in the investor's monetary position both at the time that the investment is made and in subsequent years.

Discounting methods make precise allowance for the distance (from the present) of receipts and payments and the notion of discounting underlies the modern methods of investment appraisal. To illustrate the problem and the discounting approach to its solution consider a simple example. Most people would value a promissory note that can be exchanged for £1 tomorrow more highly than one which could be exchanged for £1 in a year's time. But how much more is the earlier dated note worth? This depends upon the objectives of the individual concerned and the opportunities that are open to him. If upon receipt of £1 tomorrow the individual would wish to invest the £1 for a year and earn 10% interest per annum, then the original £1 would have become £1 + £0.1 = £1.1 after one year, and it is this sum that should be compared with the longer dated note. If the investor had received £1/1.1 immediately this would have become £(1/1.1)(1.1) = £1 in one year's time. The guaranteed receipt of £1 in one year's time has a 'present value' of £1/1.1 = £0.9091. Equivalently with the same one year horizon and an interest rate of 10%, £0.9091 can be said to have a *terminal* value (sometimes called future value) of £1. Table 1 shows the terminal value of an initial £1 invested for n years at $100r\%$.

In terms of the promissory note which 'matures' in a year's time, an individual whose best alternative was investment at 10% would just be prepared to pay £0.9091 for the note; it being assumed that there is no possibility of default. Also, transaction costs, which can be important, are

1

assumed to be zero. In other words, a receipt of £1 one year hence if discounted at 10% has a present value of £0.9091. The figure 0.9091 is referred to as the *discount factor* or present value factor and is obtained by reference
to tables of such factors. Here, 0.9091 will be seen to be the first entry
(for $n = 1$) in the column headed $r = 0.1$ (the column) of Table 2 (p. 000).

By a continuation of the argument £1 invested for two years at 10%
with annual compounding, would become $£1 \times (1.1) \times (1.1) = £1.21$ and
a receipt of £1 postponed for two years would have a present value of
$£1/1.21 = £0.8264$. Figure 1.1 extends the results to apply to more general
circumstances.

	Year 0	1	2	3	4	. . .	n
A	1	1.1	$(1.1)^2$	$(1.1)^3$	$(1.1)^4$	. . .	$(1.1)^n$
B	1	1.1	1.21	1.331	1.4641	. . .	
C	1	$(1+r)$	$(1+r)^2$	$(1+r)^3$	$(1+r)^4$	. . .	$(1+r)^n$
D	S	$S(1+r)$	$S(1+r)^2$	$S(1+r)^3$	$S(1+r)^4$	. . .	$S(1+r)^n$
E	S	$S/(1+r)$	$S/(1+r)^2$	$S/(1+r)^3$	$S/(1+r)^4$	. . .	$S/(1+r)^n$

Figure 1.1

Rows A and B show what one pound will amount to with annual compounding (at 10%) at the end of various numbers of years. Row C
generalizes row A for an arbitrary rate of interest of $100r\%$ (e.g. for 25%
$r = 0.25$). Row D shows what a sum of £S invested now would amount to
and row E shows the present value of a receipt of £S for a rate of discount
of $100r\%$.

1.2 Net Present Value and the Individual Project

Investment projects typically generate a series of returns rather than just
one and we might label the returns to a hypothetical project S as S_t, where
the t subscript gives the timing of the return. So that if there are n returns
in all they could be written out in full as $S_1, S_2, S_3, S_4, \ldots$, where S_1 is the
return after one year, S_2 the return after two years and so on. We shall
think of 'returns' as accruing at equally spaced intervals of time and being
the change in the cash flows in various years that are attributed to a particular investment.

The present value of the entire stream is the sum of the individual present values. Thus the present value of the entire n year stream is given
by equation (1.1):

$$\text{present value} = \frac{S_1}{(1+r)} + \frac{S_2}{(1+r)^2} + \frac{S_3}{(1+r)^3} + \frac{S_4}{(1+r)^4} \cdots \frac{S_n}{(1+r)^n} \quad (1.1)$$

which can be written more concisely as

$$\text{present value} = \sum_{t=1}^{n} S_t(1+r)^{-t} \quad (1.2)$$

The terms S_t in general might not all be positive. In order to secure them it will be necessary to invest money in one or more years. If an investment of £K now is required to secure the returns S_t then (1.2) is said to be the *gross present value* (GPV) of the investment and the GPV minus K (the initial outlay) is called the *net present value* (NPV), that is

$$NPV = \sum_{t=1}^{n} S_t (1 + r)^{-t} - K \qquad (1.3)$$

In relation to an individual investment opportunity the single project *NPV decision rule* R1, is as follows:

(R1) Invest in the project if the NPV is positive. Do not invest if the NPV is negative.

It should be noted that if NPV $= 0$ it makes no difference to the investor, so far as present value is concerned, whether the project is accepted or rejected. The rationale of (R1) is that if for a particular investment opportunity NPV is positive this must mean that GPV $> K$. Now GPV is the present value of the returns—it is a sum of money which if received now is equivalent to all the returns in the sense that if it was invested at $100r\%$ it would just generate the stream; an amount S_t could be withdrawn from the investment of GPV in the tth year. £K is that sum of money which has to be forgone now in order to secure the returns. Thus if GPV $> K$ and therefore NPV > 0 this means the present value of the stream of returns exceeds the present value of the money required to secure them. If, on the other hand, GPV $< K$ then the outlay required at the present moment exceeds the present value of the returns that it is expected to generate. The objective of the exercise is to compare like with like, GPV is a single-figure equivalent of the stream of returns.

As an illustration of the use of (R1) consider the following investment opportunity. A company has the opportunity to purchse a machine at the price of £2,200. It will have a productive lifetime of three years, and the net additions to cash flows (after tax and including scrap value at the end of the third year) at the end of each of three years are respectively £770, £968 and £1,331. The company has sufficient funds to buy the machine without recourse to borrowing and the best alternative is investment elsewhere at an annually compounded interest rate of 10%. Should the machine be bought? Insertion of the data given into equation (1.3) gives the NPV of the investment in the machine. It is

$$\frac{770}{1.1} + \frac{968}{(1.1)^2} + \frac{1,331}{(1.1)^3} - 2,200 = 300$$

So that by (R1) the investment is worth while, that is, the machine should be bought.

Of course, projects may generate inconvenient patterns of cash flow, or give returns at monthly rather than yearly intervals and interest may be compounded half-yearly, monthly or even continuously. These are simple enough technical problems to resolve. Modifications would need to be made to the formulae but not the principles of the approach.

The discount rate is clearly very important to the NPV decision rule. For example if the discount rate employed to evaluate the investment in the machine had been 20% $(r = 0.2)$ instead of 10% $(r = 0.1)$, then the NPV of the project would have been

$$770 \times 0.8333 + 968 \times 0.6944 + 1{,}331 \times 0.5787 - 2.200 = -115.9$$

where

$$0.8333 = \frac{1}{1.2}, \qquad 0.6944 = \frac{1}{(1.2)^2} \quad \text{and} \quad 0.5787 = \frac{1}{(1.2)^3}$$

and the project should have been rejected. It should be noted that although the investment in the machine is profitable in its own right in the sense that the undiscounted sum of the returns that it would generate exceeds the cost of the machine, *it is not profitable enough* when there is the opportunity to earn 20% on the money that would be needed to buy the machine. In other words, the discount rate should reflect such forgone opportunities when an investment is accepted. It represents an *opportunity cost* of the investment.

Normally a table of discount factors such as Table 2 is used in the calculation of present value. The following example illustrates a convenient layout for the use of such a table. Below is a schedule of the net receipts and outlays (including tax payments) that would arise if a particular project is undertaken. The receipt in year 5 includes the residual value of the project at that time.

			Year			
	0	1	2	3	4	5
Initial outlay	500					
Net receipts		150	150	150	150	225

The NPV of the project is determined by discounting the receipts and outgoings arising from the project, (i.e. multiplying each figure by the appropriate discount factor) and summing the discounted figures.

Year	Receipt (outlay)	Present value factor 10%	Present value factor 20%	Present value at 10%	Present value at 20%
0	(500)	1.00	1.00	(500)	(500)
1	150	0.9091	0.8333	136	125
2	150	0.8264	0.6944	124	104
3	150	0.7513	0.5787	113	87
4	150	0.6830	0.4823	102	72
5	225	0.6209	0.4019	140	90
			Net present value	£115	−£22

1.3 Terminal Value

In some circumstances *net terminal value* (NTV), is a more convenient yard-stick for projects than NPV. Both measures give the same accept or reject decision for a single project. We define NTV as that sum of money that the investor will have at the end of the project in excess of the amount that would have been obtained had the project not been undertaken. Suppose in the first case above the firm considering the purchase of the machine had had £3,000 available for investment. If the investment is undertaken £800 will remain and can therefore be invested at 10% becoming £880 after one year, when it is added to the first receipt from the project, £770, and carried forward at 10%. After three years of this reinvestment process, at the end of the project the investor will have

$$\{ [(3,000 - 2,200)(1.1) + 770](1.1) + 968\}(1.1) + 1,331 = 4392.3$$

Subtraction from this sum of the amount that would have been obtained had the project not been undertaken $3,000 (1.1)^3 = 3,993$ gives the NTV of the project, that is

$$NTV = 4,392.3 - 3,993 = 399.3$$

Notice that this sum is $300 (1.1)^3$, illustrating the relationship between NTV and NPV. In the single discount rate case and for an n period project this is given by equation (1.4)

$$NTV = NPV(1 + r)^n \qquad (1.4)$$

The example illustrates a point in connection with NPV. If the NPV formula is to be appropriate, funds as they accrue must be reinvested at the rate of discount. This is valid in the case of finance by borrowing too; the returns being used to repay both capital and interest on the borrowed sum. NTV was obtained assuming a reinvestment process, and NPV is obtained from NTV by dividing by $(1 + r)^n$.

1.4 Yield on Investments

The yield of a project, known also as the internal rate of return (IRR) or DCF (discounted cash flow) rate of return, is defined as that rate of discount for which the NPV of a project would be zero. It is that rate of discount, which if appropriate, would cause the investor to be indifferent between investing in the project and not investing in it. In general, yield is i or $100i\%$ where i is given by

$$\sum_{t=1}^{n} S_t(1 + i)^{-t} - K = 0 \qquad (1.5)$$

If this approach to project evacuation is adopted, the yield when calculated is compared with an appropriate 'external' rate—the rate of discount that would have been used to determine NPV. The single project yield decision rule is as follows:

(R2) If the yield of the project exceeds the comparison rate then undertake the investment. If the yield is less than the comparison rate reject it.

It is not always a simple matter to determine the yield of a project since, as can be seen for (1.5), an nth order equation has to be solved. Discount tables can be employed to give an approximate answer, in which case trial values for i are used to discount the project and interpolation can be used between the adjacent rates of discount which give NPV either side of zero. By this means the reader may verify that the yield for the project $-2,200$, 770, 968, $1,331$ is a little under 17%. Figure 1.2 illustrates how (R2) is used.

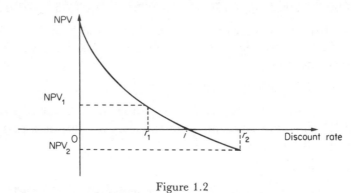

Figure 1.2

The NPV of a 'well-behaved' project is graphed against the discount rate. The figure shows that the yield and present value (and also terminal value) decision rules (R1) and (R2) must be consistent in the one project case. If the rate used to determine NPV was $100r_1\%$, then the project's NPV is NPV_1 which is positive, indicating acceptance by (R1). Also the yield of the project, $100i\%$, exceeds the 'external' discount rate $100r_1\%$ so that the yield rule would also indicate acceptance of the project. If the NPV discount rate was $100r_2\%$ NPV is NPV_2 which, being negative, indicates rejection of the project. Since the project's yield is less than $100r_2\%$ the project would be rejected by (R2) also. The two approaches however, need to be applied with care when several projects are being ranked, but detailed discussion of this point is deferred to section 1.8.

1.5 Multiple Rates of Return

It is possible that a project can have more than one IRR as defined by (1.5), if some of the returns S_t are negative. In such a case of multiple rates it is necessary to obtain a modified IRR for comparison with the external rate. One method of approach to the problem would be to discount positive and negative terms separately. In formula (1.6) terms with subscript h refer to positive components of the stream of returns, and terms with subscript L are 'losses'. Thus NPV can be written as

$$\sum_h S_h(1+r)^{-h} - \left\{K + \sum_L S_L(1+r)^{-L}\right\} \tag{1.6}$$

where the bracketed term is the initial outlay plus the present value of the losses. The expression (1.6) is the 'modified' project for which we determine the yield, i^*, from

$$\sum_h S_h(1+i^*)^{-h} - \left\{K + \sum_L S_L(1+r)^{-L}\right\} = 0 \tag{1.7}$$

Now if the expression (1.7) is positive, (1.6) and (1.7) together yield

$$\sum_h S_h[(1+r)^{-h} - (1+i^*)^{-h}] > 0 \tag{1.8}$$

Therefore $i^* > r$. The converse applies if expression (1.6) is negative.

Figure 1.3 illustrates this method. The vertical axes show net present value, the horizontal axes discount rate. The distance OA is

$$\sum_h S_h - \left\{K + \sum_L S_L\right\}$$

and the distance OA' is

$$\sum S_h - \left\{K + \sum_L S_L(1+r)^{-L}\right\}$$

Note that the NPV of the stream at the external rate is unchanged and that since in this illustration NPV is positive at r then i^* exceeds r.

As an example of a case of multiple rates consider the project

$$-1{,}000 \quad 3{,}600 \quad -4{,}310 \quad 1{,}716$$

Yield is found by solving the equation:

$$1{,}000 = \frac{3{,}600}{(1+i)} - \frac{4{,}310}{(1+i)^2} + \frac{1{,}716}{(1+i)^3}$$

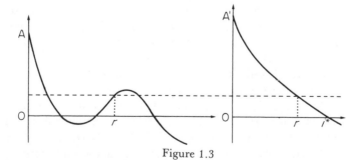

Figure 1.3

Three values emerge: 0.1, 0.2 and 0.3. Now suppose that the appropriate discount rate for determining NPV is 15%; NPV is (slightly) negative at this rate. Equation (1.7) with $r = 0.15$ should now be solved for i^* which emerges as slightly less than 0.15. Thus the comparison of the single, modified IRR, i^*, with the NPV discount rate 0.15 tells us that the project is not worth while. The *extended yield method* discounts the negative returns back only as far as is necessary to obtain a modified stream with no negative components. This method also provides an IRR decision consistent with NPV. For instance consider the project:

$$-200 \quad 120 \quad 194 \quad -55$$

(the initial outlay is 200) where the NPV discount rate is 10%. The extended yield method discounts the negative return in year 3 back to year 2 at 10%. Thus a revised stream

$$-200 \quad 120 \quad 144$$

is obtained, where $144 = 194 - (55/1.1)$. The IRR is found for the revised stream, which in this case is 20%. This exceeds the NPV discount rate so the project is worth while. Both approaches become rather involved when more than one rate of interest has to be used, and add little extra valuable information to NPV.

1.6 Data Input

There are two problems that could properly be considered under this heading. Firstly there is the problem of actually obtaining data by search, calculation and estimation and deciding how reliable are the data. The estimating of costs and revenues in future periods usually involves the use of statistical methods of forecasting, as may the determination of the discount rate to be employed.

There is also the question of the costs involved in obtaining data. Information is not a free good and the quality as well as the quantity of information may depend upon the effort and money put into obtaining it. Although this problem could be formulated as a capital budgeting problem, this is not a particularly useful way to tackle it. We shall assume here that the information expenditure problem has been resolved prior to the other investment decisions being made. Experience may give a good guide to what is about the right level of expenditure in this area and, for some companies at least, the sums involved may be small relative to the other costs associated with the making of capital investments.

The second problem is that of deciding what is the relevant data to include in NPV calculations. The two decision rules that have been examined so far are sometimes referred to as DCF decision rules. What this means is that the data employed in the NPV or yield calculation should ideally be all the receipts and outflows of money associated with a project.

The timing of each receipt and outflow will, given the discount rates, determine the discount factor to be employed for it. In practice it is necessary to use annual or in some cases half-yearly or quarterly forecasts of the excess of revenues over costs associated with the proposed investments. There may be a good deal of doubt about the precision of such estimates, but they are nevertheless preferable to figures distorted by arbitrary non-cash-flow items such as depreciation. A factor such as depreciation can effect cash flow via its influence on tax payments. Only such direct affects on cash flow are considered.

Except where taxation is explicitly mentioned, it will be assumed in the examples employed that the data are net of tax. In reality 'netting the data of tax' may be an involved process. For instance consider just one of the returns to an investment—say S_3, the return in the third year—if the company as a whole is in a healthy profit-making situation then S_3 will be added to taxable earnings. There will then be a cash outflow of $t \cdot S_3$ (where t is the rate of profits tax) when the tax is payable. If S_3 had represented a loss then if the company is earning a profit on other activities the tax bill in total will be reduced by $t \cdot S_3$. On the other hand if the company was not making any taxable profits then, the project would add the full amount S_3 to earnings with no offsetting additions to tax. However, it is clear that at least in principle tax payments can be treated in the same way as other cash flows. The following example illustrates how taxation can be included in a DCF calculation. The data and the tax structure are artificial

An investment project requires the purchase of a machine now at a cost of £10,000. The project will give net returns (revenues minus operating

Year	0	1	2	3	4	5
Outlay and net returns	− 10,000	5,000	5,000	5,000	5,000	
Working capital[a]	− 500				+ 500	
Investment grant[b]		+ 2,000				
Taxation[b]			− 1,500	− 1,500	− 1,500	− 1,500
Net cash flow	− 10,500	+ 7,000	+ 3,500	+ 3,500	+ 4,000	− 1,500
Discount factor[c]		0.8929	0.7972	0.7118	0.6355	0.5674

Notes

[a]Throughout its lifetime the project needs a sum of £500 cash to be set aside for day-to-day contingencies. £500 is taken out of other uses in year zero and replaced at the end of the final year.

[b]Tax payable is computed as follows. Although the investment grant is in fact received after one year, the Government assumes an immediate outlay by the company of £8,000 and allows it, for the purposes of assessing taxation, 'straight line' depreciation of £2,000 in each of the four years of the project's life. Tax payable (lagged by one year) is 50% of net return minus depreciation, i.e. each year's tax will be £0.5 (5,000 minus 2,000) = £1,500. Thus depreciation is relevant to cash flow calculations in so far as it affects tax payments.

[c]In determining these weights the usual assumption is made that returns occur at year-ends, e.g. the £7,000 comes in one year after the project is started.

Figure 1.4

costs) of £5,000 in each of the next four years. The problem is to decide whether the investment is worth while after having made allowance for taxation and investment grant, and provision for working capital. By including working capital it is being assumed that there will be minor cash flow items that it is not possible to include in the original NPV calculation. The rate of discount employed is 12% ($r = 0.12$). As can be seen from Figure 1.4 the data that are eventually used for the DCF calculations are rather different from the original outlay and return figures.

The NPV of the project is therefore £7,000 × 0.8929 + 3,500 × 0.7972 + 3,500 × 0.7118 + 4,000 × 0.6355 − 1.500 × 0.5674 − 1.0 × 10,500 = £2722.7 and the investment in the machine is justified.

If the project is to be evaluated using (R2) then the yield, $100i\%$, would have to be found by numerical methods. The equation is

$$- 10,500(1 + i)^5 + 7,000(1 + i)^4 + 3,500(1 + i)^3$$
$$+ 3,500(1 + i)^2 + 4,000(1 + i) - 1,500 = 0 \qquad (1.9)$$

The emergent value of i is 0.268, in percentage terms the yield of the investment is 26.8%, well in excess of the discount rate, 12%, so that the project should be accepted.

Data should allow for any external effects than an investment may have elsewhere in the firm. For example, if a manufacturer established a new plant to produce a new product, the annual net cash flows on which were estimated at £1m. but the product competed with other models in the range consequently reducing cash flows elsewhere in the organization by £150,000 then the appropriate figure to use in an NPV assessment of the new plant is £850,000.

Opportunity costs should be taken into account. The opportunity cost of a course of action is defined as the value of the best alternative that is forgone. For instance, if a firm could, with the resources at its disposal, manufacture either monochrome TV sets or colour TV sets, but to manufacture both was impracticable, then the opportunity cost of producing monochrome sets is the cash flows that would have resulted from in the manufacture of colour sets.

To illustrate how opportunity costs can be included in the data within a single project framework, consider the case of a firm that has a building which can be either used to house extra machinery of its own or rented out for three years at £250 a year as storage space to an outsider. The machinery would cost £1,000 and last for three years and give net returns of £600 in each year. But if the machinery is installed the rental moneys are forgone, so that the returns from the machinery each year over and above what would otherwise have been made are £350. The firm therefore should evaluate the single project (C).

	Year 0	Year 1	Year 2	Year 3
C:	− 1,000	350	350	350

which comes to exactly the same thing as choosing between the original
projects of

A:	– 1,000	600	600	600

and

B:	0	250	250	250

If a 10% rate of discount (which itself represents an opportunity cost)
is appropriate the firm is best advised to rent out the building since the
NPV of C emerges as – 129.6. This is not to say that the machinery will
make an over-the-counter loss, in fact the NPV of A is + 492.1. The point
is that A is not profitable enough since if it is adopted then B is forgone
and B has an NPV of + 621.7. A further example in the context of make
or buy is given on page 44.

1.7 The Discount Rate

In section 1.3 we saw that the viability of a project could hinge crucially
on the value of the discount rate that was applied in the present value
calculations. In section 1.2 we introduced an example where the investor
had retained earnings. A yield of 10% could be achieved as an alternative
to investment in the project. It is natural to argue that if no superior alternatives exist, a desirable project should show a positive NPV when discounted at this rate—the *opportunity cost* rate. In fact certain conditions
need to be met before such a step is taken. These relate to the unrestricted
possibility of movement of funds through time at the discount rate. These
conditions are discussed in section 2.3.

Except where risk and uncertainty are explicitly discussed (mainly
Chapters 8, 9 and 10) we shall be assuming 'effective certainty'. By this
we mean either that (a) the micro-environment in which the investment
decision is set has stochastic components which are so small as to be safely
disregardable, or that (b) the investor initially treats the environment *as
if* it were certain (uses point estimate data). Under (b) we do not say that
the risk component is ignored, but that it is treated in judgemental
fashion or by use of post-optimality (sensitivity) analysis. Case (b) would
represent a pragmatic operating decision of the investor. Under conditions of effective certainty the choice of discount rate will be a relatively
straightforward matter—as in the case of the example of section 1.2.

Outside of 'effective certainty' the discount rate or *cost of capital* problem is rarely so simple. It is a 'tangled skein viewed darkly'. There are
various sources of money, frequently with interdependent costs. These
costs themselves, and how they are related, cannot always be clearly identified. In actual usage any approach—be it cost of capital or capital asset
pricing model— will require numerous assumptions and approximations.
Gordon's (1962) broad brush definition is that the cost of capital to a firm
is that discount rate with the property than an investment which has a

yield above (below) this rate will raise (lower) the value of the firm. Few would query this in principle, but there is no single agreed method by which a precise figure can be arrived at.

In practice it is most common to use a *weighted average* approach to the cost of capital problem. When there are several sources of funds the overall cost is obtained by weighting the cost from each source by the preportion of the total funds that it constitutes. The three principal sources of long-term funds are retained earnings, equity (share capital) and debt. When real-world factors such as taxation are taken into account the balance between the sources (the capital structure) is important. The reader is referred to Samuels and Wilkes (1981) for full description of the cost of capital problem. However, as a résumé of the weighted average approach, the overall cost of capital would be $100r\%$, where

$$r = \sum_{i=1}^{n} w_i r_i \tag{1.10}$$

and where $100r_i\%$ is the cost of the ith source, w_i being the proportion of total funds made up by the ith source. Where equity (share capital) and debt (fixed interest loan stock) are the two sources the particular form of (1.10) would be most conveniently expressed as

$$r = \frac{v_1 r_1 + v_2 r_2}{v_1 + v_2} \tag{1.11}$$

where, in (1.11), $r_1 =$ cost of equity capital, $r_2 =$ cost of debt capital, $v_1 =$ market value of equity, $v_2 =$ market value of debt, $r =$ overall weighted average cost (WACC). In relation to (1.10):

$$w_1 = \frac{v_1}{v_1 + v_2}, \qquad w_2 = \frac{v_2}{v_1 + v_2}$$

There are numerous measurement problems, both in terms of the costs of the sources and the market values. There are many intermediate types of securities (preference shares, convertibles) which can rarely be costed with precision. The costs of the various sources may be project-specific and will be interdependent. For example, we can write

$$r_1 = f(r_1^0, g) \tag{1.12}$$

where, in (1.12), g is the *gearing ratio*, given by

$$g = \frac{v_2}{v_1} \tag{1.13}$$

and where r_1^0 is the cost of equity with zero gearing. Equity costs will rise as gearing rises due to the compensation necessary for increased variability of funds available for dividend after fixed commitments have been met. That is:

$$\frac{dr_1}{dg} > 0 \tag{1.14}$$

Substitution of (1.12) and (1.13) into (1.11) produces:

$$
\begin{aligned}
r &= \frac{v_1 f(r_1^0, g) + v_2 r_2}{v_1 + v_2} \\
&= \frac{v_1 f(r_1^0, g) + g v_1 r_2}{v_1 + g v_1} \\
&= \frac{f(r_1^0, g) + g r_2}{(1 + g)}
\end{aligned} \tag{1.15}
$$

In (1.15) the only variable is g. Proponents of the cost of capital model argue that r should now be minimised with respect to g. Thus:

$$\frac{dr}{dg} = \frac{(1 + g)\left(\dfrac{dr_1}{dg} + r_2\right) - [f(r_1^0, g) + g r_2]}{(1 + g)^2} = 0 \tag{1.16}$$

Opponents of the cost of capital model (such as Modigliani and Miller in the first instance) have argued that (1.16) is not an equilibrium condition but a truism. For a hypothetical perfect market in a taxless world this is indeed the case; the relative costs of debt and equity change in such a way as to keep the overall average constant. In the real world it is *not* the case, and the value of dr/dg is a matter for empirical measurement. Continuing on from (1.16), since $(1 + g) \neq 0$, at the optimal level of gearing

$$(1 + g)\left(\frac{dr_1}{dg} + r_2\right) - [f(r_1^0, g) + g r_2] = 0 \tag{1.17}$$

On re-arrangement, (1.17) gives:

$$\frac{dr_1}{dg} + r_2 = \frac{f(r_1^0, g) + g r_2}{(1 + g)} \tag{1.18}$$

That is:

$$r = \frac{dr_1}{dg} + r_2 \tag{1.19}$$

In (1.19) the right hand side is the marginal cost of increased gearing, and (1.19) as a whole states the result that for the average to be at a minimum, marginal must equal average. (1.19) is the equilibrium requirement for minimum average cost of capital.

The present book is not a text on general financial management (see, for example, Samuels and Wilkes) and we shall not go further into the cost of capital debate. Rather we are here concerned with quantitative techniques in the deployment of funds and r will be assumed to have been determined as appropriate to the circumstances of the investor. This is not to say that we shall be ignoring the consequences of uncertainties regarding r or variability in r. Stochastic discount rates are discussed in section 9.4, and the sensitivity analysis approach to interest rate uncertainties is discussed in section 9.1. The consequences of a known *term structure* of rates are adduced under 1.10 while discount rates and dual values in capital rationing are discussed in section 4.1. The cost of capital and asset pricing approaches are compared in section 10.7.

1.8 The Ranking of Projects

Both the NPV and yield decision rules can be extended to apply to problems involving choices from amongst several projects. The problem of choice may be that of selecting all worthwhile projects or choosing from amongst mutually exclusive ones. Using an NPV rule in the former case, all projects with positive NPV are selected and in the latter case the projects with the greater NPVs are preferred. These rules can be stated formally as:

(R3) Accept all projects with positive NPV. Reject those with negative NPV.

(R4) If m projects are to be selected from a group of n, select those

m projects which have the greatest NPVs.

In stating (R4) as above it is being assumed that the m projects selected all have positive (or at least non-negative NPVs). This assumption can be dropped in the case where m projects *must* be accepted

Using a yield approach all projects with yields greater than the NPV discount rate would be worthwhile

(R5) Accept all projects with yields greater than the comparison discount rate. Reject projects with yields less than the comparison rate.

The yield approach to mutually exclusive projects is via the incremental yield method discussed below.

To illustrate the use of the rules (R3) to (R5) consider the four projects shown in Figure 1.5.

The first entry in each row of the 'Returns' column is the initial outlay

Project	Returns			NPV (10%)	NPV (25%)	NPV (30%)	NPV (35%)	IRR (%)
A	−100	80	60	22.3	2.4	−3	−7.8	27.2
B	−120	40	100	−1.0	−24.0	−30.1	−35.5	9.5
C	−60	40	50	17.7	4.0	0.4	−2.9	30.5
D	−30	30	20	13.8	6.8	4.9	3.2	45.7

Figure 1.5

in pounds for the project concerned and the two positive returns arrive after one and two years respectively. Recalling that the NPV discount rate is the comparison rate for the yields, both (R3) and (R5) would select A, C, and D and reject project B at either the 10% or 25% rates of discount. When the discount rate is 30% both would select C and D and at 35% both would choose only project D. There is no conflict between the two rules when all worthwhile projects can be accepted. At the 10% discount rate the full ordering by NPV is A, C, D, B, whilst at the 25%, 30% and 35% rates the ordering in terms of NPV is D, C, A, B. That the NPV ordering changes does not discredit the NPV rule since conditions have changed. The changed discount rate affects different projects to different degrees. In general, projects with their greater returns in the more distant future will be affected more by a rise in the discount rate than projects with the larger returns near to the starts of the projects. If two projects were to be selected from the four with the 10% discount rate (R4) would select projects A and C. This will also be the outcome of a correctly applied yield approach.

Suppose that A and C were mutually exclusive and the discount rate was 10%. A might be 'build the warehouse for the Midlands area in Nottingham' and C 'build the warehouse for the Midlands area in Leicester', only one warehouse being required. Consequently, if one project is to be chosen from the group comprising A and C then the (R4) would select A if the discount rate was 10%, Figure 1.6 illustrates the choice situation.

The incremental yield method gives decisions consistent with the NPV rule. A is the more expensive of the two in that it requires an extra £40 immediate investment. Define the incremental project as A *minus* C. Call this project I, that is

	A	− 100	80	60
	C	− 60	40	50
A − C =	I	− 40	40	10

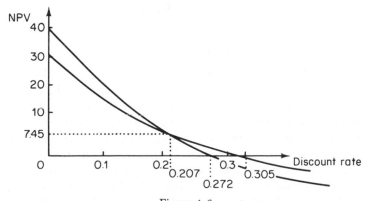

Figure 1.6

The yield of the incremental project is now determined and this rate is compared to the NPV discount rate. If the yield of I exceeds the discount rate the more expensive of the projects is preferred otherwise the cheaper project will be chosen. The rationale is that the extra money required to finance A rather than C (i.e. the 'outlay' for the incremental project) is worth spending if the return on it exceeds the discount rate. In the case above the yield of I is 20.7% so that A would be preferred any discount rate below this. If 10% was the cost of capital and therefore all projects had to earn this amount then the project I is worthwhile. In other words, if both I and C could be adopted they would be—but this would be the same as project A. (R6) is a decision rule based on the incremental yield method.

> (R6) Of two projects, select the more expensive one if the yield of the incremental project exceeds the comparison discount rate. Select the less expensive one if the yield of the incremental project is less than the discount rate.

Quite apart from the fact that in some cases the extended yield method, or an equivalent device, may have to be applied to the incremental project, the incremental yield method itself can be time consuming if there are more than two projects to be considered. For instance in the four project situation shown in Figure 1.5 suppose two projects were to be chosen. Not only are the incremental yields of A, B and C over D required but also further applications of the method for A and B over C—all to get a result that would have been given by (R4) to begin with.

The recommendation that is made here is that (R3) and (R4) should be used. That is, in the absence of financial or other constraints, between non-mutually exclusive projects those projects that have NPV > 0 are worthwhile and should be undertaken. When choosing between mutually exclusive projects those projects should be undertaken that have the greatest NPVs. (R3) and (R4) are widely used rules, or at least they form the basis of many capital budgeting decisions.

1.9 Non-discounting Methods

Non-discounting methods of investment appraisal are still employed today. That the use of these methods should have persisted as long as it has is perplexing, but is partly accounted for by reluctance to change and the fact that survival, or even a good living is possible with poor decisions if the quality of competition is low enough. It would be as well to point out some of the ideas and indicate their shortcomings, which in fact provide the justification for the rational methods of investment appraisal.

Firstly consider the *payback period* method. The payback period of an investment is the length of time required by the investment project to return

Year	Project one Cash flow	ΣCash flow	Project two Cash flow	ΣCash flow
0	− 20,000	− 20,000	− 20,000	− 20,000
1	11,000	− 9,000	1,000	− 19,000
2	5,000	− 4,000	3,000	− 16,000
3	2,000	− 2,000	5,000	− 11.000
4	1,000	− 1,000	11,000	0
5	2,000	+ 1,000	5,000	
6	7,000		3,000	
7	9,000		1,000	

Figure 1.7

its initial outlay. For evaluation for an individual project a predetermined maximum payback period (say p^* years) would be compared with the payback period of the project in question (say p_1 years). If $p_1 < p^*$ the project would be accepted and if $p_1 < p^*$ the project would be rejected. As between two mutually exclusive projects the project with the shorter payback period would be preferred. Consider the data of figure 1.7. A choice is to be made between the two projects on the basis of payback period. The payback period for each project can be determined by accumulating the cash flow items. As soon as the cumulative cash flows becomes non-negative the project has 'paid back'. Thus project one pays back in five years ($p_1 = 5$), while project two pays back in four ($p_2 = 4$). Hence since $p_2 < p_1$ the second project would be preferred by the payback criterion. Cash flows after the payback year are ignored. If the projects had been compared on the basis of NPV then project one, with NPV = £6,130 at 10% would have been selected. Indeed project two is not worthwhile at all having NPV = − £31 at 10%. It is worth noting that project one has greater NPV than project two at *any* discount rate and that project one has 'paid back' 80% of its cpaital outlay after only two years, whereas project two has paid back only 20% at this stage. The payback method is discredited by its two major characteristics, namely that the timing of cash flows within the payback period are ignored and that cash flows outside of what turns out to be the payback period are not considered.

One justification for the use of payback method that has been forwarded is that in situations of considerable risk the project that returns its outlay sooner is to be preferred since there is less risk overall attached to it. What justification is there for implicitly assuming that returns up to the payback period (itself an unknown quantity until calculations are made) are certain and that thereafter returns will be assumed to have zero expectations in each year. Equally it will not do to argue on grounds of anticipated capital shortage within the next few years after a project has been undertaken. The argument carries no weight because payback ignores the timing of returns within the payback period and in any case the NPV approach would take account of this in the discount rate or rates used or in more involved circumstances a capital rationing approach would be indicated. In this connection also the payback method takes no account of interest charges if the initial capital sum was borrowed. A veneer of respectability can be stuck on to the payback philosophy if the payback period is determined using the discounted cash flow items, but many objections remain including that of the problem of how an appropriate value for payback period is to be determined.

A method of investment appraisal with some similarities to payback period but which employs discounting is the *Finite Horizon Method*. In this approach returns after a predetermined period are assumed to make negligible contributions to present value. Discounting is employed and individual projects are assessed and mutually exclusive projects compared within the same horizon. In assessing some hydroelectric projects in the United States the public authorities used a horizon of fifty years. With half-plausible interest rates the discount factors for greater than fifty years are zero to two or more decimal places so that with such a long horizon there will be no practical difference between finite horizon decisions and straightforward NPV decisions. If however, for some reason the horizon was 'short' similar criticisms to those applied to payback period would apply.

The other category of non-discounting methods goes under the heading of 'return on capital'. The number of possible measures of this concept is the product of the number of possible definitions of 'return' and the number of possible definitions of 'capital'. Usually the 'rate' of return on capital is expressed as the ratio of average return to 'average' capital. For example in respect of the projects one and two of Figure 1.7 if average capital is taken to be one half of initial capital in either case and average return is taken as the total of undiscounted returns divided by project duration then returns on capital for the two projects are:

$$\frac{100(5,286)\%}{10,000} = 52.86\% \quad \text{and} \quad \frac{100(4,143)\%}{10,000} = 41.43\%$$

The decision rules based on returns on capital would accept an individual project if its return exceeded the target figure and of a mutually exclusive pair would select the project with the greater return on capital figure. Thus project one would be selected here. If initial capital is used in place of average capital the return figures are halved but the decision between the projects by return on capital is unaffected. Inclusion of scrap (non-zero terminal capital) in a measure of average capital would make no difference to the result if in each case scrap value was the same percentage of original capital.

Although return on capital does consider returns over the whole lifetime of projects it nevertheless, like payback period, ignores the timing of returns. The claim that once definitional problems are overcome, rate of return on capital has the advantage of simplicity of calculation seems rather pathetic when set against the substantial losses that may result

from its use as a decision making tool. If the ratio of the total of discounted returns to initial outlay had been taken then a measure would
have been produced which could be useful in a capital rationing context.
This topic is discussed at the end of chapter two.

In summary non-discounting methods such as payback period and
return on capital have no points in their favour that are not better met
by present value methods. Non-discounting methods have such serious
shortcomings that their use should be confined to financial reporting.

1.10 Many Interest Rates

If it is known that the cost of capital to a firm is not constant over time,
how can this be taken into account in the DCF calculations? Where the
changes in rate are known in advance the NPV formula can be modified
accordingly. If r_1 is the rate appropriate in the first year, r_2 in the second
and so on, the NPV formula becomes:

$$\text{NPV} = \frac{S_1}{(1 + r_1)} + \frac{S_2}{(1 + r_2)(1 + r_2)} + \frac{S_3}{(1 + r_1)(1 + r_2)(1 + r_3)} + \ldots$$

$$\ldots + \frac{S_n}{\prod_{t=1}^{n} (1 + r_t)} - K \tag{1.20}$$

where

$$\prod_{t=1}^{n} (1 + r_t)$$

in equation, (1.20), represents the product of all discount factors. That
is $(1 + r_1) \cdot (1 + r_2) \cdot (1 + r_3) \ldots (1 + r_{n-1}) \cdot (1 + r_n)$. As an example, suppose
it was required to calculate the NPV of the project $- 500, 300, 400, 200$
where $r_1 = 0.10$ (first year discount rate of 10%) $r_2 = 0.13$ and $r_3 = 0.11$.
Then, by substitution into equation (2.1)

$$\text{NPV} = \frac{300}{(1.10)} + \frac{400}{(1.10)(1.13)} + \frac{200}{(1.10)(1.13)(1.11)} - 500 = 239.5$$

Net terminal value is given by:

$$\text{NTV} = 300(1.13)(1.11) + 400(1.11) + 200 - 500(1.10)(1.13)(1.11)$$

$$= 330.4 = 239.5(1.10)(1.13)(1.11)$$

It is noteworthy that if, somewhat arbitrarily, the project had been discounted at the arithmetic mean of the three rates, i.e. $[(1.10) +
(1.13) + (1.11)] \div 3 = 1.113$ then the resulting NPV is 237.5, an error of
0.84%. The smallness of this error suggests that single interest rate approximations may be expected to be good enough in practice. However,
it should be pointed out that the percentage error in estimation of NPV

is heavily influenced by the size of the initial outlay. It is perhaps better to look at the percentage error in GPV which in the example cited here is 0.24% and might reasonably be expected to be below 1% for plausible variations in interest rates.

Another case where more than one interest rate may need to be used is the case where in any given time period several rates of interest may be relevant. As we have seen in section seven there may be a cost of capital problem. Frequently an average rate would be employed, but sometimes it is possible to be more precise. The simplest case is where there are two distinct interest rates. An example will illustrate the complication that is brought about and how the problem may be tackled.

A company providing warehousing facilities has a lease on one particular warehouse with two years to run. It can either leave the warehouse as it is, or build a temporary extension at a cost of £17,000. The company estimates that the extension would add £10,000 to the excess of income over operating costs in each of the two years but would have zero residual value. It has £9,000 'cash' available for which the only alternative use would be investment in securities giving a yield of 7%, and any future surpluses may also be invested at 7%. If it decides on the extension, the other £8,000 required can be borrowed on bank overdraft at 9%. The company wishes to adopt that course of action which would cause it to have the most money after two years when it plans to purchase a replacement warehouse. Should the extension be adopted?

If the extension was *not* built the company would invest the £9,000 and obtain (in addition to its other monies) £9,000 $(1.07)^2$. On the other hand if the extension *was* built the company would obtain

$$[- 8,000(1.09) + 10,000] (1.07) + 10,000 = 11,369.6$$

The square bracketed term above is the cash position after one year. The company has borrowed £8,000 at 9% but the first year's extra 'profit' of £10,000 enables both principal and interest to be repaid and leave some over (the contents of the square brackets) for investment in securities at 7% yield. The investment is clearly worthwhile, the NTV of the decision to invest being:

$$[- 8,000(1.09) + 10,000] (1.07) + 10,000 - 9,000(1.07)^2 = 1,065.5$$
$$(1.21)$$

which means that the company ends up with £1,065.5 more than it would have done if it had not built the extension.

Two interest rates enter into the NTV expression and strictly speaking, it would have been incorrect to assess the project using one or other rate alone. There *is* an interest rate which could be applied to the project $- 17,000, 10,000\ 10,000$ to give an NTV of 1,065.5, but this cannot be known in advance of the calculation (1.21). This interest rate is about 7.65%.

If the investment costs K and gives returns of S_1 and S_2; if the firm has M of its own resources and can borrow at $100i\%$ and invest surpluses at $100r\%$ where $i > r$; if $K > M$ and $S_1 \geqslant (K - M)(1 + i)$ then the NTV of the project would be

$$\text{NTV} = [(M - K)(1 + i) + S_1](1 + r) + S_2 - M(I + r)^2 \qquad (1.22)$$

from which it can be seen that if $i \neq r$ the term in M does not cancel out if $M < K$. If $M > K$ only r would enter into (1.22) but there is no reason why this should always be the case. If however, either $i = r$ of $M > K$ the NTV would be given by

$$\text{NTV} = [(M - K)(1 + r) + S_1](1 + r) + S_2 - M(1 + r)^2 \qquad (1.23)$$

and cancellation of the term in M and division through by $(1 + r)^2$ would give

$$- K + \frac{S_1}{(1 + r)} + \frac{S_2}{(1 + r)^2} = \text{NPV} \qquad (1.24)$$

In general the use of several discount rates in the calculation of NPV and NTV may suggest unlikely precision, but for the smaller company or the private individual for whom interest rates are more clearly defined, the exercise can be practicable. For more advanced work in this area and the development of appropriate decision rules see Wilkes (1983).

1.11 The Time Horizon

The lifetimes of alternative investments may differ considerably and the investor may have a time horizon which is different from any of these. Should projects be compared over four years or five or ten or twenty-five? In some cases, the choice of horizon may be important.

As an example consider the two mutually exclusive projects

A:	$- 100$	180	20

and

B:	$- 100$	180

It is clear that Project A will be preferred to B on either a yield or a present value basis at any discount rate. But suppose now that each project could be repeated—that is, project A could be replaced after two years and project B after one year. Assuming that project A is not to be cut short after one year then with a two year horizon the choice would be between A_2 and B_2:

t	0	1	2
A_2:	$- 100$	180	20
B_2:	$- 100$	80	180

since B can be started again after one year (the figure 80 is 180 minus the 100 reinvestment). B_2 will be preferred by (R4) at any discount rate below 60%. If the time horizon was four years there would be time to repeat A once and B three times and the choice is between A_4 and B_4.

t	0	1	2	3	4
A_4:	– 100	180	– 80	180	20
B_4:	– 100	80	80	80	180

and once again the 'B series'is preferable at any plausible discount rate by (R4). It is important that the same time horizon be chosen for both projects such that cycles of investments can be completed.

The question of how any post-horizon returns are to be treated can be crucial. The Finite Horizon method simply ignores post horizon returns. The more distant the horizon and the larger the discount rate the less this will matter, but a more attractive approach is to discount the post horizon returns back to the horizon itself. The discount rate to be applied in such a process can be important. For example, consider the two projects A and B below.

t	0	1	2
A:	– 100	140	200
B:	– 100	270	50

Suppose that both projects are financed by borrowing at 20%. Reinvestment of returns not used to repay borrowing is at 10%. If the horizon is at $t = 1$, what are the post horizon returns of 200 or 50 worth? If they are worth that amount which may be borrowed in exchange for them (i.e. 200/1.2 and 50/1.2 respectively), then the 'terminal' values of the projects at $t = 1$ would be given by:

$$(\text{NTV A})_{t=1} = -100(1.2) + 140 + 200(1.2)^{-1} = 186.67$$

and

$$(\text{NTV B})_{t=1} = -100(1.2) + 270 + 50(1.2)^{-1} = 191.67$$

so that project B would be preferred by a 'terminal' value rule. B would also be preferred by (R4) at $t = 0$ (which is the horizon if the investor wants immediate cash and can borrow on the strength of the projects) since NPV A (at 20%) = 155.56 and NVP B (at 20%) = 159.72. But if the horizon is set at $t = 2$ then on the basis of our assumptions and the interest rate specified, project A would be selected by the appropriate (based on R4) terminal value rule since:

$$(\text{NTV A})_{t=2} = [-100(1.2) + 140](1.1) + 200 = 222$$

whilst

$$(\text{NTV B})_{t=2} = [-100(1.2) + 270](1.1) + 50 = 215$$

Unless further information is forthcoming in respect of the investor's preferences it is not possible to say what is the 'correct' horizon to take.

1.12 Annuities

An income stream where the sum to be received is the same in each year is called an annuity. Examples of annuities in business life are: hire-purchase contracts, leases, 'consols', endowment policies and mortgages. The present value of an annuity could be found as for an 'irregular' income stream, but there is a shorter method. Consider an annuity of £100 for four years at 10% interest. Assume that the first payment will be made after one year. Using the discount factor table the present value is:

$$100 \times 0.9091 + 100 \times 0.8264 + 100 \times 0.7513 + 100 \times 0.6830$$

$$= 100(0.9091 + 0.8264 + 0.7513 + 0.6830)$$

$$= 100 \times 3.1699$$

$$= 316.99$$

The significant line of workings above is the second. All that has to be done is to multiply the amount involved, £100, by the sum of the first four discount factors: 3.1699. (The last digit of this sum is nine rather than eight due to the rounding of the discount factors.) Table 3 (p. 000) is the annuity table and entries here are the sum of the discount factors up to n years. Hence the entries give the present value of an annuity of £1. An annuity where the first payment is made after one year is called an *immediate annuity*. Where the first payment occurs at once this is called an *annuity due* and the appropriate entries of Table 3 must be increased by one to obtain the present value in this case.

As a concrete example of the use of annuities consider the following case. A company enters a contract to lease a building for ten years for an annual payment of £10,000; the first payment to be made a year hence. At a 16% rate of interest what is the present cost of the contract? This is £10,000 × 4.8332 = £48,332. The present cost figure of under £50,000 gives an idea of the impact of discount factors on distant payments and would be of value in considering alternative courses of action to leasing.

A special case of an annuity is where a contract runs indefinitely—there being no end to the payments. This is called a *perpetuity*. Perpetuities are rare phenomena in the private sector, but certain government securities are undated—for instance, Consols and War Loan. There is a very simple formula for calculating the present value of a perpetuity, being simply the sum involved divided by the interest rate as a decimal. If the annual sum is £S and the interest rate is $100r\%$ then

$$PV = \frac{S}{r}$$

Observe that although the income stream is infinite the present value is finite. Thus at a 10% rate of interest a perpetuity of £50 has a present value of £500 and if the security is negotiable we might expect it to change hands at around this price. For instance, what should be the price of a unit of $3\frac{1}{2}$% War Loan stock if the current market rate of interest for this kind of very low risk security is 12%? War Loan is quoted in units of £100 nominal value and the annual interest payment is $3\frac{1}{2}$% of this figure, i.e. £3.50. Assuming for simplicity a single annual payment the price should be PV given by

$$PV = \frac{3.5}{0.12} = £29.17$$

Still on the subject of annuities it is often useful to know the *terminal value* of an annuity. This occurs, for instance, in loan repayments. Suppose £1 is set aside at the end of each of four years how much will be on hand after four years, bearing in mind interest earned at the compound rate of $100r$% per annum? The first pound gathers interest for three years and so becomes $(1 + r)^3$, the second is interest earning for two years and so becomes $(1 + r)^2$, the third becomes $(1 + r)$ and the fourth pound is placed in the account at the day of reckoning so that the terminal value at $t = 4$ is

$$(1 + r)^3 + (1 + r)^2 + (1 + r) + 1$$

at a 10% rate of interest this would be

$$1.331 + 1.21 + 1.1 + 1 = 4.6410$$

Table 4 (p. 000) gives terminal values of an annuity of £1 for various values of interest rate and number of years.

In loan repayments the closely related idea of a *sinking fund* is most useful. Table 5 (pp. 398–9), the sinking fund table, shows how much must be set aside each year in order to achieve a terminal value of £1. Thus the entries in the sinking fund table are the reciprocals of the corresponding entries in Table 4. Referring to the table, with a 12% rate of interest, £0.0813 would need to be set aside annually in order to give a total of £1 after eight years. Consider an example. A company has loan stock of £750,000 due to mature in seven years' time. The company does not wish to make an issue of fresh stock at this time but rather to pay off the debt. At an interest rate of 10% how much should be set aside annually to meet the liability when it falls due? To give a terminal value of £1 after seven years at 10%, £0.1054 must be put aside each year; thus to finish with £750,000 the amount required annually is £750,000 × 0.1054 = £79,050.

In the analysis of certain problems it is helpful to convert a lump sum to a series of equal payments over time (i.e. an annuity) with the same present value. Thus a lump sum of £1 is equivalent to an immediate annuity for two years at 10% of £0.5762. Table 6 (p.000), the *annual equivalent annuity* table, shows the size of annuity required to give a present value of £1 for various rates of interest and numbers of years. To illustrate the use of the table suppose that the capital cost of a machine tool is £25,000 and that the expected life of the equipment is 10 years. At an interest rate of 8% the lump sum is equivalent, in present value terms to an annual charge of £25,000 × 0.1490 = £3,725. The figure of £3,725 could be compared with an annual charge resulting from alternative financing arrangements and also would represent the gross amount of the depreciation which would be charged on the equipment using the annuity method of depreciation. It will be noted that the entries in Table 6 are the reciprocals of corresponding entries in Table 3. Annual equivalents can be used as a means of project appraisal and are particularly useful in the context of the repair–replace problem to be discussed later on. For the moment, consider an exercise in the conversion of cash flow to annuity form. Suppose that it was required to find the annual equivalent annuity for two years at 10% for a project which produces the cash flow:

$t = 0$	$t = 1$	$t = 2$
− 700	650	800

First find the NPV for the project in the usual manner:

Year	Sum	Discount factor	PV
0	− 700	1	− 700
1	650	0.9091	590.92
2	800	0.8264	661.12
		NPV =	552.04

Second, convert the 'lump sum' NPV to the annual equivalent figure for two years at 10%. This will be £552.04 × 0.5762 = £318.09.

References

Gordon, M. J. (1962), *The Investment, Financing and Valuation of the Corporation*, Irwin, Homewood, Ill.

Samuels, J. M., and Wilkes, F. M. (1980), *Management of Company Finance* (3rd edn.), Nelson, London.

Wilkes, F. M., 'Dominance Criteria for the Ranking of Projects with an Imperfect Capital Market,' *Journal of Business Finance and Accounting*, **10**, Spring 1983.

Further Reading

Bromwich, M., 'Capital budgeting — a survey', *Journal of Business Finance*, **2**, No. 3, 1970.

Bromwich, M., *The Economics of Capital Budgeting*, Penguin books, 1976.

Fremgen, J. M., 'Capital budgeting practices: a survey', *Management Accounting*, **1973** (May).

Jean, W. J., 'Terminal value or present value in capital budgeting programmes?', *Journal of Financial and Quantitative Analysis*, **6**, January, 1971.

Levy, H., and Sarnat, M., *Capital Investment and Financial Decisions*, Prentice-Hall, Englewood Cliffs, NJ, 1978.

Lumby, S., *Investment Appraisal and Related Decisions*, Nelson, London, 1981.

Mao, J. C. T., 'Survey of capital budgeting: theory and practice', *Journal of Finance*, May **1970**.

More, R. F. de la, 'An investigation into the discounting formulae used in capital budgeting', *Journal of Business Finance and Accounting*, **2**, No. 2, Summer 1975.

Neuhauser, J. J., and Viscoine, J. A., 'How managers feel about advanced capital budgeting methods', *Management Review*, **1973** (November).

Samuels, J. M., and Wilkes, F. M., *Management of Company Finance, Students Manual*, Nelson, London, 1981.

Sarnat, M., and Levy, H., 'The relationships of rules of thumb to the internal rate of return', *Journal of Finance*, **24**, June 1969.

Teichroew, D., Robichek, A. A., and Montalbano, M., 'An analysis of criteria for investment and financing decisions under certainty', *Management Science*, **11**, November 1965.

Wilkes, F. M., 'On multiple rates of return', *Journal of Business Finance and Accounting*, **7**, No. 4, Winter 1980.

CHAPTER 2

Additional Topics

Overview
After description of the various types of compounding procedure, the subject of data inaccuracies is considered. This is followed by the first of several references to inflation and the capital budgeting process. Choise of starting date for projects, the make or buy problem, cost−benefit ratios and the repair/replace problem form the subject-matter of the next four sections. The final section introduces the topic of capital ration-ing and for the single constraint problem shows a non-programming solution procedure. The section and the chapter conclude with a programming formulation of the single constraint problem.

2.1 Alternative Compounding Schemes

It is normally assumed that returns arise and interest is compounded at the end of each year. For most purposes this is a perfectly satisfactory approach. There are some occasions, however, when it is worth explicitly taking account of departures from the standard pattern. The most com monly arising instance of this is in the half-yearly payment of interest or charging of accounts. For instance, the rate of interest on a deposit ac-count may be stated to be 14% per annum; but if 7% is paid after six months and compounded, then the true annual rate is nearly $14\frac{1}{2}$%. An original £1 would have become £$(1.07)^2$ − £1.1449 at the year's end

To take another familiar instance, suppose that interest on a personal loan is 2% per month compound. This will be equivalent to just over 26.82% per annum. The relationship is

$$(1.02)^{12} \simeq 1.2682$$

In general, if compounding is n times per year at a nominal yearly rate of $100r$% (for instance, the 14% in the case of the earlier bank deposit example), then the true annual rate would be given by

$$\text{true rate} = \left[\left(1 + \frac{r}{n} \right)^n - 1 \right] 100\% \tag{2.1}$$

The limiting case of this is when compounding approaches continuity as n increases indefinitely. As this happens:

$$\lim_{n \to \infty} \left(1 + \frac{r}{n}\right)^n = e^r \tag{2.2}$$

So that £1 would become e^r pounds after one year— rather than $(1 + r)$ pounds in the once-a-year discrete case. Naturally, for any given discrete annual compounding rate $100r\%$ there is a continuous compounding rate that gives the same effect. This would be $100s\%$ where $e^s = (1 + r)$ thus $s = \log_e(1 + r)$. However, with continuous compounding at the nominal rate $100r\%$, after n years an original £1 would have become e^{nr} pounds. Conversely, the present value of £1 to be received n years hence would be e^{-nr} pounds under continuous compounding. Similarly the present value of a stream of annual receipts would be

$$PV = \sum_{t=1}^{n} R_t e^{-tr} \tag{2.3}$$

where R_t is the receipt at the end of the tth year. Figure 2.1 gives a comparison of the discount factors at 10% for the discrete case and for the continuous case. Note that the difference is more marked in the later years.

n	Discrete: $(1 + r)^{-n}$	Continuous: e^{-nr}
1	0.9091	0.9048
2	0.8264	0.8187
3	0.7513	0.7408
4	0.6830	0.6703
5	0.6209	0.6065
6	0.5645	0.5488
7	0.5132	0.4966
8	0.4665	0.4493
9	0.4241	0.4066
10	0.3855	0.3679

Figure 2.1

Now consider the case of annuities under continuous compounding. The case in mind here is of the usual immediate annual annuity with lump sums at the end of each year, but with continuous compounding within the year. It can be shown that the present value of an annuity of £1 for n years in this case is given by

$$PV = \frac{1 - e^{-nr}}{e^r - 1} \tag{2.4}$$

Thus at 10% the present value of an annuity of 100 for 10 years would be £601.04. In contrast, the present value under the usual discrete compounding would be £614.46. In the extreme, with a perpetuity in these circumstances the present value is given by

$$PV(\text{perpetuity}) = \frac{1}{e^r - 1} \qquad (2.5)$$

which contrasts with the usual r^{-1}. At 10% the continuous compounding would give 9.5083 for a perpetuity of 1 instead of the more usual value of 10.

The last case to consider is when the returns, as well as the compounding, are continuous. Any real circumstances could only approximate to this situation. Suppose that in year 1 a total of R_1 pounds is to be received, but in n evenly spaced equal instalments throughout the year. Assume that compounding takes place at the time of each instalment. The present value of the year's return would then be

$$PV = \frac{R_1/n}{\left(1 + \dfrac{r}{n}\right)} + \frac{R_1/n}{\left(1 + \dfrac{r}{n}\right)^2} + \frac{R_1/n}{\left(1 + \dfrac{r}{n}\right)^3} + \ldots + \frac{R_1/n}{\left(1 + \dfrac{r}{n}\right)^n}$$

This sum can be expressed more succinctly. The sum, s_n, of n terms of a geometric series (which is what the above expression is) is given by

$$s_n = \frac{a(1 - d^n)}{1 - d}$$

where a is the first term in the series, and d the factor of difference. So in this case (where s_n will be PV)

$$a = \frac{R_1/n}{\left(1 + \dfrac{r}{n}\right)} \qquad d = \frac{1}{\left(1 + \dfrac{r}{n}\right)}$$

Substituting these values in the formula gives

$$PV = \frac{R_1}{r}\left[1 - \left(1 + \frac{r}{n}\right)^{-n}\right]$$

and as n increases without limit (the R_1 is spread evenly over the whole year and compounding is continuous)

$$PV = \frac{R_1}{r}(1 - e^{-r})$$

Now suppose that a different amount, R_2, was to be received in the second year. Again start from the point where there are n equal instalments. The total present value of the two years' returns would then be

$$\frac{R_1/n}{\left(1+\dfrac{r}{n}\right)} + \frac{R_1/n}{\left(1+\dfrac{r}{n}\right)^2} + \ldots +$$

$$\ldots + \frac{R_1/n}{\left(1+\dfrac{r}{n}\right)^n} + \frac{R_2/n}{\left(1+\dfrac{r}{n}\right)^{n+1}} + \frac{R_2/n}{\left(1+\dfrac{r}{n}\right)^{n+2}} + \ldots$$

$$\ldots + \frac{R_2/n}{\left(1+\dfrac{r}{n}\right)^{2n}}$$

Summation produces

$$\frac{R_1}{r}\left[1-\left(1+\frac{r}{n}\right)^{-n}\right] + \left(1+\frac{r}{n}\right)^{-n}\left[\frac{R_2}{r}\left[1-\left(1+\frac{r}{n}\right)^{-n}\right]\right]$$

and the process becomes continuous ($n \to \infty$):

$$\frac{R_1}{r}[1-e^{-r}] + e^{-r}\left[\frac{R_2}{r}[1-e^{-r}]\right]$$

If there was a third year, in which a total of R_3 was to be received, then the present value overall would be

$$\frac{R_1}{r}[1-e^{-r}] + e^{-r}\frac{R_2}{r}[1-e^{-r}] + e^{-2r}\frac{R_3}{r}[1-e^{-r}]$$

The general expression is

$$\mathrm{PV} = \frac{1-e^{-r}}{r}\sum_{t=1}^{n} R_t\, e^{-(t-1)r} \tag{2.6}$$

So this case of continuous compounding *and* continuous receipts is less convenient than the usual discrete case.

A comparison between the discount factors in this case with the usual discrete compounding factors is very interesting. Selected values are given in the Figure 2.2 below (for an interest rate of 10%, that is $r = 0.1$). Note that there is a large difference in the early years. For instance, £10,000 received as a lump sum at the end of one year is worth £9,091 in present terms. If it were received continuously throughout the year the present value would be £9,516, an increase of 4.67%. However, beyond 10 years the continuous factors are *less* than the discrete factors. In the early years the greater size of the continuous factors is due to the very significantly earlier receipt of some of the money (e.g. after 0.1 and 0.2 year rather than 1 year). In later years the differences in timing between the two schemes have only marginal effect (e.g. some cash after 20.1 and

n	$(1+r)^{-r}$	$\dfrac{(1-e^{-r})}{r}e^{-(n-1)r}$
1	0.9091	0.9516
2	0.8264	0.8611
3	0.7513	0.7791
4	0.6830	0.7050
5	0.6209	0.6379
6	0.5645	0.5772
7	0.5132	0.5223
8	0.4665	0.4726
9	0.4241	0.4276
10	0.3855	0.3869
11	0.3505	0.3501
12	0.3186	0.3168
13	0.2897	0.2866
20	0.1486	0.1423
30	0.0573	0.0524
40	0.0221	0.0193
50	0.0085	0.0071

Figure 2.2

20.2 years rather than all after 21 years) and this is outweighed by the increased impact of compounding continuously. It is interesting to note that over an infinite horizon the two schemes give the same value of a perpetuity—the more 'severe' discounting is precisely compensated for by the earlier receipts.

Now consider the continuous analogue of an annuity. Payment would be at the constant *rate* of £R per year, with continuous compounding. Now if $R_t = R$ in (2.6) it can be summed to give the result

$$PV = \frac{R}{r}(1 - e^{-nr}) \tag{2.7}$$

in which it will be noted that for the perpetuity case the result is the same as in the yearly returns—yearly compounding case. Thus the continuous analogue of a perpetuity would also be worth R/r. Figure 2.3 gives values

n	Discrete: $\dfrac{1-(1+r)^{-n}}{r}$	Continuous: $\dfrac{1-e^{-nr}}{r}$
1	0.9091	0.9516
2	1.7355	1.8127
3	2.4869	2.5918
4	3.1699	3.2968
5	3.7908	3.9347
10	6.1446	6.3212
20	8.5136	8.6466
30	9.4269	9.5021
40	9.7791	9.8168
50	9.9148	9.9326
100	9.9993	9.9995

Figure 2.3

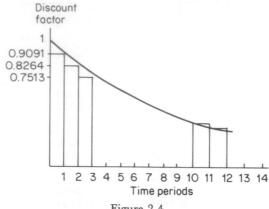

Figure 2.4

for the ordinary discrete annuity at 10% and for the continuous analogue at 10%.

From Figure 2.3 it is evident that while there is a considerable difference in the present values for short annuities, as the time period lengthens the two values come nearer to coincidence. The situation is shown as a graph in Figure 2.4. The present value of the discrete annuity is the area of the appropriate number of columns, the first three of which are shown. The present value of the continuous annuity is the area under the curve. The curve is completely above the columns at first, begins to meet them around the 10-year mark and is completely below the tops of the columns by the 35-year point.

2.2 Effects of Errors in Data

For any decision-making technique it is of value to know the possible effects of less than perfect information. Rarely will the data used be precisely accurate. In this section we shall consider the effects on estimates of GPV, NPV, and the yield of incorrect information regarding discount rate, project lifetime, initial outlay and project returns. Each case will be treated separately, but indications will be given about the changes in magnitude of the errors for qualitative changes in some of the other parameters.

(i) Incorrect Estimation of the Discount Rate

If all project returns are non-negative, underestimation of the discount rate leads to overestimation of NPV and this will be the larger in absolute terms the longer the project. If NPV and GPV refer to the supposed net and gross values, and RNPV and RGPV to the correct net and gross present values then GPV/RGPV will increase with increasing project length

α	$s=0.05$ $n=10$	$s=0.05$ $n=50$	$s=0.2$ $n=10$	$s=0.2$ $n=50$ (approx)
1.2	1.05	1.16	1.14	1.2
1.6	1.15	1.49	1.43	1.6
2.0	1.26	1.84	1.74	2.0

s = estimated discount rate; n = project length.

Figure 2.5

provided the further returns are all positive, but NPV/RNPV could move either way. Figure 2.5 illustrates the proportionate overestimation of GPV for a project yielding equal returns in each period, where although s is the supposed rate of discount, the true rate is αs. Thus, if $s = 0.05$ and $\alpha = 1.2$ then the true rate $\alpha s = 0.06$.

In this constant-returns case the proportionate error in GPV is less than the corresponding proportionate error in the discount rate, and unless the larger returns clustered towards the end of the project this would be the general case. For instance, the entry 1.15 for $\alpha = 1.6$, $s = 0.05$, and $n = 10$ means that if the discount rate assumed for the calculation of GPV was 5% but in fact it turned out to be 8%, then the proportionate error in GPV would be 15%. That is to say, GPV at a 5% discount rate exceeds GPV at an 8% discount rate by 15%. If several projects are being evaluated, incorrect estimation of the discount rate can result in the wrong ordering. This applies to both present value and yield methods.

(ii) Incorrect Estimation of Project Lifetime

If n is the number of periods for which a project will run and if all returns are positive, if ΔNPV and ΔGPV represent the changes in NPV and GPV consequent upon a change in n of Δn then

$$\frac{\Delta \text{NPV}}{\Delta n} = \frac{\Delta \text{GPV}}{\Delta n} > 0$$

and of course the larger is n(for all positive returns) the greater will be the yield of a project. That is

$$\frac{\Delta \text{IRR}}{\Delta n} > 0$$

Somewhat less obviously it can be shown that the proportionate error in GPV consequent upon incorrect estimation of project lifetime becomes smaller as the rate of discount for the project increases, but the proportionate error in NPV could move either way as the discount rate changes. Also, it can be shown that the proportionate error in yield diminishes as n increases in the case of equal returns.

The effect of incorrect estimation of project lifetime can be illustrated

Estimated	n	r	True n 6	10	11	20	21	40
	5	0.05	1.172	1.783				
	5	0.2	1.112	1.402				
	10	0.05			1.076	1.614		
	10	0.2			1.032	1.161		
	20	0.05					1.029	1.377
	20	0.2					1.004	1.026

Figure 2.6

by reference to GPV, which is not affected by the size of the initial outlay. Letting GPV_2 correspond to the true project lifetime and GPV_1 correspond to the estimated lifetime, Figure 2.6 gives GPV_2/GPV_1 in some different circumstances for a project yielding equal returns in each period.

In the constant-returns case if a project has an estimated lifetime of five years and in fact runs for six with a discount rate of 5%, then

$$\frac{GPV_2}{GPV_1} = 1.172$$

That is to say, GPV would be 17.2% greater than anticipated.

As regards selection between several projects, since each in general may be affected differently by incorrect estimation of life, incorrect selection on the basis of any of the criteria is possible.

(iii) Incorrect Estimation of the Initial Outlay for a Project

Errors in estimation of initial outlay k affect NPV and IRR. Obviously $\Delta NPV/\Delta k = -1$ and the proportionate error in NPV is smaller for an extended project (as n increases to include further positive returns) and larger for a larger discount rate. However, the proportionate variation in yield would have to be determined numerically.

For project ranking the nature of the errors in estimation of the initial outlays is important. If, for example, there is the same proportionate error in the estimate of the outlay in each case then both yield and NPV rules can give wrong orderings. If the error is the same absolutely in all cases, the yield rule may still give an incorrect ordering, but NPV will preserve the correct ordering. This point can be illustrated with a numerical example.

A choice is to be made of one or other of the two following projects. Both will cost the same amount k, to initiate, the first (A) runs for two periods yielding 1,000 at the end of each period and the second (B) for five periods yielding 500 at the end of each period and $r = 0.1$. Figure 2.7 gives the NPV and yield (approximately) of each project for different estimates of k. Project B always has the higher NPV, but the ordering by yield changes as the estimate of k nears 1,600. Thus, if $k = 1,400$ the yield method would rank project A above project B, but if $k = 1,600$ it would prefer B to A.

k	IRR_A	IRR_B	NPV_A	NPV_B
1,400	0,272	0.226	335	495
1,500	0.215	0.200	235	395
1,600	0.162	0.169	135	295
1,700	0.115	0.144	35	195
1,900	0.035	0.099	−165	−5

Figure 2.7

(iv) Incorrect Estimation of Project Returns

The relative effects on GPV, NPV and yield of incorrect estimates of returns depend upon the nature of errors. Let $\overline{GPV}$ be the Proportionate error in estimate of GPV, $\overline{NPV}$ represent the Proportionate error in estimate of NPV and let $\overline{IRR}$ be the Proportionate error in estimate of yield. If the errors are the same numerically in each year (say a constant overestimate), then $\overline{GPV}$ will be less than $\overline{NPV}$, but $\overline{IRR}$ could exceed or be less than either of these. But if several projects are involved GPV and NPV still preserve the true ordering when the projects concerned have the same lifetime, whereas yield in general does not. If the errors in returns are proportionately the same, then more definite relationships exist between $\overline{GPV}$, $\overline{NPV}$ and $\overline{IRR}$ namely (a) in the equal returns case $\overline{NPV} > \overline{IRR} > \overline{GPV}$ and (b) in the non-equal returns case $\overline{NPV} > \overline{IRR}$, $\overline{NPV} > \overline{GPV}$, but $\overline{IRR} \leqslant \overline{GPV}$. In all cases the proportionate error in GPV will be the same as the proportionate error in the returns. To illustrate the point that $\overline{IRR}$ can be less than $\overline{GPV}$ consider the case where the project $-1, 0, 0, 3$ is estimated as $-1, 0, 0, 6$, then GPV is overestimated by 100% but yield is overestimated by less than 85%. It is therefore, apparent that if the larger returns are clustered towards the end of the project, $\overline{IRR}$ may be less than $\overline{GPV}$, but otherwise not.

Figure 2.8 gives some examples for the equal returns case. The project returns are actually R per period, but are estimated as $R(1 + p)$. A rate of interest of 5% is appropriate to the calculation of GVPs and NPVs, and the initial outlay is set so as to give a true yield of 10% in each case. Entries in Figure 2.8 give $\overline{GPV}$, $\overline{NPV}$ and $\overline{IRR}$ for two values of p and three of n (length of project). As an example, for $p = 0.5$ (which is a 50% overestimate of all the returns) and for $n = 5$ (a five-year project) the 2.81 in the $\overline{IRR}$ column means that the estimated yield is 2.81

	$\overline{GPV}$	$\overline{IRR}$	$\overline{NPV}$	
$p = 0.1$	1.1	1.38	1.80	$n = 5$
$p = 0.5$	1.5	2.81	5.02	
$p = 0.1$	1.1	1.15	1.32	$n = 20$
$p = 0.5$	1.5	1.68	2.58	
$p = 0.1$	1.1	1.1	1.2	$n \to \infty$
$p = 0.5$	1.5	1.5	2	

Figure 2.8

times the true yield, and the 5.02 in the $\overline{\text{NPV}}$ column means that estimated NPV is 5.02 times the true NPV. Figue 2.8 gives an approximate indication of the magnitudes of $\overline{\text{NPV}}$ and $\overline{\text{IRR}}$ for cases similar to that on which the table is based. $,\overline{\text{NPV}}$ would diminish if the rate of discount was increased and $\overline{\text{IRR}}$ would fall as the true yield rose.

(v) Conclusions

It is important to remember that the present value and yield decision-making methods are not alone in being affected by data errors. Any quantitative procedure would be affected. Judgement methods also depend upon information input and it must be emphasized that the justification for the use of a procedure is that it improves on *what else would have been done* and does not depend on the finding of the precise 'true' solution. The word 'incorrect' has been used from time to time in this section but the context is important. An 'incorrect' decision (e.g. choosing project A rather than project B) may mean only a marginal drop in profits—and a drop compared with the 'true' maximum at that. The profits made by a theoretically suboptimal project may be much greater than those that would have been made from projects selected by unscientific procedures for which the consequences of error cannot, in any case, be evaluated.

2.3 Inflation and Capital Budgeting

In this section we shall see how inflation may affect the desirability of investment projects and comparisons between them. We shall not be concerned with the social evils of the arbitrary redistribution of goods and services or with the employment and balance of payments problems that may follow sustained general increases in the price level. The questions we shall answer are of the kind: 'How do we allow for inflation in investment decision making?' or 'What adjustments for inflation should be made in discounted cash flow calculations?' or 'Will this investment still be worth while after inflation?'

Consider an ultra-simple example to begin with. An individual can choose between the project

$$t = 0 \qquad t = 1$$
$$-100 \qquad 110$$

or investment in bank deposit at 5%. If NPV is an appropriate criterion the decision is clear. The NPV of the project is $+4.76$ so that it is worth while. Now suppose that there is inflation at 15% p.a. By this we mean that an appropriate weighted average of prices rises by 15% during the course of the year. Suppose also that the cash flow and interest rate are unaltered (we shall drop this unlikely assumption shortly). Is the project still attractive? The sacrifice of £100 at $t = 0$ produces £110 at $t = 1$, but each of the $t = 1$ pounds has less purchasing power than the $t = 0$ pounds. In fact in terms of the $t = 0$ situation the £110 at $t = 1$ will only buy £110 ÷ (1.15) = £95.65 worth of goods. Does this mean that the project should be rejected? Would it be better to bank the money? Clearly not. The $t = 1$ choices would be even worse. Goods to the tune of £105 ÷ (1.15) = £91.30 could be bought in $t = 0$ terms. So the project is still preferable to the bank alternative. Both project and bank are superior to putting the money under the bed (which would amount to the project—100,100) so the alternative is to increase current expenditure and consumption.

One of the conditions underlying the use of NPV technique is that the discount rate employed should ideally apply to *all* interperiod transfers of funds, i.e. it should be a uniform rate of borrowings and investments of any surpluses. The result of this is that if the investor is ultimately concerned with consuming real goods, the project with the higher NPV, obtained in the usual fashion, will allow superior consumption (more of all goods) in all time periods. *Thus the decision between alternatives is independent of any subjective rate of 'time preference' of the particular investor.* Thus the project

$$t = 0 \quad t = 1$$
$$-100 \quad 110$$

would allow 104.76 to be obtained immediately by borrowing at 5% on the strength of the $t = 1$ return of 110. Thus the project is still preferable to no project which would simply release 100 for current consumption. This is a most important result and deserves formal examination.

Consider in general a choice between two projects A and B running for n years with a uniform interest rate of $100r\%$ Let the NPV of the projects A and B be N_A and N_B respectively. Because of the possibility of borrowing, the returns to the projects would allow the sums of money N_A and N_B *actually to be obtained* at $t = 0$ if the only condition for borrowing is the ability to repay. The investor need not 'consume' the entire amounts N_A and N_B immediately but could add to other income available for consumption (or the payment of dividends in the case of a company) any time pattern of cash sums that satisfy (2.8) or (2.9) respectively:

$$\sum_{t=1}^{n}(1 - y_t)N_A, y_1(1 + r)N_A, y_2(1 + r)^2 N_A, \ldots,$$

$$y_{n-1}(1 + r)^{n-1}N_A, y_n(1 + r)^n N_A \tag{2.8}$$

$$\sum_{t=1}^{n}(1 - z_t)N_B, z_1(1 + r)N_B, z_2(1 + r)^2 N_B, \ldots,$$

$$z_{n-1}(1 + r)^{n-1}N_B, z_n(1 + r)^n N_B \tag{2.9}$$

where y_t and z_1 are arbitrary constants. Now suppose $N_A > N_B$. Clearly for any set of z_t, equal y_t could be chosen so that the investor's cash position in every one of the n years is better with project A than it is with project B. If inflation is present (assuming returns are unchanged) then if the interest rate r is unaffected all that happens is that each correspondng pair of terms in (2.10) and (2.11) is worth, in reality, proportionately less. If inflation is at the annual rate of $100\alpha\%$ then the tth term in each of the series is deflated by $(1 + \alpha)^t$. Project A in other words gives superior nominal spending power *and* superior real spending power. There is no reason to reverse the original pre-inflation preference for A.

In our original example with the y_t and z_t equated the moneys available for expenditure in the cases of the three alternatives (project, bank, nothing) at $t = 1$ and $t = 2$ are given by:

$$(1 - y_1)104.76, y_1(1.05)104.76 \qquad \dots \text{project}$$
$$(1 - y_1)100, \qquad y_1(1.05)100 \qquad \dots \text{bank}$$
$$(1 - y_1)100, \qquad y_1 100 \qquad \dots \text{neither}$$

Thus, no matter what pattern of current or future expenditure is desired the project is the best arrangement. With the 15% inflation the expenditures allowed in 'real' terms would be

$$(1 - y_1)104.76, y_1(1.05)104.76(1.15)^{-1} \qquad \dots \text{project}$$
$$(1 - y_1)100, \qquad y_1(1.05)100(1.15)^{-1} \qquad \dots \text{bank}$$
$$(1 - y_1)100, \qquad y_1 100(1.15)^{-1} \qquad \dots \text{neither}$$

Again the project must be preferred. There can be no logical reason for altering the original decision.

In general as the inflation rate changes (for instance moving from zero to a positive value) this will affect the project's cash flow and the discount rate. We were taking as our measure of inflation the movement of a weighted *average* of prices (for instance the retail price index). In other words not all prices need necessarily inflate at the same rate. Specifically, suppose that the project's return inflates at $100\beta\%$ p.a. Now what of the discount rate? If $\hat{r}$ represents the inflation discount rate there will be a relationship

$$\hat{r} = f(r, \alpha) \tag{2.10}$$

the details of which are vague. In (2.10) r is the discounting interest rate in the absence of inflation and $100\alpha\%$ is the inflation rate. Generally $\hat{r}$ will be an increasing function of α.

In these circumstances the NPV of the project in the presence of inflation becomes

$$-100 + \frac{110(1 + \beta)}{(1 + \hat{r})} \tag{2.11}$$

which may be less than or greater than 4.76. The project's money (nominal) cash flow is

$$-100 \qquad 110(1 + \beta)$$

and this is evaluated in the familiar fashion, using r. The nominal interest rate or cost of capital is, $100r\%$ and if the assumption stands that this rate applies to all financial transactions then it follows (from the y_t, z_t line of reasoning) that *projects should be compared by discounting nominal returns at the nominal interest rate.* An individual project is assessed in similar fashion.

Thus the investor is faced with estimating future cash flow items in terms of the prices that will prevail in future. This is the only 'allowance' that is made for inflation. The best estimates are obtained of cash flow items in nominal terms and the estimated nominal cost of capital is used to discount them.

It is sometimes said that a business will not invest unless there is a positive 'real' return and that cut-off rates (nominal yields) are raised to ensure this. What is meant by the 'real' return on an investment? The 'real yield', $100e\%$, is defined as

$$\sum_{t=1}^{n} R_t (1 + e)^{-t} (1 + \alpha)^{-t} - k = 0 \qquad (2.12)$$

where $(1 + e)(1 + \alpha) = (1 + i)$ where $100i\%$ is the nominal yield and where the R_t are the *nominal* returns. Thus:

$$e = \frac{(1 + i)}{(1 + \alpha)} - 1$$

and will be negative if $i < \alpha$. So if the nominal yield on an investment is less than the inflation rate the yield in so-called 'real' terms is negative. This would be too bad, but it is entirely irrelevant to the investment decision. Once again the '$y_t z_t$' reasoning can be used to shoot down the assertion that positive real yields ought to be obtained. Refusal to accept the best alternative available (whether or not it has a positive real yield) leads to suboptimal decisions. Setting a high threshold which is itself as arbitrary as the rate of inflation will lead to the rejection of worthwhile projects.

The vogue for thinking in 'real' terms seems to be coming to an end, but present value calculations can be expressed in 'real' terms if desired provided that the 'real' interest rate is used. Thus a project would be acceptable if

$$\sum R_t (1 + s)^{-t} (1 + \alpha)^{-t} - k > 0 \qquad (2.13)$$

where s, the real interest rate, is defined by

$$(1 + s) = \frac{(1 + r)}{(1 + \alpha)}$$

and where the R_t are the money returns. The use of (2.13) has been called 'double discounting' where first of all the R_t are converted to 'real' terms (expressed in terms of base year purchasing power) by discounting $100\alpha\%$ to give the 'real' cash flow

$$-k \quad R_1(1+\alpha)^{-1}, R_2(1+\alpha)^{-2} \ldots R_n(1+\alpha)^{-n}$$

which is then discounted using the real rate of interest, $100s\%$. Note that it would be completely wrong to discount the R_t first using α and then $\hat{r}$. There are two alternatives which come to the same thing. Either everything is in money terms or everything is in real terms. There can be no mixing the two.

The methods described relate to inflation that is anticipated. By definition there exists no technique that correctly allows (in all cases) for unanticipated inflation. Unanticipated anything (technical snags for instance) is a source of error. All that the decision-makers can do is make correct *ex-ante* decisions. What actually transpires *ex post* is irrelevant to the original decision-making problem.

Of course inflation, anticipated or otherwise, is a more complex phenomenon than we have allowed so far. High among the unbounded perversity of its ways must rank 'cash flow problems'. In short, this means that the precise timing of cash flow items can assume crucial importance or may be affected unfavourably. If in inflated outflow is to be incurred one week before an inflated inflow it may be that uninflated cash reserves (perhaps already drained by inflation) are inadequate and a liquidity crisis results. Theoretically, this circumstance can be met within the NPV framework with an alteration of the interest rate (or the inclusion of several rates) but the procedure is rather contrived. If the cash flow problems were anticipable then they would be included in the problem structure—perhaps as constraints in a capital rationing format. If they were not anticipated this is harsh reality and the techniques cannot allow for this.

The discussion so far has taken for its theoretical underpinning the assumption that all financial transactions can occur at the uniform discounting interest rate. What if this is not the case?

In contrast to the single interest rate case, the presence of different borrowing and investment interst rates prohibits (at an exact, theoretical level) the use of an NPV and NTV criterion. The investor has a formidable combinatorial problem to solve. One way of expressing the problem is

maximize $\qquad U(W_t)$

subject to $\qquad \displaystyle\sum_{t=0}^{n} (R_t + I_t - W_t)(1+i)^{y_t}(1+j)^{y_t} \geqslant T$

or $\qquad \displaystyle\sum_{t=0}^{n} (S_t + I_t - W_t)(1+i)y_t(1+j)z_t \geqslant T$

where the R_t and S_t are the returns to two alternative projects, the I_t are the existing income stream, W_t are withdrawals for consumption (or the payment of dividends), i and j are the borrowing and investment rates of interest (as decimals), T is the requisite value of retained income at the horizon y_t is the number of periods including and beyond t in which the investor is a net borrower and z_t is the number of periods including and beyond t in which the invesor is a net creditor. The values of y_t and z_t depend upon the values of W_t chosen; thus the terminal value of a project

$$\text{NTV}^R = \sum_{t=0}^{n} R_t (1 + i)^{y_t} (1 + j)^{z_t}$$

and consequently the present value cannot be expressed independently of the particular W_t chosen.

Moreover, if a choice between two projects is considered (a) before inflation and (b) afterwards, even when the returns and interest rates are unaffected (i.e. the inflation is external to the project) but there we consider the ultimate sources of utility—the goods and services bought with the money; there can be different decisions. If project R is preferred in the absence of inflation it is entirely possible that S would be preferred with it.

However, it does not follow from all this that NPV methods should be abandoned. The percentage approximation in GPV through assuming a uniform interest rate rather than several will, usually be slight. The single rate used may be an average (as the weighted average cost of capital) or one of the specific values if the project is heavily biased in that direction (e.g. always in the red until the last return comes in). In the presence of inflation, unless there is obvious reason for doing otherwise, the projects should be compared on the basis of nominal NPV's discounted at an averaged nominal rate (i.e. somewhere between i and j). Occasionally it may be appropriate to use different averages for different projects, but if the projects are not too dissimilar this will not be warranted.

In the foregoing discussion we have been taking it that project returns are affected by inflation in a predetermined fashion (viz. alternatively inflating at zero or $100\beta\%$). This may not always be an appropriate assumption—for example where the enterprise does not seek to maximize NPV but merely achieve a given NPV or yield target value. Circumstances may be such that the target is initially well within reach. If inflation now enters the picture the enterprise may be able to 'adminster' the cash flow in such a way as retain the achievement of its objective. The following example also serves to illustrate the interrelated nature of the investment and pricing decisions.

A water board is to supply water to a large industrial enterprise in each of three years. The requirements of the enterprise in the three years are for 3,000, 4,000 and 5,000 million gallons respectively. There are two technically different ways the board can supply the water. Method one would imply costs (estimated on the basis of present prices) of £400,000, £500,000 and £650,000 occurring at the end of the three years respectively. Method two would imply costs of £600,000, £500,000 and £500,000. However, it is known that costs will inflate at 5% per year, and the board's cost of capital is 10%. Public policy decrees that the board should aim to 'break even' after the three years. The same price (expressed as per 1,000 gallons) is to be charged to the industrial concern in each of the three years. It is assumed that no further costs and revenues occur subsequently. Which method would enable the board to supply the water at the lowest price?

The 'break-even' condition here means zero NTV for the board after three years. Thus we shall express the NTV's for the board as functions of price for each of the two possible methods, equate the NTV's to zero, and solve for the prices.

For method one, with a price of P_1, we obtain

$$\begin{aligned}
\text{NTV}_1 = [\ \{ &- 400,000(1.05) + 3,000,000P_1\}(1.1) \\
&- 500,000(1.05)^2 + 4,000,000P_1](1.1) \\
&- 650,000(1.05)^3 + 5,000,000P_1 \\
= 0&
\end{aligned}$$

and for method two, where the price would be P_2, we obtain

$$\begin{aligned}
\text{NTV}_2 = [\ \{ &- 600,000(1.05) + 3,000,000P_2\}(1.1) \\
&- 500,000(1.05)^2 + 4,000,000P_2](1.1) \\
&- 500,000(1.05)^3 + 5,000,000P_2 \\
= 0&
\end{aligned}$$

Soving for P_1 and P_2 we obtain $P_1 \approx £0.143$ and $P_2 \approx £0.149$. Thus, method one will supply the water at a lower price and would be preferred.

2.4 Choosing the Starting Date

These days there is rarely a great deal of choice as to *when* a large project should be begun. Both inflation and political considerations (especially in the case of public utilities), as well as commerical factors, combine to dictate timings. However, it should not be forgotten that the choice of starting date for a project is at least a theoretical option for the decision-maker. The present value of a project may change, and in particular change its sign, if the starting date is altered. This is because the outlay and returns may be asymmetrically affected by the changed timing. For instance, postponement will (inflation aside) reduce the present value of the initial outlay, and this may more than offset the reduction in the present value of the returns. The influence of calendar time is particularly important in this connection. A numerical example will illustrate this point.

The Government is considering the construction of a small power-

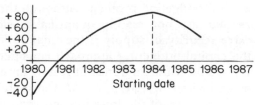

Figure 2.9

station. It can build the station in 1980 or 1990. The cost of construction will be £400m. if the station is built in 1980 or £500 million if it is built in 1990. In either case the station has a lifetime of 20 years from the date of construction. Demand and cost conditions are such that the net returns at the end of each of the 10 years 1980 to 1990 would be £40m., from 1990 to 2000 £60m. per annum, and from 2000 to 2010 £80m. per annum. The cost of capital is 10%. When should the Government build the station?

It will be assumed that the choice of date will be influenced more by the NPVs that would be obtained in each case, and less by political expediency. It is as if two mutually exclusive projects A_1 and A_2 were being considered. The cash flows in each case are as follows:

Calendar date:	1980	1990	2000	2010
A_1:	– 400 + 40 p.a.		+ 60 p.a.	
A_2:		– 500 + 60 p.a.		+ 80 p.a.

The present values of these projects at 1980 are – £12.08 million for A_1 and + £22.44m. for A_2. It is therefore preferable on financial grounds to construct the power-station in 1990. Needless to say the result will not always be in favour of the later starting date; it will depend upon the particular demand and cost conditions that obtain. But here is a case where the NPV of a project not only changes in magnitude as a result of a changed starting date, but also changes in sign.

The graph of NPV (1980) of a project against starting date may in general have any shape, depending on the nature of the returns. One possibility is illustrated in Figure 2.9, where it can be seen the NPV of the project if started in 1980 is negative and that the optimum starting date is 1984. The graph of NPV against starting date for a project with constant returns and constant outlay would tend uniformly to zero—that is, the earlier the starting date the better if NPV (1980) was positive, and the later the better if NPV (1980) was negative.

2.5 Make or Buy

Sometimes a firm may have the choice of making an item it needs or buying in supplies of the item manufactured elsewhere. The costs in each case usually have a different temporal distribution. The problem can often be formulated as a capital-budgeting problem, although there may be some important factors that are not readily quantifiable—for instance, the benefits of any extra security of supply if the 'make' decision is taken.

To illustrate the capital-budgeting approach consider the case where the 'make' decision would entail an outlay of K now for equipment which would last n years, and where $M_1, M_2, \ldots, M_n$ represent the costs of producing the requisite numbers of the item in each year and $B_1, B_2, \ldots, B_n$ are the alternative buying-in costs. Then the project to be evaluated is

$$- K, (B_1 - M_1), (B_2 - M_2), \ldots, (B_n - M_n + S_n)$$

where S_n represents scrap value of equipment at n.

As a numerical example, consider the case of a firm which is considering manufacturing for itself a component it needs in an assembly operation. In order to do the manufacturing it would need to buy a machine for £4,000 which would last for four years with (solely for simplicity) no scrap value. Manufacturing costs in each of the four years would be £6,000, £7,000, £8,000 and £10,000 respectively. If the firm obtained the components from a supplier the costs would be £9,000, £10,000, £11,000 and £14,000 respectively, in each of the four years. However, the machine would occupy floor space which could have been used for another machine which could be hired at no initial cost to manufacture an item, the sales of which would produce net cash flows in each of the four years of £2,000. It is impossible to find room for both machines and there are no other external effects. The cost of capital is 10%. Should the firm make the component or buy from the supplier?

Te stream of costs (in £1,000s) associated with manufacture are

(i) 4 6 7 8 10

and those associated with buying are

(ii) 0 9 10 11 14

thus the savings in costs of making rather than buying (ii) – (i) are

(iii) – 4 3 3 3 4

but if the firm manufactures the component, it forgoes a profit of £2,000 in each year, thus the true savings are

  – 4 1 1 1 2

so that we wish to find the value of

$$- 4 + \frac{1}{1.1} + \frac{1}{(1.1)^2} + \frac{1}{(1.1)^3} + \frac{2}{(1.1)^4}$$

which is – 0.15. Thus the firm should buy the component from the supplier and use the floor space for the other manufacturing process.

2.6 Cost–benefit Ratios

Frequently in the public sector the approach to investment decision-making that is adopted is cost–benefit analysis. Measurement of the benefits and costs of a public utility is both difficult and in practice imprecise. Much of the literature on cost–benefit analysis rightly dwells on the theoretical and practical difficulties of benefit and cost evaluation, but here we are concerned with the decision making tool itself.

In principle, if B represents the present value of future revenues b_t and C represents the present value of future costs C_t (including operating costs) associated with an n-year project, with a discount rate of $100r\%$ then, when the first 'benefit' occurs after one year:

$$B = \sum_{t=1}^{n} b_t(1+r)^{-t}$$

and where the first cost is incurred immediately;

$$C = \sum_{t=0}^{n} c_t(1+r)^{-t}$$

where c_0 is the initial outlay on the project, then the *aggregate benefit–cost ratio* is defined as $R_A = B/C$. A project with $R_A > 1$ would be accepted. In public utilities especially, the terms c_t and b_t often include monetary estimates of 'social' benefits and 'social' costs—the external effects of the project on the community and the environment, as well as outflows and inflows of hard cash. Note that the net present value of the project is $B - C$.

In many case, large projects require cash outlays for more than one year before inflows of cash occur. If such outlays are required during the first m of the n years we can write $C = C_1 + C_2$ where

$$C_1 = \sum_{t=0}^{m} c_t(1+r)^{-t}$$

and, for the operating costs after m;

$$C_2 = \sum_{t=m+1}^{n} c_t(1+r)^{-t}$$

The present value of the stream of benefits is

$$B = \sum_{t=m+1}^{n} b_t(1+r)^{-t}$$

which is B defined as previously except that the first m of the b_t are zero. The *netted benefit–cost ratio*, R_N, is defined as

$$R_N = \frac{B - C_2}{C_1}$$

By this criterion projects with $R_N > 1$ are accepted and those with

$R_N < 1$ are rejected. In summary then, $\text{NPV} = B - C_1 - C_2$, $R_A = B/(C_1 + C_2)$, $R_N = (B - C_2)/C_1$. Where a single project is being assessed with the object of providing a 'yes' or 'no' answer to the question 'should we invest?', the three criteria will give the same answer, for clearly if $\text{NPV} > 0$ this is because $B > C_1 + C_2$ so that $R_A > 1$ and also $B - C_2 > C_1$ so that $R_N > 1$ as well. But when the projects are to be ranked, or a choice made between mutually exclusive projects the R_A and R_N rules can contradict each other and either may be at variance with the NPV rankings, a point which the reader may easily verify by appropriately choosing values for B, C_1 and C_2. Which rule is to be preferred?

Like yield, both benefit—cost ratios can be blind to the scale of profit to be made: they are, by definition, more concerned with the ratios of benefits received to costs outlaid rather than the magnitude of the excess of benefits over costs. For instance consider two projects I and II. For project I let $B = 3$ and $C_2 = C_1 = 1$, and for II let $B = 11$ and $C_2 = C_1 = 4$ (say, millions of pounds). Both benefit—cost ratios would indicate acceptance of the smaller project I which gives a profit (in present-value terms) of £1m. rather than project II which gives a profit of £3 million. This illustrates the crucial difference between the NPV and benefit—cost approach. A profit-minded organization should not decline course of action leading to £3 million profit in favour of one which yields £1m. Costs of capital and/or opportunities for investment elsewhere are taken account of by the discount rates used. Also when risk is allowed for, as Schwab and Lusztig have shown, claims for the superiority of the netted ratio over NPV cannot be supported, and that in any circumstances the aggregate benefit—cost ratio should be rejected. Thus the use of benefit—cost ratios is a questionable procedure and it is preferable to employ the NPV approach once the major problem of data collection has been overcome.

2.7 Repair or Replace

When should an asset be scrapped and with what, if anything, should it be replaced? As equipment ages the operating and maintenance costs are likely to rise and in some cases the quality of output produced may fall causing reduced revenues. However, the longer an asset is kept the more is postponed the capital outlay associated with replacement. The problem is to strike the best balance between these opposing factors. In principle the problem is one of capital budgeting although there are a number of complicating factors in actual use of methods. There are considerable data problems (interdependencies and forecasting costs) and the impact of inflation may be considerable. We shall start by examining problems in which the replacing machinery is financially identical to the outgoing asset and then consider cases where this is not so. Throughout the description it will be assumed that the data are net of tax and such capital allowances as may be appropriate.

(i) Financially Identical Replacements

In those cases in which a particular item of capital equipment will be replaced by 'financially identical' equipment when it is scrapped the problem is to determine the optimal interval between the installation of new machinery; the length of replacement cycle. The term 'financially identical' means that the cash flows produced by the replacing equipment are the same as those produced by the equipment that is replaced. As we have said, there may be considerable data problems. It is not 'simply' a matter of estimating future cash flows, there will also be interdependencies to untangle. For instance, some of the costs may be joint costs, machines may 'compete' for resources and may be complementary or competitive on the revenue side. The data that are required are as follows:

(i) A table of residual values of the asset (net of expense of changeover);

(ii) Capital cost of new asset;

(iii) Operating costs and maintenance expenses ('O and M');

(iv) The revenues produced in each period.

The problem can be expressed either as one in which the objective is to maximize the present value of net revenues or one in which the present value of costs is minimized. The latter formulation is rather more convenient and in this case any differences in revenues produced by machines of different ages are incorporated in the 'operating costs' as opportunity costs. Given the choice of the cost-based formulation there still remain several ways of expressing the problem; these are:

(a) The annual equivalent annuity method (AE);

(b) The lowest common multiple method (LCM);

(c) The 'finite horizon' method (FH).

The finite horizon method is unnecessary in the simpler cases with which we shall commence, but can come into its own in the problems discussed under (ii).

First consider the AE method. Suppose that a firm operates one machine of a certain type and that all such machines, existing asset and replacements, have a maximum life of four years with the specific data as shown in Figure 2.10. The discount rate is 10% and the objective is

Time (years) t		0	1	2	3	4
Initial outlay	(£)	10,000				
O and M	(£)		3,000	4,000	5,000	6,000
Residual value	(£)		6,000	4,500	3,000	1,000

Figure 2.10

t =	1 year	2 years	3 years	4 years
0	10,000	10,000	10,000	10,000
1	−3,000	3,000	3,000	3,000
2		−500	4,000	4,000
3			2,000	5,000
4				5,000
PV at 10%	7,272.72	12,314.05	17,535.69	23,204.70

Figure 2.11

to choose the length of replacement cycle which minimizes the present value of costs.

First compute the total present values of 'costs' (some will be negative) associated with keeping the first machine for different lengths of time. The workings are shown in Figure 2.11.

The 1 year column of Figure 2.11 contains the cash flows associated with keeping the initial asset for just one year. Thus an outlay of £10,000 is required at $t = 0$, but at $t = 1$ the machine is scrapped for £6,000 and only incurs O and M costs of £3,000. Thus the net figure for 'costs' is −£3,000. Similarly in the 2-year column at $t = 2$ in this case O and M costs are £4,000, but scrapping at this point produced £4,500, a net inflow of £500, i.e. a 'cost' of −£500. Other entries are similarly determined and the present values of each cash flow calculated.

Each of the numbers in the last row of Figure 2.11 'covers' the firm for a different period. In the case where the machine is retained for just one year a new machine will be required at $t = 1$ which will again (if kept for one year) produce a stream of costs which will give a 'present value' at $t = 1$ of 7,272.72. One way of comparing these different length cycles is to find that constant annual sum (the annual equivalent annuity) which would give a present value at $t = 0$ equal to indefinitely repeated cycles of the given lengths. For instance, in the case of a cycle length of one year a payment of £8,000 at $t = 1$ would give a PV of 7,272.72, and an annual payment of £8,000 is equivalent in PV terms to the actual cash flow pattern of a one-year cycle obtained in Figure 2.12.

In the two-year cycle length case the annual equivalent annuity for two years at 10% that would produce a PV of 12,314.05 is 7,095.24. In each case the AE figure is obtained by multiplying the PV entry in Figure 2.10 by the AE factor for £1 at $100r\%$ for n years which is obtained from Table 6. The results are shown in Figure 2.13.

t =	0	1	2	3	4	5
Machine 1	10,000	−3,000				
Machine 2		10,000	−3,000			
Machine 3			10,000	−3,000		
Machine 4				10,000	−3,000	etc.
Machine 5, etc.					10,000	etc.
Net cash flow	10,000	7,000	7,000	7,000	7,000	etc.

Figure 2.12

Cycle length (years)	PV of one cycle	AE factor	AE annuity
1	7,272.72	1.1000	8,000.00
2	12,314.05	0.5762	7,095.36
3	17,535.69	0.4021	7,051.10
4	23,204.70	0.3155	7,321.08

Figure 2.13

Thus a three-year cycle length is optimal; each machine is scrapped and replaced by a financially identical machine after three years. Over an infinite horizon the total present value of costs under this alternative will be £70,511, the lowest figure that can be achieved. The actual cost data produced by a three-year cycle are

10,000   3,000   4,000   12,000   3,000   4,000   12,000, etc.

After the initial 10,000 there are triennial perpetuities of 3,000, 4,000 and 12,000 and the 70,511 figure can be obtained (difference due to rounding) as

$$\frac{12,000}{0.331} + \frac{4,000(1.1)}{0.331} + \frac{3,000(1.1)^2}{0.331} + 10,000 = 70,514$$

In the case of the 4,000 and 3,000 flows these begin at $t = 1$ and $t = 2$ respectively rather than at $t = 3$. However, a triennial flow of 4,000 starting at $t = 2$ has the same present value as a triennial flow of $4,000(1.1)$ starting at $t = 3$. Also, a triennial flow of 3,000 starting at $t = 1$ has the same present value as a triennial flow of $3,000(1.1)^2$ starting at $t = 3$. With these adjustments we can consider all flows (apart from the original 10,000) as being triennial and starting at $t = 3$. In calculating the present value the discount factors would be $1/(1.1)^3$, $1/(1.1)^6$, $1/(1.1)^9$ and so on which can be thought of as $1/1.331$, $1/(1.331)^2$, $1/(1.331)^3$, etc. Hence the division by 0.331 above.

Finally, we can obtain the 70,514 figure in one more way. If we consider the costs in the three-year case to be equivalent to a sum of 17,535.69 expended every third year, starting at $t = 0$, the total present value works out as

$$\frac{17,535.69(1.331)}{0.331} = 70,514$$

The AE method can thus turn up in a variety of guises. The alternative to it is the LCM method in which the cycle length alternatives are compared on size of present value of costs over a horizon equal to the lowest common multiple of the cycle lengths. In the numerical example above, the horizon would be 12 years. The AE method will be the most efficient in all but near-trivial cases although by astute use of standard tables the LCM method is not so bad as may appear from an 8, 9, 10-year cycle alternative LCM of 360 years. For instance if PV_8 is the present value of the first one of the 8-year cycles the entire present value over 360 years is

$$PV_8\left[1 + \frac{1}{(1+r)^8}\right] + \left[\frac{1}{(1+r)^{16}}\right] + \cdots + \left[\frac{1}{(1+r)^{352}}\right]$$

$$= PV_8\left[\frac{1-(1+r)^{-360}}{1-(1+r)^{-8}}\right]$$

$$\simeq \left[\frac{PV_8(1+r)^8}{(1+r)^8 - 1}\right]$$

where the last term above will be accurate enough for practical purposes. The method must give the same result as the AE method, since for the exact, middle term of the above it is the denominator only that counts; since for all three values of PV_m the numerator is common.

(ii) Non-identical Replacements

Under this head we consider those problems in which machines are not financially identical. Two particular cases are worth identifying. They are:

> (i) Replacement of an existing machine by a different type of machine

> (ii) Uniform inflation.

In the first of these cases the question that is raised is when to break into the cycle for the existing type of equipment and introduce the optimal cycle with the superior machines. Again an enumerative approach (considering all of the possible alternatives) is employed. Consider a numerical example.

A firm's existing machine of an old design has O and M costs and scrap value as follows:

Time (years) $t =$	0	1	2	3
O and M(£)	0	3,600	4,800	6,000
Residual value(£)	3,500	2,000	1,000	0

The column headed 0 means that if the old machine was scrapped at once there would be no O and M costs associated with it and that a scrap value of £3,500 could be realized. If scrapping occurred after one year there would be a single net outflow of £1,600 at $t = 1$.

The old machine can be scrapped at any of the four values of t and replaced permanently by machines with the cost structure of Figure 2.10 for which we have seen that a three-year replacement cycle is optimal. The total present value of costs for the new machines was £70,511 *from the date of introduction of these machines*. Thus if the new cycle was brought in at $t = 2$ (i.e. scrapping the old machine at this time) the present value

Replace	Cash flow $t=$				Total present value
	0	1	2	3	
$t=0$	$-3,500$				
	70,511				67,011
$t=1$	0	1,600			
		70,511			65,556
$t=2$	0	3,600	3,800		
			70,511		64,683
$t=3$	0	3,600	4,800	6,000	
				70,511	64,722

Figure 2.14

of costs on the new machines at $t = 0$ would be £70,511 × 0.8264 = £58,270. The whole picture is presented in Figure 2.14.

Thus the optimal policy is to keep the old machine for two years and then replace with the three-year cycle on the new machines. The figure 64,683 being 3600 × 0.9091 + (3800 + 70,511) × 0.8264. The other figures in the present value column being obtained in similar fashion and it is evident that there is little practical difference between the two-year and three-year options—just £39 in present value terms.

Now, what of the second case, that of 'uniform' inflation? By uniform inflation is meant a situation where it is known that outlay, costs and residual values will all inflate at $100i\%$ per annum commencing at $t = 0$. Thus if Figure 2.10 gives financial data for $i = 0$, with $i = 0.2$, a 20% rate of inflation, the data would be as given in Figure 2.15.

We shall assume that it remains the objective of the firm to minimize the present value of costs. As will be seen the problem is a good deal more complex than in the no-inflation case. Consider the problem in general terms to see the main difficulties that arise. The information is given in Figure 2.16 where $£k$ is the cost of the machine at time zero. The c_t^0 and s_t^0 are respectively O and M and residual values in each year of the machine's life *in the absence of inflation*. Thus, for instance, the O and M cost of the machine in the third year of its life, but at time t, would be

Time $t=$	0	1	2	3	4
Initial outlay	10,000				
O and M		3,600	5,760	8,640	12,441.6
Residual value		7,200	6,480	5,184	2,073.6
Replacement cost		12,000	14,400	17,280	20,736

Figure 2.15

Time $t=$	0	1	2	3	4	5	etc.
Initial outlay	k						
O and M		c_1^0	c_2^0	c_3^0	c_4^0	c_5^0	etc.
Residual value		s_1^0	s_2^0	s_3^0	s_4^0	s_5^0	etc.
Replacement cost		$k(1+i)$	$k(1+i)^2$	$k(1+i)^3$	$k(1+i)^4$	$k(1+i)^5$	etc.

Figure 2.16

$c_3^0(1+i)^t$. Remember that t need not equal 3 here—we could be dealing with the fourth or fifth entire cycle.

Consider a two-year cycle in these circumstances. The cash flow for the first four years would be

$t=0$	$t=1$	$t=2$	$t=3$	$t=4$
k	$c_1^0(1+i)$	$(c_2^0-s_2^0)(1+i)^2$	$c_1^0(1+i)^3$	$(c_2^0-s_2^0)(1+i)^4$
		$k(1+i)^2$		$k(1+i)^4$

Now consider the first sequence (the original machine's cash flows). Call the annual equivalent annuity for this one sequence AE_2^i. The second machine would produce an annual equivalent annuity for two years commencing at $t=3$ of $AE_2^i(1+i)^2$, the third machine would generate $AE_2^i(1+i)^4$ and so on. The total present value of all these streams will be

$$\frac{AE_2^i}{(1+r)}\left| 1+\frac{1}{(1+r)}+\frac{(1+i)^2}{(1+r)^2}+\frac{(1+i)^3}{(1+r)^3}\right.$$

$$\left.+\frac{(1+i)^4}{(1+r)^4}+\frac{(1+i)^5}{(1+r)^5}+\ldots\right|$$

$$=\frac{AE_2^i}{(1+r)}\left| s_2+\frac{(1+i)^2}{(1+r)^2}s_2+\frac{(1+i)^4}{(1+r)^4}s_2+\ldots\right|$$

where $s_2=1+[1/(1+r)]$, which we should note for future reference is equal to

$$\frac{1-\dfrac{1}{(1+r)^2}}{1-\dfrac{1}{(1+r)}}$$

Now in general, for a cycle of length m years, the total present value would be

$$\frac{AE_m^i}{(1+r)}\left| s_m+\frac{(1+i)^m}{(1+r)^m}s_m+\frac{(1+i)^{2m}}{(1+r)^{2m}}s_m+\ldots\right| \tag{2.14}$$

Obviously (2.14) will be unbounded if $i\geqslant r$, but consider the partial sum over a T year horizon (where T is any whole number multiple of the LCM of the alternative cycle lengths). For an m year cycle length there will be $n=T/m$ terms in (2.14) which sums to $(V_m)_T$ given by

$$(V_m)_T=\frac{AE_m^i}{(1+r)}\left[\frac{1-\dfrac{1}{(1+r)^m}}{1-\dfrac{1}{(1+r)}}\right]\left[\frac{1-\dfrac{(1+i)^T}{(1+r)^T}}{1-\dfrac{(1+i)^m}{(1+r)^m}}\right]$$

From which it is evident that a choice between cycle lengths can no longer be made simply on the basis of the AE_m^i alone. This figure needs to be weighted by a factor which is a function of m. This contrasts with the no inflation case. In fact the formulation (2.14) is not the most convenient one for computational purposes. The product of the first two terms in (2.14) is the present value of the inflation adjusted cash flows for the first of the m year cycles. Call this PV_m^i. We can then re-express $(V_m)_T$ as

$$(V_m)_T = \frac{(1+r)^m PV_m^i}{(1+i)^m - (1+r)^m} \left[\frac{(1+i)^T}{(1+r)^T} - 1 \right] \cdots \qquad (2.15)$$

where in (2.15) the important thing is that the square-bracketed term is independent of m so that a choice between the alternative cycle lengths can be made on the basis of the absolute value of its coefficient. Incidentally, in (2.15) note that $(1+r)^m PV_m^i \equiv NTV_m^i$. Hence, it would be convenient to work in terminal values.

As a numerical example, consider again the data of Figure 2.15. As we have just observed, the square-bracketed term in (2.15) is common to all values of m so we need only determine the values of the term in PV_m^i. For instance, if a three-year cycle is being evaluated then

$$(1+r)^m = (1.1)^3 = 1.331$$
$$(1+i)^m = (1.2)^3 = 1.728$$

and

$$\begin{aligned} PV_3^i &= 3,600 \times 0.9091 + 5,760 \times 0.8264 \\ &\quad + (8,640 - 5,184) \times 0.7513 + 10,000 \\ &= 20,629 \end{aligned}$$

Thus the coefficient of the square-bracketed term in (2.15) is

$$\frac{1.331 \times 20,629}{1.728 - 1.331} = 69,162$$

If we consider a 12-year horizon, i.e. $T = 12$, the total present value of costs in the three year cycle case is found by multiplying £69,162 by

$$\frac{(1.2)^{12}}{(1.1)^{12}} - 1$$

Thus total present value of costs in this case works out at £69,162 $\times$ 1.8409 = £127,320. Figure 2.17 gives the full results. The decision can be taken on the basis of the coefficient figure alone, but the total PV

m	Coefficient	Total PV $(T = 12)$
1	74,000	136,227
2	66,696	122,781
3	69,162	127,320
4	75,920	139,761

Figure 2.17

figures for $T = 12$ are also shown for comprative purposes. Thus in this case a two-year cycle is best showing, for any value of T, a 3.57% cost reduction in present terms over the next-best, three-year, alternative.

When machines are not financially identical and where the costs over time do not vary in a systematic and convenient fashion then there will be no alternative to the crude FH method. In this approach a large value of T is selected (perhaps between 20 and 50) the best available forecasts of the cash flows are made and the NPVs are calculated for each possible case. The alternative giving the smallest NPV of costs is then selected.

2.8 Single-constraint Capital Rationing

In Chapter 1 present value and yield-based criteria for project selection were developed. It was stated then that these rules would not apply in a situation of capital rationing. Capital rationing arises when there are insufficient funds to finance all attractive projects. We shall see that this situation causes a number of difficulties in project selection. The capital-rationing situation is a particular case of problems in which projects are selected under *constraints*. These constraints may relate to the consumption of any scarce resource required by all or some of the projects—for instance, capital in one or more periods, labour, materials, machinery, space and so on. In addition there may be requirements to be met in relation to reported profits, share price and certain financial statistics. We shall here consider the simplest case when there is only one constraint. A simple method of solution can usually be applied in such cases. For concreteness the discussion here will be in terms of problems in which the only constraint relates to the total amount spent initially—a single-period capital constraint. The method described could equally well be applied to problems in which the scarce resource was something other than capital—materials for example.

The method will be explained in the context of a numerical example.

A company's cost of capital is 10%. It has £215,000 for outlay on six investments. The objective is to select that group of investment which maximize NPV overall. There are no other investment opportunities available. The cash flows from the investments, the net present values at

	Investment					
Year	1	2	3	4	5	6
0	−25,000	−60,000	−90,000	−100,000	−120,000	−35,000
1	7,500	17,500	25,000	0	75,000	40,000
2	7,500	17,500	25,000	0	75,000	0
3	7,500	17,500	25,000	50,000	0	0
4	7,500	17,500	25,000	50,000	0	0
5	7,500	17,500	25,000	50,000	0	0
NPV (10%)	3,431	6,339	4,770	2,759	10,163	1,364
Yield (%)	15.2	14.1	12.1	11.6	16.3	14.3

Figure 2.18

10% and the yields on the investments are shown in Figure 2.18. It is evident from the figure that all projects are desirable in their own right on the basis of either NPV or yield. How is a decision to be made between the investments?

A sensible-sounding procedure would be to rank the projects by size of NPV and then work down this list until the budget was exhausted. The result would be as follows

Project	NPV	Outlay	Total expended
5	10,163	120,000	120,000
2	6,339	60,000	180,000
7/18 of 3	1,855	35,000	215,000
1			
4			
6			

$$18,357 = \text{TOTAL NPV}$$

The projects are ranked in the order 5, 2, 3, 1, 4 and those selected would be 5, 2 and 7/18 of 3. for the time being we shall assume that such fractional projects are permissible. The overall NPV figure produced by this selection is £18,357.

A possible alternative procedure would be to rank by size of yield and work down that list. The outcome in this case is as follows:

Project	Yield	NPV	Outlay	Total expended
5	16.3	10,163	120,000	120,000
1	15.2	3,431	25,000	145,000
6	14.3	1,364	35,000	180,000
7/12 of 2	14.1	3,698	35,000	215,000
3				
4				

$$18,656$$

The result is a total NPV of £18,656, a superior result to the ranking by NPV case. This is merely chance—it could be better than NPV or worse; neither are optimal. The correct procedure is to rank projects by *ratio of NPV to outlay*. Jusification for this method will be given presently. First consider the results.

Project	Ratio	NPV	Outlay	Total expended
1	0.137	3,431	25,000	25,000
2	0.106	6,339	60,000	85,000
5	0.085	10,163	120,000	205,000
1/9 of 3	0.053	530	10,000	215,000
6	0.039			
4	0.028			

$$20,463$$

A substantial improvement is effected by this means, being almost 10% greater than the yield result. Indeed, even without the fractional project three, total NPV is greater than in the two former cases. The ratio method works because the project at the top of the list has the *highest achievement of objective per unit of scarce resource*. Indeed, if it was possible to take more than 100% of an investment *only* project one would be accepted. We should then take 8.6 units of investment one producing an NPV of £29,507. However, with the 100% limit and project one removed from the scene project two makes best use of the scarce resource. If it was now possible to take several units of this project, the best plan would be to set $x_1 = 1$, $x_2 = 3\frac{1}{6}$ and achieve an NPV of £23,505. The process of working down the ratio list always ensures that the best possible use is made of remaining funds.

R. N. Anthony (1961) forms the ratio of GPV to outlay and calls the result a *profitability index* (PI). The use of GPV/outlay ratio gives exactly the same results as use of the NPV/outlay ratio, since as between two projects A and B the condition

$$\frac{NPV_A}{K_A} > \frac{NPV_B}{K_B}$$

can be written

$$\frac{GPV_A - K_A}{K_A} > \frac{GPV_B - K_B}{K_B}$$

$$\frac{GPV_A}{K_A} - 1 > \frac{GPV_B}{K_B} - 1$$

and adding one to both sides gives

$$\frac{GPV_A}{K_A} > \frac{GPV_B}{K_B}$$

Using PI the desirable projects have $PI > 1$ which corresponds to $NPV > 0$, the NPV/outlay ratio also being positive.

Now suppose that among the overall group of projects there is a mutually exclusive pair. Can the ratio method still be applied? Some care is necessary here. Consider the following problem. The following four investment possibilities face a company:

	Outlay (£m.)	PI
A	1 m	1.4
B	0.1 m	1.45
C	1 m	1.1
D	0.1 m	1.35

The company has £1.1m. available for investment. Projects A and B are mutually exclusive. All projects are divisible. Which group of projects maximizes NPV? What is the NPV figure thus obtained?

First note that it would be quite incorrect to eliminate project A to start with on the grounds that B has the greater PI. If this was done the projects selected would be B, D and 9/10 of C and total NPV achieved would be

$$100,000 \times 0.45 + 100,000 \times 0.35 + 0.9 \times 1,000,000 \times 0.1 = 170,000$$

The optimal solution is to take A and D, producing an NPV figure of £435,000. When there is a mutually exclusive pair two sub-problems have to be solved—one containing A and the other B:

Sub-problem 1	Sub-problem 2
A	B
C	C
D	D

Sub-problem 1 produces the £435,000 result and sub-problem 2 gives £170,000 as the best answer. The overall solution is the best answer from either sub-problem. With several mutually exclusive pairs many sub-problems would be formed and the procedure would become rather complicated. There is no avoiding this if an exact answer is sought—the problem contains a *combinatorial* element.

Now consider the problem of fractional projects; suppose that a project must be accepted or rejected in its entirety. Strictly speaking this requirement also produces a combinatorial problem which can rapidly assume formidable proportions. For instance if there were 20 investments there may be upwards of 100,000 groups of projects that could be selected. Consider the optimal solution to the six investment problem. This called for 1/9 of project three. Suppose this is ruled out—what can be done? In practice there is rarely an *absolutely inflexible* budget limit. If the budget could be stretched to round up the last, fractional, project then the best result would be achieved. However, this budget stretching must not affect the cost of capital or a suboptimal position may be obtained. In the six-project case an extra £50,000 is called for—an increase in the budget of over 23%—unlikely perhaps in the private sector. Note, however, that it is easy to determine how much could be paid for these extra funds; 8/9 of project three has the same yield as 9/9 of project three—12.1%. If the additional funds can be obtained at anything less than this cost this will be worth while. Note also that at worst there will only ever be one fractional project to deal with—the last one to be accepted. If the budget will not stretch enough then either (a) a combinatorial problem must be solved, or (b) an approximate solution will have to be accepted.

An approximate solution procedure that is simple to apply and may be expected to give an NPV value within a few per cent of the theoretical maximum (although possibly with a quite different combination of projects) is as follows. First select the project with the greatest PI (if its outlay does not exceed the limit), then take the project with next greatest PI (if the two outlays do not exceed the limit) and so on until a point is arrived at where the project with the next greatest PI would cause the budgetary limit to be exceeded. Projects with lower PIs are then examined and the one with the greatest PI *that can be afforded* is chosen. The list is then searched for the project with the greatest PI that can be afforded from the funds which then remain. Selection is completed when the cheapest project (of those remaining) cannot be financed from the funds yet unused.

As alternatives to the ratio methods there are a number of programming algorithms available to solve the problem, but it is not always worth while using these methods especially for problems involving only a small number of variables; the investor would have to decide whether the extra expense involved in the use of these more sophisticated methods was worth while. As a general rule, ratio metods can be used only in one-constraint problems. There are some rather specially structured two-constraint cases to which the methods can be applied but these are not typical. Systematic solution procedures for such problems rely on programming methods.

Where the net present value of investments is to be maximized subject to the choice of investments satisfying the condition that the initial outlays on the investments do not exceed a predetermined limit, where no investment may be undertaken at more than unit level the problem has come to be known as a *Lorie–Savage* problem. To express the problem in symbolic terms suppose that there are n possible investments, the numbers of units taken of each investment being represented by the variables x_j for $j = 1, 2, \ldots, n$. Let N_j represent the NPV, per unit of the jth investment and K_j represent the initial outlay, per unit, of the jth investment and let L represent the amount of money that is available for investment. The problem can be written as

$$\text{Maximize } N = \sum_{j=1}^{n} N_j x_j \tag{2.16}$$

where

$$\sum_{j=1}^{n} K_j x_j \leqslant L \tag{2.17}$$

and

$$x_j \geqslant 0 \qquad j = 1, 2, \ldots, n \tag{2.18}$$

and

$$x_j \leqslant 1 \qquad j = 1, 2, \ldots, n \tag{2.19}$$

Expression (2.16) is called the *objective function* and (2.17) is referred to as a *constraint*. Conditions (2.18) are *sign requirements* which rule out the possiblity of negative investments and (2.19) are constraints which impose the condition that no more than one unit of any project may be taken.

Reference

Anthony, R. N. (1961), *Management Accounting* (rev. edn.), Irwin.

Further Reading

Bromwich, M., 'Inflation and the capital budgeting process', *Journal of Business Finance,* **1969** (autumn).

Cowan, T. K., 'The maintenance of financial viability under inflationary conditions', *Journal of Business Finance and Accounting,* **2**, No. 3, Autumn 1975.

Foster, E. M., 'The impact of inflation on capital budgeting decisions', *Quarterly Review of Economics and Business Studies,* **10**, No. 3, Autumn 1970.

Grinyer, J. R., 'Inflation and capital budgeting decisions: a comment', *Journal of Business Finance and Accounting,* **1**, No. 1, Spring 1974.

Lorie, J. H., and Savage, C. J., 'Three problems in rationing capital', *Journal of Business,* **28**, No. 4, October 1955.

More, R. F. de la, 'An investigation into the discounting formulae used in capital budgeting', *Journal of Business Finance and Accounting,* **2**, No. 2, Summer 1975.

Nichols, D. A., 'A note on inflation and common stock values', *The Journal of Finance,* **23**, No. 4, September 1978.

Samuels, J. M., and Wilkes, F. M., *Management of Company Finance* (3rd edn.), Nelson, London, 1980.

Samuels, J. M., and Wilkes, F. M., *Management of Company Finance, Students Manual,* Nelson, London, 1981.

Scholefield, H. H., McBain, N. S., and Bagwell, J., 'The effects of inflation on investment appraisal', *Journal of Business Finance,* Summer **1973**.

Schwab, B., and Lusztig, P. (1969), 'A comparative analysis of the NPV and the benefit cost ratio as measures of the economic desirability of investments', *Journal of Finance,* **1969** (June).

Walters, A. A., 'A note on the choice of interest rates in cost benefit analysis', *Economica,* **1970** (February).

Wilkes, F. M., 'Inflation and capital budgeting decisions', *Journal of Business Finance,* **1972** (Autumn).

Wilkie, A. D., 'Discounting formulae use in capital budgeting: a comment', *Journal of Business Finance and Accounting,* **3**, No. 2, September 1976.

CHAPTER 3

Investment Decisions and Linear Programming

Overview

The chapter deals with linear programming in its relationship to present value maximization. The computational procedure is introduced and explained in the context of an investment problem, first with limited funds only and subsequently with other resource limitations. A discussion of duality and its interpretation in an investment context prepares the ground for the important topic of sensitivity analysis.

3.1 Introduction

This chapter introduces a type of problem the character of which is central to the remainder of this book and a simple problem structure is presented and examined. We begin with some generalities concerning project selection under constraints.

In the case of an already established company using buildings, materials and machinery and employing various categories of labour to manufacture one or several products, in any given period of time there are limits (upper bounds in particular) to the amounts of the factors of production such as materials, machine time, floor space, that it can call upon. Finance too is a scarce resource—unlimited amounts cannot be obtained at a given cost, there are conventional constraints on the mix of finance from various sources and some sources may impose conditions on the use of the money they supply.

Furthermore there are year-to-year (or more frequent) changes in the financial position of a firm and the financial positions and outlooks of the providers of finance. Large projects or continuing investment programmes will require capital inputs over long periods of time so that changes in the financial constraints that are faced by a firm may be expected.

If a company is establishing a new plant or if a completely new company is to be formed, we may expect fewer physical constraints (in the shape of plant size, number and types of machines) and more financial ones. In this case the investment projects are the first to be undertaken so that we need not be concerned with interactive effects with existing projects. If 'the investor' is an individual person rather than a company, his problem may be that of selecting or building a portfolio of investments in the form of stocks and bonds. Apart from time, it is unlikely that there will be effective physical constraints, but there will be quite explicit financial constraints. Financial and physical constraints are part and parcel of the environment in which investment decisions are made so that technique of project selection must be able to take them into account. But before proceeding to the development of these techniques the character of programming problems should be introduced.

A programming problem is a problem in which there is an objective to be achieved, but where there are constraints on the courses of action available which restrict the degree of achievement of the objective. Thus in this general sense many aspects of day-to-day behaviour can be viewed as programming problems.

Before programming methods can be of any help it is necessary to be able to measure the degree of achievement of the objective or objectives and to quantify the constraints. This is possible across a broad spectrum of business problems. For example the objective may be to choose the most profitable product range and the levels of production of these products subject to restrictions in the form of limits on floor space, machine time, labour time, raw materials supply and so on. Also of course there will be the requirement that no product is to be produced in a negative amount! In the investment context that concerns us here the objective will be to choose that investment programme which maximizes terminal value, present value, rate of growth or whatever is the objective subject to the physical and financial constraints already referred to. Additional constraints may be that investments be made only in whole number units and in some problems the only whole numbers permitted may be zero (don't invest) and one (invest). In general there will also be constraints relating to mutual exclusion, to which we have already referred and contingency (only consider project C if project B is decided upon) and other such constraints. A linear programming approach to the solution of some of these problems will now be explained.

3.2 A One-constraint Problem

Many of the essential features of large programming problems can be illustrated in the context of quite small ones. The major part of this chapter examines a problem in which there is one 'physical' constraint and one financial constraint and a predetermined rate of discount. We begin however, with examination of a one-constraint problem which is later expanded.

The problem is to determine the numbers to be purchased of machines of two types so as to maximize the present value of the returns that the machines generate. Capital outlays on the machines are not to exceed a predetermined level. It is assumed that all relevant data is to hand. Call the machines type 1 and type 2, and let the numbers purchased of each type be represented by x_1 and x_2 respectively. Forecasts suggest that the NPV of each machine of type 1 is £6,000 and the NPV of each machine of type 2 is £4,000. Total NPV, N, is then given (in £1,000 units) by equation (3.1).

$$N = 6x_1 + 4x_2 \tag{3.1}$$

Equation (3.1) is called the *objective function*. Suppose that each machine of type 1 costs £4,000 and each machine of type 2 costs £2,000. The firm's budget for expenditure on these new machines is £16,000 so that the budget constraint is

$$4x_1 + 2x_2 \leqslant 16 \tag{3.2}$$

It is being assumed in the formulation (3.1) of the objective function that any remainder from the amount 16 is not added to present value. This would be the case if 16 was an allocation from 'headquarters', any remainder being distributed elsewhere.

Also, we shall assume that only purchases rather than sales of machines are being considered and that apart from (3.2) there is no restriction on the numbers that may be bought. Therefore the specification of the problem is completed by the sign requirements. It should be noted that the sign requirements are not of a different nature to the constraint (3.2). The sign requirement for x_1 could be written as $-x_1 + 0.x_2 \leqslant 0$. The complete problem is to

Maximize $N = 6x_1 + 4x_2$

subject to $4x_1 + 2x_2 \geqslant 16$

and $x_1 \geqslant 0, \ x_2 \geqslant 0$

The solution of this problem is rather obvious and it is unnecessary to devise a computational procedure to solve it. Incidentally, the word 'solution' can be employed in two senses. The problems can be said to be 'solved' when the maximum value of the objective function has been found. This is the sense in which the word is used in the immediate context. Below, 'solution' will also be used to refer to a set of values of the variables which satisfy both the constraint and the sign requirements, i.e. any point in OAB in Figure 3.1 can, in this sense, be said to be a 'solution'. The context should make clear the sense in which the word is being used. The very obviousness of the solution, however, may help in understanding the *simplex method* of computation. But before the Simplex method is discussed, let us consider a graph of the problem.

The shaded region OAB, in Figure 3.1 is called the *feasible area*. Other names for the feasible area are :'opportunity set', 'feasible production set' and 'set of attainable combinations'. The feasible area contains all com-

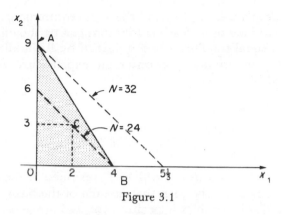

Figure 3.1

binations of x_1 and x_2 that satisfy (3.2) and the sign requirements and are therefore 'feasible'. Points on the line AB correspond to (3.2) holding as a strict equality whilst points below the line mean that a strict inequality holds in (3.2). The dashed lines in the Figure 3.1 are iso-present value (IPV) lines and represent combinations of the xs which give equal values of N. For example, the $N = 24$ line has end points $x_1 = 4$, $x_2 = 0$ and $x_1 = 0$, $x_2 = 6$, both of which clearly give $N = 24$ as does point C ($x_1 = 2$, $x_2 = 3$). The IPV lines all have the same slope, 6/4, since (3.1) can be rewritten as

$$x_2 = \frac{N}{4} - \frac{6}{4}x_1 \tag{3.3}$$

A higher value of N corresponds to an IPV line further from the origin and the problem can be described as that of finding a point somewhere in the feasible area that is on the highest IPV line. This is at point A where $x_1 = 0$, $x_2 = 8$ and $N = 32$. This is the *optimal solution* to the problem.

Whether point A or point B or somewhere in between is the optimal solution can be seen to depend upon the relative slopes of IPV lines and the constraint. The slope of the constraint is -2. The line AB is defined by $x_2 = (16/2) - (4/2)x_1$. If the IPV lines were steeper (in an absolute sense) than the constraint then point B would be optimal. This would correspond to the case where machine one had a relatively larger present value or relatively reduced intial outlay *vis-à-vis* the current situation. It is evident that points between A and B can never be superior to both A and B. They can be equally good only in the case of a coincidence of slope between the IPV lines and constraint. In this case it does not matter what combination of purchases is made as long as the budget is exhausted. The optimal solution is said to be *non-unique*.

The investor can simplify matters for himself by considering only three points A, B and O. The origin would be optimal in the case where both present values were negative. These three points have the common characteristic of being corner points of the feasible area. They are referred to as *basic feasible solutions* to (3.2) and the sign requirements. A most important property of the basic feasible solutions can be shown if (3.2) is re-expressed as an equality. This is accomplished by the addition of a *slack variable, s_1*, being the unused portion of the expenditure allowance and formally defined by

$$S_1 = 16 - 4x_1 - 2x_2 \tag{3.4}$$

so that (3.2) can be rewritten as

$$4x_1 + 2x_2 + s_1 = 16 \tag{3.5}$$

provided that $s_1 \geqslant 0$, a condition which is appended to the existing sign requirements. It can now be seen that at each of the basic feasible solutions *one* of the three variables is positive and *two* are zero. At O $x_1 = 0$, $x_2 = 0$, $s_1 > 0$. In a one-constraint problem each basic feasible solution will have one positive variable. In general, at a basic feasible solution there will be *no more positive variables than there are constraints*. Normally the number of positive variables will equal the number of constraints. In a *degenerate solution* there will be fewer positive variables than constraints. These facts, that only the basic feasible solutions need be considered, and that at these solutions there is an upper limit to the number of positive variables, are exploited by the Simplex method.

3.3   The Simplex Method

An apparently naïve but systematic method of solution of the problem can be based on the method of substitution. The objective function, including s_1 with a zero coefficient is

$$N = 6x_1 + 4x_2 + 0s_1 \tag{3.6}$$

The first step is to solve the constraint (3.5) for s_1 [giving (3.4)] and substitute this expression for s_1 into (3.6). The result is

$$N = 6x_1 + 4x_2 + 0(16 - 4x_1 - 2x_2) = 0 + 6x_1 + 4x_2 \tag{3.7}$$

The value of the objective function is zero if both xs are zero (and consequently $s_1 = 16$ by 3.4) and the coefficients of the xs can be interpreted as meaning that if either were raised from zero level then the value of the objective function would increase by the coefficient of the variable. Since x_1 has the greater coefficient, repeat the above procedure for x_1, solving (3.5) for x_1 gives

$$x_1 = 4 - \frac{1}{2}x_2 - \frac{1}{4}s_1 \tag{3.8}$$

Notice that (3.8) can be obtained by changing the positions of $4x_1$ and s_1 in (3.4) and dividing by four. Now substitute (3.8) into (3.6). The result

is

$$N = 6\left(4 - \frac{1}{2}x_2 - \frac{1}{4}s_1\right) + 4x_2 + 0s_1 = 24 + x_2 - \frac{6}{4}s_1 \tag{3.9}$$

which means that if x_2 and s_1 are zero and therefore x_1 is at its maximum
level the value of the objective function is 24. If x_2 is raised to unit level
then N will increase by the coefficient of x_2 in (3.9), i.e. by one. The important point is that this increase is *net* of the drop in the objective function caused by the necessary reduction in x_1. This is because the relationship between x_1 and x_2 in (3.8) has been incorporated into (3.9) and is implicit in the far right-hand side (RHS) of (3.9). The coefficient of s_1 in
(3.9), 6/4, means that if s_1 was raised to unit level N would *decrease* by 6/4.
The value of the solution $x_1 = 3\frac{3}{4}$, $s_1 = 1$ [from (3.8)] is $24 - 6/4 = 22\frac{1}{2}$. It
is clear that s_1 should be left at zero level and x_2 raised. Since the problem
is entirely linear each and every unit by which x_2 is raised increases the
objective function by one, so we clearly wish to 'introduce' x_2 to the maximum extent. Now, repeating the procedure above, changing the positions
of $\frac{1}{2}x_2$ and x_1 in (3.8) and dividing through by one-half [equivalent to solving (3.5) for x_2] gives

$$x_2 = 8 - 2x_1 - \tfrac{1}{2}s_1 \tag{3.10}$$

amd substitution of (3.10) into (3.6) gives

$$N = 6x_1 + 4(8 - 2x_1 - \tfrac{1}{2}s_1) = 32 - 2x_1 - 2s_1 \tag{3.11}$$

If x_1 and s_1 are both zero [and therefore $x_2 = 8$ from (3.10)] then $N = 32$.
The negative coefficients of x_1 and s_1 in (3.11) show that if they are raised
from zero level then N will fall. Since x_1 and s_1 cannot be lowered because
of the sign requirements, 32 is the maximum value of N and the optimal
solution ($x_1 = 0$, $x_2 = 8$, $s_1 = 0$) has been found. We shall now repeat the
calculations in tableau format. Figure 3.2 describes the first solution that
was tried above (with s_1 positive and x_1 and x_2 zero).

To form the tableau first write down the problem variables then, above
each one, write its objective function coefficient and below each variable
write its coefficient in the constraint equation. Then select the variable
that is to be set at a positive level (the basis variable) and write this in to
the left of the constraint coefficient row. To the right of the basis variable

Figure 3.2

write in its value and to the left put the objective function coefficient of the basis variable. Before coming to the 'index row' it should be noted that the constraint coefficients can be regarded as rates of exchange between the basis variable and the 'non-basis' variable in question. For example, 4, under x_1, means that each time x_1 is raised by one unit s_1 must be *lowered* by four units. Similarly each time x_2 is raised by one unit s_1 must be lowered by two units. The figure 1, under s_1, can be considered a 'self with self' exchange rate. Since only the basis variable is positive the value of N can quickly be found by multiplying the figure to the right of the basis variable (its level, 16) by the figure to the left (the objective function coefficient). The result goes at the bottom of the value column.

Numbers in the index row show how much the objective function would *decrease* by if the corresponding variable at the head of the column was raised to unit level. In some ways it is unfortunate that it is standard practice to form the index row and the rates of exchange so that the numbers are of the intuitively 'wrong' sign. For example, the figure -6 means that if x_1 was raised to unit level then N would increase by $+6$. Because of the one-for-one exchange rate with itself the basis variable will have a zero index row number. The index row numbers are calculated as follows. If x_1 is raised to unit level then s_1 must diminish by four each unit of which contributes zero to the objective function, while a unit of x_1 in its own right adds six. The excess of the drop in N due to reduction of s_1 over the increase in x_1 is $4 \times 0 - 6 = -6$ meaning that there is a net increase in N. By the same arguments the index row number for x_2 is $2 \times 0 - 4 = -4$ and for s_1 itself $1 \times 0 - 0 = 0$.

Each basic feasible solution that is arrived at will be described with the same tableau format as in Figure 3.2. An index row will be calculated and negative numbers in the index row will mean that the objective function can be increased by introducing a variable with a negative index row number. When a solution is obtained for which the index row is all non-negative the optimum has been reached. The next step in the procedure is to move from the solution described in the initial tableau to an improved solution.

As we have seen, in a one-constraint problem only solutions with one positive variable need be considered so that if x_1 or x_2 is raised to a positive level then this level must be such that s_1 falls to zero. But which variable should be introduced? The most frequently applied decision rule is that that variable should become a basis variable that has the 'most negative' index row number, i.e. shows the greatest per unit improvement in the objective function, x_1 in this case. figure 3.3 extends the tableau of figure 3.2 to show the first iteration.

The variable x_1 has become the basis variable and the lower half of Figure 3.3 is formed by first writing in x_1 in the position occupied by the basis variable. Then to the left of this is written its objective function coefficient. The elements of the 'main row' are the elements of the old con-

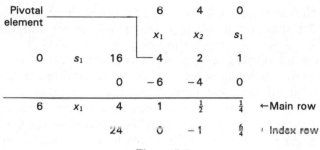

Figure 3.3

straint coefficient row divided by what is termed the *pivotal element*. The pivotal element is the rate of exchange between the variable leaving the basis and the variable entering it. Division of the constraint coefficient row by the pivotal element and changing the position of x_1 and s_1 is equivalent to the formation of equation (3.8) above. The only difference is the change of sign—it should be remembered that in the tableau rates of exchange refer to *decreases* in the outgoing variable. The new index row is formed in the same way as before. For example the -1 under x_2 is $1/2 \times 6 - 4$ and the element $6/4$ is $1/4 \times 6 - 0$. The solution described in full is $x_1 = 6$, $x_2 = 0$, $s_1 = 0$ and $N = 24$ ($= 6 \times 4$). Remember that all variables except the basis variable are at zero level.

Further improvement can be effected by the introduction of x_2. Figure 3.4 includes the next and final iteration. x_2 replaces x_1 as basis variable (since only x_2 has a negative index row number) and its objective function coefficient is 4 entered to the left of x_2. Main row elements in one-constraint problems are the old main row elements divided by the pivotal element, but in larger problems, with more than one constraint, it is not always the main row of a tableau that is divided by the pivotal element to form the new main row. We shall come to this presently. The new in-

			6	4	0	
			x_1	x_2	s_1	
0	s_1	16	4	2	1	
		0	-6	-4	0	
6	x_1	4	1	($\frac{1}{2}$)	$\frac{1}{4}$	Pivotal element
		24	0	-1	$\frac{6}{4}$	
4	x_2	8	2	1	$\frac{1}{2}$ ←Main row
		32	2	0	2 ←Index row

Figure 3.4

dex row is all non-negative indicating that the optimal solution has been reached. This solution in full is $x_1 = 0$, $x_2 = 8$, $s_1 = 0$ and consequently $N = 32$.

The reason for starting with a 'slack variable solution' is that it is an easy one to find. The Simplex method works by starting with a basic feasible solution (in principle *any* basic feasible solution will do) and subsequently moving to improved basic feasible solutions if such exist. It is therefore essential to have a basic feasible solution to start with, and in somewhat larger problems it can be a lengthy task to find a superior starting solution. The Simplex method guarantees that, if a finite optimum exists to a problem, this solution will be reached in a finite number of iterations. There are important further reasons for using the Simplex method. The principal one being that the calculations generate a large amount of valuable economic information. Also, the effects of changes in some of the parameters of the problem can be quickly deduced without having to start the problem again from scratch. This is the field of *sensitivity analysis*. Also, further variables may be added to the problem (perhaps representing new opportunities) at any stage of the calculations. The method is also ideally suited for use by computers—which is essential for really large problems.

More detailed examination of Figure 3.4, particularly in respect of the optimal solution, yields some potentially valuable information. Consider the number in the final index row under s_1. We have already seen that it means that if s_1 was raised to unit level then N would drop by two units to 30. However, since the problem is linear it also means that if s_1 was *lowered* to a level of minus one then N would *increase* to 34. Now $s_1 = -1$ is not permitted but $s_1 = -1$ and an expenditure limit of 16 is equivalent to $s_1 = 0$ and an expenditure limit of 17. Setting $s_1 = -1$ tells us what would happen if the expenditure limit could be stretched by one (thousand pounds) and would enable the evaluation of borrowing opportunities. It should be noted that N can only increase by 2 if the constraint level goes up to 17 and x_2 can be set at the level of $8\frac{1}{2}$. The rate of exchange between x_2 and s_1 tells us this—the figure $\frac{1}{2}$ also operates both ways, if s_1 is *reduced* to -1 then x_2 *increases* by $\frac{1}{2}$. Of course it might not be possible to buy a half-share in a machine, in which case the index row number under s_1 would have to be interpreted in an average sense. If the expenditure limit could be raised by two units to 18 then x_2 would go up to 9 and N to 36. The extra two units of expenditure then have raised N by four. Equally, of course, a cutting back of the expenditure limit to 14 would cause a reduction of N by four. The index row allows the consequences of budget 'economies' to be quickly evaluated. The *shadow price* of funds at $t = 0$ (the present time) is two. This shadow price relates directly to the value (or cost) *to the investor* of extra (or decreased) funds at the margin.

It should be noted, too, that the value of the objective function at each solution is the shadow price of funds multiplied by the amount of funds—

the index row number under the slack variable times the constraint level. In the optimal solution $32 = 2 \times 16$ in the previous solution, where less effective use is made of money available, $24 = (6/4) \times 16$. The shadow price can be thought of as a valuation of funds *on average* as well as at the margin—each and every unit decrease in money available (equivalent to raising s_1 by one unit) reduces N by two in the optimal solution.

The shadow price should be clearly distinguished from the 'over the counter' price that would have to be paid to secure extra funds. For instance if money over and above the original £16,000 could be borrowed from outside at 10% interest, if the discount rate used to determine the NPVs from the machines was 15% and if cash flow from the projects allowed repayment after one year then we can quickly compute the change in total net present value. It would be $2 - (1.1/1.15)$. Clearly, it is worth the companies while to find a source of extra funds. In the extreme, in order to secure an extra £1,000 now it would be prepared to pay back after one year up to £2,300 (since $2 - (2.3/1.15) = 0$)—an implied maximum borrowing interest rate of 30%.

The index row number 2 under x_1 can also tell us quite a lot. For example if the company, because of a contract or to promote goodwill, felt that it was obliged to buy one machine of type one then present value would be reduced by 2—this is the cost to the company of maintaining the goodwill. This is not to say that the company physically loses money when it buys a type one machine, the cost is an *opportunity cost*: it loses the opportunity to make an extra £2,000 in present value terms. The index row number also shows what would happen if it was possible to *disinvest* in x_1. If the company had a stock of type one machines and could sell each one for £4,000 then this provides capital for the purchase of further type two machines with the net result that N increases by two.

The *basis* of the solution to a linear programming problem is the matrix of coefficients in the original constraints of the variables which are positive. In the present one-constraint example the basis is the coefficient of the basis variable. In the first solution, with s_1 positive the basis is unity. In the second solution the basis is four and in the final solution the basis is two. The rate of exchange between the basis variable and the slack variable s_1 is the inverse of the basis. This is a valuable piece of information because the inverse of the basis, along with the constraint level, determines the level of the positive variable in the solution. For example, consider the solution with x_2 as basis variable. The constraint can be written as

$$2x_2 = 16 - 4x_1 - s_1$$

or

$$1x_2 = (\tfrac{1}{2})16 - (\tfrac{1}{2})4x_1 - (\tfrac{1}{2})s_1$$

The inverse of the basis is $\tfrac{1}{2}$ and the product of the basis inverse and constraint level gives the value of x_2. It is evident that since the coefficient of the slack variable in the original form of the constraint is unity, then the rate of exchange with x_2 must be the inverse of the basis. Using the inverse of the basis it is possible to calculate quickly the consequences of changes in the constraint level. If £20,000 were available initially the new level of x_2 would be $(\frac{1}{2})20 = 10$.

With the existing alternatives there is no way of improving on the optimal solution to the example problem shown in Figure 3.4, $x_1 = 0$, $x_2 = 8$, $s_1 = 0$ is the equilibrium solution—provided that circumstances do not change. But suppose that two further investment possibilities arise—purchase of machines of types three and four. Each machine of type three costs £5,000 and the present value of the returns generated is £9,000. Each machine of type four costs £1,600 and the present value of returns generated is £3,500. Can the hitherto optimal investment programme be improved?

To answer this question it is not necessary to solve a new problem right from scratch. All that needs to be done is to add two extra columns, corresponding to the new investment opportunities, to Figure 3.4. In fact this need be done only for the last part of the tableau in respect of the optimal solution, but for completeness this has been done throughout in Figure 3.5. It is evident that x_3 is, in an opportunity sense, not a profitable investment. Each type three machine bought would, because of the necessary reduction in numbers of type two machines, cause N to fall by one unit. However, the type four machines are, in both an absolute and a relative sense, profitable. This is shown by the index row number $-3/10$. The solution with x_2 as basis variable is no longer optimal, but the new optimum with x_4 as basis variable is obtained in one iteration taking the original optimum as the starting-point.

			6	4	9	3.5	0
			x_1	x_2	x_3	x_4	S_1
0	s_1	16	4	2	5	1.6	1
		0	-6	-4	-9	-3.5	0
6	x_1	4	1	$\frac{1}{2}$	$\frac{5}{4}$	$\frac{2}{5}$	$\frac{1}{4}$
		24	0	-1	$-\frac{6}{4}$	$-11/10$	$\frac{6}{4}$
4	x_2	8	2	1	$\frac{5}{2}$	$\frac{4}{5}$	$\frac{1}{2}$
		32	2	0	1	$-3/10$	2
3.5	x_4	10	$\frac{5}{2}$	$\frac{5}{4}$	25/8	1	$\frac{5}{8}$
		35	11/4	$\frac{3}{8}$	31/16	0	35/16

Figure 3.5

3.4 Two Constraints

With the original two alternative machine types, suppose that each machine of type one requires 20 sq. ft of floorspace and each machine of type two requires 300 sq. ft. There are 1,200 sq. ft of floorspace available. What now is the optimal investment package? The floorspace constraint can be written as

$$2x_1 + 3x_2 \leqslant 12 \qquad (3.12)$$

or, with a slack variable, s_2 specific to this constraint as

$$2x_1 + 3x_2 + s_2 = 12 \qquad (3.13)$$

s_2 is, required to be non-negative and has a zero objective function coefficient on the assumption that unused floorspace has no alternative use of value. Recalling that the Simplex procedure required a basic feasible solution to start with, and that the easiest one to find is the origin, Figure 3.6 presents this solution and the first iteration.

Variable x_1 has the 'lowest' index row number, and so will be a basis variable in the next solution. The x_1 rates of exchange form the *pivot column*. In a two-constraint problem only two variables will be positive in any basic feasible solution, that that if x_1 is brought in either s_1 or s_2 must drop out. So there are two candidates for *pivot row*. The pivot row is selected by forming the ratios of elements in the value column and rates of exchange in the same row in the pivot column i.e. 16/4 and 12/2. Whichever of these is the smaller determines the pivot row. Recall that the rate of exchange, 4, between s_1 and x_1 means that each time x_1 is raised by one unit s_1 must diminish by four units. Since s_1 is at the level 16 and must not be negative in any solution, the maximum extent to which x_1 can be introduced on this account is 16/4. Similarly, to ensure that s_2 is non-negative x_1 must not be greater than 12/2. Since both s_1 and s_2 are the be non-negative, the smaller ratio determines the variable that is leaving the basis.

			6	4	0	0	
Pivot column			x_1	x_2	s_1	s_2	
0	s_1	16	4	2	1	0	Pivot row
0	s_2	12	2	3	0	1	
		0	-6	-4	0	0	Index row
6	x_1	4	1	$\frac{1}{2}$	$\frac{1}{4}$	0	Main row
0	s_2	4	0	2	$-\frac{1}{2}$	1	
		24	0	-1	$\frac{6}{4}$	0	

Figure 3.6

The next basic feasible solution will have x_1 and s_2 as basis variables. We can begin by writing these in and to the left of them and their objective function coefficients can be written. The main row in the new tableau is in the same position as the key row in the old one and, as was the case in the one-constraint problem, it is obtained by dividing the pivot row by the pivot element. Now consider the new rate of exchange between x_2 and s_2. The effects of any change in value of x_2 in both constraint equations need to be considered. The rate of exchange between x_2 and s_2 was originally 3, this being determined from the second constraint alone. However, since x_1 also appears in the new solution the effects of the change in x_2 on x_1 have to be allowed for. If x_2 is set at unit level then, as can be seen from the main row, x_1 must be reduced by $\frac{1}{2}$ and reference back to the original solution and the rate of exchange between x_1 and s_2 tells us that if x_1 is reduced by $\frac{1}{2}$ then s_2 will *increase* by 1 on this account. So the net change in s_2 is $3 - \frac{1}{2} \times 2 = 2$ and this is the new rate of exchange. All remaining rates of exchange and the new level of s_2 can be found by a similar process which can be summarized as

'new' number = 'old' number – corresponding main row number
× corresponding pivot column number

The 'new' number is the number in the new tableau in the same position as a given number in the previous tableau—the 'old' number. In the example above, 3 is the 'old' number and 2 is the 'new' number. The 'corresponding main row number' is the number in the main row of the new tableau in the same column as the new number, i.e. $\frac{1}{2}$ in the example. The 'corresponding pivot column number' is the number in the pivot column of the old tableau in the same row as the old number, i.e. 2 in the example. The remaining numbers are: level of $s_2 = 12 - 4 \times 2 = 4$; x_1, s_2 rate of exchange $= 2 - 1 \times 2 = 0$; s_2, s_2 rate of exchange $= 0 - \frac{1}{4} \times 2 = -\frac{1}{2}$; s_2, s_2 rate of exchange $= 1 - 0 \times 2 = 1$. Three points should be noted. Firstly, for a basis variable (such as x_1 in the second tableau) the column of rates of exchange consists of unit for the 'self with self' exchange rate and zero elsewhere. Secondly, the rate of exchange $-\frac{1}{2}$ between s_1 and s_2 means that as s_1 is raised by one unit s_2 will increase by $\frac{1}{2}$. Thirdly, the index row numbers may be calculated using the new/old number formula.

Clearly the x_1, s_2 solution is not optimal since introductions of x_2 would effect improvement. Figure 3.7 shows the next, and final iteration. The optimal solution of the problem is therefore $x_1 = 3$, $x_2 = 2$, $s_1 = 0$, $s_2 = 0$ and $N = 26$. This solution can now be compared with the one-constraint case. The optimal value of the objective function has, of course, diminished since adding extra constraints will, if they are at all effective, cut down the feasible solution set and as is the case here cut out the original optimum as shown in Figure 3.8. The original optimum (now labelled D) is 'cut off' by the addition of the floorspace constraint AE. The new feasi-

			6	4	0	0
			x_1	x_2	s_1	s_2
0	s_1	16	4	2	1	0
0	s_2	12	2	3	0	1
		0	-6	-4	0	0
6	x_1	4	1	$\frac{1}{2}$	$\frac{1}{4}$	0
0	s_2	4	0	2	$-\frac{1}{2}$	1 Pivot row
		24	0	-1	$\frac{6}{4}$	0
6	x_1	3	1	0	$\frac{3}{8}$	$-\frac{1}{4}$
4	x_1	2	0	1	$-\frac{1}{4}$	$\frac{1}{2}$
		26	0	0	$\frac{5}{4}$	$\frac{1}{2}$

Figure 3.7

ble area is OABC and the new optimum is B. Note that B is preferred to A, the solution where only type two machines are bought. Although type two machines are economical in their use of finance, they are relatively extravagant consumers of floorspace. Type one machines although costly to purchase are economical users of floorspace. The optimum represents levels of x_1 and x_2 such that best use is made of *both* resources.

The Simplex method examined solutions O, C and B respectively. The reader may verify that solution A would be as described in Figure 3.9. With the presence of the floorspace requirement the opportunity cost of buying only as many 'profitable' type 2 machines as could be accommodated is $26 - 16 = 10$. It can be seen from the index row of Figure 3.9 that each type one machine would add 10/3 to N. This figure provides a check on the calculations since if x_1 can be set at $8 \div \frac{8}{3} = 3$ the value of N in the next solution should be $16 + 3 \times \frac{10}{3} = 26$.

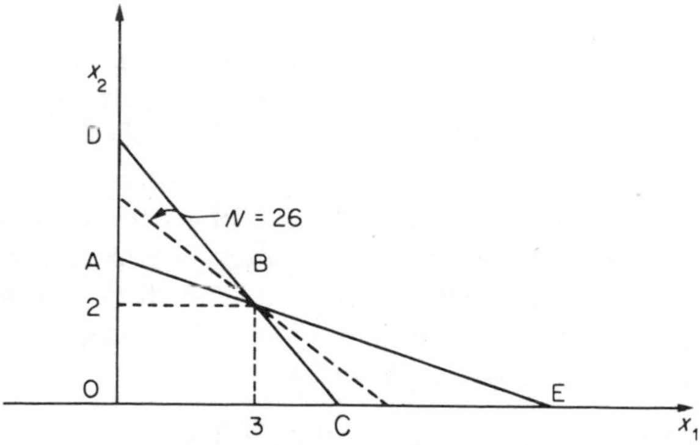

Figure 3.8

0	s_1	8	$\frac{8}{3}$	0	1	$-\frac{2}{3}$
4	x_2	4	$\frac{2}{3}$	1	0	$\frac{1}{3}$
		16	$-\frac{10}{3}$	0	0	$\frac{4}{3}$

Figure 3.9

The final index row of Figure 3.7 gives optimal shadow prices for both resources. Provided that fractional values of the xs are meaningful an extra £1,000 expended optimally would add £1,250 to present value, whilst an extra 100 sq. ft of floorspace would add £500 to N. Note that if floorspace is fixed, but more money becomes available, x_1 goes up whilst x_2 decreases. With an extra £1,000 available the optimal value of x_1 is $3\frac{3}{8}$ and the optimal value of x_2 is $1\frac{3}{4}$. Because of the floorspace requirement, the extra finance could be put to work effectively only by buying type one machines. The requisite floorspace is obtained by having fewer type two machines. If more floorspace is available this is put to best use by having more type two machines. The requisite financial resources are freed by having fewer type one machines. With an additional 100 sq. ft of floorspace the optimal values of xs are $x_1 = 2\frac{3}{4}$ and $x_2 = 2\frac{1}{2}$.

3.5 Contextual Examples

Portfolio problems are frequently suitably structured for solution by programming methods. The usefulness of a programming approach to this type of problem can be illustrated with relatively simple examples.

The financial manager of a company with cash resources has to decide on the percentages of a given sum to invest in various other companies. The yields per pound invested in each company are given below.

	Unit trusts		Chemicals		Stores		Mines	
Company No.	1	2	3	4	5	6	7	8
Yield (%)	4.8	5.4	7.5	8.5	9	10	15	18

Company policy does not give the investment manager a completely free hand. At least 30% of any portfolio must be in unit trusts; no more than 25% may be invested in mining; at least 10% must be in chemicals; and no more than 20% of the portfolio may be invested in any single company. The objective is to maximize the yield on the total sum invested. How should the portfolio be divided amongst the candidate companies?

Letting x_j represent the percentage of the portfolio invested in the jth company, yield on the total sum is a weighted average of the individual yields. The problem can be expressed as

$$\text{maximize } F = 4.8x_1 + 5.4x_2 + 7.5x_3 + 8.5x_4 + 9x_5 + 10x_6 + 15x_7 + 18x_8$$

subject to

$$
\begin{array}{llll}
x_1 + x_2 + x_3 + x_4 + x_5 + x_6 + x_7 + x_8 & = & 100 \\
x_1 + x_2 & \geqslant & 30 \\
x_7 + x_8 & \leqslant & 25 \\
x_3 + x_4 & \geqslant & 10 \\
x_1 & \leqslant & 20 \\
x_2 & \leqslant & 20 \\
x_3 & \leqslant & 20 \\
x_4 & \leqslant & 20 \\
x_5 & \leqslant & 20 \\
x_6 & \leqslant & 20 \\
x_7 & \leqslant & 20 \\
x_8 & \leqslant & 20
\end{array}
$$

The special structure of this problem (a 'sparse' matrix of coefficients and all non-zero coefficients being unity) enables a quick solution by inspection to be obtained. Company eight is the most lucrative investment and x_8 is set at 20. Company seven is the next most attractive, but x_7 may not exceed 5 because of constraint three. Clearly the best way of satisfying constraint two is to set x_2 equal to 20 and x_1 equal to 10. Constraint three is met by setting x_4 equal to 10. Constraint one then allows x_6 to be set at 20 and x_5 at 15. The solution is then: $x_1 = 10$, $x_2 = 20$, $x_3 = 0$, $x_4 = 10$, $x_5 = 15$, $x_6 = 20$, $x_7 = 5$, $x_8 = 20$.

The index row of the final Simplex tableau would enable evaluation of the elements of the companies investment policy which were predetermined. It would reveal the effects of relaxing some of the constraints. For example, if the policy was changed to the extent that 35% of the portfolio could be in minimg, then the new optimal levels of x_5 and x_7 would be 5 and 15 respectively and average yield would be up from 10.11% to 10.71%.

The constraints of this problem are an attempt to take into account the riskiness of investments. Management required at least a minimum investment in the relatively safe unit trust whilst a maximum was specified for the higher risk mining industry; furthermore, the eggs had to be divided among at least five baskets. In this instance risk itself was not quantified. The suceeding example includes a very simple measure of risk.

A finance company is considering lending up to a total of £100,000 to five prospective clients. The rates of interest that the potential customers are prepared to pay and the finance companies estimate of the default risk in each case is given below. In the event of default the entire loan will be written off. The objective is to maximize the rate of interest earned on the £100,000, if there are no defaulters, subject to 'expected loss' not exceeding £1,000.

Company	1	2	3	4	5
Interest rate (%)	6.5	7	8.6	9.5	11.5
Default probability	0.006	0.008	0.013	0.015	0.024

Letting x_j represent the amount advanced to each company, the expected loss constraint is

$$0.006x_1 + 0.008x_2 + 0.013x_3 + 0.015x_4 + 0.024x_5 \leqslant 1{,}000$$

Changing units of measure to £1,000 and multiplying both sides of the expected loss constraint by 1,000 the two constraints are

$$6x_1 + 8x_2 + 13x_3 + 15x_4 + 24x_5 \leqslant 1{,}000$$
$$x_1 + x_2 + x_3 + x_4 + x_5 \leqslant 100$$

and the objective function is

$$F = 6.5x_1 + 7x_2 + 8.5x_5 + 9.5x_4 + 11.5x_5$$

Figure 3.10 presents the solution of this problem by the Simplex method.

To obtain the average interest rate in percentage terms the value of F should be divided by 100. At the optimum an average rate of just over 7.83% is earned. Note that the selection of pivot columns was not detrmined in the usual fashion. This was because it is obvious that larger improvements in the objective function are possible by introduction of the variables indicated because of the extent to which they can be introduced. The number of iterations required can often be reduced in this way.

			6.5	7	8.5	9.5	11.5	0	0
			x_1	x_2	x_3	x_4	x_5	s_1	s_2
0	s_1	1,000	6	8	13	15	24	1	1
0	s_2	100	1	1	1	1	1	0	1
		0	-6.5	-7	-8.5	-9.5	-11.5	0	0
0	s_1	200	-2	0	5	7	16	1	-8
7	x_2	100	1	1	1	1	1	0	1
		700	0.5	0	-1.5	-2.5	-4.5	0	7
9.5	x_4	200/7	$-\frac{2}{7}$	0	$\frac{5}{7}$	1	16/7	$\frac{1}{7}$	$-\frac{8}{7}$
7	x_2	500/7	$\frac{9}{7}$	1	$\frac{2}{7}$	0	$-\frac{9}{7}$	$-\frac{1}{7}$	15/7
		5,400/7	$-3/14$	0	$\frac{2}{7}$	0	17/14	5/14	29/17
9.5	x_4	400/9	0	$\frac{2}{9}$	$\frac{7}{9}$	1	2	$\frac{1}{9}$	$-\frac{6}{9}$
6.5	x_1	500/9	1	$\frac{7}{9}$	$\frac{2}{9}$	0	-1	$-\frac{1}{9}$	15/9
		7,050/9	0	1.5/9	$\frac{3}{9}$	0	1	$\frac{3}{9}$	40.5/9

Figure 3.10

The optimal solution consists of $x_4 = 400/9$ and $x_1 = 500/9$. Only two of the five possible client companies should be lent money. This result was evident from the number of constraints in the problem. The final index row enables some evaluation of the risk policy of the finance company to be made. Each time the expected loss figure is raised by £100, x_4 increases by 100/9, x_1 decreases by 100/9 and F increases by 300/9. Alternatively, if risk had been ignored completely a sum of £68,116 [= 7,050 ÷ (9 × 11.5)] lent to company five alone would have given a return of 7.83% on the total of £100,000.

Realistic complicating considerations that this example ignores are the interdependence of risk from separate investments; the possibility that risk in an individual case may depend on the amount invested and the possibility that the rate of return required by the investor may affect the riskiness of the investment. Significant interrelations of risk must be taken into account. How this can be accomplished is explained in later chapters.

3.6 A Lorie–Savage Problem

Let us solve a small and convenient problem by the Simplex method. The problem is to

maximize $N = 9x_1 + 17x_2 + 12x_3 + s_0$
subject to
$$5x_1 + 10x_2 + 6x_3 + s_0 = 11$$
$$x_1 + s_1 = 1$$
$$x_2 + s_2 = 1$$
$$x_3 + s_3 = 1$$
$$x_1, x_2, x_3, s_0, s_1, s_2, s_3 \geqslant 0$$

Slack variables have been included for all constraints including the $x_j \leqslant 1$ constraints. In formulating the objective function it has been assumed that the £11 is the investor's own money and any unspent remainder is added to present value. Thus s_0 has a coefficient of unity in the objective function. An alternative formulation of the objective function in this case would have been $N = (9 - 5)x_1 + (17 - 10)x_2 + (12 - 6)x_3 + 0s_1 + 11$. The coefficients of the xs are now how much is added to N by investment in the xs over the 'autonomous' amount £11. For instance if an extra £5 was available, if spent on x_1, this could increase N by £9, but N would have increased by £5 'autonomously' since it cannot be less than £16; so investment in x_1 adds a further £4 to the autonomous increase. With the original formulation of the objective function, Figure 3.11 shows the solution of the problem by the Simplex method.

The optimal solution is, *degenerate*—although there are *four* constraints in the problem only *three* variables are positive at the optimum. This occurrence is noticed in the preceding solution when a tie occurred for the selection of the pivot row; both the x_2 and s_1 rows could have been chosen.

			9	17	12	1	0	0	0
			x_1	x_2	x_3	s_0	s_1	s_2	s_3
1	s_0	11	5	10	6	1	0	0	0
0	s_1	1	1	0	0	0	1	0	0
0	s_2	1	0	1	0	0	0	1	0
0	s_3	1	0	0	1	0	0	0	1
		11	−4	−7	−6	0	0	0	0
1	s_0	1	5	0	6	1	0	−10	0
0	s_1	1	1	0	0	0	1	0	0
17	x_2	1	0	1	0	0	0	1	0
0	s_3	1	0	0	1	0	0	0	1
		18	−4	0	−6	0	0	7	0
12	x_3	$\frac{1}{6}$	$\frac{5}{6}$	0	1	$\frac{1}{6}$	0	−10/6	0
0	s_1	1	1	0	0	0	1	0	0
17	x_2	1	0	1	0	0	0	1	0
0	s_3	$\frac{5}{6}$	$\frac{5}{6}$	0	0	$-\frac{1}{6}$	0	10/6	1
		19	1	0	0	1	0	−3	0
12	x_3	1	0	0	1	0	0	0	1
0	s_1	1	1	0	0	0	1	0	0
17	x_2	$\frac{1}{2}$	$\frac{1}{2}$	1	0	1/10	0	0	−6/10
0	s_2	$\frac{1}{2}$	$-\frac{1}{2}$	0	0	−1/10	0	1	6/10
		41/2	$-\frac{1}{2}$	0	0	7/10	0	0	18/10
12	x_3	1	0	0	1	0	0	0	1
9	x_1	1	1	0	0	0	1	0	0
17	x_2	0	0	1	0	1/10	$-\frac{1}{2}$	0	−6/10
0	s_2	1	0	0	0	−1/10	$\frac{1}{2}$	1	6/10
		21	0	0	0	7/10	$-\frac{1}{2}$	0	18/10

Figure 3.11

Degeneracy is not much of a problem in hand computation, but it is possible that mechanistic adherance to the rule for selecting the pivotal column can cause the problem to 'cycle'. Charnes, Cooper and Henderson have suggested a simple method of resolving a tied situation that eliminates the possibility of cycling. For the tied variables each rate of exchange in the row is divided by the pivot column number. These ratios are then compared column by column working from left to right starting

		x_1	x_2	x_3	s_0	s_1	s_2	s_3
12	x_3	1	0	0	1	0	0	1
0	s_1	0	0	−2	−2/10	1	0	12/10
9	x_1	1	1	2	2/10	0	0	−12/10
0	s_2	1	0	1	0	0	1	0
		21	0	1	8/10	0	0	12/10

Figure 3.12

with the slack variables and then proceeding, if necessary, with the structural variables. As soon as these ratios are unequal the tie is broken and that variable leaves the basis which has the algebraically smaller ratio. In the present case the tie is broken at once in the s_0 column. For s_1 the ratio is $0/1 = 0$ while for x_2 the ratio is $\frac{1}{2} \div \frac{1}{10} = 5$.

Interpretation of index row numbers requires some care. An extra £1 available for investment will only increase NPV by $17/10\{ = (7/10 + 1\}$ if x_2 can be set at the level $\frac{1}{10}$. An increase in available funds of £10 would of course, increase NPV by 17 since x_2 could then be set at unit level.

In the present problem in the optimum was intergral. Although this will not always be the case, the number of fractional projects at the optimum will not exceed the number of constraints (excluding the upper bounds and sign requirements). Thus the number of fractional projects that have to be dealt with may be quite small in relation to the total number of projects.

The optimal basic feasible solution $x_1 = 1$, $x_2 = 0$, $x_3 = 1$, $s_0 = 0$, $s_1 = 0$, $s_2 = 1$, $s_3 = 0$, could be described in tabular form in an alternative manner to that given in Figure 3.11. This would correspond to the selection of the x_2 row as pivot row in the preceding solution. The alternative presentation is given in Figure 3.12.

Although the value of the solution and the magnitudes of the variables are the same as in Figure 3.11, the index row numbers are different. In a degenerate solution the shadow prices are non-unique, both are valid *but for movements in one direction* only. The figure 7/10 for instance correctly states what would happen if one further unit of funds was available; x_2 would go up by 1/10, s_2 would decrease by 1/10 and N would rise by 7/10 over the autonomous increase of one. But 7/10 does not apply to decreases in available finance for, as can be seen from the rates of exchange, if s_0 was introduced to unit level (equivalent to a unit decrease of funds) x_2 would have to decrease to − 1/10, which is not feasible. Figure 3.12 describes the situation for decreases in funds; x_1 would decrease by 2/10 and s_1 increase by that amount. N would diminish by 18/10, i.e. 8/10 more than the autonomous decrease of 1. Degeneracy is a knife-edge situation and shadow prices are only appropriate for movements in particular directions.

3.7 Duality

With every LP problem there is associated, in a symmetrical relationship, a *dual* problem. Consider the two-constraint, two-structural variable problem:

$$\text{maximize } F = 10x_1 + 12x_2$$
$$\text{subject to} \quad 4x_1 + 2x_2 \leqslant 76$$
$$3x_1 + 5x_2 \leqslant 85$$
$$x_1, x_2 \geqslant 0$$

The dual to this problem is

$$\text{minimize } G = 76y_1 + 85y_2$$
$$\text{subject to} \quad 4y_1 + 3y_2 \geqslant 10$$
$$2y_1 + 5y_2 \geqslant 12$$
$$y_1, y_2 \geqslant 0$$

The maximization problem is usually referred to as the *primal* problem and the minimization problem as the dual, although they are duals of each other. The dual problem employs all the data of the primal problem but in a different arrangement. The coefficients of the objective function of the primal are the constraint levels of the dual; the constraint levels of the primal are the objective function coefficients of the dual; *columns* of constraint coefficients in the primal become *rows* of constraint coefficients in the dual. If 'primal' and 'dual' are interchanged in the previous sentence the statements are still valid; that is, there is *no asymmetry* between the problems. The primal and dual problems are graphed in Figure 3.13(a) and (b). The feasible area for the primal problem is OABC and the optimum is at joint B with the objective function shown as a dashed line. The feasible area for the dual is the open area with lower bound given by E'B'D'. The optimal solution is at point B' which minimizes the dual objective function G. Each basic feasible solution (bfs) of the primal

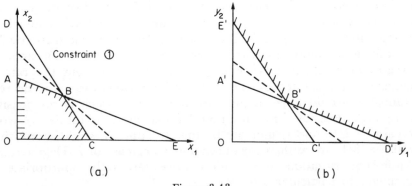

(a)   (b)

Figure 3.13

problem has a corresponding basic (not necessarily feasible) solution in the dual. Indeed it turns out that there is only one bfs in the primal problem that corresponds to a bfs in the dual. These corresponding bfs are also optimal! This point is true in general. The dual constraints can be converted to equality form by *subtraction* of slack variables, viz:

$$4y_1 + 3y_2 - t_1 = 10$$
$$2y_1 + 5y_2 - t_2 = 12$$

Apart from the symmetrical relationship between primal and dual, why should the dual be of interest? Firstly, the dual structural variables, y, turn out to be the *shadow prices* of the primal problem, i.e. the index row numbers under the slack variables. Thus the dual has great importance for economic interpretation and sensitivity analysis. Secondly, just as the optimal values of the dual variables can be found from the solution to the primal problem (being index row numbers) so also can the optimal values of primal variables be found from the solution to the dual problem. This is an important property since sometimes it is easier to solve the dual of a problem than the original problem.

In order to solve the dual problem, computational devices must be found to deal with (a) a minimizing objective function, and (b) $\geqslant$ constraints. Problem (a) is easily resolved—simply multiply the objective function through by -1. To deal with problem (b), after the subtraction of slack variables, *artificial variables* must be added in. This is so that the Simplex method may work with positive solution values. So the constraints would appear as

$$4y_1 + 3y_2 - t_1 + u_1 = 10$$
$$2y_1 + 5y_2 - t_2 + u_2 = 12$$

			10	12	0	0
			x_1	x_2	s_1	s_2
0	s_1	76	4	2	1	0
0	s_2	85	3	5	0	1
		0	-10	-12	0	0
0	s_1	42	14/5	0	1	$-2/5$
12	x_2	17	3/5	1	0	1/5
		204	$-14/5$	0	0	12/5
10	x_1	15	1	0	5/14	$-2/14$
12	x_2	8	0	1	$-3/14$	4/14
		246	0	0	1	2

Figure 3.14

		−76	−85	0	0	−M	−M
		y_1	y_2	t_1	t_2	u_1	u_2
−M u_1	10	4	3	−1	0	1	0
−M u_2	12	2	5	0	−1	0	1
	−22M	−6M + 76	−8M + 85	+M	+M	0	0
−M u_1	14/5	14/5	0	−1	3/5	1	−3/5
−85 y_2	12/5	2/5	1	0	−1/5	0	1/5
	−14/5M − 204	−14/5M + 42	0	+M	−3/5M + 17	0	8/5M − 17
−76 y_1	1	1	0	−5/14	3/14	5/14	−3/14
−85 y_2	2	0	1	2/14	−4/14	−2/14	4/14
	−246	0	0	15	8	−15 + M	−8 + M

Figure 3.15

But the artificial variables are merely computational devices for finding a non-negative starting solution. They must not appear in any optimum. They are ruled out of contention for optimality by attachment of penalty coefficients M in the minimizing objective function. Here, M is large enough to dominate other numbers so that no solution containing u_1 or u_2 at positive level can be optimal. In the index row any number containing a term in M with negative coefficient is negative. The solutions in tableau form, to primal and dual, are given in Figures 3.14 and 3.15 respectively.

The maximum value of the primal objective function is achieved by setting $x_1 = 15$, $x_2 = 8$, $s_1 = 0$, $s_2 = 0$ for a value of F of 246. The shadow prices of the resources are 1 for resource one and 2 for resource two. The optimal solution to the dual problem is to set $y_1 = 1$, $y_2 = 2$, $t_1 = 0$, $t_2 = 0$ for a value of G of 246. The minus sign attached to 246 in Figure 3.15 results from the computational device of negation the objective function. The equality of the optimal values of primal and dual objective functions is the case in general. All feasible solutions to the dual have values of G greater than or equal to all values of F for feasible solutions to the primal problem, with the equality holding only at the optimum. The dual 'shadow prices' are 15 for 'resource' one and 8 'for resource' two. The dual index row numbers under the artificial variables may be ignored; save for noting that they are both positive since $M > 15$.

The full extent of the primal–dual symmetry is now apparent. In the primal problem the optimal values of the structure variables, y, may be found in the final index row under the primal *slack* variables, hence $y_1 = 1$ and $y_2 = 2$. The optimal values of the dual slack variables, t, may be found in the final index row of the primal problem under the primal *structural* variables, hence $t_1 = 0$ and $t_2 = 0$. The same statements apply in respect of the solution to the dual problem. The optimal values of the primal structural variables may be found from the final index row of the dual problem under the dual slack variables, hence $x_1 = 15$ and $x_2 = 8$. The optimal values of the primal slack variables are found in the final index row of the dual problem under the structural variables. Note that finding an optimal solution to the primal problem (finding a solution with a non-negative index row) is finding a feasible solution to the dual problem. If the dual was being solved the process would be equivalent to finding a feasible solution to the primal problem.

The optimal solutions illustrate a further aspect of the symmetrical relationship between primal and dual. This is the *complementary slackness* condition:

(a) $s_1 y_1 = 0$ and (c) $x_1 t_1 = 0$

(b) $s_2 y_2 = 0$ (d) $x_2 t_2 = 0$

The products of corresponding pairs of primal structural variables and dual slack variables dual structural and primal slack variables must be zero at an optimum. Expression (a) states that if $s_1 > 0$, $y_1 = 0$, i.e. in a production context if any of the first resources is left over the shadow price (marginal value) of that resource is zero. Also if $y_1 > 0$ then $s_1 = 0$, that is, any resource with positive value at the margin must be fully used. The condition (c) states that if $x_1 > 0$ then $t_1 = 0$, i.e. if the first primal structural variable is positive then the first dual slack variable is zero. Dual slack variables can be interpreted as 'opportunity losses'. Consider the first dual constraint. It is

$$4y_1 + 3y_2 \geqslant 10 \tag{3.14}$$

Where t_1 is the difference between the LHS and the RHS of (3.14). The coefficients 4 and 3 are the amounts of resources one and two tied up in the acquisition of one unit of x_1 whilst the magnitudes of y_1 and y_2 are the values per unit of each resource *if resources are used optimally*. In other words each unit of resource one can make a profit of y_1 and each unit of resource two can be used to make a profit of y_2. Consequently the LHS of (3.14) is the *opportunity cost* of producing one unit of x_1—it is therefore the profit forgone in using resources to produce x_1. Obviously, if the strict inequality holds in (3.14) this means that the profit forgone in producing x_1 is greater than the profit obtained on x_1. That is, if $t_1 > 0$ there is a positive opportunity loss involved in production of x_1, the optimal value of which must then be zero. So, only when equality obtains in (3.14) will x_1 be positive. Note that in the nature of things there can never be an *opportunity profit*. y_1 and y_2 are determined by the *best* use of resources—these values allocate *all* profit to resources (the value of the dual objective function equals the value of the primal). In mathematical terms at best an equality can obtain in (3.14) in which case x_1 can be positive. All this is not to say that an *accounting profit* cannot be made but simply that there is no *better* use of resources than the best! When $t_1 > 0$ therefore, the optimal value of $x_1 = 0$, although we should recall that x_1 may still make an accounting profit.

We can best illustrate the economic interpretation of dual problems by examination of the duals to the problems considered earlier. The first problem was

$$\text{maximize } N = 6x_1 + 4x_2$$
$$\text{subject to } \quad 4x_1 + 2x_2 \leqslant 16$$

where the coefficients of the objective function were present values and the constraint was on financial outlay. The dual problem is

$$\text{minimize } G = 16y$$
$$\text{subject to } \quad 4y \geqslant 6$$
$$2y \geqslant 4$$
$$\text{and} \quad\quad y \geqslant 0$$

Evidently the first constraint is redundant. The second holds with equality at an optimum giving the minimum value of G as 32 for $y = 2$. An extra £1,000 on the firm's capital expenditure budget would enable present value to be increased by £2,000. The opportunity loss on each machine of type one is given by the optimal value of dual slack variable one. Since $y = 2$, $t_1 = 2$. So although each machine of type one would make an accounting profit (in NPV terms) of £6,000 if one such machine is bought, then an opportunity is forgone to increase profits by another £2,000. The full solution to the dual is read from the index row in Figure 3.16 from which it is seen that $t_1 = 2$, $t_2 = 0$ and $y = 2$. The advent of additional investment opportunities as shown in Figure 3.17 alters the dual solution. The first three machines (including the previously optimal type two) all now show opportunity losses ($t_1 = 11/4$, $t_2 = 3/8$, $t_3 = 31/16$) and, since we have moved to a superior solution and there is only one scarce resource the marginal value of that resource *must* have risen ($y = 35/16$), and management will exert greater pressure to relax the financial constraint. Note that the change in optimal value of the objective function, 3, is equal to 3/8 multiplied by the value of x_2 in the previous solution and is also equal to the index row number of x_4 in the 'x_2 solution', 3/10 (ignoring sign) multiplied by the optimal value of x_4 in the final solution.

In section 3.4 an additional constraint was introduced. The original optimum is now infeasible. This means that the total value of resources ($16y_1 + 12y_2$) must be lower than previously and therefore the marginal *valuation of capital must fall*. It is now 5/4—an extra £1,000 on the budget constraint would now increase NPV by only £1,250. This is because it cannot be used as effectively as before because of the new constraint. It is now optimal to purchase three machines of type one so, of course, the dual slack variable $t_1 = 0$ as can be seen from the final index row. The accounting profit of x_1 is unchanged and so is the accounting profit of x_2 but the reduced total imputed value of the resources $((5/4)16 + \frac{1}{2} \times 12)$ has caused the opportunity loss on x_1 to fall to zero. As a last point on this problem it can be seen from Figure 3.9 that the dual infeasibility $(t_1 = -10/3)$ does not imply primal infeasibility. If the original programme of buying only two type two machines is adhered to a suboptimal solution is arrived at. Marginal valuation of funds is zero (only the floorspace constraint is binding), and total imputed value of resources is $0 \times 16 + (4/3)12 = 16$. The dual to the choice of shares problem is

$$\text{minimize} \quad G = 100y_1 - 30y_2 + 25y_3 - 10y_4 + 20 \sum_{i=5}^{i=12} y_i$$

subject to

$y_1 - y_2$		$+ y_5$			≥ 4.8
$y_1 - y_2$		$+ y_6$			≥ 5.4
y_1	$- y_4$	$+ y_7$			≥ 7.5
y_1	$- y_4$	$+ y_8$			≥ 8.5
y_1		$+ y_9$			≥ 9
y_1			$+ y_{10}$		≥ 10
y_1	$+ y_3$		$+ y_{11}$		≥ 15
y_1	$+ y_3$			$+ y_{12}$	≥ 18

$$y_i \geq 0, i = 1, 2, \ldots, 12.$$

The solution is (positive variables only) $y_1 = 9$, $y_2 = 4.2$, $y_3 = 6$, $t_3 = 1$, $y_4 = 0.5$, $y_6 = 0.6$, $y_{10} = 1$, $y_{12} = 3$ and $G = 1,011$ (i.e. average yield $= 10.11\%$). The value of $y_1 = 9$ means that for each 1% of the total budget left unspent yield (over the *whole* budget including unspent balance) would be down by 0.09%. This corresponds to a reduction of x_5 to the level of 14. The value 4.2 for y_2 means that if only 29% of the total budget had to be kept in unit trusts average yield would increase by 0.042% (x_5 increased to 16, x_1 decreased to 9). $y_3 = 6$ means that if 26% of the budget could be invested in mines then yield would be up by 0.06%.

The dual to the finance company problem is

$$\text{minimize} \quad G = 1,000y_1 + 100y_2$$

subject to

$$6y_1 + y_2 \geq 6.5$$
$$8y_1 + y_2 \geq 7$$
$$13y_1 + y_2 \geq 8.5$$
$$15y_1 + y_2 \geq 9.5$$
$$24y_1 + y_2 \geq 11.5$$

$$y_1, y_2 \geq 0$$

The optimal solution is $t_2 = 1.5/9$, $t_3 = 3/9$, $t_5 = 1$, $y_1 = 3/9$, $y_2 = 40.5/9$. The value of y_1 means that if the maximum expected loss figure was raised to £1,100 the average rate earned would increase by one third of a percentage point. The value for y_2 means that if an extra £1,000 was available for loaning then the total earnings would increase to 7090.5/9 but note that this would mean that *average* earnings would decline since

$$\frac{7090.5}{9(101)} < \frac{7,050}{9(100)}$$

This is due to the fact that the absolute level of expected loss remains unchanged.

3.8 Sensitivity Analysis

Sensitivity analysis examines the consequences of parameter variation upon the optimal solution. We may be concerned with finding the maximum permitted range of variation in a parameter (for example NPV or available funds) such that the original investment programme remains feasible and optimal. Groups of parameters can also be dealt with.

If there is a specific functional relationship between the parameters, sensitivity analysis can be conducted on the parameters of the functional relationship! We shall concentrate upon changes in objective function coefficients and changes in right-hand side elements (available finance). Consider the problem solved in Figure 3.14. The optimum has $x_1 = 15$ and $x_2 = 8$ giving $F = 246$ with $y_1 = 1$ and $y_2 = 2$. Now suppose the objective function coefficient of $x_1(\pi_1)$ goes down to 8; only optimality, not feasibility is in doubt. All that needs to be done is to recalculate the index row of the 'optimal' solution. The result is shown in Figure 3.16. The new index row is all non-negative and so the original solution remains optimal (i.e. the *dual* remains feasible). When objective function coefficients change, to check optimality all that needs to be done is to recalculate the index row. Now suppose that π_1 had dropped to 6, Figure 3.17 shows that the new index row has $y_1 = -6/14$ and the original optimum is no longer optimal. To obtain the new optimum the problem need not be started again from scratch. The x_1, x_2 solution is still *feasible* and the Simplex method can begin with any bfs, x_1 dropping out. In larger pro-

			8	12	0	0
			x_1	x_2	s_1	s_2
8	x_1	15	1	0	5/14	− 1/7
12	x_2	8	0	1	− 3/14	2/7
		216	0	0	2/7	16/7

Figure 3.16

			6	12	0	0
			x_1	x_2	s_1	s_2
6	x_1	15	1	0	5/14	−1/7
12	x_2	8	0	1	−3/14	2/7
		196	0	0	−6/14	18/7
0	s_1	42	14/5	0	1	−2/5
12	x_2	17	3/5	1	0	1/5
		204	6/5	0	0	12/5

Figure 3.17

blems this need not happen, but if the basis changes the new level of the less profitable variable will be lower. So, the procedure is relatively straight forward. Step one is to recalculate the index row. If this contains negative numbers reiterate to new optimum using the original optimum as initial bfs.

Maximum ranges of variations can be calculated for π_1 and π_2. For either coefficient all index row numbers must remain non-negative. So, for π_1 and $\pi_2 = 12$,

$$(5/14)\pi_1 - 3/14(12) \geqslant 0$$

and

$$(-1/7)\pi_1 + 2/7(12) \geqslant 0$$

which means that the original solution remains optimal so long as

$$7.2 \leqslant \pi_1 \leqslant 24$$

with $\pi_1 = 10$ the permitted range of π_2 is

$$5 \leqslant \pi_2 \leqslant 50/3$$

As a final point it should be noted that if the objective function coefficient of a non-basic variable changes then the only index row number that is affected is its own. Thus if the coefficient of s_2 became $+2$ (unused units of resource two have salvage value), then its index row number becomes $+2/7$; no other index row numbers change.

Changes in the RHS are a little more complicated to deal with. Figure 3.18 details the optimal solution of the dual problem (artificial variables omitted). Recall that the index row numbers under the dual slack variables are the optimal values of the x's. If it is also recalled that constraint level variation in the primal is equivalent to objective function coefficient variation in the dual, it is clear that all that has to be done is to repeat the preceding analysis for the dual problem! If the coefficient of y_1 (level of resource one) becomes 90 then x_1 (the t_1 index row number)

			y_1	y_2	t_1	t_2
-76	y_1	1	1	0	$-5/14$	$3/14$
-85	y_2	2	0	1	$1/7$	$-2/7$
		-246	0	0	15	8

Figure 3.18

becomes:

$$(-90)(-5/14) + (-85)(1/7) = 20$$

and the new level of x_2 is

$$(-90)(3/14) + (-85)(-2/7) = 5$$

Thus the dual solution is still optimal, i.e. the primal is still feasible with $x_1 = 20$, $x_2 = 5$ and $F = G = 260$. Maximum ranges of variation can now be worked out for each resource individually. If b_1 represents the level of resource one then,

$$-b_1(-5/14) - 85(1/7) \geqslant 0 \quad \text{and} \quad -b_1(3/14) - 85(-2/7) \geqslant 0$$

Thus,

$$34 \leqslant b_1 \leqslant 113\tfrac{1}{3}$$

In a similar manner with $b_1 = 76$ the range of values for b_2 that keep both x_1 and x_2 non-negative (i.e. keep point B in the non-negative quadrant) is found to be:

$$57 \leqslant b_2 \leqslant 190$$

The effects of changes in RHS elements of the primal can be obtained directly from the primal tableau by using the facts that:

(i) The levels of variables in the solution are the RHS elements premultiplied by the inverse of the basis.
(ii) The inverse of the basis is the matrix of exchange rates under the slack variables.

That is

$$\begin{pmatrix} 5/14 & -2/14 \\ -3/14 & 4/14 \end{pmatrix} \begin{pmatrix} 76 \\ 85 \end{pmatrix} = \begin{pmatrix} 15 \\ 8 \end{pmatrix}$$

Now substituting an unknown b_0 for 76 in the above will enable limits to be found for b_0 such that the solution values remain non-negative. When RHS elements are changes it is *feasibility* of the primal that is in question. Optimality is not affected since index row numbers are independent of the RHS elements. Thus it is required that

$$\begin{pmatrix} 5/14 & -2/14 \\ -3/14 & 4/14 \end{pmatrix} \begin{pmatrix} b_0 \\ 85 \end{pmatrix} \geqslant \begin{pmatrix} 0 \\ 0 \end{pmatrix}$$

Thus to ensure non-negativity of x_1,

$$5b_0 - 170 \geqslant 0$$

and to retain non-negativity for x_2,

$$-3b_0 + 340 \geqslant 0$$

resulting in

$$34 \leqslant b_0 \leqslant \frac{340}{3}$$

In a similar manner, with $b_0 = 76$, the permitted range for b_1 (originally 85) would be

$$57 \leqslant b_1 \leqslant 190$$

The solution is said to 'remain unchanged' so long as the same group of variables is positive. The actual *levels* of the variables change as the RHS elements alter. If b_1 remains in its permitted interval, then the company will know that both investments should still be undertaken.

Joint analysis on b_0 and b_1 is possible. We have (after multiplication by 14)

$$\begin{pmatrix} 5 & -2 \\ -3 & 4 \end{pmatrix} \begin{pmatrix} b_0 \\ b_1 \end{pmatrix} \geqslant \begin{pmatrix} 0 \\ 0 \end{pmatrix}$$

From which it emerges that

$$0.75b_0 \leqslant b_1 \leqslant 2.5b_0$$

so that as long as funds available at time one are not less than three-quarters of funds at time zero, and not more than two and one-half times the $t = 0$ funds, then both investments should be undertaken to some level.

What happens, however, if the new optimal level of one of the variables in the solution is negative? The problem need not be started again from scratch. The *dual Simplex method* can be applied with guaranteed success. However, at this stage an intuitive rule will be suggested. Suppose that (with the original objective function coefficients) the level of resource one was raised to 120. The resulting values of x_1 and x_2 are

$$\begin{pmatrix} x_1 \\ x_2 \end{pmatrix} = \begin{pmatrix} \dfrac{5}{14} & -\dfrac{2}{14} \\ \dfrac{-3}{14} & \dfrac{4}{14} \end{pmatrix} \begin{pmatrix} 120 \\ 85 \end{pmatrix} = \begin{pmatrix} \dfrac{215}{7} \\ -\dfrac{10}{7} \end{pmatrix}$$

This infeasible solution and the return to feasibility is detailed in Figure 3.19. The negative x_2 has been *raised* to zero level by the introduction of s_1 which has a negative rate of exchange with x_2. The negative pivot ele-

			10	12	0	0
			x_1	x_2	s_1	s_2
10	x_1	215/7	1	0	5/14	-2/14
12	x_2	-10/7	0	1	-3/14	4/14
		1910/7	0	0	1	2
10	x_1	85/3	1	5/3	0	1/3
0	s_1	20/3	0	-14/3	1	-4/3
		850/3	0	14/3	0	10/3

Figure 3.19

ment, $-3/14$, means that the variable replacing x_2 will be positive. The new optimum is arrived at in one iteration. Note that $850/3 < 1910/7$. This is because s_1 has a positive index row number. However, it is not always the case that only one iteration is required to get back to a feasible solution.

Reference

Charnes, A., and Cooper, W. W. (1961), *Management Models and Industrial Applications of Linear Programming* (2 vols.,), Wiley, New York.
Charnes, A., Cooper, W. W., and Henderson, A. (1953), *Introduction to Linear Programming*, Wiley, New York.

Further Reading

Baumol, W. J., *Economic Theory and Operations Analysis* (2nd Edn.), Prentice-Hall, Englewood Cliffs, NJ, 1965.
Bellman, R., *Introduction to Matrix Analysis*, McGraw-Hill, New York, 1960.
Bhaskar, K. N., 'Linear programming and capital budgeting: a re-appraisal', *Journal of Business Finance and Accounting*, 3, No. 3, Autumn 1976.
Carleton, W. T., 'Linear programming and capital budgeting models: a new interpretation', *Journal of Finance*, 25, December 1969.
Dantzig, G. B., *Linear Programming and Extensions*, University Press, Princeton, NJ, 1963.
Intriligator, M. D., *Mathematical Optimisation and Economic Theory*, Prentice-Hall, Englewood Cliffs, NJ, 1971.
Metzger, R. W., *Elementary Mathematical Programming*, Wiley, New York, 1958.
Norstrom, C. J., 'A comment on two simple decision rules in capital rationing', *Journal of Business Finance and Accounting*, 3, Summer 1976.
Salkin, G., and Kornbluth, J., *Linear Programming and Financial Planning*, Haymarket Publishing, London, 1973.
Weingartner, H. M. 'Criteria for programming investment project selection', *Journal of Industrial Economics*, 15, November 1966.
Wilkes, F. M., *Elements of Operational Research*, McGraw-Hill, New York, 1980.

CHAPTER 4

Capital Rationing and Financial Planning

Overview
Multiconstraint capital-rationing models are introduced commencing with two models employing a terminal value objective. The discounted dividend approach is then discussed with an extensive worked example. The subject of financial planning is a natural extension of capital rationing and Chambers' model is used to introduce the topic. Financial planning is itself a lead-in to the more general subject of corporate modelling, which is introduced via a description of two practical models.

4.1 Net Terminal Valve Formulations

A capital-rationing problem is one where not all projects with positive present values—determined at the pre-rationing discount rate—can be taken up because of limits on funds available for investment. It is also a situation in which some projects with negative present or terminal values—at the pre-rationing discount rate—may be accepted if they generate funds at crucial times. An interrelationship exists between projects because of the consumption of a common scarce resource: capital. Within the context of rationing models it is possible to include interrelationships due to the consumption of *any* scarce resource or resources. Although there can be difficulties in defining NPV and NTV, we shall frequently be concerned with the NTV or yield of feasible groups of projects with the idea of maximizing terminal or present value *overall*.

Consider the problem facing an investor who has the choice of either, both or neither of two projects. In order to obtain one unit of project one, a sum of money K_{01} is required immediately, and subsequently a further sum K_{11} is required at the end of one year. The corresponding amounts for one unit of project two are K_{02} and K_{12}. Each unit of project one yields returns of R_{11} and R_{21} at the end of the first and second years respectively. Similarly project two yields R_{12} and R_{22} per unit. The investor has a sum of money of b_0 immediately available and a further sum b_1 available after one year. All or part of these funds may be invested in short-term securities at a rate of return of $100j\%$. The investor does not wish to raise

$t=2$	R_{21}	R_{22}	
$t=1$	R_{11}	R_{12}	
	x_1	x_2	
$t=0$	K_{01}	K_{02}	b_0
$t=1$	K_{11}	K_{12}	b_1

Figure 4.1

further funds elsewhere, and seeks to maximize the terminal value of investments after two years. The data for the problem is presented in Figure 4.1 with the timing of outflows and inflows shown to the left.

First the constraints must be formulated. For the initial period, zero, the constraint is

$$K_{01}x_1 + K_{02}x_2 \leqslant b_0$$

or with the slack variable included:

$$K_{01}x_1 + K_{02}x_2 + s_0 = b_0$$

Now after one year the investor will have not only b_1 available, but also any unused funds from $t = 0$ invested at $100j\%$ plus the first returns from the projects. So the total amount available is

$$b_1 + R_{11}x_1 + R_{12}x_2 + s_0(1 + j)$$

and the period one constraint can be written as

$$K_{11}x_1 + K_{12}x_2 + s_1 = b_1 + R_{11}x_1 + R_{12}x_2 + s_0(1 + j)$$

or:

$$(K_{11} - R_{11})x_1 + (K_{12} - R_{12})x_2 - s_0(1 + j) + s_1 = b_1 \tag{4.1}$$

The coefficients of the xs in (4.1) are then the *net* inputs required per unit of each project.

Terminal value at $t = 2$ is return from the projects in year two, $R_{21}x_1 + R_{22}x_2$, plus any sum unspent from year one invested at $100j\%$. The objective function is

$$F = R_{21}x_1 + R_{22}x_2 + s_1(1 + j)$$

or, since

$$s_1 = b_1 + (R_{11} - K_{11})x_1 + (R_{12} - K_{12})x_2 + s_0(1 + j)$$

and

$$s_0 = b_0 - K_{01}x_1 - K_{02}x_2$$

it can be written as

$$F = \pi_1 x_1 + \pi_2 x_2 + A$$

where

$$\left.\begin{array}{l} \pi_1 = R_{21} + (R_{11} - K_{11})(1 + j) - K_{01}(1 + j)^2 \\ \pi_2 = R_{22} + (R_{12} - K_{12})(1 + j) - K_{02}(1 + j)^2 \\ A = b_0(1 + j)^2 + b_1(1 + j) \end{array}\right\} \quad (4.2)$$

The coefficients π_1 and π_2 are the per unit NTVs of x_1 and x_2 and A is the autonomous terminal value arising from zero internal investments. Division of F by a positive constant is allowable and if F is divided by $(1 + j)^2 > 0$ the present value formulation is obtained since

$$\pi_1(1 + j)^{-2} = R_{21}(1 + j)^{-2} + (R_{11} - K_{11})(1 + j)^{-1} - K_{01} = N_1$$
$$\pi_2(1 + j)^{-2} = R_{22}(1 + j)^{-2} + (R_{12} - K_{12})(1 + j)^{-1} - K_{02} = N_2$$

Using the terminal value formulations the full problem is

$$\left.\begin{array}{ll} \text{maximize } F = \pi_1 x_1 + \pi_2 x_2 + A \\ \text{subject to} \quad K_{01}x_1 + K_{02}x_2 + s_0 = h_0 \\ \quad (K_{11} - R_{11})x_1 + (K_{12} - R_{12})X_2 - s_0(1 + j) + s_1 = b_1 \\ \quad x_1, x_2, s_0, s_1 \geqslant 0 \end{array}\right\} \quad (4.3)$$

Consider a numerical example. Let $j = 0.1$ and in the layout of Figure 4.1 the returns, costs and available fund data be

$t = 2$	14	25	
$t = 1$	12	9	
	x_1	x_2	
$t = 0$	10	4	260
$t = 1$	7	17	120

Use of (4.2) and (4.3) results in the problem:

$$\begin{array}{ll} \text{maximize } F = 7.4x_1 + 11.36x_2 + 446.6 \\ \text{subject to} \quad 10x_1 + 4x_2 + s_0 = 260 \\ \quad -5x_1 + 8x_2 - 1.1s_0 + s_1 = 120 \\ \quad x_1, x_2, s_0, s_1 \geqslant 0 \end{array}$$

Now since s_0 appears with non-zero coefficient in another constraint it is necessary to introduce an artificial variable u_0 into the first constraint in order to obtain a starting solution. This done, the problem is solved via the Simplex method. The result is laid out in Figure 4.2 Investment in 16 units of x_1 and 25 of x_2 would add 402.4 to the autonomous value of F of 446.6. Terminal value at $t = 2$ is then 849. The values of the dual structural variables are 1.16 and 0.84.

			7.4	11.36	0	$-M$	0
			x_1	x_2	s_0	u_0	s_1
$-M$	u_0	260	10	4	1	1	0
0	s_1	120	-5	8	-1.1	0	1
		$-260M$	$-10M-7.4$	$-4M-11.36$	$-M$	0	0
7.4	x_1	26	1	0.4	0.1	0.1	0
0	s_1	250	0	10	-0.6	0.5	1
		192.4	0	-8.4	0.74	$0.74+M$	0
7.4	x_1	16	1	0	0.124	0.08	-0.04
11.36	x_2	25	0	1	-0.06	0.05	0.1
		402.4	0	0	0.236	$1.16+M$	0.84

Figure 4.2

A diagram reveals some interesting features of the problem. In Figure 4.3 the lines CE and AG show the two constraints with slack variables zero. The feasible region would appear to be the cross-hatched area OADE, but this is not the case. The variable s_0 appears with negative coefficient in constraint one. If s_0 is made positive funds are transferred to the second period. The $t = 0$ constraint, represented by line CE moves inwards as indicated by the arrow while AG moves upwards. The point of inter section moves along the line DB towards the x_2-axis. Thus points in ABD are also feasible and the total feasible region is OBDE. If borrowing from the supply in period two was possible at the same interest rate (i.e. if s_0 could be made negative) then the directions of movement of the constraints would be reversed and the intercept term D would move along

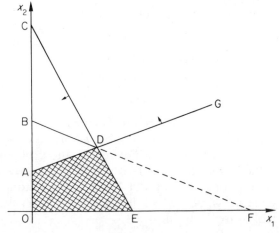

Figure 4.3

the dashed line segment towards F. In the event of this possibility the total feasible region is OBF. The ability to transfer funds thus increases the feasible region. The two constraints are not independent and only determine the area OADE for the particular value of s_0 of zero. If s_0 does not have this lower bound there is in effect only one constraint; the two original constraints joining to form the line BF. The implication of this is quite striking. If there is no lower bound on s_0 and no upper bounds on the xs then only one project will be taken. This is not to predict that in reality we shall find companies in capital rationing situations with all their eggs in one basket. Quite apart from considerations of risk there will be upper bounds on variables, borrowing limits, diminishing returns (an instance of non-linearity in the problem) and differential external borrowing and investment conditions.

We turn now to interpretation of the optimal solution. The index row number of artificial variable u_0 has a meaning once the M is removed. This is because in this problem u_0 is acting as the 'genuine' slack variable for constraint one. s_0 appears with a non-zero coefficient in the second constraint so that its column of rates of exchange cannot be elements of the inverse of the basis. This *is*, however, true of the u_0 column. The non-autonomous part of the dual objective function is

$$(1.16)260 + (0.84)120 = 240.4$$

An extra £1 available at $t = 0$ would increase value at $t = 2$ by £1.16 over and above the autonomous increase of £1.21. The gross change in value at $t = 2$ is then £$(1.16 + 1.21)$ = £2.37. Likewise, an extra £1 available at $t = 1$ would increase value at $t = 2$ by £0.84 over and above the autonomous increase of £1.1. The total change in this case is therefore £1.94.

It is these gross figures that enable maximum borrowing rates of interest to be calculated when the repayment date is $t = 2$. Clearly, for £1 borrowed from an outside source at $t = 0$ the investor would be prepared to pay anything up to a maximum of £2.37 at $t = 2$. This means that the interest, annually compounded, charged on the loan could be up to 54%. If borrowing occurred at $t = 1$ with repayment at $t = 2$ the maximum borrowing rate would be 94%. If repayment of the loan had to be made prior to $t = 2$, dual values enable rapid evaluation of such schemes. If there is £1 borrowed at $t = 0$ and £D_2 repaid at $t = 2$ then the change in F, ΔF, is given by

$$\Delta F = (1.16 \ \ 0.84)\binom{+1}{0} + (1.21 \ \ 1.1)\binom{+1}{0} - D_2$$

in which case D can be up to 2.37. If, on the other hand, a sum of money D_1 was repaid at $t = 1$ the change in F would be given by

$$\Delta F = (1.16 \ \ 0.84)\binom{+1}{-D_1} + (1.21 \ \ 1.1)\binom{+1}{-D_1} = 2.37 - 1.94D_1$$

So, in order that $\Delta F > 0$ it is required that $D_1 < 2.37/1.94$ implying a maximum borrowing rate of interest between $t = 0$ and $t = 1$ of 22.2%. The dual values enable any borrowing and repayment stream to be rapidly assessed. For arbitrary D_0 D_1 and D_2 we require

$$\Delta F = (2.37 \quad 1.94)\begin{pmatrix} D_0 \\ D_1 \end{pmatrix} - D_2 \geqslant 0 \tag{4.4}$$

ΔF may be thought of as the negative of the opportunity loss on one unit of a new variable x_0 with coefficients in the constraints of $-D_0$ and $-D_1$ respectively, and a coefficient of $-D_2$ in the objective function. If ΔF in (4.4) is positive the borrowing scheme is worth while and x_0 should be brought into the solution.

The problem will now be represented in a format which does not include the NTVs of individual projects and has more general applicability in that it can be used in cases where there is no preassigned interest rate. Formulation two has constraints as before but the form of objective function is $F = R_{21}x_1 + R_{22}x_2 + s_1(1 + j)$. The solution to the problem is shown in Figure 4.4. In this formulation the 'full' shadow price for funds in period zero is given. However since s_1 has an objective function coefficient of 1.1 this has to be added to the s_1 index row number, 0.84, to give the marginal value for funds at $t = 1$.

In formulation two the NTVs of the projects are not shown individually although it is terminal value that it is the objective to maximize. There is in fact no unambiguous value that can be put on terminal value or present value of a project in a multiproject context with multiperiod constraints. The contribution of a given stream of costs and returns to terminal value depends upon the streams of returns on other projects and the capital constraints. This will change if the project is added to either

			14	25	0	$-M$	1.1
			x_1	x_2	s_0	u_0	s_1
$-M$	u_0	260	10	4	1	1	0
1.1	s_1	120	-5	8	-1.1	0	1
		$132 - 260M$	$-10M - 19.5$	$-4M - 16.2$	$-M - 1.21$	0	0
14	x_1	26	1	0.4	0.1	0.1	0
1.1	s_1	250	0	10	-0.6	0.5	1
		639	0	-8.4	0.74	$1.95 + M$	0
14	x_1	16	1	0	0.124	0.08	-0.04
25	x_2	25	0	1	-0.06	0.05	0.1
		849	0	0	0.236	$2.37 + M$	0.84

Figure 4.4

a different set of other possible projects or a different set of constraints. An asset *cannot* be valued in isolation from other assets to which it can be adjoined or from the constraints which apply to its use.

Now consider a borrowing possibility. The investor must repay £0.35 at $t = 2$ and £1 at $t = 1$ for each £1 borrowed at $t = 0$. No limit is set on the amount borrowed other than by the ability to repay. The borrowing scheme may be viewed as an additional investment project and adjoined to the constraint set and objective function of the problem. The problem becomes

maximize $F = 14x_1 + 25x_2 - 0.35x_3 + 1.1s_1 - Mu_0$

subject to $\quad 10x_1 + 4x_2 - x_3 + s_0 = 260$

$$-5x_1 + 8x_2 + x_3 - 1.1s_0 + s_1 = 120$$
$$x_1, x_2, s_1, s_0 \geqslant 0$$

The new optimum is shown in Figure 4.5. Extensive borrowing at $t = 0$ is indicated and only x_1 is invested in. If there had been an upper bound on borrowing of less than 500 then x_2 would have remained in the solution at a reduced level. The marginal valuations of funds are 2.45 at $t = 0$ and $2.1 (= 1 + 1.1)$ at $t = 1$. It should be noted that x_3 has been introduced into the solution despite having a negative NTV (NTV $= -0.24$, NPV $= -0.198$). Furthermore, it has been introduced in preference to a project with NTV $= 11.36$. The reason is that x_3 provides funds at the right time. Its value in conjunction with x_1 is much greater than its value alone. NTV calculated with the discount rate of 10% does not measure the ability of the project to contribute to value at $t = 2$.

While there is no *true* NTV for x_3, the index row number in the previous optimum shows the terminal value per unit of x_3 in conjunction with the asset set $A = (x_1, x_2)$ as 0.08. The solution also provides discount factors (or 'appreciation factors' in an NTV context) which allow this figure to be arrived at. These factors are of course the shadow prices, the

			14	25	−0.35	0	−M	1.1
			x_1	x_2	x_3	s_0	u_0	s_1
14	x_1	16	1	0	−0.12	0.124	0.08	−0.04
25	x_2	25	0	1	0.05	−0.06	0.05	0.1
		849	0	0	−0.8	0.236	2.37 + M	0.1
14	x_1	76	1	2.4	0	−0.02	0.2	0.2
−0.35	x_3	500	0	20	1	−1.2	1	2
		889	0	1.6	0	0.14	2.45 + M	1

Figure 4.5

opportunity loss on x_3 in the original optimum is t_3 where

$$(2.37) \times 1 - (1.94) \times 1 - t_3 = -0.35$$

therefore $t_3 = -0.08$. This is the third constraint of the dual problem. Consequently the appropriate weights to attach to the stream of costs and income associated with x_3 are the marginal values of money given by the optimal solution. These marginal values can be broken down into implied interest rates from period to period. The equations to solve are

$$(1 + i_0)(1 + i_1) = 2.37$$
$$(1 + i_1) = 1.94$$

where $100i_0\%$ is the implied interest rate prevailing from $t = 0$ to $t = 1$ and $100i_1\%$ prevails from $t = 1$ until $t = 2$. The rates are 22.16% and 94% respectively. NTV of x_3 with asset set A is then

$$[1(1 + i_0) - 1](1 + i_1) - 0.35 = 0.08$$

In a similar fashion present value with asset set A is

$$\frac{-0.35}{(1 + i_0)(1 + i_1)} \frac{-1}{(1 + i_1)} + 1 = 0.0337$$

Once again it should be recalled that these figures for 'terminal value' and 'present value' are not NTV and NPV in the usual senses. The values for TV and PV for x_1 and x_2 obtained by using the dual discount factors illustrate this—they are both zero. In other words only invest in those projects with zero present value! This is clearly *not* a conventional view of present values, but discounting by shadow prices will give optimal accept/reject decisions for additional projects since the shadow prices are the opportunity costs of capital. A distinction should be made between NPV in an accounting sense and NPV for decision making. Further projects can be assessed using shadow prices as discount rates. Acceptable projects have zero or positive NPV at these rates. New maximum NPV will be zero using the new opportunity cost discount rates emerging from the optimal solution. Projects can only have positive NPVs when discounted with suboptimal opportunity cost discount factors.

Now consider the problem of borrowing from outside sources at predetermined interest rates. If a uniform interest rate applies to both borrowing and lending only one project will be undertaken unless there are additional constraints. This will not necessarily be the case if borrowing and investment rates of interest differ. Let investment be possible at $100j\%$ and let $J = (1 + j)$. Borrowing is possible at $100i\%$ and $I = (1 + i)$. It is assumed that repayment is at will rather than at a specified date. Let $\hat{s}_t$ represent surplus cash at period t and $\bar{s}_t$ represent the level of borrowing at period t. New borrowing at t is $\bar{s}_t - \bar{s}_{t-1}$. In our current context the constraints are

$$(K_{01} - R_{01})x_1 + (K_{02} - R_{02})x_2 + \hat{s}_0 - \bar{s}_0 = b_0$$

$$(K_{11} - R_{11})x_1 + (K_{12} - R_{12})x_2 - J\hat{s}_0 + I\bar{s}_0 + \hat{s}_1 - \bar{s}_1 = b_1$$

where $R_{01} = R_{02} = 0$. In a larger problem with n investment opportunities the constraint for the tth period would be

$$\sum_{h=1}^{n} (K_{th} - R_{th})x_h + J\hat{s}_{t-1} - I\bar{s}_{t-1} + \hat{s}_t - \bar{s}_t = b_t$$

In the two constraint example the objective function will be

$$\text{maximize } F = R_{21}x_1 + R_{22}x_2 + J\hat{s}_1 - I\bar{s}_1$$

In a problem with horizon at $t = m$ the objective function would be

$$\text{maximize } F = \sum_{h=1}^{n} (R_{mh} - K_{mh})x_h + J\hat{s}_{m-1} - I\bar{s}_{m-1}$$

In such a problem, if there were constraints until only the $(M-p)$th period where $p \geqslant 2$ then 'part way' values of the objective function would have to be defined. For instance if $m = 6$ and $p = 2$ we should define.

$$F_5 = \sum_{h=1}^{n} (R_{5h} - K_{5h})x_h + J\hat{s}_4 - I\bar{s}_4$$

and constrain

$$F_5 - \hat{s}_5 + \bar{s}_5 = 0$$

which would be added to the list of constraints. This has to be done since *a priori* it is not known at what rate of interest to carry forward the sum F_5 into period six. If F_5 is positive, it should go forward at $100j\%$; if negative, the company is in debt and must pay interest at $100i\%$. $\hat{s}_5$ and $\bar{s}_5$ cannot both be positive *at an optimum* and optimality (and feasibility) considerations will select the values of the variables in the course of solution of the problem. In the context of the numerical example let $i - 0.3$ and suppose that the maximum debt allowable at any time is 100. The problem is to

$$\text{maximize } F - 14x_1 + 25x_2 + 1.1\hat{s}_1 - 1.3\bar{s}_1 - Mu_0 - Mu_1$$

$$\text{subject to} \quad 10x_1 + 4x_2 + \hat{s}_0 - \bar{s}_0 + u_0 = 260$$

$$- 5x_1 + 8x_2 - 1.1\hat{s}_0 + 1.3\bar{s}_0 + \hat{s}_1 - \bar{s}_1 + u_1 = 120$$

$$\bar{s}_0 + \overset{*}{s}_0 = 100$$

$$\bar{s}_0 + \overset{*}{s}_1 = 100$$

$$x_1, x_2, \hat{s}_0, \bar{s}_0, \hat{s}_1, \bar{s}_1, u_0, u_1, \overset{*}{s}_0, \overset{*}{s}_1 \geqslant 0$$

c_B	Basis	Value	14 x_1	25 x_2	0 $\hat{s}_0$	0 $\bar{s}_0$	1.1 $\hat{s}_1$	−1.3 $\bar{s}_1$	−M u_0	−M u_1	0 s_0^*	0 s_1^*
−M	u_0	260	(10)	4	1	−1	0	0	1	0	0	0
−M	u_1	120	−5	8	−1.1	1.3	1	−1	0	1	0	0
0	s_0^*	100	0	0	0	1	0	0	0	0	1	0
0	s_1^*	100	0	0	0	0	0	1	0	0	0	1
		(−380M)	(−5M−14)	(−12M−25)	(0.1M)	(−0.3M)	(−M−1.1)	(M+1.3)	0	0	0	0
14	x_1	26	1	0.4	0.1	−0.1	0	0	0.1	0	0	0
−M	u_1	250	0	10	−0.6	0.8	1	−1	0.5	1	0	0
0	s_0^*	100	0	0	0	(1)	0	0	0	0	1	0
0	s_1^*	100	0	0	0	0	0	1	0	0	0	1
		(364−250M)	0	(−19.4−10M)	(1.4+0.6M)	(−1.4−0.8M)	(−M−1.1)	(M+1.3)	(1.4+0.5M)	0	0	0
14	x_1	36	1	0.4	0.1	0	0	0	0.1	0	0.1	0
−M	u_1	170	0	(10)	−0.6	0	1	−1	0.5	1	−0.8	0
0	$\bar{s}_0$	100	0	0	0	1	0	0	0	0	1	0
0	s_1^*	100	0	0	0	0	0	1	0	0	0	1
		504−170M	0	(−19.4−10M)	(1.4+0.6M)	0	−1.1−M	M+13	(1.4+0.5M)	0	(1.4+0.8M)	0

14	x_1	29.2	1	0	0.124	0	-0.04	0.04	0.08	-0.04	0.132	0
25	x_2	17	0	1	-0.06	0	0.1	-0.1	0.05	0.1	-0.08	0
0	$\bar{s}_0$	100	0	0	0	1	0	0	0	0	1	0
0	s_1^*	100	0	0	0	0	0	(1)	0	0	0	1
		833.8	0	0	0.236	0	0.84	-0.64	2.37-M	1.94+M	-0.152	0

14	x_1	25.2	1	0	0.124	0	-0.04	0	0.08	-0.04	0.132	-0.04
25	x_2	27	0	1	-0.06	0	0.1	0	0.05	0.1	-0.08	0.1
0	$\bar{s}_0$	100	0	0	0	1	0	0	0	0	(1)	0
-1.3	$\bar{s}_1$	100	0	0	0	0	0	1	0	0	0	1
		897.8	0	0	0.236	0	0.84	0	2.37+M	1.94+M	-0.152	0.64

14	x_1	12	1	0	0.124	-0.132	-0.04	0	0.08	-0.04	0	-0.04
25	x_2	35	0	1	-0.06	0.08	0.1	0	0.5	0.1	0	0.1
0	s_0^*	100	0	0	0	1	0	0	0	0	1	0
-1.3	$\bar{s}_1$	100	0	0	0	0	0	1	0	0	0	1
		913	0	0	0.236	0.152	0.84	0	2.37+M	1.94+M	0	0.64

Figure 4.6

The slack variables in the upper bound restrictions have been distinguished by *. A second artificial variable, u_1, has been added in so that index row numbers can be used as they stand. The solution to the problem is given in Figure 4.6. Pivotal elements are circled.

The borrowing opportunity raises F to 913; x_2 being raised to 35 and x_1 lowered to 12 in contrast to the 'x_3' borrowing scheme with compulsory part repayment at $t = 1$ in which x_1 (the $t = 1$ money generator) was raised to 76. Note that the marginal valuations of extra internal capital (2.37 and 1.94.) are unchanged. Why then is it not worth setting $\bar{s}_0 = 1$ and having to repay only £1.69 at $t = 2$ when the extra £1 at $t = 0$ should increase TV by £2.37? The correct evaluation of $\bar{s}_0 = 1$ is shown to be -0.152, i.e. F would decrease by 0.152. This can be deduced from the marginal valuations of capital in the following way. An extra £1 at $t = 0$ would increase F by £2.37 but the LHS of the constraint at $t = 1$ would have to be reduced by 1.3 because of the limit on $\bar{s}_1$ and on this account F would decline by $(1.3).(1.94) = 2.522$ making a net decrease of $2.522 - 2.37 = 0.152$. The figure 2.37 then shows how F would increase if £1 more of *internal* funds was available at $t = 0$.

The problem is graphed in Figure 4.7. The original optimum with no borrowing or investment is D with optimal objective function line OO indicated. The borrowing of 100 from outside sources moves constraint two upwards to A'G but leaves the original constraint unaltered at CE and the new optimum is at D'. The objective function through the point D' can be thought of as having the same slope as through D but with 130 [= (100)1.3] deducted from its value or it can be envisaged as having different slope with an addition. The latter formulation is arrived at by

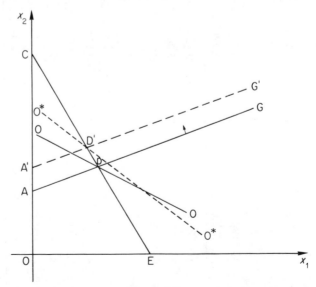

Figure 4.7

writing F as

$$F' = 14x_1 + 25x_2 - 1.3(8x_2 - 5x_1 - 120) = 20.5x + 14.6x_2 + 156$$

since $8x_2 - 5x_1 - 120 = \bar{s}_1$ provided that all other ss are zero. This is the form used for objective function line O*O* and the constraints show that borrowing will always be up to the limit as this is raised. Point D' remains optimal and moves up constraint CE towards C as the limit on $\bar{s}_1$ is raised. It should be recalled that, because of the non-zero ofcs (objective function coefficients) of slack variables and the autonomous components thus produced, the relative slope condition is no longer sufficient to prove optimality of D'. The autonomous components have to be considered too.

4.2   The Discounted Dividend Model

There is a further formulation of capital-rationing problems that has many attractive features. The foregoing formulations would appear to have much to commend them in respect of the individual investor and unquoted company. Following the practice established earlier in the book we have also been presuming an environment of 'effective certainty'. For companies with issued share capital operating in more risk-conscious circumstances the *discounted dividend* model would be apposite. To an extent, this model blurs the distinction that we have been at pains to preserve between effective certainty situations and risky environments. Some linkage is, therefore, welcome. There is also a natural lead-in to the area of financial planning models.

It will be assumed that the objective of the investing company is the maximization of shareholder wealth. More specifically, we shall assume that shareholder wealth is measured by the current value of equity and that the value of equity is the present value of future dividend payments. The appropriate discount rate for dividends is the cost of equity capital. The undertaking of an investment programme will mean that changes in the future dividend stream are brought about. These changes are of two kinds. There may be years in which dividend is depressed through higher than usual retentions to finance the investments. Then there will be years in which increased dividends can be paid because of the returns from the investments coming in. We shall take it to be the case that the present value of the set of dividend changes must be positive for an investment programme to be worthwhile. We can write the requirement formally as

$$\Delta D_0 + \frac{\Delta D_1}{(1+e)} + \frac{\Delta D_2}{(1+e)^2} + \ldots + \frac{\Delta D_n}{(1+e)^n} > 0 \tag{4.5}$$

where the ΔD_t are the dividend changes brought about over an n year horizon and $100e\%$ is the cost of equity. The objective of the investing company will then be to choose a group of investments (that can be afforded in all years) so as to maximize (4.5).

	Capital inputs required per unit of investment			Sum available for investment
Time	1	2	3	
$t = 0$	k_{01}	k_{02}	k_{03}	b_0
$t = 1$	k_{11}	k_{12}	k_{13}	b_1
	Return per unit of investment undertaken			Short-term interest rate
Time	1	2	3	
$t = 0$	0	0	0	$100r\%$
$t = 1$	R_{11}	R_{12}	R_{13}	$100r\%$
$t = 2$	R_{21}	R_{22}	R_{23}	

Figure 4.8

Now consider the nature of the financial constraints themselves. Suppose as before that capital inputs are required in each of two years—the present moment (year zero) and also after one year (year one). We shall again simplify matters by assuming that a decision has already been taken to set aside given amounts for investment at $t = 0$ and $t = 1$. Suppose that there are three investments under consideration. The notational scheme is shown in Figure 4.8.

It is assumed that any unused funds at $t = 0$ can be transferred to $t = 1$ at a rate of interest of $100r\%$. This rate may be bank deposit interest rate or the rate of return on one year government securities, and will normally differ from the cost of equity.

With ΔD_0 representing any change in current dividend the $t = 0$ constraint is

$$k_{01}x_1 + k_{02}x_2 + k_{03}x_3 + \Delta D_0 + s_0 = b_0 \qquad (4.6)$$

Equation 4.6 is the initial constraint.

Now at $t = 1$ we can write in similar fashion

$$E_1 = k_{11}x_1 + k_{12}x_2 + k_{13}x_3$$

and letting ΔD_1 represent the increased dividend at this point and s_1 any surplus transferred to $t = 2$ at $100r\%$ the total sum called for at $t = 1$ will be

$$k_{11}x_1 + k_{12}x_2 + k_{13}x_3 + \Delta D_1 + s_1$$

Now the sum available for expenditure at $t = 1$ will include what, if anything, was surplus to requirements at $t = 0$ (compounded at $100r\%$) plus the first year returns from the investments undertaken. Thus total funds available will be

$$b_1 + s_0(1 + r) + R_{11}x_1 + R_{12}x_2 + R_{13}x_3$$

so that the $t = 1$ constraint can be written as

$$(k_{11} - R_{11})x_1 + (k_{12} - R_{12})x_2 + (k_{13} - R_{13})x_3 - s_0(1 + r)$$
$$+ \Delta D_1 + s_1 = b_1$$

Finally, the dividend increase allowed in year two will be the returns from investments at that time plus any surplus, s_1, invested at $100r\%$ at $t = 1$. So that

$$\Delta D_2 = R_{21}x_1 + R_{22}x_2 + R_{23}x_3 + s_1(1 + r)$$

The full problem is, then, to

maximize $F = \Delta D_0 + \dfrac{\Delta D_1}{(1 + e)} + \dfrac{\Delta D_2}{(1 + e)^2}$

subject to $k_{01}x_1 + k_{02}x_2 + k_{03}x_3 + \Delta D_0 + s_0 = b_0$
$(k_{11} - R_{11})x_1 + (k_{12} - R_{12})x_2 + (k_{13} - R_{13})x_3$
$\quad - s_0(1 + r) + \Delta D_1 + s_1 = b_1$

$\quad\quad - R_{21}x_1 - R_{22}x_2 - R_{23}x_3 - s_1(1 + r)$
$\quad\quad + \Delta D_2 = 0$

$\left.\begin{array}{r}\\\\\\\\\\\\\end{array}\right\}$ (4.7)

where $x_1 \geqslant 0, x_2 \geqslant 0, x_3 \geqslant 0, s_0 \geqslant 0,\ s_1 \geq 0, \Delta D_0$
$\geqslant 0, \Delta D_1 \geqslant 0, \Delta D_2 \geq 0$

The scheme 4.7 can be built upon. As examples of further constraints there may be:

(i)   Upper limits (possibly unity) on the investment levels.
(ii)   Physical resource constraints.
(iii)   'Balance sheet' constraints.
(iv)   Interdependencies between the investments.

Constraints of type (i) at unity level would prohibit repetition of an investment. In (iii) are included requirements that the investment programme be such as to leave certain crucial financial statistics within given bounds. Further, there may be limits on the relative sizes or dividends of dividend changes. Under (iv) would be included mutual exclusiveness between investments or one investment being a precondition for another. Further opportunities might include:

(i) Further borrowing possibilities.
ii) Delayed start or repetition of completed projects.
(iii) Consideration of alterntive objectives.

Consider the following problem. A company is settling its capital budget for 1982 and 1983 against a background which suggests the likelihood of a shortage of cash resources during the period. It is estimated that the established operations of the company will generate a cash surplus of £250,000 on 1 January 1982 ($t = 0$) and of £240,000 on 1 January 1983 ($t = 1$) available for payment of a dividend and for financing new investments. Market conditions are thought to rule out the raising of additional capital from external sources during the period, but conditions are expected to improve during 1984 and it is expected that the company will no longer face a rationing situation. Six investments are available (which are continuously divisible but not repeatable), the financial data for which are

Project	1	2	3	4	5	6
Outlays required ($£1,000$):						
$t = 0$	30	40	20	40	60	—
$t = 1$	—	—	40	40	40	80
Return at $t = 2$	72	72	96	132	168	144

The objective of the company is to maximize the value of its equity at $t = 0$ and equity value is determined by the discounted dividend model. The cost of equity capital represents the appropriate discount rate for dividends and is 20%. The company can invest unused funds elsewhere at 15%. The previously determined dividends of £100,000 at $t = 0$ and £105,00 at $t = 1$ may be added to but not decreased. There is no restriction on dividend at $t = 2$ nor are the relative sizes of dividend payments restricted.

Let ΔD_t represent the increase, if any, in the otherwise planned dividend at $t = 1, 2, 3,$. The increase in current value of equity that would result is then

$$\Delta V = \Delta D_0 + \frac{\Delta D_1}{1.2} + \frac{\Delta D_2}{(1.2)^2} \tag{4.8}$$

and it is desired to maximize ΔV.

Now, as regards the constraints, expenditure on the investments at $t = 0$ must not exceed £150,000. This is because while £250,000 is available at this time £100,000 has already been earmarked for dividend. So, we can write

$$30x_1 + 40x_2 + 20x_3 + 40x_4 + 60x_5 + 0x_6 + s_0 + \Delta D_0 = 150 \tag{4.9}$$

in which x_1 to x_6 represent the number of units taken of each investment. At time $t = 1$ funds outlaid on the projects must not exceed £135,000 (= £240,000 – £105,000) *plus* any unused funds from $t = 0$ invested at 15%. The constraint would then be

$$0x_1 + 0x_2 + 40x_3 + 40x_4 + 40x_5 + 80x_6 + \Delta D_1 \leqslant 135 + s_0(1.15)$$

and re-expressed with variables on the LHS only and with slack variables included we have

$$0x_1 + 0x_2 + 40x_3 + 40x_4 + 40x_5 + 80x_6 - 1.15s_0 + s_1 + \Delta D_1 = 135 \tag{4.10}$$

Now, unlimited extra dividends cannot be paid at time $t = 2$. The increase in dividend that is possible at that time depends on the returns coming in from the investments and any surplus funds from $t = 1$ invested at

15%. So that ΔD_2 is limited by

$$72x_1 + 72x_2 + 96x_3 + 132x_4 + 168x_5 + 144x_6 + 1.15s_1 - \Delta D_2 = 0$$
$$(4.11)$$

Finally there are the upper bounds on the x's

$$x_1 \leqslant 1, \; x_2 \leqslant 1, \; x_3 \leqslant 1, \; x_4 \leqslant 1, \; x_5 \leqslant 1, \; x_6 \leqslant 1 \qquad (4.12)$$

The full problem would now be to maximize (4.8) subject to (4.9), (4.10), (4.11), (4.12) and the sign requirements on all variables.

Now from (4.11) we can obtain ΔD_2 in terms of the x's and s_1:

$$\Delta D_2 = 72x_1 + 72x_2 + 96x_3 + 132x_4 + 168x_5 + 144x_6 + 1.15s_1 \qquad (4.13)$$

However, it will be noted that s_1 cannot be strictly positive at an optimum. If s_1 is positive this means that funds are being transferred from $t = 1$ to $t = 2$ at 15%. The x's are being cut back or ΔD_2 is being increased at the expense of ΔD_1. Reductions in the x's as a result of positive s_1 may have even more serious consequences in terms of V, we cannot tell at the outset, but *at the very least* £1 transferred from $t = 1$ to $t = 2$ will cause V to decline by $1/1.2 - 1.15/1.44$ hence s_1 is zero at an optimum.

Now let us employ this information to simplify the problem. With ΔD_2 as given by (4.13) and with $s_1 = 0$, we can substitute for ΔD_2 in (4.8) producing the form of objective function (4.14):

$$V = 20x_1 + 50x_2 + 66\tfrac{2}{3}x_3 + 91\tfrac{2}{3}x_4 + 116\tfrac{2}{3}x_5$$

$$+ \; 100x_6 + \Delta D_0 + \frac{\Delta D_1}{1.2} \qquad (4.14)$$

which is to be maximized subject to

$$30x_1 + 40x_2 + 20x_3 + 40x_4 + 60x_5 + 0x_6 + s_0$$
$$+ \Delta D_0 = 150$$

$$0x_1 + 0x_2 + 40x_3 + 40x_4 + 40x_5 + 80x_6 - 1.15s_0$$
$$+ 0\Delta D_0 + \Delta D_1 = 135$$

and $\qquad\qquad\qquad\qquad\qquad\qquad\qquad\qquad\qquad\qquad\qquad (4.15)$

$$x_1 \leqslant 1, \; x_2 \leqslant 1, \; x_3 \leqslant 1, \; x_4 \leqslant 1, \; x_5 \leqslant 1, \; x_6 \leqslant 1$$

for

$$x_1, \; x_2, \; x_3, \; x_4, \; x_5, \; x_6, \; s_0, \; \Delta D_0, \; \Delta D_1 \geqslant 0$$

If surplus funds could be transferred from $t = 0$ to $t = 1$ at 20% instead of 15%, then both ΔD_0 and ΔD_1 could be substituted out of the objective function and the resulting coefficients of the x's would in fact have been the net present values of the projects discounted at 20%. But since more than one interest rate applies in this case this substitution cannot be made. It is instructive to see what would have been the solution had there been no upper bounds. At once six constraints are lost from (4.15), but in addition some of the xs can be dispensed with now that repeatability is allowed.

To start with, x_1 clearly *dominates* x_2 since it has the same objective function coefficient (per unit contribution to V) as x_2 and requires a smaller outlay. Less obviously x_4 is dominated by $x_3 + \frac{2}{3}x_1$; this combination requiring the same outlays as one unit of x_4 but yielding 100 in the objective function in comparison to $91\frac{2}{3}$. Also x_5 is dominated by $x_3 + \frac{4}{3}x_1$ while x_3 itself is inferior to $\frac{1}{2}x_6 + \frac{2}{3}x_1$. The problem has now been reduced to

maximize $\Delta V + 50x_1 + 100x_6 + \Delta D_0 + 0.833\Delta D_1$

subject to $30x_1 + s_0 + \Delta D_0 = 150$

$\qquad\qquad 80x_6 - 1.15s_0 + \Delta D_1 = 135$

$\qquad\qquad x_1 \geqslant 0, \ x_6 \geqslant 0, \ s_0 \geqslant 0, \ D_0 \geqslant 0, \ D_1 \geqslant 0$

But yet further shrinkage is possible. It will be seen that ΔD_0 is dominated by $\frac{1}{30}x_1$ and ΔD_1 is dominated by $\frac{1}{80}x_6$ so that all that is left is

Maximize $\Delta V = 50x_1 + 100x_6$

subject to $30x_1 + s_0 = 150$

$\qquad\qquad 80x_6 - 1.15s_0 = 135$

$\qquad\qquad x_1 \geqslant 0, \ x_6 \geqslant 0, \ s_0 \geqslant 0$

Now from the first of the constraints

$s_0 = 150 - 30x_1$

and substitution into the second gives

$80x_6 - 1.15(150 - 30x_1) = 135$

which on rearrangement becomes

$80x_6 + 34.5x_1 = 307.5$

Solving this for x_6 produces

$x_6 = 3.84375 - 0.43125x_1$ \hfill (4.16)

and substituting into the objective function gives

$\Delta V = 50x_1 + 384.375 - 43.125x_1$

$\qquad = 6.875x_1 + 384.375$ \hfill (4.17)

Now the important thing about the objective function as presented in (4.17) is that the coefficient of x_1 is positive. The constraints are implicitly included, so that it means that for each unit that x_1 is raised *after allowing for the changes in the other variables*, ΔV will increase by 6.875. Consequently the optimum is produced by making x_1 as large as possible. The largest value that x_1 can take is when $s_0 = 0$ and $x_1 = 5$ ($= 150 \div 30$) and by substitution into (4.16) $x_6 = 1.6875$. Substituting these values into (4.17) produces $\Delta V = 418.75$. This implies that $\Delta D_0 = 0$, $\Delta D_1 = 0$ (as we have already seen, they are dominated) and by substitution of the optimal values of x_1 and x_6 into (4.13) (everything else in the equation is zero) gives $\Delta D_2 = 603$. As a check, substituting these values of the dividend increases into (4.8) gives

$$\Delta V = 0 + \frac{0}{1.2} + \frac{603}{1.44} = 418.75$$

Thus in the absence of upper limits of units on investment size, the optimal policy would be to take five units of the first investment, nothing of the second to fifth investments, take one and eleven sixteenths of investment six, transfer no money from 1 January 1982 to 1 January 1983, pay the minimum dividends of £100,000 in 1978 and £105,000 in 1983 and increase the dividend by £603,000 in 1984. Of course this may represent an unacceptable dividend policy in practice, in which case further constraints relating ΔD_0, ΔD_1 and ΔD_2 should be included. The value of the firm's equity will rise by £418,750.

Now consider the upper bounds. If no more than one unit of each investment is possible we cannot eliminate any of the investments *ex-ante*. The full problem has to be solved. Figure 4.9 shows the initial tableau for solution by the Simplex method and Figure 4.10 shows the final tableau. The optimal solution requires full participation in investments one, two, five and six, an approximately 44% share in investment four while investment three is ignored. Note that £2,326 are to be transferred at 15% from period zero to period one. ΔD_0 and ΔD_1 are at zero level and by substitution of the levels of the x's into (6), ΔD_2 is found to be 8846.4/17.2 which produces a value of ΔV of 6143.33/17.2 = 357.17. The presence of the upper bound constraints has caused ΔV to drop by 61.58. The opportunity loss of taking one unit of x_3 is 8.33/17.2.

In the optimal solution to the problem with upper bounds included, a 'loan' was made for one period which superficially yielded less than the cost of capital. The *nominal* yield of £1 invested at 15% in these conditions is 15% but the true yield is, it turns out, much greater than this. Investing at 15% at $t - 0$ makes money available at $t - 1$ when it is particularly valuable. This enables a superior investment programme to be undertaken allowing bigger returns and $t = 2$ dividend to be paid. To determine the implied yield on the marginal £1 invested at 15% proceed in the following manner. An additional constraint would be appended limiting the value of s_0 to 22.8/17.2 (i.e. 40/17.2 – 1) and the new optimum value of ΔV determined. The difference between the two values of ΔV is the increase in present value of dividends obtainable by investing the marginal £1 at a nominal 15% rather than using the £1 in the best alternative manner. This difference turns out to be 0.3958, meaning that the increase in ΔD_2 with $s_0 = 40/17.2$ instead of 22.8/17.2 is 0.5700 (= 0.3958 × 1.44). Now in the new solution with restricted s_0, the value of an extra £1 available at $t = 0$ (the new bracketed index row number

			x_1	x_2	x_3	x_4	x_5	x_6	s_0	D_0	D_1	s_1	s_2	s_3	s_4	s_5	s_6
			50	50	$66.\overline{66}$	$91.\overline{66}$	$116.\overline{66}$	100	0	1	$0.8\overline{33}$	0	0	0	0	0	0
1	D_0	150	30	40	20	40	60	0	1	1	0	0	0	0	0	0	0
0.833	D_1	135	0	0	40	40	40	80	−1.15	0	1	0	0	0	0	0	0
0	s_1		1	0	0	0	0	0	0	0	0	1	0	0	0	0	0
0	s_2		0	1	0	0	0	0	0	0	0	0	1	0	0	0	0
0	s_3		0	0	1	0	0	0	0	0	0	0	0	1	0	0	0
0	s_4		0	0	0	1	0	0	0	0	0	0	0	0	1	0	0
0	s_5		0	0	0	0	1	0	0	0	0	0	0	0	0	1	0
0	s_6		0	0	0	0	0	1	0	0	0	0	0	0	0	0	1
			−20	−10	−13.33	−18.33	−23.33	−33.33	0.04	0	0	0	0	0	0	0	0

Figure 4.9

			50	50	66.66	91.66	116.66	100	0	1	0.833	0	0	0	0	0	0
			x_1	x_2	x_3	x_4	x_5	x_6	s_0	ΔD_0	ΔD_1	s_1	s_2	s_3	s_4	s_5	s_6
0	s_5	$\frac{40}{17.2}$	0	0	$-\frac{160}{17.2}$	0	0	0	1	$\frac{8}{17.2}$	$-\frac{8}{17.2}$	$-\frac{240}{17.2}$	$-\frac{320}{17.2}$	0	0	$-\frac{160}{17.2}$	$\frac{640}{17.2}$
116.66	x_5	1	0	0	0	0	1	0	0	0	0	0	0	0	0	1	0
50	x_1	1	1	0	0	0	0	0	0	0	0	1	0	0	0	0	0
50	x_2	1	0	1	0	0	0	0	0	0	0	0	1	0	0	0	0
91.66	x_4	$\frac{7.6}{17.2}$	0	0	$\frac{12.6}{17.2}$	1	0	0	0	$\frac{.23}{17.2}$	$\frac{0.2}{17.2}$	$-\frac{6.9}{17.2}$	$-\frac{9.2}{17.2}$	0	0	$-\frac{21.8}{17.2}$	$-\frac{16}{17.2}$
0	s_4	$\frac{9.6}{17.2}$	0	0	$-\frac{12.6}{17.2}$	0	0	0	0	$-\frac{.23}{17.2}$	$-\frac{0.2}{17.2}$	$\frac{6.9}{17.2}$	$\frac{9.2}{17.2}$	0	1	$\frac{21.8}{17.2}$	$\frac{16}{17.2}$
0	s_3	1	0	0	1	0	0	0	0	0	0	0	0	1	0	0	0
100	x_6	1	0	0	0	0	0	1	0	0	0	0	0	0	0	0	1
		$\frac{6143.33}{17.2}$	0	0	$\frac{8.33}{17.2}$	0	0	0	0	$\frac{3.8833}{17.2}$	$\frac{4}{17.2}$	$\frac{227.5}{17.2}$	$\frac{16.66}{17.2}$	0	0	$\frac{8.33}{17.2}$	$\frac{253.33}{17.2}$
										$\frac{21.0833}{17.2}$	$\frac{18.33}{17.2}$						

Figure 4.10

under ΔD_0) is 1.0417 which means that a further £1 available at $t = 0$ and *not used to* increase s_0 would allow ΔD_2 to rise by 1.5 (= 1.0417 × 1.44). So, the total change in ΔD_2 that is effected by putting the marginal £1 into the one-year investment at 15% nominal, is £2.07 (= 1.5 + 0.57) which implies a yield of 43.87%; well in excess of the cost of capital. All this information can in fact be squeezed out of the tableau of Figure 4.10, but let us turn now to interpretation of the remainder of the index row.

When slack variables have non-zero objective function coefficients, the value of further units of the corresponding resource is found by adding back the objective function coefficient to the index row number. So that the value of a further £1 at $t = 0$ is 21.0833/17.2 and a further £1 available at $t = 1$ would produce an increase of 18.33/17.2 in ΔV. Recalling that ΔV is in present value terms, the increases in $t = 2$ divided that would be effected, per unit, by further money at $t = 0$ and $t = 1$ are 30.36/17.2 and 26.4/17.2 respectively. These values are the figures in present value terms multiplied by 1.44. Using this data, implied period-to-period interest rates can now be determined, viz

$$(1 + i_1)(1 + i_2) = 30.36/17.2$$
$$(1 + i_2) = 26.4/17.2$$

where i_1 is the maximum interest rate (as a decimal) that the company would be prepared pay to borrow £1 at $t = 0$ and repay at $t = 1$. Similarly, i_2 is the maximum rate at which the firm would be prepared to borrow at $t = 1$ to repay at $t = 2$. These rates work out at 15% and 53.49% respectively. For borrowing at $t = 0$ to repay at $t = 2$ the overall, annually compounded interest rate is 32.86%. The 15% figure for $t = 0$ to $t = 1$ borrowing arises, rather obviously, from the fact that all that would be allowed by extra money at $t = 0$ to be repaid plus 15% at $t = 2$ is an increase in s_0—investment elsewhere at 15%.

The index row numbers corresponding to the slack variables in the upper bound constraints show what would happen if these constraints were relaxed. For example, suppose that x_1 could be set at the level 1.1 then ΔV would increase by 22.75/17.2. There is a limit to the range of variation in the constraint levels for which these numbers are relevant. In the case of x_1, the ndex row number remains relevant only so long as the maximum level of x_1 does not exceed

$$1\tfrac{1}{6}\left(= 1 + \frac{40}{17.2} \div \frac{240}{17.2} \right)$$

It is interesting to work out the overall yield that is obtained on the sums invested. With the upper bounds imposed, the yield that is achieved is given by

$$150(1 + e)^2 + 135(1 + e) - \frac{8846.4}{17.2} = 0$$

which solves to give $e = 0.4556$. That is, the equivalent annually compounded rate of interest is 45.56%. Without the upper bounds, yield is obtained by solving

$$150(1 + e)^2 + 135(1 + e) - 603 = 0$$

which produces a result of 60.49%. The effect of the upper bounds then is to cut the yield that can be achieved by almost 15 percentage points.

4.3 Financial Planning: Chambers' Model

The past few years have seen the larger companies making increasing use of full-scale financial planning models. The problems of capital budgeting, capital structure, short-term financial management and cash management can be seen as sub-problems in the broader setting of overall financial planning. Ideally a financial planning model brings these sub-problems together and seeks to obtain a complementary set of decisions.

Normative models, based on mathematical programming, will seek optimal decisions—an ideal set of mutually consistent decisions in all the sub-problem areas. These can be vastly complicated models (even though uncertainties are dealt with indrectly via the constraints and objectives) and as yet are relatively little used even in the United States. In the UK, one of the most impressive of these models was the FIRM model designed for British Petroleum (in this case producton decisions were included too). One of the earliest applications in the UK was reported by Chambers (1967). It has been suggested by Smith (1973) that financial modelling should initially be used in a restricted area to tackle a well-specified problem and the work of Chambers would be consistent with this. Myers (1976) has described the use of optimization models as a way of sifting through alternative strategies, identifying good ones, and projecting their consequences.

Simulating models are positive in that they are based upon actual accountancy practice. Again, these models produce the results that would follow given courses of action under specified assumptions about the future. The models in use are deterministic and use as inputs forecasts and decisions from the various departments in the enterprise; the models produce the financial statements that would follow. The models can be used to provide management with derived information—rather as in 'sensitivity analysis'. The relative emphasis placed upon the financial statistics produced and the final decision is left to the executives.

Chambers' model in some ways represents optimization models at their best—an actual application at a manageable level of sophistication in circumstances that suit the model. Management of the company for which the model was designed wished to take account of the way that the allocation of investments fund affected other published financial results besides cash flows. Further, they considered that an important part of their skill in financial management lay in dovetailing projects so that funds were released by some investments as they were required by others. In the former respect '. . . they (the managers) were unwilling altogether to neglect the changes which the project would bring about in other parts of the published accounts, derived on the basis not of cash flows but of accruals. They regarded the accounting convention of assigning costs and revenues to the periods judged to give rise to them as defining rules of a game in which they wanted a good score.'

The company prescribed that three financial measures should not fall below specified lower limits. They were earnings after tax; return (before tax) on gross assets; and the ratio of current assets to current liabilities. If these constraints were violated 'the price of the firm's shares and its ability to raise new funds might be impaired, and it might fall into the financial trap of not being able to finance projects essential to improving subsequent performance'. Of course it would be difficult to calculate precise values of the lower limits, and ideally the functional relationship between these variables and the objective function would have been specified. This was not practicable however.

The first financial constraint to be considered is the value taken by the 'current ratio', for which a predetermined minimum value was set. The constraint can be written as

$$\frac{\text{current assets}}{\text{current liabilities}} \geqslant K \tag{4.18}$$

Now, current assets, V_t, are defined as

$$V_t = V_t^0 + \sum_{j=1}^{n} \sum_{s=0}^{t} V_{js} x_j \tag{4.19}$$

where V_t^0 is the amount of current assets in period t attributable to investments undertaken before the commencement of the current planning period at $t = 0$. These investments will be referred to as 'old' investments which give rise to 'old' assets and 'old' liabilities. There are n new investments to choose from and x_j represents the level of the jth investment (in some cases x_j might only be allowed the values 0 or 1 but will be regarded as a continuous variable here) where $j = 1, 2, \ldots, n$. The coefficient V_{js} is the increase in current assets arising in the sth period per unit of investment j undertaken. The coefficients V_{js} are assumed constant, that is there are no economies or diseconomies of scale in this (or indeed any other) respect. The summation term in (4.19) then, is an unweighted sum of increase in current assets due to new investments in all periods from zero up to and including t. Current liabilities, b_t, are defined as

$$B_t = B_t^0 + \sum_{j=1}^{n} \sum_{s=0}^{t} b_{js} x_j \tag{4.20}$$

where B_t^0 is the level of old current liabilities and b_{js} is the increase in current liabilities in the sth period per unit of project j. Substitution of (4.20) and (4.19) into (4.18) and rearrangement gives the form of the current ratio restriction most convenient for purposes of computation. It is

$$\sum_{j=1}^{n} \sum_{s=0}^{t} (Kb_{js} - V_{js})x_j \leqslant V_t^0 - KB_t^0 \tag{4.21}$$

The next requirement for a financial statistic is the rate of return, pre-tax, on gross assets. Total gross assets in period t are defined as A_t where

$$A_t = A_t^0 + \sum_{j=1}^{n} \sum_{s=0}^{t} k_{js}x_j + \sum_{j=1}^{n} \sum_{s=0}^{t} (V_{js} - b_{js})x_j \tag{4.22}$$

where A_t^0 is the value in period t of gross assets acquired before $t = 0$ and not scrapped by period t. The coefficient k_{js} is the outlay in period s per unit of project j and the second summation term is new current assets minus new current liabilities in period t. Clearly (4.22) can be re-expressed concisely as

$$A_t = A_t^0 + \sum_{j=1}^{n} \sum_{s=0}^{t} (k_{js} + V_{js} - b_{js})x_j \tag{4.23}$$

Now the rate of return on these assets in the tth period is defined as the ratio of earnings in this period to gross assets. Earnings (pre-tax and depreciation) in the tth period, R_t, are given by

$$R_t = R_t^0 + \sum_{j=1}^{n} r_{jt}x_j \tag{4.24}$$

where R is the contribution to earnings (before tax and depreciation) in period t from old investments and the r_{jt} are the contributions to earnings (before tax and depreciation) expected to occur in period t per unit of project j. The r_{jt} are the 'net returns' of previous acquaintance in earlier models. The rate of return restriction is then given by

$$\frac{R_t}{A_t} \geqslant I \tag{4.25}$$

As a percentage the rate of return is $100i\%$ where: $I = (1 + i)$. Substitution of (4.24) and (4.23) into (4.25) and re-expression gives

$$I \sum_{j=1}^{n} \sum_{s=0}^{t} (k_{js} + V_{js} - b_{js})x_j + \sum_{j=1}^{n} r_{jt}x_j \leqslant R_t^0 - IA_t^0 \tag{4.26}$$

Chambers' third financial requirement was a series of restrictions (one for each value of t as for (4.21) and (4.26) on earnings themselves. It was required that total earnings in each period net of tax and depreciation should not be less than a predetermined amount. This condition can be written as

$$E_t = E_t^0 + \sum_{j=1}^{n} e_{jt}x_j \geqslant E_t^* \tag{4.27}$$

where E_t is post-tax and depreciation earnings in period t, E_t^0 is that part of the total attributable to existing projects; the e_{jt} are the tax and depreciation netted r_{jt} and E_t^* is the assigned minimum value.

In addition to the three sets of restrictions above there are the familiar budget constraints in each period. These can be expressed as

$$\sum_{j=1}^{n} k_{jt}x_j + D_t \leqslant F_t^0 + \sum_{j=1}^{n} f_{jt}x_j + N_t \tag{4.28}$$

where D_t are dividends to be paid in period t; the f_{jt} are the contributions to the flow of funds in period t per unit of project j; F_t^0 is the contribution to flow of funds in period t from old investments and N_t is the level of new long-term finance becoming available during period t. The dividends D_t are set at a proportion of earnings post-tax and depreciation in each period that is

$$D_t = d^{-1}E_t \tag{4.29}$$

Substitution of (4.27) into (4.29) and the result into (4.28) and rearrangement gives

$$\sum_{j=1}^{n} (k_{jt} - f_{jt} + d^{-1}e_{jt})x_j \leqslant F_t^0 + N_t - d^{-1}E_t^0 \tag{4.30}$$

The constraint set is completed by the usual sign requirements and upper limits on the scale of investment in each project, that is

$$0 \leqslant x_j \leqslant x_j^* \quad j = 1, 2, \ldots, n$$

We now turn to consideration of the objective function. This is expressed in present value terms as the discounted sum of dividends to be paid over the planning period and the discounted value of 'wealth' at the horizon. The result, divided by the number of shares, would give share price according to a familiar model of share valuation. The objective function is written as

$$\text{PV} = \sum_{j=0}^{H} D_t(1 + r)^{-t} + W_H(1 + r)^{-H} \tag{4.31}$$

where H is the predetermined horizon date. Now wealth at the horizon is defined as the discounted value at the horizon of post-horizon cash flow from both old and new investments, that is

$$W_H = \sum_{t=H+1}^{L} \sum_{j=1}^{n} f_{jt}x_j(1 + r)^{H-t} + W_H^0 \tag{4.32}$$

where L is the lifetime of the longest-running new project and W_H^0 determined in a similar manner to the 'new' component of W_H but not spelled out here) in the discounted value of flow of funds from old investments. Now define:

$$W_j = \sum_{t=H+1}^{L} f_{jt}(1+r)^{H-t} \tag{4.33}$$

and substitute (4.17) into (4.30) and the result and (4.33) into (4.32) and rearranging, the objective function becomes

$$PV = \sum_{j=1}^{n} \left(\sum_{t=0}^{H} d^{-1} e_{jt}(1+r)^{-t} + W_j(1+r)^{-H} \right) x_j + C \tag{4.34}$$

where the constant term C is the present value due to old investments and is given by

$$C = d^{-1} \sum_{t=0}^{H} E_t^0(1+r)^{-t} + W_H^0(1+r)^{-H} \tag{4.35}$$

The complete problem is:

maximize

$$PV = \sum_{j=1}^{n} \left(\sum_{t=0}^{H} d^{-1} e_{jt}(1+r)^{-t} + W_j(1+r)^{-H} \right) x_j + C$$

subject to

$$\left. \begin{array}{l} \displaystyle\sum_{j=1}^{n} \sum_{s=0}^{t} (Kb_{js} - V_{js})x_j \leqslant V_t^0 - KB_t^0 \\[2ex] \displaystyle\sum_{j=1}^{n} \left(r_{jt} + I\sum_{s=0}^{t} (k_{js} + V_{js} - b_{js}) \right) x_j \leqslant R_t^0 - IA_t^0 \\[2ex] \displaystyle\sum_{j=1}^{n} (k_{jt} - f_{jt} + d^{-1} e_{jt})x_j \leqslant F_t^0 + N_t - d^{-1} E_t^0 \end{array} \right\} \quad t = 0, 1, \ldots, H$$

$$0 \leqslant x_j \leqslant x_j^* \qquad j = 1, 2, \ldots, n \tag{4.36}$$

The various coefficients of the x_j are not of course independently determined but arise from various manipulations of the costs for and returns from the individual projects. For instance, the after tax net cash flow figures f_{jt} are given by $f_{jt} = r_{jt} - \text{tax}(1) + \text{grant}(1) + V_{jt} + b_{jt} - k_{jt}$, and the after tax earnings (profit) $e_{jt} = r_{jt} - \text{tax}(2) + \text{grant}(2) - \text{depreciation}$. The terms tax (1) and grant (1) are respectively tax paid and grant received per unit of x_j and tax (2) and grant (2) are tax accrued and grant accrued. Depreciation is, as always an arbitrary figure being a proportion of previous capital outlays. The model could therefore be re-expressed in various ways eliminating many of the coefficients in (4.36) by substitution from the linear relationships defined above. The choice of formulation is a matter of convenience or aesthetics and makes no difference to the problem.

Despite the relative complexity of the model a considerable number of simplifying assumptions are embodied in it. Among these are:

(i) The pre-set horizon date.
(ii) The predetermined discount rate for dividends, wealth and post-horizon returns.
(iii) The predetermined critical values of financial statistics.
(iv) The predetermined amounts of long-term capital to be available in each year.
(v) The assumption that profits and taxes can be attributed to particular projects.
(vi) The absence of interactive affects between projects.
(vii) The absence of uncertainty.
(viii) The invariance of per unit project returns and costs with scale.
(ix) The exclusion of whole number requirements for the x_j.

To be of use all models must bring a real-world problem down to manageable proportions. Simplifying assumptions must be made and it is worth repeating that the relevant test of a model is whether or not it improves decision-making—not whether it produces a global optimum.

The appearance of arbitrary depreciation figures in a decision-making model (rather than in innocuous matters of report) may appear incongruous. So long as important institutions and individuals set stock by figures including depreciation then they must be included in the model. This is the environment within which economic decisions are to be made. Of course, depreciation data can be directly relevant to cash flows in so far as liability for taxation is partly dependent upon what is allowed by the tax authorities for depreciation purposes.

Suppose an investment problem is structured as in (4.36) and solved, a *sensitivity analysis* of the solution should then be undertaken. Whenever assumptions have to be made about particular values of the parameters of a problem it is as well to see what consequences would follow from changes in the values of some of the more important of these parameters. The numbers N_t, representing increases in amounts of long-term finance available at various times, would ideally be considered as decision variables themselves. Different values of at least some of the N_t could be assumed and the effects of these changes on the optimal investment programme derived by the sensitivity analysis methods discussed in Chapter 3. The dual solution of course has as structural variables the effect of marginal variations in the RHS in (4.36) on the total present value. Those coefficients of the N_t which are positive indicate times at which it may be worth raising additional capital. The word 'may' is used because the marginal cost of funds may be in excess of the average cost of the exising amounts N_t. Those N_t which have zero shadow prices indicate times at which more funds than can be used are available. Consequently unless (a) the commitment to raise these funds is irrevocable or (b) substantial additional amounts are to be raised in periods in which finance is short, PV can be increased by reductions in the original levels of long term finance to be raised in such periods.

The sensitivity of the solution could also be examined in response to alternative values of the discount rate used in the objective function. There is as implicit assumption in the model that the investment programme decided upon does not alter the discount rate employed by the market to evaluate the company's future dividend stream. Changes in the value of r affect the objective function coefficients of the x_j and the final index row of the problem would be recalculated for different values of r.

The effect of a changed planning period can, in principle, also be determined. This will be a more involved process if (as is the case in the present model) the size of the constraint set is a function of H. In those cases in which only the objective function coefficients depend on H the matter is simpler. The higher the original value of H the less likely the solution is to be sensitive to marginal changes of horizon date but in any event the usual procedure for changes in objective function coefficients can be employed.

Changes in the profitability of projects, in that these affect the technical coefficients of the problem, are much more troublesome. If there are only one or two such changes anticipated then the problem need not be recomputed afresh but additonal columns can be appended to the solution tableau. Another possibility is that all the r_{jt} are affected by changed external circumstances—say the overall state of the economy. In this event it might be useful to have (say) three runs of the programme for a 'most likely' outcome for a 'pessimistic' outcome and for an 'optimistic' outcome. It may then transpire that there is a 'core' of investments that would be desirable for all the economic scenarios. Plans could then be implemented to undertake these investments and a more detailed study (perhaps by way of a second stage, subsidiary problem) undertaken of the relative desirability of the remaining alternatives.

Apart from the property of being readily amenable to sensitivity analysis, financial planning models also enable predictions to be made of important financial statistics and balance sheet items or indeed comprehensive balance sheets. These forecasts derive from the optimal investment programme and will of necessity fall within the prescribed limits. In his article Chambers used his model to calculate reported after-tax earnings, return on gross assets (per annum) and the value of the current ratio over a period of five years. Furthermore, once this has been done the years in which these variables are at the minimum permitted levels '... identify occasions on which the need to satisfy the corresponding financial restriction keeps the firm from exploiting investment possibilities

which would increase the value of the whole programme. Valuable op-
portnities are excluded by the requirement that reported results should
always meet the states standards.' In his post-optimally analysis
Chambers points out that the results '. . . suggest interesting motives for
making these investments, and these are not motives which appear pro-
minently in the orthodox canon of investment theory'. Some projects pro-
ved attractive because they added to before tax earnings without adding
to the asset base whilst another was undertaken because it would 'give a
quick boost to after-tax earnings'. Chambers concluded that each of the
projects undertaken offered '. . . a particular way of shifting profits, or
return, or changes in current ratio, from one year to another. financial
managers can make use of these transformations to make published
results more consistent from year to year. Such possibilities come as no
news to the financial manager; what is novel in the current method is that
it includes them in the formal analysis'. finally, Chambers showed how
the question of the allocation of funds to projects could be related to other
important management decisions; how 'a firm may so plan its borrowing
as to escape from the trap of having to allocate funds to relatively unprofitable projects in order to meet short-term restrictions on reported
results' and detailed a method by which the effects of alternative dividend
policies on the optimal investment programme may be deduced.

From the model developed by David Chambers we now turn to consideration of a larger financial planning model which although following
the capital rationing and linear programming line of approach is more
comprehensive in its consideration of the financing decision and taxation
implications.

4.4 Corporate Models—An Example

A corporate model is one which, as the name implies, can include all the
principal activities of the corporation from long-term financial planning
to production planning and cash management. In the case of an enterprise that is a group of companies there may be a group model with submodels for individual firms or particular purposes. These submodels are
not independent of the group model but are interlinked with it so that
there are no inconsistencies either in objectives or constraints and
parameters.

The 'FIRM' model (or rather set of models) produced by Deam,
Bennett and Leather (1975) was produced with reference to a large
petroleum company with worldwide operations. The description given
here will be confined to a broad outline of the major model along with
some discussion of the scope of application and some reference to corporate models in general. Before the FIRM model proper is introduced
it would be constructive to consider a simpler model produced by Deam,
Bennett and Leather (1975, pp. 35–37), which includes constraints
relating to cash, labour, machine and new capital availability and output

and dividend policy constraints. This particular formulation might prove useful to smaller-scale enterprises (with adaptations to suit). The parameters of this model are:

Z = horizon data,
r = shareholders' discount rate,
q_{ji} = value at the horizon of project i available at time j,
v_j = horizon value of machine purchased at time j
p_j = price of new machines at time j,
g_{ji} = net cash receipt per unit of product i at time j (selling price less unit variable cost),
f_j = fixed costs at time j,
a_{jik} = cash receipt (positive) or outlay (negative) at time k on project i available for acceptance at time j,
B_{ji} = net contribution to cash per unit of product i at time j,
b_{ji} = labour hours required per unit of product i at time j,
L = lifetime of machines,
s_{ji} = machine hours required per unit of product i at time j,
t_j = hours of service available from a machine j years after purchase ($t_j = 0$ for > 1),
B = initial cash available (at $j = 0$),
H_j = labour hours available at time j,
Y_{ji} = maximum possible sales of product i at time j,
d_{-1} = dividend paid one year before time $j = 0$
C_j = maximum cash that can be raised by the issue of ordinary shares at time j to existing shareholders,
m = number of investment projects available,
n = number of products in product range.

Note that C_j could be set at zero level if no new issue (restricted to existing shareholders in this model), of equity capital was being considered. In the g_{ji} it is assumed that there is no significant time lag between incurring costs and securing revenue from sales. The parameters q_{ji} and v_j (referred to by the authors as terminal value) are 'the value at the horizon date of cash flows associated with the item subsequently'. In other words post-horizon moneys are treated in the usual way by discounting back to the horizon; in this case at $100r\%$. The authors make the point that: 'This procedure involves an element of approximation: for example, projects available before the horizon are not exposed to competition with a project which might become available just after the horizon. Such approximation is inevitable, however. It is likely to be less serious, the further ahead the horizon is set.'

The decision variables of the model are:

b_j = cash balance carried forward on current account from time j,
c_j = cash raised from the issue of ordinary shares to existing shareholders at time j,

d_j = ordinary dividend at time j,
w_j = number of new machines purchased at time j,
x_{ji} = number of units taken of project i at time j,
y_{ji} = sales (and production) of product i at time j.

All decision variables are constrained to be non-negative. Sales are directly from production (no change in inventory). Here, c_j can be thought of as a deduction from dividend at time j. Issue costs are ignored. 'Projects' and 'machines' are distinguished. The machines relate to the normal productive activity of the firm, whilst projects are separate entities which consume only financial resources and unscarce physical resources. The 'projects' may be no more than the $\hat{s}$ and s of previous acquaintance or they may be physical assets which do not compete with 'machines' for anything other than finance. Upper bounds may be required on some of the x_{ji} and some may be restricted to integral values. The problem is to

maximize

$$F = \sum_{j=0} (d_j - c_j)(1 - r)^{-j} + (1 + r)^{-z} \sum_{j=0}^{z-1} \sum_{i=1}^{m} q_{ji} x_{ji} + \sum_{j=z-L}^{z-1} V_j w_j$$

(4.37)

$$b_0 + d_0 + p_0 w_0 - \sum_{i=1}^{m} a_{0i0} x_{0i} \leqslant B$$

(4.38)

$$b_k + d_k + f_k + p_k w_k + c_k - b_{k-1} - \sum_{j=0}^{k} \sum_{i=1}^{m} a_{jik} x_{ji} - \sum_{i=1}^{n} g_{ki} y_{ki} \leqslant 0$$

$$(k = 1, 2, \ldots, z - 1, z)$$

(4.39)

$$\sum_{i=1}^{n} h_{ji} y_{ji} \leqslant H_j \qquad (j = 1, 2, \ldots, z - 1, z)$$

(4.40)

$$\sum_{i=1}^{n} S_{ji} Y_{ji} - \sum_{k=0}^{j-1} t_{j-k} w_k \leqslant 0 \qquad (j = 1, 2, \ldots, z - 1, z)$$

(4.41)

$$y_{ji} - Y_{ji} \leqslant 0 \qquad (j = 1, 2, \ldots, z - 1, z)$$

(4.42)

$$d_{j-1} - d_j \leqslant 0 \qquad (j = 0, 1, 2, \ldots, z - 1, z)$$

(4.43)

$$c_j - C_j \leqslant 0 \qquad (j = 1, 2, \ldots, z - 2, z - 1)$$

(4.44)

$$b_j, c_j, d_j, w_j, x_{ji}, y_{ji} \geqslant 0$$

(4.45)

The objective function (4.37) is the present value of current and future divdends net of new capital raised from the shareholders, plus the present value of the horizon value of projects and assets. The financial constraints are defined by (4.38) and (4.39) all of which, incidentally, will be satisfied as equalities in an optimal solution. This is because if the time j constraint was satisfied as a strict inequality then d_j or a future dividend could be increased thus increasing the value of F. It would not necessarily be the case that d_j could be increased, because of the dividend constraints (4.43), but there is no explicit upper bound on d_z which could always be raised by inter-period transfers via the b_j. The dividend constraints (4.43) prevent dividend cuts which are normally eschewed.

The physical constraints are defined by the remainder of the constraint set. The expressions of (4.40) relate to labour availability, the limit of which is predetermined for each period in any one run of the model whilst (4.41) relate to machine services availability and include the decision variables w_j thus there are no explicit upper bounds in this case. Production takes place from time one onwards and (4.42) are the upper bounds on sales. In the words of the authors: 'This would amount to a fairly crude representation of an assumed sales price–volume relationship, i.e. the assumption that price is fixed as a policy decision and there is some maximum volume that can be sold at that price. Although crude, such a view of pricing policy is often adopted in practice.' Constraints (4.45) are the familiar sign requirements in addition to which (omitted here) the authors placed the requirement that some of the $x_{ij} \leqslant 1$ 'shares' in a project limited to 100% participation are often admissible, for instance where a contract is made jointly with another company and as a matter of course in insurance underwriting. Of particular interest in sensitivity analysis would be an examination of the effects of changes in some of the financial variables and parameters. The effects of changed market discount rate in the objective function—perhaps allowing for changes in this rate over time, the effects of changing the upper limit on new capital c_j and the initial funds available, B and the effects of changed dividend policy requirements.

In connection with data requirements Deam, Bennett and Leather (1975) point out that: 'The estimation of the numerical data is likely to be a much more costly exercise than the formulation of the mathematical model the first time a linear programming exercise is undertaken. On subsequent occasions, much of the existing data can be reused subject to critical review and revision in the light of new information.' The objection that '. . . in practice the estimates of the data may seem so speculative that management may have little confidence in the exercise', is invalid. The exercise can be repeated '. . . for a range of different estimates to discover which decisions are unaltered within the range of assumptions – and hence should be adopted with high confidence – and which are 'marginal' and require further investigation'. In addition, 'All the data required is relevant and some assumption about it is implied by any decision; the model building process requires the assumptions to be made explicit so that the consequences of the best estimates possible can be studied systematically.'

The FIRM model proper whilst on a substantially larger scale than the model just described has a number of structural similarities. It is an optimizing rather than a simulating corporate model and seeks to maximize the NPV of after-tax cash flows to shareholders. All operating (existing production) and investment activities are expressed in terms of cash flows and a series of financial matrices provides the linkage between successive time periods. To quote:

> within each period opportunities are represented by a static linear programming formulation. In any period net cash flow is equal to Revenue less Operating Costs (excluding Depreciation), Loan Interest and Company Tax, and may be invested, carried forward or paid out as dividend. It may be supplemented by New Share issues and net borrowing. Whilst the model is a cash flow model it does have the ability to report by years the projected conventional financial statement data (and tax information) associated with each solution. FIRM simultaneously determines optimal production, refining and marketing plans for each specific year together with their implicit investment decisions. Interrelationships between proposed investments and existing facilties, interrelationships between operations and equipment capacities, and interrelationships between investment, operations and finance are examined in an integrated manner which permits the interrelationships to be resolved automatically.

In addition:

> Financial policy is examined in a manner which recognizes the effect of debt on the required yield on equity capital and which also relates financial policy to the overall corporate plan. It does not associate the interest rate on incremental debt with the evalution of any incremental investment opportunity.

This latter point, as we have already seen in the capital-rationing discussion is an essential difference between rationing models and non-rationing discussion NPV maximization problems.

Deam, Bennett and Leather (1975) produced a number of models including an overall Group FIRM model and associate models. The Group model is in reference to an international petroleum company with activities in many areas. To lead up to a description of this model we should start with what would be termed by the authors a 'static, long term planning, single area model' the structure of which is given in Figure 4.11. In the figure, columns represent activities and rows constraints and the shaded areas denote the presence of non-zero coefficients. The RHS of the constraints is separated off and the objective function is at the bottom. As can be seen, three types of activity are distinguished: refining marketing and investment with subdivision within each category. In the objective function it will be seen that there are non-zero coefficients under all but the contractual marketing activities. The term produced by these activities is a constant and so does not affect the maximization exercise. The objective function is 'optimal revenues' less variable costs less anual

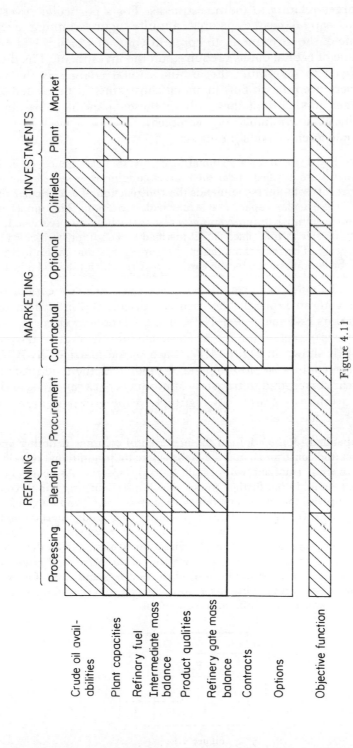

Figure 4.11

capital charges relating to the investments. For a particular investment the 'annual capital charge' is that annuity figure running over the expected life of the investment, the present value of which is equal to the present value of capital outlays required on the investment. The discount rate employed to determine the annual capital charges is the cost of capital. There are no cash flow financial constraints incorporated as yet. In the larger models to follow, where these financial constraints are included the objective function is changed.

How would such a model be used?

> ... the model is run for a terminal year, say six years hence, to find what investments are justified under the market conditions projected. Let us suppose that this solution recommends the construction of a particular refinery unit of a particular capacity at a particular location. The model is then rerun for a number of intervening years, in each case to see whether that unit of that size in that place is still justified by conditions projected for the earlier years. The recommendation that emerges is that the unit is built in time to be commissioned by the earliest year in which the model justifies it.

In a sense this model is intermediate between the cash flow capital-rationing models with an explicitly represented horizon and intermediate cash flow constraints and the earlier NPV maximization models.

The larger group planning model (restricted for illustrative purposes to four areas), is shown in Figure 4.12. Each of the matrices **A, B, C** and **D** are constructed as for the single area model. Elements outside of the lettered areas correspond to transfers of products between areas and coefficients in overall constraints. In Figure 4.13 the group planning model of Figure 4.12 has been

> ... expanded by the addition to each area of columns denoting financial balances and constraints, and the areas where these additional rows and columns overlap (marked with small letters), are the Associate financial matrices. In addition, further rows and columns depicting parent company and Group variables and constraints are added, the Group financial matrix being marked **G**. The possibilities of transferring funds internationally are also represented. These are by way of dividend payments from Associates to the parent company, by loans, by direct investment and by the extending or shortening of credit terms on international movements of crude oil and products. Each method will be subject to restraints and costs, for example, exchange costs, withholding taxes on dividends, interest charges on loans, and upper and lower limits on credit terms.

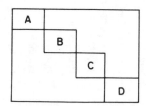

Figure 4.12

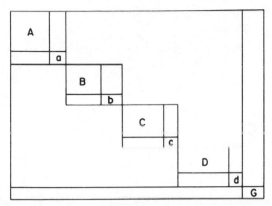

Figure 4.13

Now, call a matrix such as that of Figure 4.14 **F**. In the full model there is an **F** matrix for each time period that the model covers. The structure of the model in a four time period case would be as shown in Figure 4.14 in which $\mathbf{F}_t$ represents the **F** matrix for the tth time period so that as is usual, all time periods are handled simultaneously. There are non-zero coefficients below the $\mathbf{F}_t$ matrices in Figure 4.14. These represent the effects in future periods of activities undertaken in any given period. The objective function employed in this model represents current share price which is expressed as the sum of a function of historical share prices over the preceding average shareholding period and a discounted sum of all future dividends after 'allowance' for income and capital gains tax effects. A more detailed description of the objective functions will be given below.

The financial matrices (small letters in Figure 4.13) are of particular interest. A representation of such is given in Figure 4.15 for an associate company in an initial year (one) and a subsequent year. The authors describe this formulation as having only superficial representation of the parent company, it being assumed that the sole operating part of the group is the associated company. Further, costs and revenues are associated with cash flows, the credit elements of transactions being ignored.

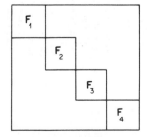

Figure 4.14

±		1. Quantity Column	2. Costs	3. Revenues	4. Crude Profit	5. Investment	6. Operating Cash	7. Flow (+ −)	8. Loan Taken	9. Loan Repaid	10. Interest Paid	11. Taxable Surplus	12. Tax Allowances Used	13. Tax Allowances C/F	14. Acc. Earnings Before (+)	15. Dividend (−)	16. Dividend	17. Acc. Earnings After Dividend	18. Cash C/F	19. Cash Surplus To Investment	20. Borrowing Excess	21. New Issues	22. Dividend	23. Retained Cash
0	1. Investment Cash	-(7)				−1			+1	−1										−1		+1		
0	2. Tax Allowances	+(8)				−(1)							+1	+1										
0	3. Operating Cash	0	−1	+1			−1	+1			−1													
+	4. Loan Availability	+(9)							+1															
0	5. Loan Repayments	−(10)							+(2)	−1														
0	6. Interest	−(11)							+(3)		−1													
0	7. Taxable Surplus	0					+1					−1	−1											
0	8. Acc. Earnings	−(12)				−(4)	+1	−1				−(5)			−1	+1								
0	9. Div ⩽ Acc. Earnings	0													−1		+1	+1						
0	10. Div ⩽ Cash Flow	+(13)					+1	−1									−1		−1	+1				
+	11. Debt/Equity Ratio	+(14)							+1	−1											−1	−(6)		
0	12. Parent Co. Cash	0			+1												+1						−1	−1
+	13. Dividend Constraint	−(15)																					−1	
			←										Year 1											→
0	16. Investment Cash	0																	+1					+1
0	17. Tax Allowances	+(8)				−(1)		−1						−1										
0	18. Operating Cash	0																						
+	19. Loan Availability	+(9)																						
0	20. Loan Repayments	−(10)							+(2)															
0	21. Interest	−(11)							+(3)															
0	22. Taxable Surplus	0																						
0	23. Acc Earnings	−(12)				−(4)										−1		+1						
0	24. Div ⩽ Acc. Earnings	0																						
0	25. Div ⩽ Cash Flow	0										−(5)												
+	26. Debt/Equity Ratio	+(14)							+1	−1						+(6)		−(6)				−(6)		
0	27. Parent Co. Cash	0																						
+	28. Dividend Constraint	0																					+1	
Objective	S Type	(18)																				+(16)−(17)		
Functions	V−D Type	(18)							+(19)+(20)−(21)													+(22)−(23)		

Figure 4.15

In the matrix of Figure 4.15 elements in the column labelled $\pm$ indicate the equation to zero (0) of the LHS of the corresponding constraint or a weak inequality (+) in which the LSH $\geqslant 0$. Elements in the matrix other than plus or minus unity are references to the explanatory notes below. A reference preceded by a minus sign indicates that the number entered is negative. To the right of the lower half of the array of coefficients in Figure 4.15 (opposite numbers 16–28), is an array identical to the upper half of the figure. These coefficients correspond to new activities undertaken in year two. The constraints 16–28 are spelled out in full after the following notes. (1) The fraction of investment allowed as depreciation, investment allowances, etc. for corporation tax purposes. (2) The fraction of loan repayable (e.g. for 20-year loans repaid in equal instalments, the figures would all be 0.05). (3) The interest rate on loans. (By replicating the columns 8, 9, 10 with different figures it is of course possible to allow the model to choose between different terms of borrowing.) (4) The fraction of investment allowed as depreciation for accounting purposes. (5) The corporation tax rate. (6) The limiting debt/equity ratio. (7) Cash b/f from previous year. (8) Tax allowances available as a result of earlier operations. (9) Loan availability. (10) Sum of repayments. (11) Interest payments, due on loans taken previously. (12) Initial value of accumulated earnings less current year's depreciation on existing assets (in year one; in subsequent years only the depreciation on existing assets is given here, since the accumulated earnings figure is carried forward by the matrix itself). (13) Tax liability on previous year's operations. (14) (Limiting debt/equity ratio) $\times$ (initial level of equity) – (initial level of debt). (15) Minimum dividend (in year one only). (16) S type objective function (see p. 132). Cost to shareholder of one unit of cash raised by a new issue (including issue charges), discounted zero years in year one, one year in two, etc. (since issue is assumed to have been made during the previous year). (17)

$$\frac{\lambda^{j-1}(1 - \beta)^{j-1}(1 - b)}{(1 + k_e^*)}$$

where b is the personal tax rate k_e^* is the shareholders' discount rate j is the year number and λ, β are correction factors for capital gains tax. Specifically β is the ratio of capital gains tax rate to shareholding period and $\lambda = 1$ in the absence of gains tax. Otherwise λ satisfies $\lambda^N v - \lambda + 1 = 0$, where $v = \beta(1 - \beta)^{N-1}(1 + k_e^*)^{-N}$. (18) A constant, the value of which will not affect the optimal strategy. (19) V–D type objective function. Loans taken are considered as involving cash flows from debt-holders in the previous period. Hence the coefficients for year j are

$$\frac{1}{(1 + k_w^*)^{j-1}} - \frac{1}{(1 + k_i^*)^{j-1}}$$

where k_w^* is a weighted average cost of capital figure with the recognition of corporate and personal taxes, and k_i^* is the interest rate on debt capital, net of tax. (20) As for (19) but shifted one year

$$\frac{1}{(1 + k_w^*)^j} - \frac{1}{(1 + k_i^*)^j}$$

(21) Debt-holders' income is subject to personal tax, so coefficients become:

$$\frac{1-b}{(1 + k_w^*)^j} - \frac{1-b}{(1 + k_i^*)^j}$$

(22), (23) As for (16), (17) but with k_w^* replacing k_e^*.

The financial constraints can now be spelled out. The first states that investment in the first year does not exceed funds available then. In the identity form as presented in the matrix this reads:

     – cash brought forward from previous year
     – (– 1 × year one investment +
         + 1 × loan taken +
         – 1 × loan repaid +
         – 1 × cash surplus to investment requirements +
         + 1 × cash raised by new share issues)
     = 0

or alternatively it may be read as:

     year one investment = cash brought forward
                   plus loan taken
                   minus loan repaid
                   plus cash from new share issues
                   minus cash surplus

It is particularly instructive to examine constraints 16–28, i.e. those applying to the second year. It will be remembered that to the right of this lower half is another first half corresponding to activities started in year two. Thus row 16 can be expressed as

     year two investment = cash brought forward
                   plus retained cash
                   plus loan taken
                   minus loan repaid
                   plus new issues

Row 17 states that:

     tax allowance (to be used in year = tax allowances on investment
     two or carried forward   (in year two, year one and
                                      earlier)
                                      plus operating loss in year one
                                      plus tax allowances b/f from
                                      year one.

In row 18 operating cash flow may be either positive or negative and is represented by two variables in each year, one being positive cash flow the other the modulus of a negative cash flow. This constraint states that:

Operating cash flow = operating revenues
minus operating costs
minus interest paid on loans

The remaining constraints state:

Row 19: Loan taken ⩽ loan availability
Row 20: Loan repayments = annual instalments due on earlier loans
Row 21: Interest paid = interest rate *times* amounts of previous loans outstanding
Row 22: Taxable surplus = operating surplus *minus* tax allowances used
Row 23: Accumulated earnings (before year two dividend) = year one accumulated earnings *plus* current operating cash flow *minus* depreciation *minus* current tax liability
Row 24: Accumulated earnings (after dividend) = accumulated earnings (before dividend) *minus* dividend
Row 25: Dividend = operating cash flow *plus* cash surplus to investment requirements *minus* payment of previous years tax liability *minus* cash carried forward
Row 26: Borrowing excess ⩾ book value of debt *minus* debt/equity limit *times* book value of equity
Row 27: Retained cash = profit to parent company (from oil sales) *plus* dividend received from associate *minus* dividend to shareholders
Row 28: Year two dividend to shareholders ⩾ year one dividend to shareholders

The 'borrowing excess' variable assumes a positive value when the debt/equity ratio is exceeded. This variable can be prevented from being positive in an optimum solution by attributing to it a suitably large, negative, objective function coefficient. On the other hand the model can allow for the possibility of the debt/equity limit being exceeded for individual years while holding on average.

The model was run with two version of the objective function, most work being done with what the authors refer to as the 'S type' function. The function is a definition of current share price which is the sum of a function of historical share prices over the past N years where N is the average shareholding period, and (b) a discounted sum of dividends over an infinite horizon after adjustment for income and gains tax effects. The S type function is given in equation (4.46) where the first summation term is (a) above and the second summation term is (b) and in which the P^* are historical share prices.

$$P_0 = \sum_{j=1}^{N} \left(\frac{\lambda(1 - \beta)}{1 + k_e^*} \right)^{j-1} \cdot \frac{\beta P_{-N+j}^*}{1 + k_e^*} + \sum_{j=1}^{\infty} \left(\frac{\lambda(1 - \beta)}{1 + k_e^*} \right)^{j-1} \cdot \frac{d_j}{1 + k_e^*} \quad (4.46)$$

P_0 as defined by (4.46) is referred to by the authors as the 'true value' of shares although the authors readily concede that capital gearing creates difficulties, since the discount rate k_e^* was determined on the assumption that the limiting debt equity ratio held. In fact in use of the model this turned out to be reasonable. The 'V–D' type objective function attempts to remedy this not-too-serious deficiency. In the V–D type function (with new issues allowed for), instead of the contribution to the objective function in year j being

$$\frac{S_j}{(1 + k_e^*)^j}$$

where S_j is the total after tax cash flow to shareholders including dividends and new issues (negative) the contribution to the objective function is expressed as

$$\frac{S_j + t_j}{(1 + k_w^*)^j} - \frac{t_j}{(1 + k_i^*)^j}$$

where t_j is the after-tax cash flow to debt-holders including interest payments, repayments and new loans (negative), k_i^* *is the after (personal) tax interest rate on debt* and k_w^* is a weighted mean cost of capital figure independent of gearing.

The prototype FIRM model with one associate company and two refining and marketing areas and covering seven one-year periods contained about 2,800 rows and 5,500 columns. The initial run of this model (even after a fairly good starting-point had been obtained piecemeal), took 15 hours. However, after the problem has been solved once it is a much smaller task to solve a slightly different problem with the original solution as the starting-point—'This, together with improvements in the computer programme over recent years, means that it is now possible to run variant cases in an hour or two'. So the single associate model is currently a practical proposition. The full-scale model described earlier is an order of magnitude larger. Based on a Group planning model of 3,000 rows with 500 financial constraints and in excess of 6,000 columns over seven time periods there would be 24,500 rows. While this scale is problematical the authors point out that 'While the possiblities for optimization clearly increase as more and more of the Group's activities are included, we feel that it is not premature to discuss openly the concept of such a model, which draws together much of the previously published work in the field of corporate financial planning,'

It is useful to see the place within an overall planning contex of pioneer models such as FIRM. A hierarchy of models can be consructed which can cover most aspects of short-, medium- and long-term planning. For instance, in the short term the problem of cash management could be approached with an appropriately designed model integrated into the overall planning system as shown in Figure 4.16 Deam, Bennett and Leather constructed such a model to cover twelve one-month periods. The model '...describes the periodic inflows and outflows of cash to and from the Group and the possible ways of investing or borrowing in the short term, the predictions of fluctuations in interest rates and exchange rates and the possible ways of transferring funds across natural boundaries, and attempts to maximize the value of the Group's current assets less current liabilities in one year's time'. In the short and medium term, production and inventory control problems can be addressed with long-term assets taken as fixed. Quarterly time periods might be convenient in such contexts. 'Such a model with, say, six time periods, three of one month and three of three months, could be used to break-down the medium term plan into short term operating patterns.'

Figure 4.16 illustrates the place of these models along with the long-term Group and Associate models in the overall planning system. 'Data would be fed to each model consisting of quantities and prices of the Group's resources as determined by the next senior model(s) in the

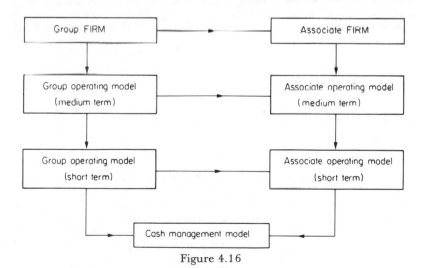

Figure 4.16

hierarchy. Thus, each aspect of the Group's activities would be optimized in a way that was subject to, and hence in accordance with, the objective of the whole. Suboptimization at the expense of the whole would thus be avoided.'

There are very many 'company' models in existence, both those that were designed by or for particular companies and those that are offered as adaptable packages by computing or consulting organizations. Those models in use in the UK are described in a survey by Grinyer and Wooller (1975). The variation in sophistication is considerable, many being little more than a series of interconnected accounting identities that would find their principal use in the projection of profit and loss accounts, balance sheets, etc. under differing assumptions (i.e. sensitivity analysis). At the other extreme are corporate models of considerable complexity and adaptability with the ability to handle financial planning over several years and production and marketing problems, project evaluations and cash flow analysis. Some packages offer built-in sensitivity analyses and considerable choice of forecasting techniques. The larger packages can handle a 1,000 or more variables with 'no practical limit' on the number of statements. Many can be interlinked and integrated with other models that the company may use.

References

Chambers, D. J. (1967) 'Programming the allocation of funds subject to restrictions on reported results', *Operations Research Quarterly*, **18**, No. 4.

Deam, R. J., Bennett, J. W., and Leather, J. (1975), *'FIRM: A Computer Model for Financial Planning'*, The Institute of Chartered Accountants Research Committee, Occasional Paper No. 5.

Grinyer, P. H., and Wooller, J. (1975), *'Corporate Models Today: A New Tool for Financial Management'*, The Institute of Chartered Accountants in England and Wales.

Jaaskelainen, V. (1975), 'Linear programming and budgeting', *Studentilitteratur*, Lund.

Myers, S. C. (ed.) (1976), *'Modern Developments in Financial Management'*, Praeger, p. 562.

Smith, P. R. (1973), 'What a chief executive should know about financial modelling', *Price-Waterhouse Review*, **18**, No. 1.

Further Reading

Amey, L. R., 'Interdependencies in capital budgeting: a survey', *Journal of Business Finance*, **4**, No. 3, Autumn 1972.

Baumol, W. J., and Quandt, R. E., 'Investment and discount rates under capital rationing: a programming approach', *Economic Journal*, **75**, 1965.

Bernhard, R. H., 'Mathematical programming models for capital budgeting: a survey, generalisation and critique', *Journal of Financial and Quantitative Analysis*, **4**, No. 2, 1969.

Bhaskar, K. N., 'Borrowing and lending in a mathematical programming model of capital budgeting', *Journal of Business Finance and Accounting*, **1**, No. 2, Summer 1974.

Bhaskar, K. N., 'Linear programming and capital budgeting: a re-appraisal', *Journal of Business Finance and Accounting*, **3**, No. 3, Autumn 1976.

Bhaskar, K. N., *Building Financial Models, A Simulation Approach*, Associated Business Programmes, London, 1978.

Bryant, J. W. (ed.) *Financial Modelling in Corporate Management*, John Wiley & Sons, Chichester, 1982.

Carleton, W. T., 'Linear programming and capital budgeting models: a new interpretation', *Journal of Finance*, **25**, December 1969.

Carleton, W. T., Dick, C. L., and Downes, D. H., 'Financial policy models: theory and practice', *Journal of Financial and Quantitative Analysis*, **8**, December 1973.

Chateau, J. P. D., 'The capital budgeting problem under conflicting financial policies', *Journal of Business Finance and Accounting*, **2**, No. 1, Spring 1975.

Elton, E. J., 'Capital rationing and external discount rates', *Journal of Finance*, **1970** (June).

Grinyer, J. R., 'Financial planning models incorporating dividend and growth elements', *Accounting and Business Research*, **1973** (Spring).

Grinyer, P. H., and Batt, C. D., 'Some tentative findings of corporate financial simulation models', *Operational Research Quarterly*, **1974** (March).

Hughes, J. S., and Lewellen, W. G., 'Programming solutions to capital rationing problems', *Journal of Business Finance and Accounting*, **1**, No. 1, Spring 1974.

Ijiri, Y., Levy, F. K., and Lyon, R. C., 'A linear programming model for budgeting and financial planning', *Journal of Accounting Research*, **1963** (Autumn).

Jaaskelainen, V., *Optimal Financing and Tax Policy of the Corporation*, Helsinki Research Institute for Business Economics, Publication No. 31, 1966.

Myers, S. C., and Pogue, G. A., 'A programming approach to corporate financial management', *Journal of Finance*, **29**, May 1974.

Naylor, T. H., *Corporate Planning Models*, Addison-Wesley, Reading, Mass., 1978.

Norstrom, C. J., 'A comment on two simple decision rules in capital rationing', *Journal of Business Finance and Accounting*, **3**, Summer 1976.

Salkin, G., and Kornbluth, J., 'Linear programming in financial planning', *Accountancy Age Books*, Haymarket Publishing, London, 1973.

Warren, J. R., and Skelton, J-P., 'A simultaneous equation approach to financial planning', *Journal of Finance*, **1971** (December).

Weingartner, H. M., *Mathematical Programming and the Analysis of Capital Budgeting Problems*, Prentice-Hall, Englewood Cliffs, NJ, 1963.

Weingartner, H. M., 'Capital budgeting of interrelated projects: survey and synthesis, *Management Science*, **12**, No. 7, 1966.

Weingartner, H. M., 'Criteria for programming investment project selection', *Journal of Industrial Economics*, **15**, No. 1, 1966.

Weingartner, H. M., 'Capital rationing: *n* authors in search of a plot', *Journal of Finance*, **1977** (December).

Wilkes, F. M., and Samuels, J. M., *'Stock Market Constraints and Objectives in Capital Investment Appraisal'*, University of Aston in Birmingham Discussion Paper in Business and Organization No. 21, July 1970.

CHAPTER 5

Integer Programming for Project Selection

Overview
This chapter introduces two of the many techniques of integer programming. The methods selected are those most relevant in an investment context. After the general character of the problems has been outlined, cutting plane methods are described. The section 5.1 explains the limited value of shadow prices in integer linear problems. Zero—one problems are of particular relevance where investments have an all-or-nothing character. These are described in section 5.5. Investment problems may contain a fixed charge element; the problems that this brings about are introduced in section 5.6. Sections 5.7 and 5.8 explain other special integrality features that may be found in investment problems, while section 5.9 outlines the branch and bound approach.

5.1 Introduction

Integer linear problems are those programming problems which would be linear were it not for the fact that some or all of the problem variables are not continuously divisible. We may come across such problems in the capital budgeting area for two reasons. First there is the obvious case where only whole numbers of units of investments may be taken. Then there are those problems in which the formulation used requires the introduction of variables, not investment levels themselves, of a discrete nature. Such is the case in problems in which some of the constraints are of an 'either-or' nature and it can be convenient from a formulation point of view (if not from the computational standpoint) in such cases to introduce special additional variables that may take only integral values, usually just zero or one. The class of discrete linear programming problems can be divided into a number of sub-types. A convenient classification is as follows:

   (i) all integer problems.
  (ii) mixed integer-continuous variable problems.
 (iii) zero—one problems.

The first category (also known as pure integer problems) consists of those problems in which all of the variables, including the slack variables, are required to take whole number values in feasible solutions. Consider the problem:

maximize $F = 6x_1 + 7x_2$

subject to $\quad 2x_1 + x_2 \leqslant 13$

$\qquad x_1 + 2x_2 \leqslant 15$

$\qquad x_1, x_2, s_1, s_2 \geqslant 0$

$\qquad x_1, x_2, s_1, s_2$ integral

This problem is graphed in Figure 5.1. Were it not for the integrality requirements the feasible area would have been the familiar convex quadrilateral OABC of the continuous linear problem. With the integrality requirements, the feasible 'area' becomes the set of integer *lattice points* bounded by OABC. It should be noted that in an all-integer problem, some of the lattice points may not be feasible since they correspond to non-integral values of the slack variables. In the problem graphed it is evident that the basic feasible solutions, A, B, C, to the linear continuous problem are not feasible in the integral case, but this will not always be so.

On the face of it, the fact that a continuum of feasible solutions has been reduced to a finite number may seem a simplification; but it is not. It will be recalled that the fundamental theorem of linear programming allows the elimination of all feasible solutions save the basic solutions at the corner points of the feasible area. With the integrality requirements in force this is no longer possible. It will be seen that there are many more feasible lattice points in the integer problem than there are bfs in the

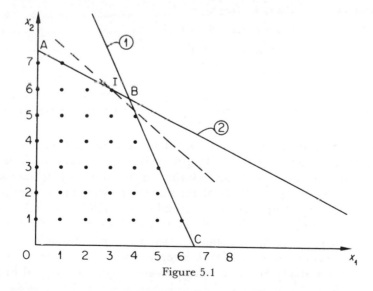

Figure 5.1

linear continuous case. This is the heart of the matter. It might be argued that only the five lattice points on the boundary of the feasible region need to be considered, the remainder could not be optimal. Whilst this is correct it would be a prodigous computational task in problems of moderate size to identify and eliminate the 'dominated' lattice points. What is a simple task in a two-dimensional problem is out of the question in problems of realistic proportions.

What alternative approaches suggest themselves? From Figure 5.1 it will be seen that the integral optimum, I, represents a rounding off of the continuous optimum at B. At point B the variables take the values $x_1 = 11/3$, $x_2 = 17/3$, $s_1 = 0$, $s_2 = 0$ and $F = 185/3$. At point I the values are $x_1 = 3$, $x_2 = 6$, $s_1 = 1$, $s_2 = 0$ and $F = 60$. It will be noted that at the integral optimum there are *three* strictly positive variables. Unless by chance the integral optimum coincides with a basic solution of the continuous problem there will be more positive variables than there are constraints in the continuous version of the problem. The integrality requirements themselves represent additional constraints which can be thought of as a set of mutually exclusive equality constraints, i.e. $x_1 = 0$, *or* $x_1 = 1$, *or* $x_1 = 2$, etc. Naturally, when constraints are added to a problem the value taken by the objective function cannot increase. While rounding off is advisable in certain cases (see below) it is not a useful approach to finding the global integral optimum. This is so for two reasons. Firstly, the integral optimum may not be a rounded-off version of the continuous optimum, and secondly, the problem of rounding off is in itself an integer programming problem. As an instance of this point, the problem of rounding off the continuous solution to the example above can be expressed as

$$\text{maximize } F = 6\Delta x_1^* + 7\Delta x_2^* + 13/3$$
$$\text{subject to} \quad 2\Delta x_1^* + \Delta x_2^* \leqslant -1$$
$$\Delta x_1^* + 2\Delta x_2^* \leqslant -1$$
$$\Delta x_1^* \Delta x_2^* \text{ integral}$$
$$\Delta x_1^* \geqslant -4\Delta x_2^* \geqslant -6$$

where $\Delta x_1^* = \Delta x_1 - \frac{1}{3}$ and $\Delta x_2^* = \Delta x_2 - \frac{1}{3}$ and where Δx_1 and Δx_2 are the changes in x_1 and x_2 respectively from their values at the continuous optimum.

The second category consists of problems in which some, but not all of the variables must take only integral values. Typically in investment applications the slack variables relating to financial constraints are not required to be integral. Physical resources are frequently continuously divisible. The set of integer-only variables is usually confined to certain of the investment possibilities and some variables introduced for formulation convenience. Figure 5.2 shows a two-structural variable problem in which only x_2 is required to take an integral value, x_1 and the slacks being continuous variables. Feasible solutions are on the horizontal lines cor-

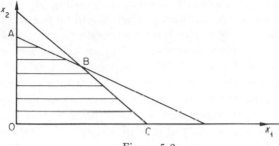

Figure 5.2

responding to integral values of x_2 bounded by the axes and the constraints. Again, there will typically be more positive variables at the optimum than there are constraints in the corresponding all-continuous problem. It should be noted that it can sometimes turn out that an apparently mixed problem is in effect an all-integer problem. For instance, in the problem of Figure 5.1 if only the structural variables were required to be integral it would always turn out that the slack variables took on integral values at a feasible solution. Clearly, in problems in which all structural variables are required to be integral and in which technical coefficients and right-hand sides are integral then slack variables will turn out to be integral too.

In zero–one problems the structural variables may assume only the values zero or one. These variables are said to be 'two state' and in an investment context would correspond to reject (zero) or accept (one). Investments which are of an all-or-nothing variety will have a two-state variable representing the investment level. The feasible set in an all-two-state n structural variable problem comprises those 'corners' of the n dimensional hypercube which do not violate the financial and other constraints. Clearly such zero–one problems are special cases of the mixed integer–continuous variable problem and could in principle, employ the same solution procedure. However, it is useful to exploit whatever special structure a problem has, and a different solution method is appropriate. There will of course be problems in which not all of the investment levels are restricted to zero or one and in some problems only variables introduced for formulative convenience will be two-state.

Obtaining the global optimum (or in many instances just a 'good' solution) in integer problems will be much more time consuming and expensive than is the case in ordinary LP problems. Thus if integrality requirements can be sidestepped or otherwise not explicitly included in the problem at hand, they should be. What such cases arise? In practice there will be some readily identifiable cases where rounding *down* is desirable. If an automobile manufacturer finds that optimal monthly output should be 1,413.2 units when rounding down this figure will be of negligible importance. In this instance the fractional component of the answer is minute compared to the integral component. Rounding down 1.4 to 1 units of an investment is another matter. If rounding off a fractional solution is straightforward and satifactory then it will be preferable to the formal incorporation of integrality requirements into the problem. Then it may be possible to redefine variables. Human beings are indivisibe but man-hours are a continuous variable; a production rate of 8.25 luxury cars per week means in reality 33 vehicles a month; investment in 1.3 computers by a department may suggest buying one and taking a 30% share in that of another department which requires 0.7 machines. Finally, there may be cases where the number of integral alternatives is so small that they can be completely enumerated. If a company has just two large-scale go/no-go possibilities and 20 continuously divisible investment opportunities then four separate ordinary LP problems could be solved, each corresponding to one pair of values of the two-state variables.

If the integrality requirements must remain, then a formal integer alogorithm must be employed. One of the earliest approaches, that of integer forms, has yet to be significantly improved upon.

5.2 A Cutting Plane Method

Figure 5.3 represents a two-by-two problem in which all $x_1 x_2$ lattice points in the non-negative orthant below ABC are feasible. It is clear that the set of feasible lattice points has a 'lower' upper bound than that defined by ABC. The polygon ODEFGHI shown in the figure is the smallest convex area that will contain all the feasible lattice points and is known as the *convex hull* of the constraint set. Clearly, the convex hull can be obtained by the addition of extra constraints which cut down the feasible area. An important characteristic of the convex hull is that the basic feasible solutions to the LP constraint set defined by the convex hull are feasible

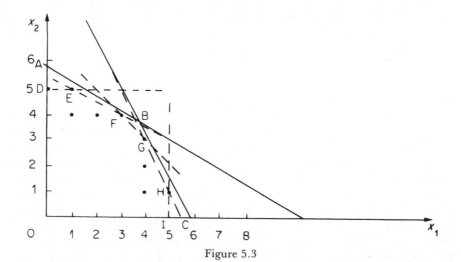

Figure 5.3

lattice points to the original integer problem. Since the objective function is linear, one of the basic feasible solutions on the convex hull will be an optimal integral solution to the original problem. Fortunately, it does not prove to be necessary to determine the entire convex hull. Additional constraints are introduced piecemeal to cut down the original area OABC towards the convex hull.

The additional constraints that are added to the original constraint set define *cutting planes*. They are of such a nature as to exclude some of the non-integral region between the convex hull and the original constraints—consequently no feasible integral solution will be ruled out. We shall solve an all integer problem using Gomory's cutting plane method. The procedure is as follows:

Step 1	Solve the problem by the Simplex method ignoring integrality requirements. If the solution to this problem (call it P_0) is integral then the optimum has been reached. If the optimal solution to P_0 is not integral, then:
Step 2	introduce one extra constraint to make the solution to P_0 infeasible but without excluding any feasible lattice points. Find the optimal feasible solution to this problem (P_1). If this solution is integral the optimum has been reached. If it is not integral, then:
Step 3	introduce a further cut and find a sign—feasible optimum to this problem (P_2). If this solution is integral it is optimal. If not, introduce a further cut—and so on. Cuts can be defined in such a way that this procedure converges on the integral optimum in a finite, if possibly very large, number of steps.

Consider the following problem:

maximize $F = 5x_1 + 3x_2$

subject to
$$2x_1 + x_2 \leqslant 15$$
$$x_1 + 3x_2 \leqslant 12$$
$$x_1, x_2 \geqslant 0$$
$$x_1, x_2 \text{ integral}$$

The problem is all integer since the slack variables will also be integral for integral x_1 and x_2. Figure 5.4 shows the solution to P_0 obtained in the usual way. The solution is non-integral, consequently stage 2 of the procedure must be entered and a cut generated. A number n_{ij} can be expressed as

$$n_{ij} = w_{ij} + f_{ij}$$

where w_{ij} is integral and f_{ij} is fractional such that $f_{ij} \geqslant 0$. Thus for

			5	3	0	0
			x_1	x_2	s_1	s_2
0	s_1	15	⟨2⟩	1	1	0
0	s_2	12	1	3	0	1
		0	−5	−3	0	0
5	x_1	7.5	1	0.5	0.5	0
0	s_2	4.5	0	⟨2.5⟩	−0.5	1
		37.5	0	−0.5	2.5	0
5	x_1	6.6	1	0	0.6	−0.2
3	x_2	1.8	0	1	−0.2	0.4
		38.4	0	0	2.4	0.2

Figure 5.4

$n_{ij} = 2.4$, $w_{ij} = 2$ and $f_{ij} = 0.4$ and for $n_{ij} = -4.2$, $w_{ij} = -5$ and $f_{ij} = 0.8$. To produce a cut, select one of the basic variables in the optimal solution to P_0 that should be integral but is not, say x_2 in the current example. Next express all numbers in the x_2 row as $w_{ij} + f_{ij}$. Thus the x_2 row from Figure 5.4 can be written as

$$1 + 0.8 \quad 0 + 0 \quad 1 + 0 \quad -1 + 0.8 \quad 0 + 0.4$$

Next take the fractional parts of these numbers and negate them producing

$$-0.8 \quad 0 \quad 0 \quad -0.8 \quad -0.4$$

The first -0.8 is the level of the slack variable in the new constraint—the first cut. The remaining numbers are the rates of exchange between this variable (call it s_3) and x_1, x_2, s_1 and s_2 in the now non-feasible solution to the extended problem, P_1. The new s_3 row and an s_3 column are added to the tableau of Figure 5.4. The problem is now one in three constraints; consequently there will be three variables in any non-degenerate basic solution. The task is to find a sign-feasible optimal solution to this problem, this is doen by the *dual Simplex method*.

The method consists in maintaining a positive index row (i.e. optimality of the primal and feasibility of the dual) and obtaining a sign-feasible solution to the primal problem. It will be recalled that in the (primal) Simplex method dual feasibility was sought whilst maintaining feasibility of the primal, where suboptimal solutions to the primal ($F < F$ max.) correspond to 'superoptimal' and infeasible solutions to the dual ($G < G$ min.). The two methods are, therefore, symmetrical. In the dual Simplex method the pivotal row is determined by a variable with negative values in the primal solution; s_3 being the only candidate in the current example.

The pivotal column is determined by selection of the smallest ratio (ignoring sign) of index row number to rate of exchange in the pivotal row, the pivotal element being negative. This will ensure that the next solution obtained has an all non-negative index row for the same reasons that selection of the pivotal row in the primal Simplex method guaranteed that the next solution obtained was primal-feasible. There is, however, no guarantee that only one iteration with the dual Simplex method will produce a sign-feasible primal. Several steps may be required before this is achieved and a particular subproblem P_t solved.

The first array of Figure 5.5 shows the additional row and column and the selection of pivotal row and column ($0.2/0.4 < 2.4/0.8$). Since s_3 is in the solution albeit at an infeasible level, it has unity rate of exchange with itself and zeros elsewhere in the new column. The objective function coefficient of s_3 is, as with the other slack variables, zero. The lower array of Figure 5.5 shows the situation with one iteration complete. Dual feasibility has been maintained, and, as it turns out, a sign and integer-feasible solution to P_1 has been obtained. The original problem has therefore been solved with the addition of just one constraint (an extra constraint would have been required to generate the convex hull). The value of the objective function is reduced by 0.4, slack variable s_2 is integral and the solution to the dual to the original problem is also integral, a result which is true for all integer problems in general. In this case it has transpired that the optimal integral solution is a rounding off of the original continuous solution.

What is the significance of the third constraint in terms of the original problem variables and why is it that a constraint so generated cannot exclude any feasible lattice points? In respect of the first question the s_3 row of the first array of Figure 5.5 states that the value of s_3 is given by

$$s_3 = -0.8 - 0x_1 - 0x_2 + 0.8s_1 + 0.4s_2$$

			5	3	0	0	0
			x_1	x_2	s_1	s_2	s_3
5	x_1	6.6	1	0	0.6	−0.2	0
3	x_2	1.8	0	1	−0.2	0.4	0
0	s_3	−0.8	0	0	−0.8	−0.4	1
		38.4	0	0	2.4	0.2	0
5	x_1	7	1	0	1	0	−0.5
3	x_2	1	0	1	−1	0	1
0	s_2	2	0	0	2	1	−2.5
		38	0	0	2	0	0.5

Figure 5.5

but from the original constraints

$$s_1 = 15 - 2x_1 - x_2 \quad \text{and} \quad s_2 = 12 - x_1 - 3x_2$$

Substituting for s_1 and s_2 in the expression for s_3 gives

$$s_3 = 16 - 2x_1 - 2x_2$$

which can be written as the inequality

$$2x_1 + 2x_2 \leqslant 16$$

which is the cut that was introduced. The problem is graphed in Figure 5.6. This displays an interesting feature of the problem in that constraint two is a convex hull constraint. The cut introduced, labelled 3 in the diagram, is another convex hull constraint, producing $(7, 1)$ by intersection with constraint one and $(6, 2)$ by intersection with the second restriction. The remaining convex hull constraint is $x_1 \leqslant 7$; this was not needed to produce the integral optimum.

What would have happened if a cut had been generated from the x_1 constraint in the solution of P_0? Figure 5.7 shows the calculations that would have resulted. The reader may verify that the constraint (corresponding to s_4) so introduced would have been

$$2x_1 + 3x_2 \leqslant 18$$

This is *not* a convex hull constraint, but does make the solution to P_0 infeasible without excluding any feasible lattice points. The problem is, in this case, not solved in one iteration. The sign-feasible solution to P_1 is not integral, so that a further cut is required. This is shown in the second

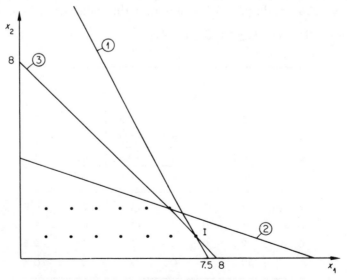

Figure 5.6

			5	3	0	0	0	0
			x_1	x_2	s_1	s_2	s_4	s_5
5	x_1	6.6	1	0	0.6	−0.2	0	
3	x_2	1.8	0	1	−0.2	0.4	0	
0	s_4	−0.6	0	0	−0.6	(−0.8)	1	
		38.4	0	0	2.4	0.2	0	
5	x_1	6.75	1	0	0.75	0	−0.25	0
3	x_2	1.5	0	1	−0.5	0	+0.5	0
0	s_2	0.75	0	0	0.75	1	(−1.25)	0
0	s_5	−0.75	0	0	−0.75	0	−0.75	1
		38.25	0	0	2.25	0	0.25	0
5	x_1	7	1	0	1	0	0	$-0.\overline{33}$
3	x_2	1	0	1	−1	0	0	$0.\overline{66}$
0	s_2	2	0	0	2	1	0	$-1.\overline{66}$
0	s_4	1	0	0	1	0	1	$-1.\overline{33}$
		38	0	0	2	0	0	$0.\overline{33}$

Figure 5.7

array and corresponds to:

$$3x_1 + 4x_2 \leqslant 26$$

This is not a convex hull constraint, but as will be seen from the third array of Figure 5.7 it does produce the integral optimum. Note that in the second array the s_5 constraint is generated either by the x_1 row or the s_2 row. In the final array the integral optimum is produced, but contains an additional slack variable since there are now four constraints; dual values for the original constraints are unaffected, however.

Why do the cuts that have been introduced not exclude any feasible lattice points? The value of a variable in any solution can be written as

$$x_i = x_i^0 - \sum n_{ij}x_j \tag{5.1}$$

where x_i^0 is the solution value of x_i shown in the tableau, the x_j represent all the variables currently in the problem including the slacks and the n_{ij} are the rates of exchange in the x_i row, n_{ij} being zero for basic variables $i \neq j$ and unity if $i = j$. Now dividing up each coefficient into whole and fractional parts (5.1) can be rewritten as

$$x_i = w_i^0 + f_i^0 - \sum (w_{ij} + f_{ij})x_j \tag{5.2}$$

where $0 \leqslant f_{ij} < 1$. That is, the fractional components are non-negative as explained above. Equation (5.2) can be re-expressed as

$$x_i = w_i^0 - \sum w_{ij}x_j + f_i^0 - \sum f_{ij}x_j \tag{5.3}$$

Now any integral solution will be such that

$$x_i - w_i^0 + \sum w_{ij}x_j = \text{integer} \tag{5.4}$$

In other words all lattice points satisfy (5.4). Therefore, if x_i is integral

$$f_i^0 - \sum f_{ij}x_j = \text{integer} \tag{5.5}$$

Now

$$\sum f_{ij}x_j \geqslant 0 \tag{5.6}$$

since $f_{ij} \geqslant 0$ and $x_j \geqslant 0$ and since by definition $f_i^0 < 1$ the integer in (5.5) cannot be positive. Therefore any integral solution (i.e. all the lattice points) must satisfy

$$f_i^0 - \sum f_{ij}x_j \leqslant 0 \tag{5.7}$$

that is

$$f_i^0 - \sum f_{ij}x_j + s_{m+1} = 0 \tag{5.8}$$

where $s_{m=1}$ is an additional slack variable and is non-negative. Equation (5.8) can be re-expressed as

$$s_{m+1} = -f_i^0 + \sum f_{ij}x_j \tag{5.9}$$

which is the form of constraint proposed by Gomory (1963) and is that which we have used.

Which row in a solution should be used to determine the cut? Convergence on the integral optimum in a finite number of steps is only *guaranteed* if the cut is generated in particular ways. However, in practice simpler rules are used. Intuitively we want any cut to be as 'deep' as possible—to exclude as much of the original feasible area as possible (remember no feasible lattice point can be excluded). In fact, ideally we should like all of the ratios f_i^0/f_{ij} to be as large as possible to ensure deepness since the larger is f_i^0/f_{ij}, the larger will have to be the extent of the introduction of some previously not included variable and the further will be the movement away from the infeasible position. Typically, however, for most rows some of the ratios are large and others small! As a rule of thumb (that has worked in practice) we simply select the largest of the f_i^0. This is the selection rule that was employed in the first instance in the numerical example above.

At first sight it would seem to be the case that the problem expands by one constraint and one variable (the new slack) every time that a cut is introduced and so rapidly that it may become daunting computationally. In fact there is an upper limit to the number of constraints that any problem P_t need have. This limit is the number of structural and slack variables, in the original problem, plus one. This is because the new Gomory constraints need *not* always be satisfied (at a non-integral solution). Consequently, if say s_5 appears as a basic variable in P_3 it has done its job in making the solution to P_2 sign infeasible and may be removed from the problem. The s_5 row and column being deleted and the original variables used to generate further cuts.

5.3 Mixed Problems

We now return to consideration of problems in which some, but not all of the variables are required to be whole numbers. A common occurrence of such a problem is when the structural variables are required to be integral but the slack variables are not. There are also of course cases where not all of the xs are required to be integral. The method of solution is the same in principle to that already described for all-integer problems. The difference lies in the manner which cuts are determined. The slack variable in the new constraint appended to any problem is given by

$$s = -f_i^0 + \sum d_{ij}x_j \tag{5.10}$$

where the terms d_{ij}, negated, will be the rates of exchange in the new row and where f_i^0 is given by a variable in the current solution which is required to be integral. Conventionally, the non-integral variable with the highest fractional component (from among those variables required to be integral) is used to determine the cut. The d_{ij} are determined as follows:

$$d_{ij} = \left. \begin{cases} n_{ij} & \text{if } n_{ij} \geqslant 0 \\ \dfrac{-n_{ij}f_i^0}{1-f_i^0} & \text{if } n_{ij} < 0 \end{cases} \right\} \text{ for variables not required to be integral}$$

$$d_{ij} = \left. \begin{cases} f_{ij} & \text{if } f_{ij} \leqslant f_i^0 \\ \dfrac{f_i^0}{1-f_i^0}(1-f_{ij}) & \text{if } f_{ij} > f_i^0 \end{cases} \right\} \begin{array}{l} \text{for variables required to be} \\ \text{integral} \end{array}$$

The n_{ij} of (5.11) are the rate of exchange in the selected row and the f_{ij} are the fractional components of the n_{ij} determined in the usual manner. Thus the d_{ij} for variables not required to be integral are determined without reference to the fractional components of the n_{ij}. The only fraction relevant here being f_i^0. For those variables that should become integral the d_{ij} are determined as for the all-integer situation provided that $f_{ij} \leqslant f_i^0$. If $f_i^0 < f_{ij}$ then the relevant d_{ij} is given by the last condition in (5.11). Note that

$$\frac{f_i^0}{1-f_i^0}(1-f_{ij}) < f_{ij}$$

148

when $f_{ij} > f_i^0$. Cuts generated in the manner (5.11) could also be employed in the all-integer case, the first half of (5.11) being irrelevant. The cuts so generated would be no shallower and often deeper than those generated in the $-f_{ij}$ manner. Consider a numerical illustration of the use of the technique:

$$\text{maximize } F = x_1 + 1.5x_2$$
$$\text{subject to} \quad 2x_1 + 2.5x_2 \leqslant 12.25$$
$$x_1 + 0.8x_2 \leqslant 5.5$$
$$x_1, \, x_2 \geqslant 0$$
$$x_2 \text{ integral}$$

The problem is graphed in Figure 5.8. The feasible set is the series of horizontal lines terminating on OABC and corresponding to integral values of x_2. The continuous optimum is at A where $x_2 = 4.9$. The 'integral' optimum is at A' with $x_2 = 4$ and $x_1 = 1.125$. Note that the optimum must be on the boundary of the feasible set for the continuous case. Since the objective function coefficient of x_1, the continous variable, is positive there can be no interior optimum. The solution of the problem by cuts is shown in Figure 5.9 where the single cut required is generated by (5.11). The x_2 row in the second array is used to generate the cut, since only x_2 is required to be integral. In this case the elements of the s_j row (the $-d_{ij}$) are easily determined, all being given by the first line of (5.11).

The optimal solution, with x_2 integral is obtained in one iteration, no further cuts being required. The cut is, in fact an upper bound on x_2 being $x_2 \leqslant 4$. Note that the dual solution is not integral.

The problems solved in this and the preceding section have required

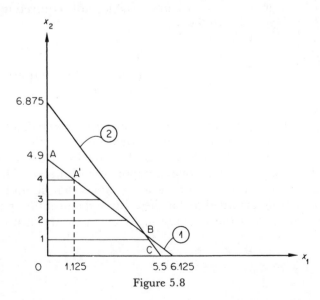

Figure 5.8

			1	1.5	0	0	0
			x_1	x_2	s_1	s_2	s_2
0	s_1	12.25	2	2.5	1	0	
0	s_2	5.5	1	0.8	0	1	
		0	−1	−1.5	0	0	
1.5	x_2	4.9	0.8	1	0.4	0	0
0	s_2	1.58	0.30	0	−0.32	1	0
0	s_3	−0.9	−0.8	0	−0.4	0	1
		7.35	0.2	0	0.6	0	0
1.5	x_2	4	0	1	0	0	1
0	s_2	1.175	0	0	−0.5	1	0.45
1	x_1	1.125	1	0	0.5	0	−1.25
		7.125	0	0	0.5	0	0.25

Figure 5.9

few iterations to achieve the integral optimum. This will by no means always be the case. Indeed the method of cut determination that we used in the all integer case does not guarantee convergence on the integral optimum in a finite number of iterations. The cuts (5.11) can be shown to lead to an optimum in a finite number of steps if the value of F is one of the variables required to be integral. This, however, would represent an artificial restriction in many investment applications. It does turn out, none the less, that the solution procedures work quite well in actual use. We must bear in mind that the problems are much *larger* than those in continuous variables. There can be difficulties if a completely automatic procedure is used to tackle integral problems. Quite aside from round-off difficulties in digital computers (only so many decimal places can be used) the 'finite-number' may be very large indeed. To quote Hadley (1964, p.281) ... it seems that in many cases the number of iterations is so large that for practical purposes convergence is not obtained'. Continuous LP problems requiring less than 20 iterations to solve have been run for 2,000 or more iterations without converging to an integer solution. The outcome depends very much on the type of problem that is tackled. The procedure does not work very well for sequencing problems—where the analytical formulation is large—but for certain investment problems the cutting plane method can often be used to advantage.

5.4 Shadow Values in Integer Problems

In the process of finding an integral solution to an otherwise linear problem, further constraints were added to the original set, the problem so arrived at is called the *augmented* LP problem has a dual problem associated with it. The optimal value of the objective function in the augmented problem will be lower than in the original problem P_0, so as regards shadow prices the total valuation of the original resources must drop. The result can be stated as

$$\sum b_0 y_0 > \sum b_0 y_0^a + \sum b^* y^* \geq \sum b_0 y_0^a \qquad (5.12)$$

where the b_0 are the resource levels, the y_0 are the associated shadow prices in the optimal solution to P_0; the y_0^a are the shadow prices of the resources in the optimal solution to the augmented problem, the b^* are the RHS of the additional constraints defined by the cuts and the y^* are the dual variables associated with the RHS of the new constraints. Except when the optimal solution to the augmented problem is degenerate, $\sum b^* y^* > 0$ so that strict inequality would hold throughout (5.12). From (5.12) it can be seen that

$$\sum b_0(y_0 - y_0^a) > 0 \qquad (5.13)$$

which allows the possibility that some of the original resources may receive *increased* valuation at the margin, although some valuations must be reduced to such an extent that there is a net decrease. This situation is shown in Figure 5.10 where the shadow price of resource two is zero at the continuous optimum C but has become positive at the discrete optimum, D. The shadow prices themselves have to be carefully interpreted in an integer problem. A zero index row number corresponding to a constraint can no longer be taken to mean *necessarily* that further units of that resource are not worth having. Ruling out the case of degeneracy, a zero index row number means that the corresponding primal variable is at a positive level in the solution. If this primal variable is a slack variable then some of that particular resource is currently left unused. Consider the optimal solution to the first integer problem of this chapter. For convenience this is reproduced in Figure 5.11.

Resource two is not fully used here ($s_2 = 2$) and the index row number under s_2 is zero. A slight increase in the amount of resource two available

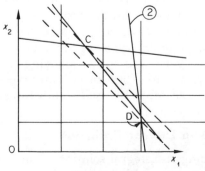

Figure 5.10

		5	3	0	0	0
		x_1	x_2	s_1	s_2	s_3
5	x_1	7	1	0	1	0	-0.5
3	x_2	1	0	1	-1	0	1
0	s_2	2	0	0	2	1	-2.5
		38	0	0	2	0	0.5

Figure 5.11

would not allow a superior integral solution to the solution $x_1 = 7$, $x_2 = 1$ to be achieved. However, if there were an extra *three* units available ($b_2 = 15$ instead of 12) then the solution $x_1 = 6$, $x_2 = 3$ becomes feasible and optimal ($F = 39$). So three or more additional units of the second resource are worth £1 (£39 – £38). This is not evident from the optimal tableau. The fact that b_2 has a positive shadow price in P_0 does not necessarily mean that there may be some large worthwhile increase in b_2 in the integer case. Figure 5.12 illustrates such a case. The optimal continuous solution is at C in which $y_2 > 0$. The integral optimum is at D where $y_2 = 0$, but there is no worthwhile increase of any magnitude in resource two from the integral position.

Positive index row numbers in integer problems are also not all that they might seem. Although in the problem of Figure 5.11 a further unit of resource one *is* worth £2, enabling the solution $x_1 = 8$, $x_2 = 0$ to be achieved, the situation is not always so convenient. The rates of exchange under the slack variable corresponding to the increasing resource must be such that solution values for basic variables alter to new feasible levels. If this is not the case then the shadow price of the resource may give no useful information as to the value of marginal units. Consider the follow-

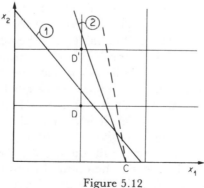

Figure 5.12

			7	3	0	0
			x_1	x_2	s_1	s_2
0	s_1	4	②	1	1	0
0	s_2	6	1	2	0	1
		0	−7	−3	0	0
7	x_1	2	1	0.5	0.5	0
0	s_2	4	0	1.5	−0.5	1
		14	0	0.5	3.5	0

Figure 5.13

ing problem:

maximize $F = 7x_1 + 3x_2$

subject to $\quad 2x_1 + x_2 \leqslant 4$

$\qquad x_1 + 2x_2 \leqslant 6$

$\qquad x_1, x_2 \geqslant 0$

$\qquad x_1, x_2, s_1, s_2$ integral

The optimal solution is shown in Figure 5.13. It will be noted that the dual solution is not integral. The dual solution could be made integral by multiplication of the RHS of the constraint set by a constant (in this case 0.5), but we shall not trouble to do this here. If the problem was continuous a further unit of resource one would be worth £3.5 since x_1 would become 2.5 and $F = 17.5$ with $s_2 = 3.5$. The fractional solution is not permitted here, but further units of resource one are of some value. Raising b_1 to 5 allows the solution $x_1 = 2$, $x_2 = 1$, to be achieved for $F = 17$. Consequently the extra unit of resource one is worth £3. In such a problem as this, in which the integral solution was arrived at without the addition of cuts, the index row numbers under the slacks provide *upper bounds* for changes in F following relaxation of the RHS of the constraints. After cuts have been introduced however, the shadow prices may *underestimate* the value of extra resources. For example, suppose that constraint one was relaxed to 5 in the first instance. The tableau of the optimal integral solution is shown in Figure 5.14. If the RHS of constraint 1 is relaxed to 6 from 5, the integral solution $x_1 = 3$, $x_2 = 0$ becomes feasible. This gives $F = 21$, an increase of £4 over the $b_1 = 5$ case rather than the £3 increase that would be indicated by the shadow price in Figure 5.14. From the rates of exchange in the s_1 column it is evident that the solution $x_1 = 2$, $x_2 = 2$ is feasible for $b_1 = 6$, $b_2 = 6$ giving $F = 20$ and an increase over the previous solution of 3. The new solution $x_1 = 2$, $x_2 = 2$ is, as we know, suboptimal, but it would appear to be optimal from the tableau since all variables are integral ($s_2 = 0$) and there is an all non-negative index row.

			7	3	0	0	0
			x_1	x_2	s_1	s_2	s_3
7	x_1	2	1	0	0	0	1
0	s_2	2	0	0	-2	1	3
3	x_2	1	0	1	1	0	-2
		17	0	0	3	0	1

Figure 5.14

The explanation lies in the fact that the cut constraints do not always have to be observed. The reader may verify the cut required to produce the Figure 5.14 solution from the continuous optimum for $b_1 = 5$, $b_2 = 6$ is $x_1 \leqslant 2$. As long as the resource levels remain at 5 and 6 then $x_1 \leqslant 2$ does not exclude any feasible lattice point, but when b_1 is relaxed to 6 the cut excludes $x_1 = 3$ which is now feasible. What information then do shadow prices in such a solution give us? The value of 3 for y_1 is in fact a *lower bound* on the change in F *provided* that the values of the variables in the solution and the s_1 column rates of exchange allow another feasible lattice point to be reached by alteration of the solution values using the rates of exchange. In our example $F = 20$ is reached for

$$x_1 = 2 + (0) = 2$$

$$s_2 = 2 + (-2) = 0$$

$$x_2 = 1 + (1) = 2$$

Figure 5.12 shows that it is possible for a resource to have zero shadow price in both the continuous optimum and the integral optimum and still it may be worth buying more of the resource if a sufficiently large increase is possible. Resource one in the diagram falls into this category. It is in surplus at both C and D but a 'large' increment would allow integral solution D' (superior to D) to be reached. There is, of course, no increment sufficient to allow the objective function to exceed its value at the continuous optimum C. All the combinations of Figure 5.15 are possible. Column 1 gives the state (positive or zero) of a shadow price at a continuous optimum. Column 2 gives the state at the integral optimum. A

1	2	3
+	+	√
+	+	×
+	0	√
+	0	×
0	+	√
0	+	×
0	0	√
0	0	×

Figure 5.15

tick in column 3 means that there are cases in which the integral solution can be improved by further units, in sufficient quantity, of the resource in question. A cross indicates that there are cases where no increment in the resource will improve the integral position. Figure 5.15 may be further complicated by separation of cases where cuts have not been required to produce the integral optimum and further by separation of those cases where an upper bound or lower bound statement may be made.

Similar possibilities exist in the case of mixed integer–continuous problems. It is possible that a shadow price be positive at an integral optimum, but nevertheless no more of the resource can be used. Figure 5.12 can be used to illustrate such a case in a mixed problem in which the slack variables are not required to be integral. In general, shadow prices may over- or understate the value of additional resources but frequently it is possible to say that the index row number represents a bound on the true value. For example consider the problem of Figure 5.9 and the index row number 0.5 in the final array—this suggests that an extra unit of the first resource would increase F to 7.625. This is not the case. If b_1 is increased by 0.25 to 12.5 the solution $x_2 = 5$, $x_1 = 0$ becomes feasible giving $F = 7.5$. Thus the ration $\Delta F/\Delta b_1 = 1.5$ in this case. If $\Delta b_1 = 1$, however, x_2 cannot be increased beyond 5 but x_1 can be set at 0.375 giving $F = 7.875$ and $\Delta F = 0.75$ over the original value. Thus $\Delta F/b_1 = 0.75$ for $\Delta b_1 = 1$. Nevertheless the figure 0.5 in the tableau does convey *some* information, being a lower bound on the increase in F since the existing solution can be adjusted by the rates of exchange in the s_1 column. If in a solution to a problem in which cuts have been required the rates of exchange cannot be used to find a new feasible position it is not possible to say *a priori* whether the shadow prices in an upper or lower bound to the true improvement. But when an integral optimum has been arrived at without cuts the shadow price will be an upper bound on the increase in F. For instance if in the first place $b_1 = 12.5$ then the optimum $x_1 = 5$, $x_2 = 0$, $s_2 = 1.5$ would have not required a cut and the index row number 0.6 under s_1, showing $\Delta F/\Delta b_1$ in the all-continuous case is an upper bound for the discrete problem. In this case if $\Delta b_1 = 1$ (from a base of 12.5) then the optimum has $x_2 = 5$, $x_1 = 0.375$ and $\Delta F = 0.375$ ($= 7.875 - 7.5$). If no cut has been required the shadow price cannot understate the true improvement.

5.5 Zero–one Problems

Frequently cases arise when an investment project has to be accepted or rejected in its entirety: that is either $x_j = 1$ or $x_j = 0$ any other values for x_j being meaningless. Also there are situations in which one or other of two projects, but not both, must be undertaken. Such a condition defines a constraint for the problem. It can be stated as

$$x_i + x_k = 1 \tag{5.14}$$

which, in conjunction with the requirements that $x_j = 0$ or 1 and $x_k = 0$ or 1 produces the only two possibilities $x_j = 1$, $x_k = 0$ and $x_j = 0$, $x_k = 1$. Additional constraints of this type (also taken in conjunction with zero–one requirements) are

$$x_j + x_k \leqslant 1 \qquad\qquad (5.15)$$

which reads 'not both of x_j and x_k'

$$x_j - x_k \geqslant 0 \qquad\qquad (5.16)$$

that is, 'undertake project k only if project j is accepted', the solution $x_k = 1$, $x_j = 0$ being excluded,

$$x_j + x_k \geqslant 1 \qquad\qquad (5.17)$$

which means accept 'either or both or' projects j and k. The restriction 'both or neither' can be accommodated by using constraint (5.16) plus

$$x_k - x_j \geqslant 0 \qquad\qquad (5.18)$$

while

$$x_j + x_k + x_L = 2 \qquad\qquad (5.19)$$

means any two of projects j, k and L and so on.

The solution procedures with cuts that have been detailed in sections 5.4 and 5.5 will work also for zero–one problems. Indeed, in problems in which most of the problem variables are not two-state, but a few are, then a cutting plane approach would prove to be amongst the better procedures for solution. But in all-zero–one problems this special two-state characteristic can be exploited by specifically designed computational procedures. There are many algorithms to choose from. The relative efficiency of the algorithms in problem solution depends on the structure and size of the problem. Algorithms especially designed for zero–one problems employ partial or implicit enumeration. Not every feasible solution is evaluated, some may be eliminated without evaluation since it is known that there is at least one superior solution in such cases.

The method selected for discussion here uses ideas from Boolean algebra—the algebra of systems of two-state variables. The technique is simple to grasp and is well suited to solution of suitable small problems by hand. It also provides a good structure for sensitivity analysis but there are disadvantages. In comparison to some other procedures relatively few solutions are not explicitly evaluated. This is of less importance the fewer in number are the feasible solutions to the problem. The technique is better suited to those problems in which the principal computational difficulty is in determining a relatively small feasible solution set. Such problems are those in which most of the technical coefficients are 'large' relative to the RHS of the constraints. The technique then, will be more efficient in larger-scale investment applications than to 'shop floor' scheduling problems for which there are superior methods.

Consider the following problem:

maximize $\quad F = 10x_1 + 6x_2 + 7x_3 - x_4 + 5x_5$

subject to (1) $\quad 5x_1 + 6x_2 - x_3 + 2x_4 + 2.5x_5 \leqslant 9$

(2) $\quad -2x_1 + 4.5x_2 + 6x_3 - 0.5x_4 + 7x_5 \geqslant 10$

(3) $\quad 4.5x_1 + 4x_2 + 1.5x_3 + 4x_4 + 3x_5 \leqslant 8.5$

$$x_1,\ x_2,\ x_3,\ x_4,\ x_5 \ 0 \text{ or } 1$$

The form of constraints (1), (2) and (3) is not the most convenient way that the restrictions can be expressed. The first step is to convert the constraints to *canonical form*—in which all coefficients are positive and the constraints are of $\geqslant$ variety. It will also prove convenient to rearrange and relabel variables so that their coefficients are in descending order of magnitude from left to right. Starting with the first constraint convert to $\geqslant$ form by multiplication through by -1. It becomes

$$-5x_1 - 6x_2 + x_3 - 2x_4 - 2.5x_5 \geqslant -9 \tag{1$'$}$$

Now define new variables y as follows:

$y_1 = 1 - x_2 \quad y_3 = 1 - x_5 \quad y_5 = x_3$

$y_2 = 1 - x_1 \quad y_4 = 1 - x_4$

It is a useful simplification to write $\bar{x}_2$ for $1 - x_2$, etc. It will be noted that where an x variable appears with negative coefficient in (1)$'$ it is replaced by a y variable that will be of opposite state, i.e. if $x_2 = 0$, $y_1 = 1$ and if $x_2 = 1$, $y_1 = 0$. The y's have been subscripted so that y_1 has the highest coefficient down to y_5 with the lowest. Substitution of y's for x's in (1)$'$ gives

$$6y_1 + 5y_2 + 2.5y_3 + 2y_4 + y_5 \geqslant 6.5 \tag{1$''$}$$

The task now is to find *basic solutions* of (1)$''$. A basic solution in this context is one in which if any variable set at unit level in the solution is changed to zero level then the constraint is violated. For example, one basic solution to (1)$''$ is $y_1 = 1$, $y_3 = 1$, $y_2, y_4, y_5 = 0$, whereas $y_1 = 1$, $y_2 = 1$, $y_3 = 1$, $y_4 = 0$, $y_5 = 0$ is non-basic. The basic solutions to (1)$''$ are tabulated below.

y_1	y_2	y_3	y_4	y_5
1	1	0	0	0
1	0	1	0	0
1	0	0	1	0
1	0	0	0	1
0	1	1	0	0
0	1	0	1	0

The basic solutions can be systematically found by first finding those which contain y_1 at unit level; next find those in which y_1 is at zero level but y_2 is at unit level and so on. The next stage in the procedure is to convert the basic solutions to the first constraint into *families* of solutions. A family of solutions comprises *fixed variables*: those which are set at zero or one and may not be altered) and *free variables* which are allowed to be zero or one. The families of solutions are

y_1	y_2	y_3	y_4	y_5
1	1	—	—	—
1	0	1	—	—
1	0	0	1	—
1	0	0	0	1
0	1	1	—	—
0	1	0	1	—

The dashes represent the free variables. It will be seen that a family is obtained from the corresponding basic solution by replacing the zero after the last unit entry in the row with dashes. It will thus follow that in each family the group of fixed variables is such that if any one of the variables at unit level is reduced to zero the constraint is violated. The constraint is satisfied whatever the values of the free variables are. Lastly, the families of solutions are reconverted to expression in the x's and each is labelled.

	x_1	x_2	x_3	x_4	x_5
a_1	0	0	—	—	—
b_1	1	0	—	—	0
c_1	1	0	—	0	1
d_1	1	0	1	1	1
e_1	0	1	—	—	0
f_1	0	1	—	0	1

The same process is now applied to the other constraints. Constraint (2) is written as

$$7y_1 + 6y_2 + 4.5y_3 + 2y_4 + 0.5y_5 \geqslant 12.5 \qquad (2)''$$

where $y_1 = x_5$, $y_2 = x_3$, $y_3 = x_2$, $y_4 = \bar{x}_1$, $y_5 = \bar{x}_4$. The transformation of x variables will differ from one constraint to the next. The y variables are used only as 'intermediaries'. The solution families to the second constraint, in terms of the y's are

y_1	y_2	y_3	y_4	y_5
1	1	—	—	—
1	0	1	1	—
0	1	1	1	—

which on reconversion to x's become

	x_1	x_2	x_3	x_4	x_5
a_2	—	—	1	—	1
b_2	0	1	0	—	1
c_2	0	1	1	—	0

Before the process is applied to the third constraint, families of solutions which are feasible for both of the first two constraints are found. Starting with a_1 appropriate setting of the free variables produces

	x_1	x_2	x_3	x_4	x_5
a_1a_2	0	0	1	—	1

a family of solutions which satisfies both a_1 and a_2. Again, by appropriate choice of free variables it will be seen that all the solutions below are members of a family of solutions to each of the constraints:

	x_1	x_2	x_3	x_4	x_5
a_1a_2	0	0	1	—	1
c_1a_2	1	0	1	0	1
d_1a_2	1	0	1	1	1
e_1c_2	0	1	1	—	0
f_1a_2	0	1	1	0	1
f_1b_2	0	1	0	0	1

So the above are families of solutions to each of the first two constraints. The third constraint can be written as

$$4.5y_1 + 4y_2 + 4y_3 + 3y_4 + 1.5y_5 \geqslant 8.5 \tag{3''}$$

where $y_1 = \bar{x}_1$, $y_2 = \bar{x}_2$, $y_3 = \bar{x}_4$, $y_4 = \bar{x}_5$, $y_5 = \bar{x}_3$. The families of solutions are

y_1	y_2	y_3	y_4	y_5
1	1	—	—	—
1	0	1	—	—
1	0	0	1	1
0	1	1	1	—
0	1	1	0	1
0	1	0	1	1
0	0	1	1	1

which are in terms of the x's

	x_1	x_2	x_3	x_4	x_5
a_3	0	0	—	—	—
b_3	0	1	—	0	—
c_3	0	1	0	1	0
d_3	1	0	—	0	0
e_3	1	0	0	0	1
f_3	1	0	0	1	0
g_3	1	1	0	0	0

Common solutions to all three constraints are then

	x_1	x_2	x_3	x_4	x_5
$a_1a_2a_3$	0	0	1	—	1
$e_1c_2b_3$	0	1	1	0	0
$f_1a_2b_3$	0	1	1	0	1
$f_1b_2b_3$	0	1	0	0	1

It is from among these solutions that the optimum will be found. At this stage, free variables in each family are set at zero or one depending on the coefficient in the objective function. The optimal solution is now obtained by evaluating each solution. In matrix form the results can be written as

$$
\begin{pmatrix}
0 & 0 & 1 & 0 & 1 \\
0 & 1 & 1 & 0 & 0 \\
0 & 1 & 1 & 0 & 1 \\
0 & 1 & 0 & 0 & 1
\end{pmatrix}
\begin{pmatrix}
10 \\
6 \\
7 \\
-1 \\
5
\end{pmatrix}
=
\begin{pmatrix}
12 \\
13 \\
18 \\
11
\end{pmatrix}
$$

The optimal solution therefore is $x_1 - 0$, $x_2 - 1$, $x_3 - 1$, $x_4 - 0$, $x_5 - 1$, giving $F = 18$.

The major problem lay in finding feasible solutions to the entire constraint set. Once the feasible solutions have been found some are eliminated without evaluation when the remaining free variables in each family are set at the appropriate state determined by the signs of objective function coefficients. All solutions that then remain have to be evaluated. Note that there is no feasible solution with $x_1 = 1$. It is instructive to see by reference back to the original constraints how difficult this fact would be to establish by an inspection procedure.

The method is particularly amenable to sensitivity analysis of the objective function coefficients. If present values of projects are changed the new values are inserted into the column vector in the evaluation stage. If the

RHS of a constraint alters then the families of solutions appropriate to the new resource level must be found and the 'intersection' of these families with the families of solutions to the other constraints determined. The new optimal solution would then be determined. If a technical coefficient changes, the effect on the optimum is calculated in a similar manner. Additional constraints can be incorporated by finding the families of solutions to the new constraints and forming the intersection of these with the existing solutions to the problem (prior to selection of values for the free variables in these solutions). Finally, if a new variable is added to the original problem then the number of basic solutions to each constraint may increase. Each existing basic solution will still be basic with the new variable at zero level, but there may be more solutions with the new variable at unit level which are basic. These new basic solutions are found and the intersection of families of solutions redetermined.

5.6 Fixed Charges in Investment Appraisal

Suppose that an investor is to select from amongst n possible investments so as to maximize total net present value. Suppose also, for the time being, that the constraint set does not include an initial capital expenditure constraint. The net present value resulting from x_j units of investment j is given by

$$
\begin{array}{ll}
N_j x_j - F_j & \text{if} \quad x_j > 0 \\
0 & \text{if} \quad x_j = 0
\end{array}
\tag{5.20}
$$

The capital outlay required for $x_j > 0$ has two components, an amount which depends upon the level of the investment and which is included in the N_j of (5.20) in the usual manner and a *fixed charge* F_j which is incurred only if the investment is undertaken at *any* positive level. The F_j may be thought of as certain of the administrative expenses connected with a project. In a production planning exercise the F_j are often described as 'set-up' costs.

What difficulties are caused by (5.20)? It is incorrect to express the objective function as:

$$
N = \sum_{j=1}^{n} N_j x_j - \sum_{j=1}^{n} F_j
\tag{5.21}
$$

since the effect of the formulation (5.21) is that the F_j are ignored by the LP optimization process. In (5.21) the F_j are included in N even if the x_j are zero, whereas we know from (5.20) that this is not the case. The difficulty is resolved in the following manner. Introduce n new variables w_j where $w_j = 0$ or 1. Redefine the objective function as:

$$
N = \sum_{j=1}^{n} N_j x_j - \sum_{j=1}^{n} F_j w_j
\tag{5.22}
$$

Now if we can ensure that $w_j = 1$ if and only if $x_j > 0$ the correct level of N will be obtained. To accomplish this introduce n new constraints of the form

$$x_j - M_j w_j \leqslant 0 \qquad j = 1, 2, \ldots, n \qquad (5.23)$$

where M_j are constants of such magnitude that $x_j \leqslant M_j$ is certainly satisfied in any optimal solution. Now observe that if $w_j = 0$ (5.23) along with the sign requirements on x_i means that $x_j = 0$ and the contribution to N is zero. If $w_j = 1$ then (5.23) means that $x_j \leqslant M_j$ which will, from the definition of M_j be an ineffective restriction and the contribution to N will be $N_j x_j - F_j$.

With the other joint constraints on x_j represented in the usual manner the full formulation of the problem is

$$\left. \begin{array}{l} \text{maximize } N = \sum_{j=1}^{n} N_j x_j - \sum_{j=1}^{n} F_j w_j \\[1em] \text{subject to} \\[0.5em] \Sigma a_{ij} x_j \leqslant b_i \qquad i = 1, 2, \ldots, m \\[0.5em] x_j - M_j w_j \leqslant 0 \qquad j = 1, 2, \ldots, n \\[0.5em] w_j \lessapprox 1 \\[0.5em] x_j, \ w_j \geqslant 0 \\[0.5em] w_j \text{ integral} \end{array} \right\} \qquad (5.25)$$

The upper (1) and lower (0) bounds on w_j conjoined with the integrality requirement that the only permissible values of the w_j are 0 and 1. It only remains to determine suitable values of the M_j. An obvious possibility would be to set $M_j = \text{Max}_i (b_i)/a_{ij}$ so that (5.23) are redundant if $w_j = 1$.

For computation a mixed integer continuous programming algorithm would be employed. The computational burden depends upon how many of the investments have a fixed charge associated with them, since for each such case a new variable, a new constraint and an integrality requirement are introduced.

Earlier on we stated that the validity of the formulation (5.24) was contingent upon there being no constraint on initial outlay. The reason for this can now be seen. If there was such a constraint a fixed charge element would be introduced into the constraint set since the outlay required for x_j units of the jth investment would be

$$K_j x_j + F_j \qquad \textit{if } x_j > 0$$
$$0 \qquad\qquad \text{if } x_j = 0$$

where K_j represents that part of outlay variable directly with x_j. In the objective function $N_j = G_j - K_j$ where G_j is the gross present value per unit of x_j. Fixed charges in a constraint may be nandled by the same device employed on the objective function. Call the initial capital constraint zero and express it thus:

$$\sum_{j=1}^{n} K_j x_j + \sum_{j=1}^{n} F_j w_j \leqslant b_0 \qquad (5.25)$$

Now simply append (5.25) to the problem given by (5.24). Any further constraints with fixed charges could be included in a similar fashion.

5.7 Singleton Two-state Projects

A special case of mixed integer continuous programming that is of interest in an investment context is the situation where there is only one project to be accepted or rejected in its entirety, but more than one source of finance and more than one potential outlet for surplus funds. In practice there will be limits to the amounts of cash that can be raised from given sources and there may be external or self-imposed limits on the amounts placed in individual institutions or bonds. The rate of return required for acceptability of the project will, in these circumstances, depend not only on the rates of interest in the problem but also upon the upper bounds. This will be the case more generally too, but the relatively simple cases considered below allow functional relationships between required yield from the project and upper bounds and rates of interest to be determined. Consider the problem:

maximize $F = 1.13x_1 + 1.11x_2 - 1.05z_1 - 1.14z_2 + R_3 x_3$

subject to $\qquad x_1 + x_2 + 1{,}000x_3 - z_1 - z_2 \leqslant 0$

$$z_1 \leqslant 800$$

$$x_1,\ x_2, z_1,\ z_2 \geqslant 0 \quad x_3 = 0 \text{ or } 1$$

The single project is represented by variable x_3 which would cost £1,000 to initiate and give a single return of R_3 after one year. The variables z represent amounts raised from the two possible sources of finance at costs of 5% and 14% and x_1 and x_2 represent deposits in financial institutions giving interest at 13% and 11%. If the project is not taken ($x_3 = 0$) F is maximized for $x_1 = 800$ and $z_1 = 800$. Therefore $\bar{F} = 800\ (1.13 - 1.05) = 64$. Now for the project to be acceptable the value of F with $x_1 = 1$ must be at least 64. With $x_3 = 1$, F is maximized for $z_1 = 800$, $z_2 = 200$ and the constraint on F is given by

$$\bar{F} = R_3 - 800(1.05) - 200(1.14) \geqslant 64$$

which means that $R_3 \geqslant 1{,}132$ for acceptability so that the requisite yield on the project is 13.2%. This yield figure, it will be noted, is different from any of the interest rates in the problem even though the horizon is only one period. This is because of the upper bound on the cheap source of finance. The required minimum return R_3 is, in fact,

$$\hat{R}_3 = 800(1.13) + 200(1.14)$$

or, with an upper bound $z_1^* \leqslant 1,000$ on z_1,

$$\hat{R}_3 = z_1^*(1.13) + (1,000 - z_1^*)(1.14)$$

in which it will be noted that $\hat{R}_3$ does not depend at all on the cost of the 'cheap' finance provided that this does not exceed 13%. The term z^* (1.13) is an opportunity cost due to the fact that the return on x_1 is not earned if $x_3 = 1$. If the cheap finance cost 13.5% then x_1 would never have been worthwhile and $\hat{R}_3$ would have been given by

$$\hat{R}_3 = x_1^*(1.135) + (1,000 - z_1^*)(1.14)$$

which is £1,136 for $z_1^* = 800$. To illustrate further the importance of bounds for requisite yield, append one further constraint to the original problem, namely $x_1 \leqslant 500$. The best alternative values of R are now

$$x_3 = 0 \quad \left.\begin{matrix} x_1 = 500 \\ x_2 = 300 \\ z_1 = 800 \end{matrix}\right\} \quad F = 500(1.13) + 300(1.11) - 800(1.05) = 58$$

$$x_3 = 1 \quad \left.\begin{matrix} x_3 = 1 \\ z_1 = 800 \\ z_2 = 200 \end{matrix}\right\} \quad F = R_3 - 800(1.05) - 200(1.14)$$

therefore $\hat{R}_3 = 500(1.13) + 300(1.11) + 200(1.14) = 1,126$ so that the minimum yield required on the project is 12.6%. That is, the required yield is less than the return on the best alternative investment forsaken (x_1).

5.8 Threshold Size and Specific Alternatives

Suppose that an investment can be varied in scale but there is a smallest possible size if the investment is to be undertaken. That is

either $x_j = 0$

or $\quad x_j \geqslant X_j$

This dichotomy can be accommodated by a means similar to that in the fixed charges problem. For each investment with minimum feasible level include two additional constraints of the form

$$\text{and} \quad \left.\begin{matrix} x_j - M_j w_j \leqslant 0 \\ x_j - X_j w_j \geqslant 0 \end{matrix}\right\} \tag{5.26}$$

where the w_j are two-state, M_j are defined as above and X_j are the minimum positive levels. If $w_j = 0$ then (5.26) restricts x_j to zero. If $w_j = 1$ the first constraint in (5.26) is redundant and the second states that $x_j \geqslant X_j$ as required.

In some problems an investment level may be restricted to zero or certain specific alternative possible values which may not be neighbouring integers. For instance, suppose that there are only three permissible positive values of investment one. Label these values

$$0, x_{11}, x_{12}, x_{13}$$

In the objective function (in place of $N_1 x_1$) write

$$N_{11} x_{11} + N_{12} x_{12} + N_{13} x_{13}$$

and in the constraints (in place of $a_{i1} x_1$) write

$$a_{i11} x_{11} + a_{i12} x_{12} + a_{i13} x_{13}$$

and add the condition that

$$x_{11} + x_{12} + x_{13} \leqslant 1$$

where the coefficients in the objective function are the net present values corresponding to the alternative levels of investment and the constraint coefficient shows resource consumptions corresponding to each level. Finally, add the requirement (in whatever form the particular algorithm requires) that x_{11}, x_{12} and x_{13} are either zero or one.

There may arise cases in which although there are m individually defined constraints only k of these need necessarily hold. Management efforts or 'mobile resources' may be employed to relax $m - k$ of the constraints as required. How can such a possibility be allowed for? The m constraints in familiar form are given by:

$$\sum a_j x_j \leqslant b_i \quad i = 1, 2, \ldots m$$

Now introduce m zero–one variables w_i and the constraint

$$\sum w_i \geqslant k$$

Define numbers M_i such that

$$\sum a_{ij} x_j \leqslant M_i \quad i = 1, 2, \ldots m \tag{5.27}$$

is satisfied in any optimal solution and rewrite the original constraints as

$$\sum a_{ij} x_j \leqslant b_i w_i + M_i (1 - w_i) \quad i = 1, 2, \ldots m \tag{5.28}$$

From (5.28) it is evident that if a particular $w_i = 1$ then the constraint in original form must be observed (it is not relaxed), but if $w_i = 0$ then (5.28) reduces to (5.27) which is ineffective. Note that the constraints (5.28) could be re-expressed in conventional form (with variables on the LHS) as

$$\sum a_{ij} x_j + (M_i - b_i) w_i \leqslant M_i$$

5.9 Branch and Bound

The most important class of computational methods not discussed so far are *branch and bound* methods. Variations on the basic theme can be applied to pure, mixed and zero–one problems. In broad terms the branch and bound approach is as follows.

For each variable required to be integral determine a lower bound and an upper bound on the value of that variable, viz. for x_j integral

$$L_j \leqslant x_j \leqslant H_j \tag{5.29}$$

where L_j and H_j are such that the optimal value of x_j will be included. Usually $L_j = 0$ and H_j need be no greater than the integer at or below $\text{Max}_i(b_i/a_{ij})$. As will be seen if the circumstances of a particular problem allow tighter bounds to be inserted in (5.29), this will diminish computational effort.

Having initially determined the optimal solution to the continuous LP problem suppose that it turns out that in this solution $x_j = 2.5$. Now clearly in the integral optimum either

$$L_j \leqslant x_j \leqslant 2 \tag{5.30}$$

or

$$3 \leqslant x_j \leqslant H_j \tag{5.31}$$

since (5.30) and (5.31) cover all permissible integral valeus of x_j. Now solve separately two LP problems with the original constraints to which is added (5.30) in one case and (5.31) in the other. If both of these problems have an optimal solution integral in the required variables then the integral optimum corresponds to the greater of the two values of the objective function. Usually one or other problem does not have an optimum solution which satisfies all of the integrality requirements. Further iterations are then required. At any stage of these iterations there is a 'master list' of problems which differ in the bounds that are placed on individual variables required to be integral. Problems are selected from and added to the master list as the bounds (5.30) and (5.31) on each variable are revised. When any problem that is solved has an integral optimum the value of the objective function for this solution is recorded. It determines a *lower bound* for the integral optimum objective function. If at some iteration a problem has an optimum solution with objective function value less than or equal to the current lower bound or there is no feasible solution then that branch need not be investigated further. If, on the other hand, a problem has an integral optimum and the value of the objective function is greater than the current lower bound, the lower bound is replaced by the new value. Comparisons cease when the master list is empty. The optimal solution corresponds to the last bound thus obtained.

This approach seems to work well for problems in which there are few integer valued variables. But, if the number of such variables is large or if the solution to the original LP problem is a long way (in terms of the values of the variables in the solutions) from the integral optimum then the number of iterations required may be impractically large. A rather obvious difficulty here is that whilst the former situation can be spotted in advance the latter cannot be. The procedure can be efficiently coded for machine computation without intervention being required. A variation of the procedure can be used to solve all zero–one problems.

In summary, we have examined the various types of integer linear programming problems. They are relevant to consideration of capital-rationing problems whenever all or some of the investment alternatives may take only certain discrete values. We have seen that interpretations of solutions to integer problems is less straightforward than in the linear continuous case—indeed the solutions are much less informative. Of the very many computational approaches possible we selected two: a pseudo-Boolean method for zero–one problems and cutting plane methods for non-zero–one mixed and all integer problems. Of these techniques not detailed the most important are branch and bound methods. On the whole, these are about as successful as the cutting plane approach, but it was not our objective to review all the algorithms in use.

Reference

Hadley, G. (1964), *Non-linear and Dynamic Programming*, Addison-Wesley, Reading, Mass.

Further Reading

Abadie, J. (ed.), *Integer and non-Linear Programming*, North-Holland, Amsterdam, 1970.

Alcaly. R. E., and Klevorick, A. K., 'A note on the dual prices of integer programs', *Econometrica*, **34**, 1966.

Balas, E., *Duality in Discrete Programming: IV Applications*, Management Sciences Research Report No. 195, Pittsburgh: Carnegie-Mellon University, October 1968.

Balinski, M. L., 'Integer programming: methods, uses, computation', *Management Science*, **12**, 1965.

Beale, E. M. L., 'Survey of integer programming', *Operational Research Quarterly*, **16**, 1965.

Cooper, L., and Drebes, C., 'An approximate solution method for the fixed charge problem', *Naval Research Logistics Quarterly*, **14**, 1967.

Faaland, R., 'An integer programming algorithm for portfolio selection', *Management Science*, **20**, Series B, 1973–74.

Geoffrion, A. M., and Marsten, R. E., 'Integer programming algorithms: a framework and state of the art survey', *Management Science*, **18**, Series A, 1972.

Gomory, R. E., 'An algorithm for integer solutions to linear programs', in Graves, R. L. and Wolfe, P. (eds.), *Recent Advances in Mathematical Programming*, McGraw-Hill, New York, 1963.

Hammer, P. L., and Rudeanu, S., 'Pseudo Boolean programming', *Operations Research*, **17**, 1969.

Hirsch, W. M., and Dantzig, G. B., 'The fixed charge problem', *Naval Research Logistics Quarterly*, **15**, 1968.

Jensen, R. E., 'Sensitivity analysis and integer programming', *The Accounting Review*, **1968**.

Kaplan, S., 'Solution of the Lorie–Savage and similar integer programming problems by the generalised Lagrange multiplier method', *Operations Research*, **XIV**, 1966.

Lawler, E. L., and Bell, M. D., 'A method for solving discrete optimisation problems', *Operations Research*, **XIV**, 1966.

Mao, J. C. T., and Wallingford, B. A., 'An extension of Lawler and Bell's method of discrete optimisation with examples from capital budgeting', *Management Science*, **XV**, No. 2, October 1968.

Salkin, H. M., *Integer Programming*, Addison-Wesley, Reading, Mass. 1975.

Trouth, C. A., and Woolsey, R. E., 'Integer linear programming: a study in computational efficiency', *Management Science*, **XV**, Series A, 1968–69.

Wagner, H. M., *Principles of Operations Research with Applications to Managerial Decisions*, Prentice-Hall, Englewood Cliffs, NJ, 1969.

Weingartner, H. M., *Mathematical Programming and the Analysis of Capital Budgeting Problems*, Prentice-Hall, Englewood Cliffs, NJ, 1963.

Weingartner, H. M., 'Capital budgeting of interrelated projects: survey and synthesis', *Management Science*, **XII**, 1966.

Woolsey, R. E. D., 'A candle to Saint Jude, or four real world applications of integer programming', *Management Science Interfaces*, **2**, No. 2, 1972.

Ziemba, W. T., 'A myopic capital budgeting model', *Journal of Financial and Quantitative Analysis*, **1970**.

CHAPTER 6

Distribution and Network Methods in Capital Budgeting

Overview
The technical preliminaries are introduced in sections 6.1–6.4. Section 6.5 gives an investment application in the context of production and movement of goods. Section 6.6 shows that certain capital-rationing problems have a distributional structure. Sections 6.7 and 6.8 give financial applications of the basic transportation model and the transhipment model respectively. Section 6.9 relates critical path method to discounted cash flow in the context of large-scale investment projects with substantial preproduction periods. Section 6.10 develops these arguments further and relates the problems to linear programming. The chapter concludes with a discussion of optimal duration for a project.

6.1 Introduction

Large corporations have a number of geographically separate production plants and trade with customers located in various regions of a country and overseas. Prior to commencement of operations there is the major investment problem of determining the scale and location of plant and buildings. Then, as demand or production conditions change further investment decisions arise as to which plants to invest capital in and to build up and which production facilities to run down. If a company is moving into a new region there will be problems of where to locate production and storage facilities or in which cities to purchase plant and equipment. Such investment problems have a distributional character. Distribution problems are particular cases of linear programming problems but their special structure allows a very efficient computational procedure to be devised. Also it will be shown, later in the chapter, that certain financial problems can be expressed as distribution problems.

Consider an example of a distribution problem. A company has, at present, three factories that produce a single product. The product is supplied to four (potential) customers. Factory one has unit costs of £2 for the product whilst in the newer factories two and three each unit of the product costs only £1 to produce. The entries in Figure 6.1 are cost data

168

(shown negative) and represent the production plus transportation cost per unit from each factory to each customer. For one unit of the product made in factory one and shipped to customer one the cost is £6. This is made up of £2 in production costs and £4 in transportation costs. The remaining entries in this row under columns 2, 3, and 4 are the production costs of £2 plus respectively £3, £1 and £3 transportation costs. The final column gives production capacity figures (for arithmetic convenience these are kept unrealistically small). Rows two and three again show production plus transportation costs from the remaining factories to the four customers. The final row shows the requirements of each customer. The price of the product p is the same to each customer and $p \geqslant 8$. The objective of the firm is the maximization of profits. Shipments from factories to customers will be determined accordingly. The profit per unit shipped from factory to a customer is selling price, p, minus unit production and transportation costs. Total profit is the sum of unit profits times shipments from each source to each destination. It should be noted that the assumption of a common price charged to all customers is not, in fact, restrictive. If the price to customer one was $p + 1$ then the same unit profit position is achieved by considering the price to be p and deducting 1 from the shipment costs.

There are, implicit in the problem, two linearity assumptions. Firstly there are the constant per-unit productive and shipment costs. There are assumed to be no economies or diseconomies of scale in either production or transportation and no divisibility problems. There are also assumed to be no 'externalities'. On the demand side it is being assumed that each customer will take any size of shipment (up to the amount entered in the demand row) at the going price. It is also assumed that price is invariant with respect to quantity taken.

The problem is clearly a linear programming problem and could be written as follows:

$$\text{maximize } F = \sum_i \sum_j (p - c_{ij}) X_{ij}$$

$$\text{subject to} \quad \left. \begin{array}{ll} \sum\limits_j x_{1j} \leqslant 10 & \sum\limits_i x_{i1} \leqslant 6 \\[2mm] \sum\limits_j x_{2j} \leqslant 8 & \sum\limits_i x_{i2} \leqslant 12 \\[2mm] \sum\limits_j x_{3j} \leqslant 14 & \sum\limits_i x_{i3} \leqslant 8 \\[2mm] & \sum\limits_i x_{i4} \leqslant 8 \\[2mm] x_j \geqslant 0 & \end{array} \right\} \qquad (6.1)$$

where x_{ij} represents the amount produced at factory i and sent to customer j.

From \ To	Cust. 1	Cust. 2	Cust. 3	Cust. 4	Supply capacity
Factory 1	-6	-5	-3	-5	10
Factory 2	-2	-7	-6	-4	8
Factory 3	-4	-8	-5	-3	14
Demand	6	12	8	8	

Figure 6.1

It would be possible to solve the problem (6.1) using the Simplex method in tableau form. This would be extravagant. It will be noted that the set of technical coefficients in the problem consists only of zeros and ones; with the vast majority being zeros. Consequently, it is not surprising that the tableau Simplex method can be bettered for problems of this type, although the method to be described is itself a disguised version of the Simplex procedure.

6.2 The Modified Distribution Method

The method of solution begins by making supply equal demand. If, as in the present example, it is demand that exceeds supply an additional row is introduced to make up the deficit. There are no costs associated with the 'dummy' factory (prohibitions on supply to certain customers can be introduced). When supply equals demand the problem is said to be one in *balanced rim conditions*. Since the problem is an LP problem the optimal solution will be a basic solution and the first requirement is to find a star-

	1	2	3	4	
1	-6	-5 ②	-3 ⑧	-5	10
2	-2 ⑥	-7 ②	-6	-4	8
3	-4	-8 ⑥	-5	-3 ⑧	14
4	0	0 ②	0	0	2
	6	12	8	8	34 Total / 34

Figure 6.2

ting basic solution. Such a a solution is shown in Figure 6.2. Circled numbers in the squares represent *assignments*—values of the x_{ij}; for example $x_{32} = 6$, $x_{13} = 8$ and so on. Since $x_{42} = 2$ customer 2 will receive in total only 10 of the 12 units that he would be prepared to take. The sum total of costs associated with this solution,

$$\sum_i \sum_j x_{ij} C_{ij}$$

is

$$2.5 + 8.3 + 6.2 + 2.7 + 6.8 + 8.3 + 2.0 = 132.$$

If we now suppose that $p = 10$ the value of F for the solution will be

$$10 \sum_{i=1}^{3} \sum_{j=1}^{4} x_{ij} - 132 = 10.32 - 132 - 188$$

It will be observed that only seven of the x_{ij} are not zero although there are eight constraints including the constraint for the fourth row $\sum_j x_{4j} \leqslant 2$. This does not mean that the solution is degenerate. The constraints are *linearly dependent*—there are only seven independent constraints. In general, if there are m rows and n columns a basic solution will have no more than $m + n - 1$ positive assignments.

To begin with, any basic solution is determined, then an optimality check is made. If the solution is not optimal a new variable is introduced at positive level and a move is made to a neighbouring basic feasible solution. This process is repeated until the optimum is reached.

The next task is therefore to check the starting solution for optimality. This is done by seeing if there are any neighbouring basic solutions that would improve the objective function. If x_{11} is set at unit level the consequent adjustments in the existing assignments are shown in Figure 6.3.

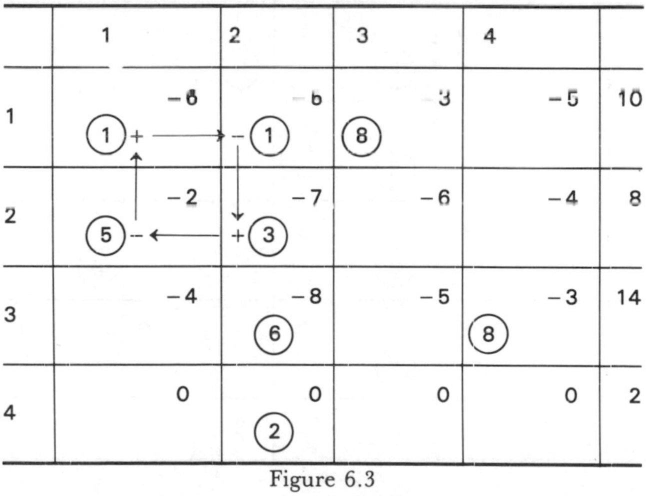

Figure 6.3

It is as if one unit had been shifted round the arrowed path; x_{11} and x_{22} increasing and x_{12} and x_{21} decreasing as indicated by the signs. Such a 'closed path' begins and ends at the same square. Has the readjustment of assignments via the closed path improved F? Revenue is unchanged but costs are altered. One unit is now shipped to customer 1 from factory one at a cost of £6, one more unit shipped from two to 2 thus adding £7 to costs here, but since x_{12} and x_{21} are both decresed by one there are savings of £5 and £2 respectively. The net change is therefore $+ 6 + 7 - 5 - 2 = 6$ so that the rearrangement adds to costs and is not worth while. There is a rapid evaluation procedure for unused routes. It is as follows. To each row and column a number, u_i for a row v_j for a column, is determined such that at each *assignment square* i, j $u_i + v_j = - c_{ij}$.

It is convenient to write in the u_i and v_j to the left of each row and at the head of each column respectively. Once that has been done, as shown in Figure 6.4 these row and column numbers can be used to determine the improvement potential of each vacant square in the solution. One u_i or v_j may be arbitrarily set (by convention $u_i = 0$).

The process of evaluation of the vacant squares is as follows. For each vacant square determine the number e_{ij} given by

$$e_{ij} = u_i + v_j + c_{ij}$$

The sign of e_{ij} indicates whether or not improvement is possible. The magnitude (if negative) gives the size of the per-unit improvement in the objective function as a result of the introduction of x_{ij} into the solution. The e_{ij} are in fact the index row numbers for the x_{ij} if the Simplex method of computation had been employed. Thus the e_{ij} are the evaluations that would be arrived at by use of individual closed paths for each square. The

	$v_1 = 0$	$v_2 = -5$	$v_3 = -3$	$v_4 = 0$	
$u_1 = 0$	-6	-5 (2)	-3 (8)	-5	10
$u_2 = -2$	-2 (6)	-7 (2)	-6	-4	8
$u_3 = -3$	-4	-8 (6)	-5	-3 (8)	14
$u_4 = +5$	0	0 (2)	0	0	2
	6	12	8	8	34

Figure 6.4

e_{ij} are as follows:

square:
$$1, 1 = \quad 0 + 0 + 6 = +6$$
$$1, 5 = \quad 0 + 0 + 5 = +5$$
$$2, 3 = -2 - 3 + 6 = +1$$
$$2, 4 = -2 + 0 + 4 = +2$$
$$3, 1 = -3 + 0 + 5 = +1$$
$$3, 3 = -3 - 3 + 5 = -1$$
$$4, 1 = +5 + 0 + 0 = +5$$
$$4, 3 = +5 - 3 + 0 = +2$$
$$4, 4 = +5 + 0 + 0 = +5$$

Thus only x_{33} has a negative index row number and will be made positive in the next solution to improve F. The evaluations would remain the same, if, say, u_3 had been set equal to an arbitrary constant M. The 'M components' of the u_i and v_j cancel out in each evaluation. Also, the evaluation of each assignment square must be zero.

Once the direction of improvement has been found in the above manner the MODI method proceeds to 'route round' the closed path the maximum amount. As soon as a solution has been found in which $u_i + v_j + c_{ij} \geqslant 0$ for all i,j an optimum has been reached. The solution of Figure 6.5 is optimal with $u_1 = 0$, the remaining row and column numbers are $u_2 = -2$, $u_3 = -2$, $u_4 = +5$, $v_1 = 0$, $v_2 = -5$, $v_3 = -3$, $v_4 = -1$ and each vacant square evaluation is accordingly positive.

It will be noted that the solution is also integral. The structure of distribution problems is such that provided the RHS of the constraints are integers all basic solutions will be integral. Unfortunately, this integrality

	$v_1 = 0$	$v_2 = -5$	$v_3 = -3$	$v_4 = -1$	
$u_1 = 0$	-6	-5 ⑧	-3 ②	-5	10
$u_2 = -2$	-2 ⑥	-7 ②	-6	-4	8
$u_3 = -2$	-4	-8 ⑥	-5 ⑧	-3	14
$u_4 = +5$	0	0 ②	0	0	2
	6	12	8	8	

Figure 6.5

property of the solutions to distribution problems cannot be exploited to provide a useful algorithm for integer problems generally.

The relationship of MODI to the Simplex method proper can be highlighted via the dual problem. Omitting the revenue side of the objective function the distribution problem can be stated as

$$\text{maximize}\, F = -\Sigma c_{ij}x_{ij}$$

subject to $\qquad \sum_j x_{ij} = s_i \forall i$

$$\sum_i x_{ij} = D_j \forall j$$

$$x_{ij} \geqslant 0 \forall i, j$$

(where the symbol ∀ means 'for all') and it will be recalled that the formulation of the problem we are using here is for balanced rim conditions. The dual problem is to:

Minimize $G = \sum_i u_i s_i + \sum_j v_j d_j$

subject to $\qquad u_i + v_j \geqslant -c_{ij} \forall ij$

$$u_i, v_j \text{ unrestricted}$$

since equality constraints in a primal problem imply corresponding dual structural variables of unrestricted sign. For a variable that is basic, the corresponding dual constraint is satisfied as a strict equality. Thus for all $x_{ij} > 0$, $u_i + v_j = -c_{ij}$. That is, $u_i + v_j + c_{ij} = 0$ which are precisely the conditions used to determine the row and column numbers above. Consequently the u_i and v_j are the shadow prices of the problem. In any LP problem the index row numbers of the primal beneath the x_{ij} are the values of the dual slack variables ($u_i + v_j + c_{ij}$) and are therefore the evaluations of squares. In a non-optimal solution to the primal problem the corresponding dual solution is infeasible (dual slacks are not unrestricted), and some of the evaluations are negative.

An improvement of the solution procedure would be effected if a starting solution could be found in 'reasonable' time that was on average superior to casual inspection. Vogel's approximation method (VAM) provides such a solution (Reinfeld and Vogel, 1958). For each row and column determine the difference between the two smallest c_{ij}-figures and attach these numbers to the row and columns. Select that row or column with the greatest such number and assign as much as possible to the square with lowest c_{ij} in that row/column. For our example problem the result is shown in Figure 6.6.

Column 2 has the largest VAM number and the smallest c_{ij} element is zero in the dummy row (remember that the data in the tableau are $-c_{ij}$). The maximum assignment that can be made to this square is two. No further assignments can be placed in row 4. At each stage of the VAM pro-

VAM Nos.	2	5	3	3	
2	−6	−5	−3	−5	10
2	−2	−7	−6	−4	8
1	−4	−8	−5	−3	14
0	0 X	0 (2)	0 X	0 X	2
	6	12	8	8	

Figure 6.6

cedure *maximal* assignments will be made being the smallest of the two figures—remaining supply and remaining demand in the row and column of the square selected. The row or column fulfilled is temporarily deleted and the process repeated—ignoring the deleted row/column. In the example row 4 is deleted and new VAM numbers calculated. These, and the next assignment are shown in Figure 6.7. There is a five-way tie for the row or column to be chosen next. One tie-breaking rule is that the assign-

	2̶ 2	5̶ 2	3̶ 2	3̶ 1	
2	−6 X	−5	−3	−5	10
2	−2 (6)	−7	−6	−4	8
1	−4 X	−8	−5	−3	14
0̶	0 X	0 (2)	0 X	0 X	2
	6	12	8	8	

Figure 6.7

ment is made to the square with the lowest c_{ij} in all of the tied rows/columns. This is square (2, 1) and the greatest assignment possible here is six. This causes column 1 to be deleted and leaves two units of supply remaining in row 2. In the next application there is again a five-way tie and the assignment of eight was accordingly made to square (1, 3) and column three deleted. The next assignment is eight to square (3, 4) deleting column 4 and the remaining assignments follow of necessity. The solution obtained turns out to be the original solution of Figure 6.2.

6.3 Sensitivity Analysis

Consider cost changes. If a cost figure in a vacant square alters then this will not affect the u_i and v_j since these are determined only by the assignment squares. All that is affected is the evaluation of the vacant square itself. If the cost changes by Δ_{ij} then the evaluation also changes by Δ_{ij}, no other squares are affected. When the cost at an assignment square alters this is equivalent to a change in the objective function coefficient of a basic variable. The u_i and v_j are affected and the evaluation of many vacant squares may change. All that is required is to recalculate the u_i and v_j for the new cost data. If it emerges that some vacant squares now show improvement, one is selected and the solution procedure reapplied.

As an example, suppose that in the context of the original problem price to customers, one, three and four was raised by £1 and price to customer two was reduced by £1 whilst all costs increased by 10%. The resultant changes in coefficients and the u_i v_j are shown in Figure 6.8.

The original solution remains optimal. It should be noted that the financial entries int he squares are no longer the $-c_{ij}$ throughout since not

	$v_1 = 0$	$v_2 = -7.5$	$v_3 = -3.3$	$v_4 = -1.1$	
$u_1 = 0$	-6.6	-7.5 ⑧	-3.3 ②	-5.5	10
$u_2 = -2.2$	-2.2 ⑥	-9.7 ②	-6.6	-4.4	8
$u_3 = -2.2$	-4.4	-10.8	-5.5 ⑥	-3.3 ⑧	14
$u_4 = 5.5$	0	-2 ②	0	0	2
	6	12	8	8	

Figure 6.8

all customers are now charged the same price. The entries are $-(c_{ij} - \Delta p_j)$ where Δp_j is the deviation for the jth customer, from the maximum price charged to any customer.

The original problem was to maximize $\Sigma_i\Sigma_j(p - c_{ij})x_{ij}$. The term $\Sigma_i\Sigma_j p x_{ij} = p\Sigma_i\Sigma_j x_{ij} = p\Sigma_j d_j$ being a constant would not influence the optimality calculation. Consequently, in the tableau only the c_{ij} appeared and $\Sigma_i\Sigma_j - c_{ij}x_{ij}$ was maximized. When prices are different between customers the objective function of the problem can be expressed as:

$$\text{maximize } F = \sum_i \sum_j (p_h - c_{ij} - \Delta p_j)x_{ij}$$

where p_h is the highest price obtained from any customer and the Δp_j are the amounts below this price charged to individual customers. Except for the dummy row, the data in Figure 6.8 are the terms $-(c_{ij} + \Delta p_j)$ where $\Delta p_j = 2$ for $j = 2$ and $\Delta p_j - 0$ otherwise. The term $p_h\Sigma_i\Sigma_j x_{ij} = d p_h$ being constant. In the original problem coefficients of zero were used in the dummy row. We could equally well have used coefficients of $-p$. There are no costs or revenues associated with dummy assignments. For $i = 4$ the objective function coefficients should, strictly, be zero. Since $c_{4j} = 0 \; \forall \; i$ we should write $\Sigma_i(p - c_{4j} - p)x_{4j}$ for the fourth row. However, adding a constant to the objective function coefficients in any row or column will not change the optimal solution and p was added throughout the dummy row.

In general, if k_j is added to the ofcs in the jth column and r_i added to the ofcs in the ith row the objective function becomes

$$F^* = \sum_i \sum_j (p + k_j + r_i - c_{ij})x_{ij}$$

so that

$$F^* = \sum_i \sum_j (p - c_j)x_{ij} + \sum_i \sum_j k_j x_{ij} = \sum_i \sum_j r_i x_j$$

but

$$\sum_i k_j x_{ij} = k_j d_j \qquad \text{therefore} \qquad \sum_j \sum_i k_j x_{ij} = \sum_j k_j d_j = \text{constant}$$

similarly since

$$\sum_j r_i x_{ij} = r_i s_i, \qquad \sum_i \sum_j r_i x_{ij} = \sum_i r_i s_i = \text{constant}$$

so that

$$F^* = \sum_i \sum_j (p - c_{ij})x_{ij} + \text{constant}$$

and the optimal x_{ij} are unchanged. Consequently, in Figure 6.8 in the second column the coefficients -5.5, -7.7, -8.8, 0 could have been used and the optimal solution would have been unaffected. Note that if the constant $+2$ is added to the coefficients in the second column only v_2 changes, becoming -5.5. All the u_i and the remaining v_j are unaltered as are all of the vacant square evaluations.

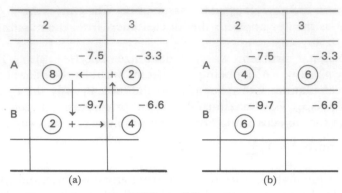

Figure 6.9

Now consider changes in the rim conditions. Suppose that there is a 'balanced' change in supplies and demands. By 'balanced' it is meant that the change in demand is equal to the change in supply. For instance let demand from customer 3 increase to 12 units and supply at plant B increase to 12 units. How can these changes best be accommodated?

For convenience, work with the financial data of Figure 6.8. The procedure is first to assign the amount of the increase in supply to the customer whose demand has also increased. Thus an assignment of four would be made in square (2, 3). There are now more assignments than necessary, but the (2,3) assignment can readily be eliminated by routing it round a closed path which initially consists entirely of assignment squares. The steps are shown in Figure 6.9 (a) and (b). Only the relevant part of the array is reproduced here, the other assignments being unchanged.

The 'new' solution must be optimal since the u_i and v_j will be unchanged. The cost of handling each such extra unit in a balanced increase for row i and column j is $u_i + v_j$ provided that the original basis does not become infeasible. An even simpler case would be where the square at the intersection of the row and column concerned was already an assignment square. All that would be required here is an increase in the assignment so conveniently located.

Balanced changes involving more than one supplier and demander can be dealt with in a similar fashion. Firstly the extra allocations are made, secondly the number of assignments is reduced to $m + n - 1$ and thirdly feasibility is restored. Not all of these steps will be necessary in each case. Unbalanced changes can be accommodated by adjustment of dummy demand and supply levels.

6.4 Transhipment Problems

Transhipment problems are distribution problems in which 'goods' may be moved through intermediate locations (i.e. transhipped). The 'goods' may be physical commodities or, as we shall see, money.

Consider the case of a retailing chain that has stores at six different locations. At present although the total amount of stocks of a certain commodity that the company has is satisfactory the distribution between stores is not as desired and a redistribution is planned. In Figure 6.10 each numbered circle represents a store and the figures alongside each store represent the excess (if positive) or deficiency (if negative) in stocks of the item that are held by the store. Thus for instance store No. 1 has a surplus of 6 units, store No. 5 requires 7 units while the stock position at store No. 4 is as desired. Movements of stock may proceed in the directions indicated by the arrows and the c_{ij} figures show the cost of moving one item of stock between adjacent stores. Note that stocks can move either way between stores 4 and 3, but we are not assuming that the costs of movement are the same in each direction.

In the tableau described here a row is designated for each 'source' and a column for each 'sink'. A 'source' is a point which has positive supply and cannot be used as a transhipment point—it is a 'pure' supply point. Thus store 1 is a source but store 3 is not. A 'sink' is a 'pure' demand point; being the end of a line. Store 6 is thus a sink. In general there may be several sources and sinks in a problem. In the rim conditions the s_i figure for a source is its supply and the d_j figure for a sink is its demand. For each transhipment point both a row and column is assigned. Now let p_k represent the initial net stock level of transhipment point k. If point k is a supply point then $p_k > 0$, if it is a demand point than $p_k < 0$. In the rim conditions we set the s_k figure at $p_k + T$ and the d_j figure at level T where T is the total therefore 10 units. Note that the net figure for point k is p_k. The reason that T is added to both supply and demand figures (one of which would otherwise be zero) is that the store may have to handle up to $p_k + T$ units due to a possible transhipment function. The device prevents negative entries in the tableau. Finally, positive x_{ij} (for $i \neq j$) are permitted only as allowed by the arrows in the original network. Thus x_{24} may be positive but x_{42} must be zero; prohibitive cost figures being entered accordingly.

The tableau layout and optimal solution are shown in Figure 6.11. Zero cost entries will be noted at the junction of the kth row and kth col-

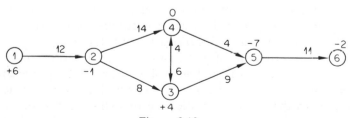

Figure 6.10

	2	3	4	5	(Sink) 6	
(Source) 1	−12 ⑥	−M	−M	−M	−M	6
2	0 ④	−8 ⑤	−14	−M	−M	9
3	− −M	0 ⑤	−4 ⑨	−9	−M	14
4	−M	−6	0 ①	−4 ⑨	−M	10
5	−M	−M	−M	0 ①	−11 ②	3
	10	10	10	10	2	

Figure 6.11

umn. Prohibited movements between adjacent points are ensured with M cost figures which are also attached to the intersection of rows and columns corresponding to non-adjacent points. The remaining c_{ij} entries are the original data. Establishment of u_i and v_j values reveals the optimum to be unique.

6.5 Investment in Plant Capacity

We shall now examine the application of the techniques developed in this chapter to problems in which a capital element is explicitly identified. In this section, investment problems set in the physical context (production and movement of goods) of transportation are considered. Firstly the problem of adjusting the sizes of existing plant is considered. This is a case of running down or increasing capacity at plants to meet changing demand (and more generally cost) conditions. Then the problem of altogether new plant at new locations is considered.

Consider the problem of expansion or contraction of production capability of existing factories. The problem is one of optimal investment in new equipment or disinvestment in existing facilities. Consider a simple example. In the original problem of this chapter two units less than the demand limit were supplied to customer two. Suppose that management wished to rectify this situation by expanding capacity at some factory by two units. Assume for the moment that the capital costs of the expansion at all factories would be zero. The objective is to supply two more units to customer 2 from a real source at lowest variable cost.

The u_i and v_j are shadow prices and for arbitrary Δd_j (changes in demand) and Δs_i (changes in supply) the minimum change in the dual (and hence the primal) objective function is $\Sigma_i u_i \Delta s_i + \Sigma_j u \Delta d_j$. Thus for a given set of Δd_j the least cost changes in supply to meet this changed demand are found by minimizing $\Sigma u_i \Delta s_i$ such that the 'appropriate' u_i and changing supply there by $\Sigma_j \Delta d_j$. For a net demand increase the appropriate u_i and changing supply there by $\Sigma_j \Delta d_j$. For a net demand increase the appropriate u_i is the greatest value. In our example we are setting $\Delta d_j = 0 \, \forall j$. Also, we wish to eliminate supply from the dummy source and so set $\Delta s_4 = -2$, consequently since $\Sigma_i \Delta s_j = 0$ then $\Sigma_{i=4} \Delta s_i = 2$. The values of the u_i in the solution were $u_1 = 0$, $u_2 = -2$, $u_3 = -2$ and $u_4 = +5$. Therefore it is optimal to increase supply at factory one. The increase in total cost will be $\Sigma_i - u_i \Delta s_i = 10$ and the increase in profits will be $2p - 10$. Consequently, production capacity should remain unchanged at factories two and three. There would be an *opportunity loss* of $2(u_2 - u_1)$ if capacity at factory two had been expanded instead.

The question of capital costs can now be considered. Suppose that the capital costs of expansion of capacity at each plant had been, K_1, K_2, K_3 respectively and that the supply and demand figures represent weekly flows. If these flows are aggregated over an interest compounding period of n weeks and the relevant interest rate is $100i\%$ the choice is between three projects that can be compared on a NPV basis. The return in each compounding period (consisting of n of the time units for which supply and demand figures are given) in the case of factory 1 would be $n(2p - 10)$ and in the case of factories 2 and 3 the return is $n(2p - 14)$. The choice between 2 and 3 would be trivial (depending only on the outlays) if the expanded capacity at both plants had the same life expectancy.

However, suppose that the new capacities at each location have different lifetimes. Investments at the three locations represent mutually exclusive alternatives and the one with the greatest NPV will be selected. The respective net present values can be calculated from a simple formula. If an investment gives a constant return R at the end of each of T years, with an interest rate of $100i\%$ then the gross present value is given by

$$\text{GPV} = R \left[\frac{1 - (1 + i)^{-T}}{i} \right] \tag{6.2}$$

so that in the present context the choice is between the NPVs as given in (6.3), where the respective lifetimes are T_1, T_2 and T_3 years.

$$n(2p - 10) \cdot \frac{1 - (1+i)^{-T_1}}{i} - K_1$$

$$n(2p - 14) \cdot \frac{1 - (1+i)^{T_2}}{i} - K_2 \qquad\qquad (6.3)$$

$$n(2p - 14) \cdot \frac{1 - (1+i)^{-T_3}}{i} - K_3$$

The next illustration concerns the choice of factory location at the planning stage of operations. Suppose a company wishes to get established in a region or country and has a range of alternative sites for production facilities. Assume that the locations of the demand points are predetermined but that the company has a number of possible sites at which to locate factories. How can the company arrive at the set of optimal factory locations? The problem is combinatorial in character and several subproblems may have to be solved. The first step, however, would be to eliminate the dominated locations. This is a trivial exercise once the relevant information has been assembled. Location X dominates location Y if costs per unit (production and shipment) at Y are greater for every destination than at X.

Several questions remain, including those of how many factories to build and where to locate them amongst the non-dominated alternative sites. To simplify the illustration assume that technological considerations dictate that the maximum production capacity at a factory in any location

Factory / Customer		$v_1 = -9$ 1	$v_2 = -5$ 2	$v_3 = -5$ 3	$v_4 = -11$ 4	$v_5 = 0$ 5	
$u_1 = 0$	1	-10	-5 (80)	-7	-15	0 (20)	100
$u_2 = +1$	2	-8 (30)	-12	-4 (70)	-14	0	100
$u_3 = 0$	3	-9 (20)	-6	-14	-12	0 (80)	100
$u_4 = +1$	4	-11	-4 (40)	-9	-10 (60)	0	100
$u_5 = 0$	5	-10	-6	-6	-12	0 (100)	100
		50	120	70	60	200	

Figure 6.12

is 100 and that there are five possible locations. Demand from each of four customers are, respectively, 50, 120, 70 and 60 units. Figure 6.12 gives the production plus transportation costs and the optimal solution to the problem where 'fixed' capital costs (the total of initial outlays) are assumed to be independent of the number of factories established. Selling price is assumed to be the same from each factory and the fifth column is the dummy customer taking up the 200 units of slack capacity.

Several results are apparent. Although only three plants are needed to supply existing customer demand, four are called for in the transportation solution. Location 5 is apparently undesired and location 1 would produce only at 80% whilst 3 has 80% unutilized capacity in the current solution. Now unless rapid expansion of demand is envisaged, if capital costs are anything near to realistic levels only three plants will be desired initially. The static decision problem where a demand of 300 is to be satisfied is how to accomplish this optimally with three plants. If capital costs differ between plant locations the problem is considerably more complicated than if capital costs are the same everywhere.

First consider the differing capital costs case. From Figure 6.12 it would appear that location 5 can be eliminated; but this is not the case as the 6.12 solution has not considered capital costs. It may well turn out that plant at 5 is not optimal but we cannot say so yet. As was mentioned earlier the problem is combinatorial and unless a rather involved integer programming formulation is employed the 5C3 = 10, possible combinations of three plants from 5 will have to be solved as separate subproblems and NPVs calculated from expression similar to those in (6.3). Although such an exercise would be rather tedious by hand it would of course take little time by computer and would certainly be a worthwhile exercise to eliminate possibilities.

One useful piece of information can readily be obtained Figure 6.12 however, and that is an upper bound (not necessarily the least upper bound in general) on the increase in variable costs of the three-plant optimum over the four-plant solution. Notice that the evaluation of vacant square 1, 1 is only + 1 and that routing 20 units round the corresponding closed path would produce a three-plant (1, 2 and 4) feasible solution (albeit degenerate) with total production plus distribution costs only 20(= 20 × 1) per 'supply and demand' period greater than in the four-plant solution.

If capital costs and lifetimes are the same in all locations, then the 1 2 4 three-plant solution is in fact optimal. This can be seen without solving the ten subproblems in the following way. Notice that no vacant square evaluation is less than + 1. This means that *any* reassignment of one unit from the solution of Figure 6.12 will cost at least one unit of money per supply and demand period. Further, at least 20 units must be reassigned from the solution of Figure 6.12 to effect a three-plant solution (in which there must be precisely two positive entries in the dummy column). Therefore 20 is the least possible increase in variable costs and the 1 2 4 solution must be an optimum. In fact 1 2 4 is the unique optimum since every other three-plant departure from the solution of Figure 6.12 must involve reassignment of more than 20 units.

6.6 Capital Rationing Problems of Distributional Form

In this section and sections 6.7 and 6.8 we examine investment problems that are set in the mathematical, rather than physical, context of transportation problems. Since distribution problems are a special class of linear programming problems, and since capital-rationing problems can be expressed in linear programming form, it is not surprising to discover that some special types of capital-rationing problem can be expressed in distributional form. Consider an example.

An individual can invest in three types of security: 'savings certificates', 'inflation bonds' and other dated stocks. A three-year horizon is adopted with a view to maximizing terminal value. The securities can be purchased at $t = 0$, $t = 1$ or $t = 2$. The yields would be as follows:

	Yield to $t = 3$ if acquired at		
	$t = 0$	$t = 1$	$t = 2$
Savings certificates (x_{t1})	16%	15%	14%
Inflation bonds (x_{t2})	15%	15%	15%
Dated stocks (x_{t3})	14%	13%	12%

Securities purchased at any date are retained until $t = 3$. The Government allows each individual a maximum of 100 (financial units of) savings certificates and 100 units of inflation bonds. There is no limit on purchases of other dated stocks. The investor's available funds are 75 units at $t = 0$, 90 at $t = 1$ and 115 at $t = 2$. All available funds in any year will be used in that year. Expressed as a capital rationing problem in linear programming form we have

maximize

$$F = (1.16)^3 x_{01} + (1.15)^3 x_{02} + (1.14)^3 x_{03} + (1.15)^2 x_{11}$$
$$+ (1.15)^2 x_{12} + (1.13)^2 x_{13} + (1.14) x_{21} + (1.15) x_{22} + (1.12) x_{23}$$

subject to

$$
\begin{aligned}
x_{01} + x_{11} + x_{21} && \leqslant 100 \\
x_{02} + x_{12} + x_{22} && \leqslant 100 \\
x_{01} \quad\quad + x_{02} \quad\quad x_{03} && = 75 \\
x_{11} \quad\quad + x_{12} \quad\quad x_{13} && = 90 \\
x_{21} \quad\quad + x_{22} \quad\quad + x_{23} && = 115
\end{aligned}
$$

$$x_{01} \geqslant 0,\ x_{11} \geqslant 0,\ x_{21} \geqslant 0,\ x_{02} \geqslant 0,\ x_{12} \geqslant 0,\ x_{22} \geqslant 0,\ x_{03} \geqslant 0,$$
$$x_{13} \geqslant 0,\ x_{23} \geqslant 0$$

(6.4)

	Certificates	Bonds	Stocks	
$t=0$	1.56 ⑦⑤	1.52	1.48	75
$t=1$	1.32 ㉕	1.32 ㉖	1.28	90
$t=2$	1.14	1.15 ㉟	1.12 ⑧⓪	115
Dummy	0	0	0 ⟨200⟩	200
	100	100	280	

Figure 6.13

The problem (6.4) *could* be solved by the Simplex method, but the sparse nature of the matrix of technical coefficients should suggest that superior methods might be available. The fact that all technical coefficients are either zero or one and the way that the constraints divide up point to the possibility of a distributional layout. The only problem appears to be the absence of a restriction on dated stocks purchase. This can be met by inserting a redundant upper bound for this column and a dummy row as shown in Figure 6.13. Objective function coefficients have been rounded to two decimal places and remain as positive numbers in the cells since the problem is one of maximization. As before, negative vacant square evaluations show improvements. The optimum is non-unique as insertion of u_i and v_j values will indicate. An alternative way of presenting the dual solution is shown in Figure 6.14. Here, the entries in the cells are the vacant square evaluations. The non-uniqueness is evident from the zero

	1.56		1.52		1.48
0		0.04		0.08	
	1.32		1.32		1.28
0		0		0.04	
	1.14		1.15		1.12
0.01		0		0	
	0		0		0
0		0		0	

Figure 6.14

entries in cells 4, 1 and 4, 2. The values of the dual structural variables, u_i and v_j can be determined from the vacant square evaluations and objective function coefficients. As regards the evaluations themselves, purchase of one financial unit of stocks at $t = 0$ will carry a penalty of 0.08 of a financial unit at $t = 3$.

In general, capital-rationing problems that may be expressed in distributional format require that a unit of each investment can be defined so that each investment requires one financial unit (a convenient multiple of the basic unit of currency) at one point in time only. Transferability of funds from one time period to another within the horizon is a counter-indication, but the effects of this possibility can be examined in the context of sensitivity analysis by comparison of the relative magnitudes of the u_i.

6.7 Holding Company Financing Problem

It is possible to formulate certain financing problems in the form of distribution problems. Consider the following example. A holding company owns three firms A, B and C. Each firm is at the point of requiring capital inputs of amounts 140, 70 and 90 capital units respectively. The holding company can obtain funds from three sources. It can issue shares in each of the companies held which will represent differing costs to existing shareholders in the holding company depending on the 'risk class' of the individual firm. There is an overall limit (imposed by the holding company) of 100 units of finance raised by equity issue. In addition, debt may be increased by up to 80 units and the holding company has 120 units of retained earnings available. Figure 6.15 shows this financing problem and its solution in a distributional format.

	Firm A	Firm B	Firm C	Sums available
Equity	− 15 (90)	− 20	− 14 (10)	100
Debt	− 12	− 15	− 10 (80)	80
RE	− 8 (50)	− 8 (70)	− 8	120
Requirements	140	70	90	300 / 300

Figure 6.15

In the figure, the cost entries are the costs to the holding company of finance for the three firms from the different sources and 'assignments' represent the amounts to be raised from each source for each firm. The intention of this example is not to suggest that all problems of sourcing finance are so conveniently formulated. A number may, however, have a number of characteristics which allow of a distributional expression. Typically, financing problems will have the structure of more complicated programming problems and indeed, ideally, the problems of optimal sources and uses of funds should be examined simultaneously. This will not always be possible, but occasionally computational techniques originally designed for quite different management applications can suit the structure of simplified financing problems. In section 6.8 an application of distribution methods to a short-term investment problem is given. The problem is considerably more involved than the example that has just been studied, but it has the character of that special class of distributional problems known as transhipment problems.

6.8 A Short-term Investment Model

V. Srinivasan (1973–74) has produced an intriguing application of distributional methods in the area of cash management. The problem of cash management '. . . is concerned with optimally financing net cash outflows and investing net inflows of a firm while simultaneously determining payment schedules for incurred liabilities'. The operational research approach to this problem has been two-pronged; inventory based models have been suggested and linear programming formulations have been produced. Srinivasan's model uses the approach of Orgler (1970), but with a distributional formulation and solution procedure. In the model four major types of decision variable are distinguished: payment schedules, short-term financing, securities transactions and the cash balance. The objective in the model is to minimize net cost (taking into account timings of receipts and payments) from the cash budget over the planning horizon. The optimization is, of course, subject to constraints (of an interperiod nature) on the decision variables.

The unusual feature of Orgler's model is that the period lengths are unequal, ranging from one day to three months in the illustration to follow. This device enables the day-to-day aspects of cash management to be taken into account without producing a model of impracticable size. In use, at the end of the first (day length) period the model is recomputed so that only the period one decisions are actually implemented but the longer-run implications of these decisions have been taken into account. Srinivasan employed the same numerical example as Orgler (for comparative purposes) but with a distributional formulation that provides greatly increased computational efficiency. Six time periods are considered. The lengths are as follows:

Period No.	Length (days)
1	1
2	1
3	10
4	20
5	60
6	90

Within this time structure decisions are to be made regarding the following:

(i) The payment schedules for predicted purchases in all periods.
(ii) The transactions to be made on the portfolio of securities that is held by the firm at the start of the planning period.
(iii) The extent of any new investments in marketable securities.
(iv) The use (or non-use) of credit facilities available to the firm.

In order to set up the tableau it is necessary to specify:

(a) The total number of sources of funds (in total P).
(b) The total number of uses of funds (in total Q).
(c) The amounts available at each of the sources (represented by a_i where $i = 1, 2 \ldots P$).
(d) The amounts required at each of the uses (i.e. the 'demands' represented by r_j where $j = 1, 2 \ldots Q$).
(e) The cost of putting one dollar from source i to use j (represented by c_{ij}).

These are the data requirements. With x_{ij} representing the amount of the ith source that is allocated to use j, the problem can be expressed as

$$
\left.
\begin{array}{l}
\text{minimize} \quad \displaystyle\sum_{i=1}^{P}\sum_{j=1}^{Q} c_{ij}x_{ij} \\[2em]
\text{subject to} \quad \displaystyle\sum_{j=1}^{Q} x_{ij} = a_i \quad (i = 1, 2, \ldots P) \\[2em]
\displaystyle\sum_{i=1}^{P} x_{ij} = r_j \quad (j = 1, 2, \ldots Q) \\[2em]
x_{ij} \geqslant 0 \quad \forall \quad i, j
\end{array}
\right\}
\qquad (6.5)
$$

In addition to the constraints of (6.5) prohibitions may be incorporated in the usual manner, viz. if source i may not be employed for use j then $c_{ij} = M$. Cash may represent a supply, for instance in the making of payments and a destination as when securities are sold to generate cash. Consequently, cash will appear in both rows and columns. In Figure 6.16 the first six rows correspond to sources of cash and the first six columns represent uses of cash in each of the periods. Rows 7–12 correspond to securities held by the firm at the start of the planning period, each having a different maturity date. For instance the unit entry in the availabilities column, seventh row corresponds to a security of $10,000 which matures at the end of the first period and so provides a sum of $10,000 available for use during the second period. It will be noted that row 12 corresponds to a security of $500,000 face value which matures after the end of the sixth period (i.e. beyond the horizon). All but the first security can be sold prior to the maturity date. Row 13 corresponds to an 'open line of credit' of $2,500,000 that may be drawn on, if desired. Row 14 is a dummy and denotes uses not satisfied during the time horizon. The figure of $1,000,000 entered in this availability column is arbitrary and can be shown not to affect the optimal solution. It is inserted so that optimum cash balance can be easily determined, otherwise it could be deleted since the model does not allow accounts payable to be postponed beyond the horizon.

The accounts payable (again in units of $10,000) are shown in the requirements row, columns 7–12. Column 13 is a dummy representing unused sources and corresponds to securities that are allowed to mature beyond the horizon and line of credit not being fully utilized. The requirement level r_{13}, shown as $6,470,000 is determined so as to balance the rim conditions, i.e.

$$\sum_{i=1}^{14} a_i - \sum_{j=1}^{13} r_j$$

The determination of this value for r_{13} comes after all the other rim conditions have been entered in. Before the rim conditions can be completed we shall need to examine the cost data. The solution is akin to that of determining the RHS of the constraints in capital rationing models. The figures that we ended up with there depended on the rate of interest at which funds may be transferred from one period to another. 'Shipments' from sources $i = 1, 2, \ldots 6$ to uses $j = 2, 3, \ldots 6$ and 13 with $i < j$ represent investments in marketable securities. For example if the firm invests $1 of first period cash in a security which matures at the beginning of the sixth period it receives 1.2 cents interest. All 'cost' figures are given in cents and are negated in our format. Investing $1 in the second period in a security which matures beyond the horizon earns 2.4 cents interest; hence the entry of 2.4 dummy column 13 row 2.

Squares with $j < i$ and $i = 2, 3, \ldots 6$ correspond to the taking of short-term loans. An assignment in square $(4, 2)$ would correspond to the taking of a loan at the beginning of period two and paying back at the start of period four. Provision is not made in the model for such loans and a figure of $-M$ is entered in squares with $j < i$ and $i = 2, 3, \ldots 6$. Where $i = j$ an assignment would represent a shipment from a cash source to a cash use hence $c_{ij} = 0$ for $i = 1, 2, \ldots 6$.

The c_{ij} for $i = 7, 8, \ldots 12$ relate to sales of securities in the initial port-

Uses Sources	Cash 1	2	3	4	5	6	Accounts Payable 7	8	9	10	11	12	Slack 13	
1	0 (2945)	0.01 (25)	0.025 (30)	0.16	0.40	1.20	2.0	-M	-M	-M	-M	-M	2.4	3,000
2	-M	0 (3000)	0.01	0.15	0.40	1.20	2.0	2.0	-M	-M	-M	-M	2.4	3,000
3	-M	-M	0 (2992)	0.13	0.40	1.20	2.0 (5)	2.0 (3)	2.0	-M	-M	-M	-M	3,000
4	-M	-M	-M	0 (2900)	0.26	1.06	0	0	2.0 (40)	2.0 (60)	-M	-M	2.26	3,000
5	-M	-M	-M	-M	0 (3000)	0.8	-M	-M	0	0	2.0 (150)	-M	2.1 (440)	3590
6	-M	-M	-M	-M	-M	0 (3000)	-M	-M	-M	-M	0	2.0 (570)	1.2 (85)	3,655
7	-.02	0 (1)	-M	-M	-M	-M	-M	-M	-M	-M	-M	-M	-M	1

							12	5	10	25	50	250	100
8	−0.04	−0.02	0 (12)	−M	−M	−M	−M	−M	−M	−M	−M	−M	−M
9	−0.21	−0.19	−0.17 (5)	0	−M	−M	−M	−M	−M	−M	−M	−M	−M
10	−0.50 (10)	−0.50	−0.50	−0.33	0	−M	−M	−M	−M	−M	−M	−M	−M
11	−1.5 (25)	−1.5	−1.5	−1.33	−1.0	0	−M	−M	−M	−M	−M	−M	−M
12	−3.0 (50)	−3.0	−3.0	−2.83	−2.5	−1.5	−M	−M	−M	−M	−M	−M	0
13	−3.6	−3.58	−3.56 (23)	−3.38 (205)	−3.0	−1.8	−M	−M	−M	−M	−M	−M	0 (22)
14	−M	−M	−M	−M	−M	−M	−M	−M	−M	−M	−M	−M	0 (100)
	3,030	3,025	3,062	3,105	3,000	3,000	5	3	40	60	150	570	647

Securities

Credit

Slack

Figure 6.16

folio prior to maturity. These costs are interpreted by Srinivasan as losses in yield—which will in general be uncertain so that expected values would have to be used. The actual nature of these c_{ij} in any situation depend upon the particular circumstances. For instance if no interest payments are due on the securities (as might be the case if interest is paid at six monthly intervals) the c_{ij} would represent discounts. It would seem desirable to keep data on an actual cash flow basis wherever possible. Since securities cannot be sold after they have matured cost figures of M are entered for all post-maturity periods for each security. Accounts are paid only from cash hence $c_{ij} = M$ for $i = 7, 8, \ldots 12$ and $j = 7, 8, \ldots 12$.

The remaining c_{ij} relate to cash-to-accounts payable assignments and credit. A 2% discount is assumed to apply if accounts are settled within 10 days. If payment is made within 10–30 days there is no discount. It is assumed accounts may not be settled beyond 30 days (the maximum period of trade credit here). Accordingly, entries of 2, 0 and $-M$ are made in squares ij for $i = 1, 2, \ldots 6$ and $j = 7, 8, \ldots 12$.

Row 13 corresponds to the line of credit on which loans can be obtained at the beginning of any period repayable after one year. Monthly simple interest is charged at 0.6%. Early repayments are prohibited. The c_{ij} for $i = 13, j = 1, 2, \ldots 6$ show the interest charges until the horizon. Accounts are settled only in cash hence $c_{13j} = M$ for $j = 7, 8, \ldots 12$. Since all credit need not be used $c_{13\,13} = 0$. In this problem all accounts payable must be settled within the horizon so that the dummy source 14 may ship only to the dummy use, 13. Thus $c_{14j} = 0$ for $j = 1, 2, \ldots 12$ and $c_{14\,13} = 0$.

We can now return to complete the rim conditions. We need data for availabilities at sources $1, 2, \ldots 6$ and requirements at use $1, 2, \ldots 6$. In this example the net exogenously determined cash flows are expected to be $-300,000$, $-260,000$, $-620,000$, $-1,050,000$ $+5,900,000$ and $+6,550,000$ in each of the periods respectively. Initial cash balance is 90,000 so that with maturing securities of 10,000 in the first period the initial cash balance may be regarded as 100,000. Now, the minimum cash balance that is to be held at any time is 100,000 and this is treated by subtracting it from the initial balance to get a zero figure. As Srinivasan points out, it is as if the initial cash balance is set aside to meet the minimum cash balance requirement.

'Cash' in all the periods represent transhipment points. Cash may be moved around from one period to another (in this case not backwards in time) as goods may be moved from one store to another (with certain prohibitions). In obtaining the a_i and r_j figures for rows 1–6 and columns 1–6, Srinivasan has simply added a large number (30,000,000) to the exogenously determined cash supply or demand. This is a minor variation on the device that we suggested in the previous section ($a_k = p_k + T$, $r_k = T$). Note that if this technique had been used with $T = 30,000,000$ the s_i figures would have been 2,970, 2,974, 2,938, 2,895, 3,590 and 3,655 respectively while all d_j figures (for columns 1–6, that is) would have been

3,000. In this case all that would have changed are the 'i to i' notional transhipment figures on the diagonal up to $i = 6$; no real cash transfers would have been affected. To complete the rim conditions r_{13} is determined so that

$$\sum_{i=1}^{14} a_i = \sum_{j=1}^{13} r_j$$

thus $r_{13} = 647$.

The solution is interpreted as follows. The accounts payable billed in periods $1, 2, \ldots 6$ are paid in full in periods 3, 3, 4, 4, 5 and 6 respectively. For example $x_{37} = 50,000$ and $x_{6,12} = 5,700,000$. Credit is drawn upon to the tune of 230,000 at the start of period three ($x_{13,3} = 230,000$) and 2,050,000 at the start of period four ($x_{13,4} = 2,050,000$). The securities maturing in periods 5 and 6 and beyond the horizon are sold in the first period; those maturing in period four are sold in period three whilst the remainder are allowed to mature. In the first period amounts of 250,000 and 300,000 are invested in securities maturing in the second and third periods respectively ($x_{12} = 250,000$ and $x_{13} = 300,000$). In the fifth and sixth periods 4,400,000 and 850,000 are invested in securities that mature beyond the horizon.

Since the problem is in distributional format sensitivity analysis may readily be undertaken. The dual solution is shown in Figure 6.17 in which the entry (a_{ii}) in each square is the sum of row and column numbers (the u_i and v_j of previous acquaintance) associated with each square. Consider the effect of having one more unit of cash in period 1. The result would be to decrease the optimum value of the objective function (i.e. reduce cost) by 3.58 cents. The appropriate d_{ij} is $d_{1,13} = +3.58$ since one more unit of cash would increase the requirement of the slack use. The extra cash helps by reducing the amount borrowed from the line of credit in period three (saving 3.56 cents) and yields 0.02 cents from investment in securities from periods 1–3.

In respect of accounts receivable by the firm some initial assumption regarding the use of credit facilities by the firm's customers must be made. Suppose payment of accounts receivable was one month beyond the due date, then $d_{45} = +1.28$ shows the effect of tightening credit policy so that bills due in period 4 (which would normally have been paid in period 5) are paid in period 4. This will increase the cash source in period 4 at the expense of period 5, it is as if the *use* in period 5 had increased. The net effect is an improvement of 1.28 in the objective function.

The d_{ij} from $j = 1, 2, \ldots 6$ with $i <$ bring out the effects of short-term loans if these were available. For instance $d_{35} = +1.46$ shows that if a loan could be obtained at the start of period 3 and repaid at the start of period 5 total cost would be reduced by 1.46 cents. This would be an alternative to the line of credit facility and determines the maximum acceptable monthly interest rate (1.46%) that would be attractive over this period.

Sources \ Uses		Cash					Accounts payable						Slack
	1	2	3	4	5	6	7	8	9	10	11	12	13
Cash 1	0	+0.01	+0.02	+0.20	+1.48	+2.38	+2.02	+2.02	+2.20	+2.20	+3.48	+4.38	+3.58
2	-0.01	0	+0.01	+0.19	+1.47	+2.37	+2.01	+2.01	+2.19	+2.19	+3.47	+4.37	+3.57
3	-0.02	-0.01	0	+0.18	+1.46	+2.36	+2.00	+2.00	+2.18	+2.18	+3.46	+4.36	+3.56
4	-0.20	-0.19	-0.18	0	+1.28	+2.18	+1.82	+1.82	+2.00	+200	+3.28	+4.18	+3.38
5	-1.48	-1.47	-1.46	-1.28	0	+0.90	+0.54	+0.54	+0.72	+0.72	+2.00	+2.90	+2.10
6	-2.38	-2.37	-2.36	-2.18	-0.90	0	-0.36	-0.36	-0.18	-0.18	+1.10	+2.00	+1.20
Securities 7	-0.01	0	+0.01	+0.19	+1.47	+2.37	+2.01	+2.01	+2.19	+2.19	+3.47	+4.37	+3.57
8	-0.02	-0.01	0	+0.18	+1.46	+2.36	+2.00	+2.00	+2.18	+2.18	+3.46	+4.36	+3.56
9	-0.19	-0.18	-0.17	+0.01	+1.29	+2.19	+1.83	+1.83	+2.01	+2.01	+3.29	+4.19	+3.39
10	-0.50	-0.49	-0.48	-0.30	+1.98	+1.88	+1.52	+1.52	+1.70	+1.70	+2.98	+3.88	+3.08
11	-1.50	-1.49	-1.48	-1.30	-0.02	+0.88	+0.52	+0.52	+0.70	+0.70	+1.98	+2.88	+2.08
12	-3.00	-2.99	-2.98	-2.80	-1.52	-0.62	-0.98	-0.98	-0.80	-0.80	-0.48	+0.38	+0.58
13	-3.58	-3.57	-3.56	-3.38	-2.10	-1.20	-1.56	-1.56	-1.38	-1.38	-0.10	+0.80	0
14	-3.58	-3.57	-3.56	-3.88	-2.10	-1.20	-1.56	-1.56	-1.38	-1.39	-0.10	+0.80	0

The d_{ij} in the fourteenth row for $j = 7, 8, \ldots 12$ show the effects on the minimal level of costs resulting from increasing the accounts payable (note that slack supply will be increased to balance the increase of the requirement r_j). Total cost would increase if these accounts payable were to increase since 'to pay the accounts payable due in period 1, for instance, a loan is obtained from the line of credit costing 3.56 cents/$ so that even after subtracting the discount of 2.0 cents/$ there is a net cost of 1.56 cents/$. However, $d_{14,12} = +0.8$ cent since the 2.0 cents/$ discount on accounts payable is more attractive than the yield of 1.2 cents/$ obtainable by investing in securities maturing beyond the horizon. The effect of postponing purchases so that accounts payable currently due in, say, the third period would be due only in, say, the sixth period is given by $+ d_{14,9} - d_{14,12} = -2.18$ cents/$. A simultaneous decrease of r_9 and increase of r_{12} is equivalent to simultaneous decrease of (a_{14}, r_9) and an increase of (a_{14}, r_{12}). Finally, note that since $d_{13,13} = 0$ increasing the line of credit limit would not reduce optimal cost.

Advantages of the distributional layout are that it may be more attractive to management (and therefore find wider use) than the LP formulation due to its 'inherent simplicity and intuitive appeal'. The approach is also attractive computationally, being 'more efficient by a factor of about 30 to 1 than the linear programming formulation of the problem. Since the model is to be recomputed daily the savings involved would be substantial.' The sole disadvantage of the transhipment formulation is that it is considerably less flexible (than the LP version) in incorporating institutional constraints on average cash balances, financial ratios, etc. If more than one such constraint was to be included 'one would have to resort to decomposition techniques with such constraints constituting the master problem and the transhipment formulation defining the subproblem'. Along with the LP approach the transhipment model requires systematic setting down of data, constraints and objectives: '...the financial manager needs to state in tabular form the varous sources and uses of funds and their timing and provide the amounts and the unit costs involved. Thus, the transhipment formulation serves as a very useful tool in organizing data in management information systems for financial control.'

In addition to the cases that we have examined in this section and sections 6.6 and 6.7, certain network problems can be formulated as distributional problems and therefore solved by distributional methods. Of particular interest in this respect is a network cash flow problem shortly to be described. The dual of this problem has the form of a transportation problem and distribution methods could be applied to its solution. Although useful insights may be gleaned by such an exercise a 'network flow' approach is more efficient as a solution procedure. The next section begins a description of these methods.

6.9 Discounted Cash Flow in Project Networks

The method of network analysis play an important part in the management of complex construction and assembly projects. The Critical Path Method (CPM) and its variants are also of value in the appraisal of such projects. In this section we explore the relationship between the critical path method and DCF methods. The essential feature of CPM is in the representation of a project in network form. The various jobs that comprise the project are linked together in a diagram which makes clear the order relationships between the jobs. CPM finds the longest—timewise—path through the network (the *critical* path) the 'float' or spare time is available in jobs and considers the problems of time reductions cost savings and resource usage. This section illustrates how a project network diagram helps in providing cash flow data and timings.

In lengthy investment projects—for which CPM is essential—several outflows of capital will be involved and the timing of the outflows will be important from both the liquidity and present value standpoints. There will also be important cash inflows at various stages of the operation representing payments for part completion, or income resulting from partial operation of plant and equipment. Consider an example. Figure 6.18, the *dependency table*, lists the fourteen distinct jobs that go to make up a certain manufacturing and assembly project. Jobs a and b represent materials collection and erection of plant whilst jobs c, f, g, and h, d, and i, e and j, represent fabrication of components. Jobs k and l are sub-assembly operation and job m represents final assembly and inspection while jobs m and n corresponds to testing and delivery. The information in the dependency table is put into network form in Figure 6.19. The vertical line segments represent the jobs. The circles are 'nodes' or 'events' which mark the completion of one task and the commencement of another. In this particular diagramatic scheme the length of the vertical

Job description	label	Duration (weeks)	Capital input	Completion payment	Weekly variable costs	Preceding job
Assemble materials	a	10	150		10	
Erect plant	b	20	150	250	10	a
Component 1	c	20	100	300	10	b
Component 2	d	15	100	75	10	b
Component 3	e	20	100	225	10	b
Component 4	f	40	200	100	10	c
Component 5	g	10	50	175	10	f
Component 6	h	10	100	650	10	g
Component 7	i	15	100	250	10	d
Component 8	j	15	150	450	10	e
Sub-assembly 1	k	10	250	125	10	i, j
Sub-assembly 2	l	20	75	150	10	k
Final assembly	m	25	250	500	10	h, l
Delivery	n	15		2,000	10	m

Figure 6.18

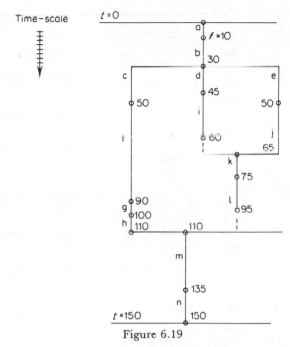

Figure 6.19

lines is proportional to the job durations. The broken lines show the amounts of *free float* in jobs i and l—the delay possible in a job such that the earliest time at which a succeeding job can begin is not affected.

The capital outlays and receipts of income associated with jobs are shown in the dependency table in units of £1,000. Data in the capital input column give capital expenditures consequent upon the commencement of each individual job. When each job is completed a payment is received from the customer. These sums are shown in the completion payments column. In the next column data for weekly variable costs are per job, so that if three jobs are being undertaken simultaneously weekly variable costs are £30,000.

In Figure 6.20 the cash flow pattern is deduced from the financial data of the project table and the network diagram of Figure 6.19. Column 1 of Figure 6.20 shows the outlays required at various times. For instance at $t = 30$ outlays of £100,000 are required on each of the jobs c, d and e; so that the total cash outflow at this time is £300,000. Column 2 of the figure shows the timing of completion payments. For example at $t = 50$ completion payments of £525,000 are due in: £225,000 for job e and £300,000 for completion of job c. Column 3 shows weekly variable costs aggregated over five-week periods. For example at $t = 35$ the bill for variable costs is £150,000 relating to expenses on three jobs (c, d and e) over a five-week period. Column 4 [$= 2 - (1 + 3)$] shows net cash flow for each value of t. For example at $t = 45$ there is a net outflow of £175,000, being £75,000—(£100,000 + £150,000).

t	1	2	3	4	5		6	7
0	150		50	−200				
5			50	−50				
10	150		50	−200				
13					(1)	−458.3	0.9709	−445.0
15			50	−50				
20			50	−50				
26					(2)	−102.0	0.9426	−96.1
30	300	250	50	0				
35			150	−150				
39					(3)	−151.4	0.9151	−138.6
40			150	−150				
45	100	75	150	−175				
50	350	525	150	+25				
52					(4)	−302.4	0.8885	−268.7
55			150	−150				
60		250	150	+100				
65	250	450	100	+100	(5)	+47.7	0.8626	+ 41.1
70			100	−100				
75	75	125	100	−50				
78					(6)	−152.2	0.8375	−127.5
80			100	−100				
85			100	−100				
90	50	100	100	−50				
91					(7)	−254.0	0.8131	−206.5
95		150	100	+50				
100	100	175	50	+25				
104					(8)	+76.3	0.7894	+ 60.2
105			50	−50				
110	250	650	50	+350				
115			50	−50				
117					(9)	+254.0	0.7664	+194.7
120			50	−50				
125			50	−50				
130			50	−50	(10)	−151.7	0.7441	−112.9
135	5	500	50	+450				
140			50	−50				
143					(11)	+408.0	0.7224	+294.7
145			50	−50				
150		2,000	50	+1,950				
156					(12)	+1,925.7	0.7014	1,350.7
							Σ=	+546.1

Figure 6.20

As regards discounting, assume that interest is compounded quarterly at the rate of 3% per quarter and that the first compounding is at $t = 13$. Column 5 brings the cash flow items forward to the next compounding point. The procedure here is one which could be adapted in any capital budgeting problem in which cash flows arise in between compounding points. It proves to be convenient to alter the cash flows to an equivalent stream of flows occurring at the compounding points. Then discount factors can be applied to this adjusted pattern of cash flows in the familiar fashion. Consider the first entry in column 5. In present value terms, a single outflow of 458.3 at the end of the first quarter is equivalent to the individual flows of 200 out at once plus 50 out after 5 weeks plus 200 out after 10 weeks. The initial -200 is carried forward at the full 3% and so would become $-200(1 + 0.03)$ at $t = 13$. The next outflow, of 50 at $t = 5$ occurs with 8/13 of the first quarter still to go. Thus the interest on this sum will be 8/13 of 3%, so that the -50 is brought forward to $t = 13$ as $-50\{1 + (8/13)0.03\}$. Finally the -200 flow at $t = 10$ occurs with 3/13 of the initial quarter remaining and so is equivalent to -200 $\{1 + (3/13)0.03\}$ at $t = 13$. All this is summarized as

$$-458.3 = -200(1 + 0.03) - 50\left(1 + \left(\frac{8}{13}\right)0.03\right) - 200\left(1 + \left(\frac{3}{13}\right)0.03\right)$$

Further applying this procedure, the equivalent cash flow at the second compounding points is given by

$$-102.0 = -50\left(1 + \left(\frac{11}{3}\right)0.03\right) - 50\left(1 + \left(\frac{6}{13}\right)0.03\right)$$

and so on for the remaining entries in column 5. Column 6 shows the present value factor associated with each compounding point. Column 7 ($= 5 \times 6$) then gives the present value of each item in the modified cash flow. Net present value is the sum of entries in column 7 and is £546,100.

Frequently in cases where CPM is employed the question arises of time savings and the speeding up of jobs. When substantial cash flows are involved the present value consequences of time changes will need to be considered. Thus it may be that although it costs money to speed up some particular job, the fact that this brings forward a substantial cash inflow may 'pay' for the speeding up in present value terms. In respect of time savings in jobs, it is important whether or not a job is 'critical'. The critical jobs are those on the longest path from start to finish. In this case the critical path consists of jobs a, b, c, f, g, h, m, n. The non-critical jobs are d, e, i, j, k, l.

First consider increases or decreases in the durations of non-critical jobs. These will not affect the overall completion time and will also have unchanged the cash flow items associated with critical jobs. To the extent that such time changes are discretionary their desirability will be determined solely by the effects on NPV. If jobs i and l, for instance, are speeded up then the completion payments associated with them are brought forward. NPV must increase on this account. If the increase in NPV as a result of the earlier payments for completion exceeds the present value of the increases (if any) in variables costs for the jobs speeded up, then (assuming that there are no deleterious effects on other jobs) the speeding up is worth while. For example suppose that job l is speeded up so that it is completed in 15 weeks instead of 20. The effect of this change is twofold. Firstly, the completion payment for l would be received at $t = 90$ instead of $t = 95$. Secondly, the weekly variable costs during the 15 weeks now required for the completion of job l may be changed. Let us suppose that variable costs for l are the same overall, viz. 200. This would mean $13\frac{1}{3}$ per week for each of the 15 weeks. Throughout this period from $t = 75$ to $t = 90$ one other job is being worked on which incurs weekly variable costs of 10. Thus, weekly variable costs now total $23\frac{1}{3}$ that is $116\frac{2}{3}$ per five-week period. The entries in column 3 for $t = 80$, 85 and 90 will now be $116\frac{2}{3}$ instead of 100. From $t = 90$ to $t = 95$ only one job will now be worked on so that variable costs for this period will be 50. This is the new $t = 95$ entry in column 3. In column 2 the $t = 95$ entry of 150 is deleted that the $t = 90$ entry is increased to 250. The change in NPV will therefore be

$$\left[-16\tfrac{2}{3}\left(1 + \left(\frac{11}{13}\right)0.03\right) - 16\tfrac{2}{3}\left(1 + \left(\frac{6}{13}\right)0.03\right) - 16\tfrac{2}{3}\left(1 + \left(\frac{1}{13}\right)0.03\right) \right.$$

$$\left. + 150\left(1 + \left(\frac{1}{13}\right)0.03\right)\right]0.8131 + \left[+50\left(1 + \left(\frac{9}{13}\right)0.03\right)\right.$$

$$\left. - 150\left(1 + \left(\frac{9}{13}\right)0.03\right)\right]0.7894 = 0.449$$

Now suppose that a *critical* job is speeded up. There are two possibilities here. Either the start times of subsequent jobs can be brought forward or some free float (equal to the time saving) is introduced for that particular job. Subsequent jobs are not automatically started earlier (unless a time constraint is to be met) since in general the effect on NPV is not known *a priori*. Ideally, alternative possibilities in the earlier starting of subsequent groups of jobs would be evaluated in terms of their effects on NPV. That rearrangement of start times which gave the maximal increase in NPV could then be adopted. This is a combinatorial problem and for large systems enumeration may be infeasible. Fortunately, in many practical problems by far the largest cash inflow will occur at the completion of the last job, as is the case in the current illustrative example, and the bringing forward of this item may be expected to dominate any adverse effects on NPV resulting from earlier capital expenditures at the commencement of preceding jobs. Alternatively, there may be only a small number of rearrangements of start times, which are possible for resource availability reasons, in which case evaluation of each rearrangement might prove to be feasible.

Suppose that a technical innovation allowed the completion of job f in 20 weeks instead of 40. The extreme alternatives are (a) to bring the start and completion of g and h forward by 20 weeks and the start of m and n forward by 15 weeks and (b) to allow 20 weeks of slack in f itself and start subsequent jobs on the critical path at the existing times. Between these extrema are compromise possibilities of allowing some slack in the critical path from f and completing n sooner by an amount of $\Delta_t < 15$ weeks. Clearly, the earlier payment of the substantial cash inflows presently scheduled for $t = 100$, $t = 135$ and $t = 150$ will dominate other considerations and alternative (a) brings the greatest improvement in NPV.

The possibility may arise of *rescheduling* jobs so as to improve NPV. Present-value favourable reschedulings do not necessarily imply time reductions overall although in practice this will often be the case. Also, there may arise the questions of delay penalties for late completion and bonuses for early delivery. The problem is one of choosing from a potentially large number of possible combinations without the possibility of expressing the objective *a priori* as a function of the possible courses of action. If the number of alternatives is small then enumeration is feasible, but otherwise fairly cavalier assumptions and simplifications may be called for.

6.10 Network Cash Flow and Linear Programming

The problem confronting the investor may be one of choosing between a number of mutually exclusive 'projects' corresponding to different timings or alternative schedulings of the original project. So far we have discussed the relationship between project networks and present value and shown how the network layout can be used to assess changes in present value in very restricted cases. Two questions remain to be considered. Firstly, can an optimizing algorithm be developed, and secondly, is such an algorithm likely to be useful on problems of practical size where the number of alternatives is large? Taking the second question first, there does not exist at present, nor is there likely to exist in the near future, an exact optimizing algorithm for present value maximization in large networks with many alternative timings and schedulings. At the end of this section we shall mention some practical possibilities for such cases.

To answer the first query, consider the problem as a programming problem for a very small network. Suppose that there are just three real jobs (labelled 1, 2, 3) with additional jobs 0 (representing the imaginary job 'start' which precedes all other jobs) and 4 (the imaginary 'finish' job, succeeding all other jobs). The system is described in the dependency table of Figure 6.21 and reproduced in the arc–node diagram of Figure 6.22. The length of the job lines has no significance in this type of diagram.

Suppose now that cash flows are associated with the occurrence of the events. For example, event 2 represents the completion of job 1 and the

Job	Predecessor	Duration
0	—	d_0
1	0	d_1
2	0	d_2
3	1	d_3
4	2, 3	d_4

Figure 6.21

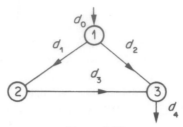

Figure 6.22

start of job 3. The cash flows at event 2 would, in the context of earlier illustrations correspond to the completion payment for job 1 and the initial outlay on job 3. With the arc–node network we can replicate any of the networks so far considered by suitable use of 'dummy' jobs. By suitable definition of jobs, cash flow items that are essentially of variable-cost nature could be made to correspond to nodes. Otherwise regular or minor cash flows may be aggregated or treated separately in an approximation approach if regular day-to-day cash flows were more or less independent of the important capital items.

Let R_i be the cash flow (positive or negative) that is associated with node i. In general the objective function would be given by (6.6)

$$V = \sum_{i=1}^{n} R_i W_i \tag{6.6}$$

where V represents NPV to be maximized. In (6.6) the W_i are discount factors determined by the rate of interest, the time of occurrence of the nodes and the nature of the compounding process. Note that V is a non-linear function of the event times t_i. In the example network the t_i observe the following restrictions (in which d_4 is assumed to take the value zero):

$$\left.\begin{array}{l} t_0 = d_0 \\ t_2 = t_1 + d_1 \\ t_3 \geqslant t_1 + d_2 \\ t_3 \geqslant t_2 + d_3 \end{array}\right\} \tag{6.7}$$

Suppose that individual job times may be varied continuously between lower and upper limits. That is

$$d_j^L \leqslant d_j \leqslant d_j^U \quad \text{for} \quad j = 0, 1, 2, 3 \tag{6.8}$$

For different values of the d_j the critical path may change, but (6.7) must always be observed. On the basis of (6.8) let d_j^* be the difference between actual job time and minimum job time for each job. Thus

$$d_j^* \geqslant 0$$
$$d_j^* \leqslant d_j^U - d_j^L \tag{6.9}$$

and the constraint set can be written as

$$
\left.
\begin{aligned}
t_1 + d_0^* &= d_0^L \\
t_2 - t_1 - d_1^* &= d_1^L \\
t_1 - t_3 + d_2^* &\leqslant -d_2^L \\
t_2 - t_3 + d_3^* &\leqslant -d_3^L \\
d_0^* &\leqslant d_0^u - d_0^L \\
d_1^* &\leqslant d_1^u - d_1^L \\
d_2^* &\leqslant d_2^u - d_2^L \\
d_3^* &\leqslant d_3^u - d_3^L \\
d_j^* &\geqslant 0 \quad \text{for} \quad j = 0, 1, 2, 3
\end{aligned}
\right\}
\tag{6.10}
$$

Now let us reconsider the objective function. If the discrete compounding process is used in (6.6) then an integer programming formulation of the problem is necessary. To avoid this eventuality assume that the compounding process is continuous, so that (6.6) may be written as

$$
V = \sum_{i-1}^{n} R_i e^{-rt_i}
\tag{6.11}
$$

If the compounding process is in fact discrete then in (6.11) we shall have made the first of two approximations. In comparison with the next approximation to be made, that in (6.11) is very minor. As an aside, it is worth noting that (6.11) could equally well have been written as

$$
V = \sum_{i=1}^{n} R_i (1 + s)^{-t_i}
\tag{6.12}
$$

where for any value of the interest rate s in (6.12) we can choose r in (6.11) such that $r = \log_e(1 + s)$ so tht (6.11) and (6.12) are equivalent.

The next stage is to develop a linear approximation to (6.11). In Figure 6.23 the declining curve graphs $V_i = R_i e^{-rt_i}$, t_i' is a 'current' value for t_i (to be further discussed shortly) and the straight line represents a linear approximation to R_i. In fact, as the linear approximation to be used here, we shall take the tangent of the V_i function at t_i'. Now the value given by the tangent, $\hat{V}_i$, will, except at t_i' itself always understate V_i. At first glance this does not seem good and it might appear preferable to use a line, such as that in Figure 6.23 which at $t_i = t_i'$ is above V_i. However, only the slope of the linear approximation is important, the position of the line relative to the origin provides a constant term in the approximated objective function and so does not affect the outcome of the maximization exercise. Use of the tangent was suggested by Russell (1970).

Russell pointed out that provided the optimal event times were sufficiently close to the current times t_i' then the approximation is valid. The computational approach is one of successive approximations in which a series of linear programming problems are solved. If—for the moment—

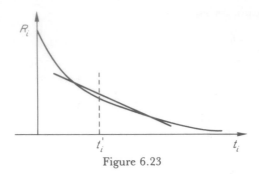

Figure 6.23

we envisage a one-stage procedure (which may be indicated for very large networks) in respect of the accuracy of the approximation we recall that a procedure is justified if it improves on what otherwise would have been done. Once an optimum has been attained with the approximated objective function the true value of V can be obtained by substitution of the event times into (6.11). This will determine (and, hopefully, verify) that an improvement has been effected.

The current event times t_i' correspond to a feasible solution to the constraint set (6.10). Assuming that such a solution has been obtained, the approximated objective function can be worked out. The present value of the cash flow associated with an individual event i is approximated as the equation of the tangent to V_i at t_i' being the linear terms in the Taylor expansion of V_i about t_i'.

$$\hat{V}_i = R_i e^{-rt_i'} + rt_i' R_i e^{-rt_i'} - rt_i R_i e^{-rt_i'} \tag{6.13}$$

Given t_i' and the interest rate, r, the first two terms in (6.13) are constants and we shall call their sum R_i^*. Labelling $R_j e^{-rt_i'}$ as R_i' the approximation to (6.11) is

$$\hat{V} = \sum_{i=1}^{n} \hat{V}_i = \sum_{i=1}^{n} R_i^* - r \sum_{i=1}^{n} t_i R_i' \tag{6.14}$$

The problem is now expressed as a continuous linear programming problem in which a maximum of (6.14) is sought subject to (6.10). In some problems it may be necessary to add an upper bound on the last event time to the constraint set (6.10). Apart from time, feasibility requirements if R_n is sufficiently large and negative PV may be maximized by setting t_n at $+\infty$.

Where computational facilities permit, it would be possible to extract a more accurate answer by the following procedure. Beginning with a feasible set of values for the t_i', form the objective function (6.13) and optimize. The resulting values of the t_i become the t_i' in the objective function of the next problem—and so on until the solution converges. Although convergence will occur in a finite number of steps in this procedure it is not clear how rapid this convergence process is in practice. We have seen the magnitude of problems that can arise in this connection in integer programming. Further, only convergence on a local optimum is guaranteed which is usually as much as can be expected of approximation procedures. However, Russell (1970) suggests a special computational procedure which appears promising. 'There should be no difficulty in solving maximum present value network problems involving several hundred nodes and arcs in a matter of a few minutes judging by Ford and Fulkerson's results.' The Simplex method would not represent a very efficient means of solution since it does not exploit the special structure of the problem at all. Russell suggests a method using a fluid flow interpretation of the dual problem.

An important conclusion of the study of network cash flow problems is that the time-critical path may not be particularly important in financial terms. To quote Russell: 'It has been shown that the critical path may not be very cost significant but that there exists a cost-critical tree of activities to each of which a marginal cost of lengthening the duration may be ascribed.' Interpreted in the context of the constraint set (6.10) there will emerge shadow prices associated with the RHS of the constraints. The shadow prices will be the present value implications of marginal alternations to the bounds on job durations. The cost of altering an optimal job duration that falls strictly within the given bounds can also be determined. In terms of an LP formulation, this latter value will be given by the sum of products of rates of exchange (in the row of the duration being altered) and corresponding index row numbers.

There is considerable scope for further research in the network cash flow area, and as Russell points out the possible applications are almost as numerous as are the applications of CPM/time. In particular Russell cites six types of problem:

(i) The pricing of delays in contractual situations.
(ii) The optimum timing of logically dependent investments.
(iii) The avoidance of payment structures which positively discourge the early completion of a project.
(iv) The identification of 'cost-critical' jobs during progress of a contract.
(v) The optimum timing of major projects in a developing national economy.
(vi) The use of the 'duration price' as the criterion for resource allocation decisions in time-cost trade-off problems.

We shall go some way to answering questions raised by (i) and (iii) in the next section.

6.11 Optimum Project Duration

In this section the question of delay penalties first raised in section 6.9 is taken up. In an earlier chapter we considered optimal delay in a project of *fixed* duration. But suppose that there is some 'temporal elasticity' in the project; how many years and months should be spent on a large construction task? To begin to answer the question it is useful to divide costs into those which increase with time and those for which $dc/dt < 0$. Into the former category would fall 'indirect' costs; costs of administration, financing, hire of plant and equipment, rent, etc. The 'direct' costs, attributable unambiguously to particular tasks would generally fall into the latter category. How can these different characteristics be optimally reconciled?

First consider the direct costs (we shall include all costs with $dc/dt < 0$ under this heading) for the project as a whole. Beginning by doing each job the long, cheap way and finding the critical path obtain one pair of values for project time and total direct costs. The objective here is to obtain the graph of total direct costs against time and in principle we should like to find the cheapest way of saving each unit of time. This problem can be formidable and the following approximate procedure is suggested. Consider just two possible times for each job—normal (cheap) time and crash (costly) time. Begin with each job assumed to be done the normal way and find what would be total cost and the critical path. Now crash the cheapest (in terms of 'crashing') job on the CP. Find the new level of total direct cost and time and the new CP. Now crash the cheapest job on this path and so on. By this means (or by an LP approach in smaller problems) time/direct cost data is obtained and a possible graph of direct costs against time can be produced. If an investment decision is being taken (whether or not to undertake the project) the cost data may be put in present value form.

A plausible shape for a graph of the present value of direct costs against time is shown in Figure 6.24 (a) while Figure 6.24 (b) shows a possible graph of the present value of total indirect costs against time. Whilst we should not conclude that discounted indirect costs are necessarily a linear function of time, a monotonic increasing relationship is to be expected. In Figure 6.25 the line $D + I$ gives the present value of total costs, direct plus indirect and the line shows the present value of the return on the project (assumed here to be a lump sum payment occurring when the project

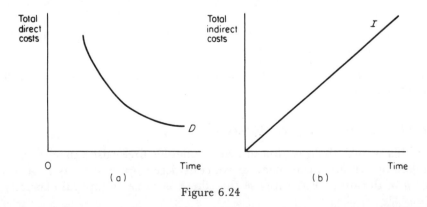

Figure 6.24

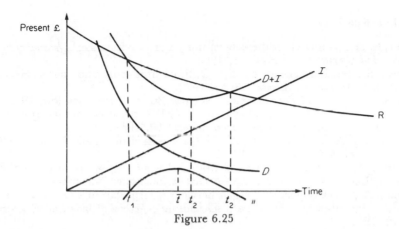

Figure 6.25

is complete). The line π shows NPV against time $[-R-(D+I)]$. This is maximized at $t = t$, the optimal duration. Breakeven durations are t_1 and t_2 while the minimum cost duration is t_3. Note that if R is a declining function of time (as in the case of a fixed payment on completion) then the minimum cost duration for the project will not be chosen if the objective is maximization of present value of profits. The cost minimizing time would only be chosen if there was provision (say by an inflation clause in the contract) to increase the terminal payment at a compound rate equal to the rate of discount, i.e. to keep the present value constant.

Figure 6.25 allows of further analysis. Suppose the company that is involved with the project is in a bidding situation, and in order to secure the contract has to promise completion by $t_4 < t$. Presumably penalty payments will be due in the event of delay. The optimum project duration in this instance would be found by subtracting the curve showing lateness penalties as a function of time from the previous profit function as given by π. The high point of this new curve would determine optimum (from the point of view of the constructor) project duration. If, as seems reasonable, the lateness penalties are an increasing function of time, the new optimum duration will be less than t. Though the argument here seem unscrupulous, if the lateness penalties reflect something in excess of the true costs of lateness to the customer, the solution would prove mutually beneficial.

References

Orgler, Y. (1970), *Cash Management: Methods and Models*, Wadsworth, Belmont, Calif.

Reinfeld, N. V., and Vogel, W. R. (1958), *Mathematical Programming*, Prentice-Hall, Englewood Cliffs, NJ.

Russell, A. H. (1970). 'Cash flows in networks', *Management Science*, **16(A)**.

Srinivasan, V. (1973–74), 'A transshipment model for cash management decisions', *Management Science*, **20(B)**.

Further Reading

Archer, S. H., 'A model for the determination of cash balances', *Journal of Financial and Quantitative Analysis*, **1**, 1966.

Arisawa, S., and Elmaghraby, S. E., 'Optimal time–cost trade-offs in Gert networks' *Management Science*, **18(A)**, 1972.

Barnetson, P., *Critical Path Planning*, Newnes-Butterworth, London, 1969.

Berman, E. C., 'Resource allocation in PERT networks under continuous time–cost functions', *Management Science*, **10**, 1964.

Carruthers, J. A., and Battersby, A., 'Advances in critical path methods', *Operations Research Quarterly*, **17**, 1966.

Chapman, C. B., *Project Planning: A General Programming Model for Practical Problems*, University of Southampton Discussion Paper No. 6804.

Charnes, A., and Cooper, W. W., 'A network interpretation and a directed subdual algorithm for critical path scheduling', *Journal of Industrial Engineering*, **12**, 1961.

Clarke, C. E., 'The optimum allocation of resources among the activities of a network', *Journal of Industrial Engineering*, **12**, 1961.

Croft, F. M., 'Putting a price tag on PERT activities', *Journal of Industrial Engineering*, **21**, 1970.

Elmaghraby, S. E., 'On the expected duration of PERT-type networks', *Management Science*, **13**, 1967.

Ford, L. R. J., and Fulkerson, D. R., *Flows in Networks*, University Press, Princeton, NJ, 1962.

Fulkerson, D. R., 'A network flow computation for project cost curve', *Management Science*, **7**, 1961.

Hill, L., 'Some cost accounting problems in PERT/cost', *Journal of Industrial Engineering*, **17**, 1966.

Hu, T. C., *Integer Programming and Network Flows*, Addison-Wesley, Reading, Mass., 1969.

Jewell, W. S., 'Optimal flow through networks with gains', *Operations Research*, **10**, 1962.

Kelly, J. E., 'Critical path planning and scheduling: mathematical basis', *Operations Research*, **9**, 1961.

Klein, M., 'A primal method for minimal cost flows with applications to the assignment and transportation problems', *Management Science*, **14**, 1967.

Muth, J. E., and Thompson, G. L. (eds.), *Industrial Scheduling*, Prentice-Hall, Englewood Cliffs, NJ., 1963.

Orden, A., 'The transshipment problem', *Management Science*, **2**, 1956.

Orgler, Y., 'Cash budgeting, the payment schedule, and short term financing by business firms', Ph.D. dissertation, Graduate School of Business, Carnegie-Mellon University, 1967.

Robichek, A. A., Teichroew, D., and Jones, J. M., 'Optimal short term financing decisions', *Management Science*, **12**, 1965.

Wagner, H. M., *Principles of Operations Research with Applications to Managerial Decisions*, Prentice-Hall, Englewood Cliffs, NJ, 1969.

Wilkes, F. M., *Elements of Operational Research*, McGraw-Hill, London, 1980.

CHAPTER 7

Investment Appraisal with Non-linear and Dynamic Programming

Overview

The chapter begins with a review of the fundamentals of calculus optimization and Kuhn–Tucker theory. Two applications of unconstrained optimization in the context of present value maximization then follow. After a quadratic programming exercise there is a discussion of non-linearities in the constraint set and a brief review of approximation techniques. The chapter concludes with an introduction to discrete dynamic programming and investment sequences.

7.1 Review of Maximization Methods

Consider the problem of finding the maximum value that a function of a single variable takes when the only constraint is that the variable is a real number. The problem can be stated as

$$\underset{x}{\text{Max}} F(x) \quad \text{s.t.} \quad x \in R \tag{7.1}$$

Consider the particular case where $F(x)$ takes the form shown in Figure 7.1. The maximizing value of x is $\bar{x}$ and in this case $\bar{x} \leqslant 0$. The maximum is characterized by the slope of the function $F(x)$ being zero:

$$\frac{\mathrm{d}F(x)}{\mathrm{d}x} = 0 \tag{7.2}$$

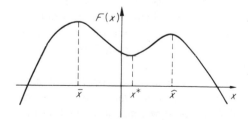

Figure 7.1

209

at a maximum. The condition of zero slope given by (7.2) is the equation to zero of the *first derivative* of $F(x)$ with respect to x. The first derivative is the rate of change of $F(x)$ as x changes. We shall be concerned only with polynomial functions. A polynomial function of a single variable x may be written as

$$F(x) = a_0 x^n + a_1 x^{n-1} + a_2 x^{n-2} + \ldots + a_{n-1} x + a_n \qquad (7.3)$$

where (7.3) represents an nth-order polynomial provided that $a_0 \neq 0$. The slope of $F(x)$ at any point is the value of the derivative of the function at that point and the derivative of a function such as (7.3) is obtained by *differentiating* each term individually and summing. For a typical term:

$$\frac{d(ax^m)}{dx} = max^{m-1} \qquad (7.4)$$

that is, the derivative with respect to x of ax^m where the coefficient, a, and the exponent, m, are constants is obtained by multiplying by the 'old' exponent and reducing the exponent by one. So the derivative of (7.3) with respect to x is

$$\frac{dF(x)}{dx} = na_0 x^{n-1} + (n-1)a_1 x^{n-2} + (n-2)a_2 x^{n-3} + \ldots + a_{n-1} \qquad (7.5)$$

and the slope of $F(x)$ for any value of x is obtained by substituting that value of x in (7.5). Thus if we wanted to find those values of x for which the slope of $F(x)$ was zero we should have to solve the $(n-1)$th-order polynomial equation:

$$\frac{dF(x)}{dx} = na_0 x^{n-1} + (n-1)a_1 x^{n-2} + (n-2)a_2 x^{n-3} + \ldots + a_{n-1} = 0 \qquad (7.6)$$

Except for some special cases, the solution of (7.6) for values of n in excess of 4 would be obtained by numerical methods. There will be $n-1$ values of x which satisfy (7.6); these are *roots*, some of which may be identical so that there may be less than $n-1$ distinct numbers. Some roots may not be real numbers (they may involve the square root of -1) but this possibility need not concern us here.

Returning to consideration of conditions for a maximum of $F(x)$ in general. Each point which satisfies (7.2) is termed a *stationary value* of the function. A stationary value, in the case of a function of a single variable, may be a maximum, a minimum or a point of *inflexion*. The condition of zero slope is necessary but is not sufficient to ensure the overall, *global maximum* of $F(x)$.

At the point $x = \hat{x}$ the function takes on a *local maximum* value. That is, small variations, increases or decreases, in x around the value $\hat{x}$ produce a reduced value of $F(x)$. A *sufficiently large* reduction in the value of x to bring it near to x, would produce a higher value of $F(x)$. Of course, a global maximum is also a local maximum. The function takes on a local minimum at $x = x^*$. This turning point is also characterized by (7.2). The distinction between local maxima and local minima is, sufficiently, that the rate of change of the slope of $F(x)$ is negative for a maximum (slope decreasing) and positive for a minimum (slope increasing).

The rate of change of the slope of a function is given by the derivative of the expression for the slope—itelf a function of x. Thus the rate of change of the slope of $F(x)$ in (7.3) is given by the derivative of (7.5). This is the *second derivative* of the original function and is given by (7.7)

$$\frac{d^2 F(x)}{dx^2} = (n-1)na_0 x^{n-2} + (n-2)(n-1)a_1 x^{n-3},$$

$$+ (n-3)(n-2)a_2 x^{n-4} + \ldots + 2a_{n-2} \tag{7.7}$$

In (7.7) it is assumed that n is at least 5. For example if $n-5$ then (7.7) in full would be

$$\frac{d^2 F(x)}{dx^2} = 20a_0 x^3 + 12a_1 x^2 + 6a_2 x + 2a_3 \tag{7.8}$$

Now for a local maximum we have stated that the rate of change of the slope of $F(x)$ should be negative. Thus (7.9) should hold for a maximum. For a local minimum (7.10) applies.

$$\frac{d^2 F(x)}{dx^2} < 0 \tag{7.9}$$

$$\frac{d^2 F(x)}{dx^2} > 0 \tag{7.10}$$

The conditions (7.2) and (7.9) apply to all local maxima and do not enable us to distinguish between local and global maxima. Unless it is known *a priori* that a local maximum is also the global maximum, the global maximum can be found by reference to the value of $F(x)$ itself, i.e. by evaluating $F(x)$ at each point satisfying (7.2) and (7.9).

Now suppose that not all real values of x are permissible. In particular, consider the case where only non-negative values of x are allowed. The problem now becomes

$$\underset{x}{\text{Max}} F(x) \quad \text{s.t.} \quad x \geqslant 0 \tag{7.11}$$

Equation (7.11) defines a non-linear programming problem (provided of course that $F(x)$ is not a linear function) the choice of real values of x is restricted. What conditions now characterize maxima? Reference to Figure 7.1 suggests that there are two types of point at which maxima can occur—a turning point of $F(x)$ such as $\hat{x}$, or a *boundary point*. The only boundary point in the current problem is $x = 0$. At $x = 0$ the only permitted direction of change in x is an increase in the value of x and it is evident from the graph that $F(x)$ diminishes for increasing x at $x = 0$. Con-

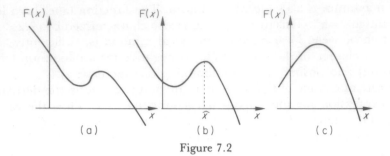

Figure 7.2

sequently, $x = 0$ is a candidate for the global maximum of $F(x)$ because of the sign requirement. If $F(x)$ had been as in Figure 7.2(a) the boundary point $x = 0$ would have provided the global maximum even though it is not a turning point of $F(x)$. In Figure 7.2(b) $x = 0$ is a local maximum since decreases in x are not allowed but $\hat{x}$, an *interior* turning point, is the global maximum. In Figure 7.2(c) the boundary point is not a local maximum since $F(x)$ is increasing for increasing x.

The local maxima in the diagrams of Figure 7.2 satisfy one or other of two sets of conditions; either

$$x = 0 \quad \text{and} \quad \frac{\mathrm{d}F(x)}{\mathrm{d}x} < 0 \tag{7.12a}$$

or

$$x > 0 \quad \text{and} \quad \frac{\mathrm{d}F(x)}{\mathrm{d}x} = 0 \tag{7.12b}$$

The local minima in the diagrams satisfy one or other of

$$x = 0 \quad \text{and} \quad \frac{\mathrm{d}F(x)}{\mathrm{d}x} > 0 \tag{7.13a}$$

or

$$x > 0 \quad \text{and} \quad \frac{\mathrm{d}F(x)}{\mathrm{d}x} = 0 \tag{7.13b}$$

It should be noted that (7.12a) and (7.13a) unambiguously identify a local maximum and a local minimum respectively, whilst (7.12b) and (7.13b) are identical. One further possibility that is not represented in Figure 7.12(b) is that a stationary value occurring at $x = 0$, that is

$$x = 0 \quad \text{and} \quad \frac{\mathrm{d}F(x)}{\mathrm{d}x} = 0 \tag{7.14}$$

Note that condition (7.14) will be satisfied if, and only if, there is no constant term in the derivative of $F(x)$.

The characteristics of a local maximum of $F(x)$ subject to $x \geqslant 0$ can be summarized as

$$\left.\begin{array}{l} x \geqslant 0 \\[2mm] \dfrac{\mathrm{d}F(x)}{\mathrm{d}x} \leqslant 0 \\[3mm] \dfrac{\mathrm{d}F(x)}{\mathrm{d}x} \cdot x = 0 \end{array}\right\} \tag{7.15}$$

Note that (7.15) includes (7.12a) and (7.12b), but since (7.15) also includes (7.13a) and (7.14) then (7.15) must be described as necessary conditions only.

Necessary first-order conditions for a minimum of $F(x)$ for non-negative x are

$$\left.\begin{array}{l} \dfrac{\mathrm{d}F(x)}{\mathrm{d}x} \geqslant 0 \\[3mm] \dfrac{\mathrm{d}F(x)}{\mathrm{d}x} \cdot x = 0 \\[3mm] x \geqslant 0 \end{array}\right\} \tag{7.16}$$

In the case of a minimum, for a boundary point to be optimal the function must be downward sloping at the boundary (i.e. decreasing with increasing x).

Situations may arise in which x was restricted to non-positive values. In this case necessary conditions for a maximum of $F(x)$ in the permitted range of values of x are:

$$\left.\begin{array}{l} \dfrac{\mathrm{d}F(x)}{\mathrm{d}x} \geqslant 0 \\[3mm] x \cdot \dfrac{\mathrm{d}F(x)}{\mathrm{d}x} = 0 \\[3mm] x \leqslant 0 \end{array}\right\} \tag{7.17}$$

Conditions (7.18) are necessary for a minimum of $F(x)$ for non-positive values of x.

$$\left.\begin{array}{l} \dfrac{\mathrm{d}F(x)}{\mathrm{d}x} \leqslant 0 \\[3mm] x \cdot \dfrac{\mathrm{d}F(x)}{\mathrm{d}x} = 0 \\[3mm] x \leqslant 0 \end{array}\right\} \tag{7.18}$$

The reader may find it instructive to check conditions (7.17) and (7.18)

214

by constructing diagrams of the type shown in Figures 7.1 and 7.2.

The conditions set out above can be readily extended to cases where the lower or upper bound on x is not zero. For instance, suppose that it is required that x be not less than some specified value x min. The conditions for a maximum subject to this requirement are

$$\left.\begin{array}{l} \dfrac{\mathrm{d}F(x)}{\mathrm{d}x} \leqslant 0 \\[2ex] (x - x\ \text{min}) \cdot \dfrac{\mathrm{d}F(x)}{\mathrm{d}x} = 0 \\[2ex] x - x\ \text{min} \geqslant 0 \end{array}\right\} \tag{7.19}$$

Now consider the extension of the results to the case of a function of two variables.

Suppose first that we wish to find an unconstrained maximum of the function:

$$F = F(x_1, x_2) \tag{7.20}$$

Consider the function of Figure 7.3. The function takes on its maximum value at the point (x_1, x_2). In the case illustrated in the figure the problem is akin to finding the coordinates of the highest point of a hill. Interpret the value of x_2 as the distance moved in a northerly direction from the origin and the value of x_1 as the distance travelled eastwards from the origin. The value of F corresponds to the height of the hill. Obviously, at the highest point the hill must have zero slope in both the northerly and eastwards directions otherwise it would be possible to gain height by moving north (or south) or/and east (or west).

These slopes are the *partial derivatives* of the function; the rates of change of the function in the *fundamental directions*, $\partial F/\partial x_2$ is the slope in the x_2 direction, there being no change in the value of x_1, and $\partial F/\partial x_1$ is the slope in the x_1 direction allowing no change in x_2. For a small change in x_1, Δx,

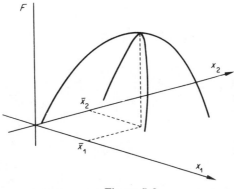

Figure 7.3

and with no change in the value of x_2 the change in F, ΔF, is approximately

$$\Delta F \simeq \frac{\partial F}{\partial x_1} \Delta x_1 \tag{7.21}$$

Similarly for a small movement x_2 in the x_2 direction alone we can write

$$\Delta F \simeq \frac{\partial F}{\partial x_2} \Delta x_2 \tag{7.22}$$

and for small movements in both directions

$$\Delta F \simeq \frac{\partial F}{\partial x_1} \Delta x_1 + \frac{\partial F}{\partial x_2} \Delta x_2 \tag{7.23}$$

This is the case since a function with continuous first-order partial derivatives in the neighbourhood of a point cannot have zero slopes in the fundamental directions and non-zero slopes in other directions at that point. If F has continuous first-order partial derivatives in a region where ϵ_1 and ϵ_2 approach zero as Δx_1 and Δx_2 approach zero, we could write as an equation

$$\Delta F = \frac{\partial F}{\partial x_1} \Delta x_1 + \frac{\partial F}{\partial x_2} \Delta x_2 + \epsilon_1 \Delta x_1 + \epsilon_2 \Delta x_2$$

The expression

$$dF = \frac{\partial F}{\partial x_1} dx_1 + \frac{\partial F}{\partial x_2} dx_2 \tag{7.24}$$

is the *total differential* of F or the *principal part* of ΔF. In (7.24) dx_1 and dx_2 are the differentials of x_1 and x_2 respectively and may be of arbitrary size (i.e. they need not be small). In general, $dF \neq \Delta F$. However, if $\Delta x = dx$ and $\Delta y = dy$ are small then dF will be a close approximation to ΔF. The partial derivatives give both the slopes of the surface in the fundamental directions and the slopes of the *tangent plane* in these directions. Thus dF is the increment in height of the tangent plane for arbitrary dx_1 and dx_2. For a function to have a stationary value at a point, dF must be zero for arbitrary dx_1 and dx_2.

As regards the mechanics of partial differentiation, when differentiating partially with respect to one variable, all terms and parts of terms in other variables are treated as constants. If

$$F = 128x_1 + 84x_2 + 5x_1x_2 - 7x_1^2 - 9x_2^2$$

then

$$\frac{\partial F}{\partial x_1} = 128 + 5x_2 - 14x_1$$

and

$$\frac{\partial F}{\partial x_2} = 84 + 5x_1 - 18x_2$$

The function F takes a stationary value when these two partial derivatives are equal to zero. This is the case for $x_1 = 12$ and $x_2 = 8$. The character of the stationary value may be determined by reference to higher order derivatives. If it was known that F was *concave* in the neighbourhood of a point satisfying first-order conditions then we should know that a *local* maximum had been obtained at that point. Intuitively, a surface is concave over a region if a straight line joining any two points on the surface above the region lies on or below the surface. If a function happens to be everywhere concave, then first-order conditions will be sufficient. The functions in this chapter are everywhere concave functions. To summarize; if an unconstrained maximum of $F(x_1, x_2)$ is sought then first-order conditions are

$$\frac{\partial F}{\partial x_1} = 0 \quad \text{and} \quad \frac{\partial F}{\partial x_2} = 0 \tag{7.25}$$

which are necessary conditions in general, but are both necessary and sufficient if $F(x_1, x_2)$ is generally concave.

Now consider the problem of maximizing $F(x_1, x_2)$ subject to the sign requirements $x_1 \geqslant 0$ and $x_2 \geqslant 0$. It turns out that first-order conditions are the obvious generalization of the conditions (7.16) in the case of a function of a single variable. They may be stated as

$$\left.\begin{array}{l} \text{(i)} \quad \dfrac{\partial F}{\partial x_1} \leqslant 0 \\[2mm] \text{(ii)} \quad \dfrac{\partial F}{\partial x_2} \leqslant 0 \\[2mm] \text{(iii)} \quad x_1 \cdot \dfrac{\partial F}{\partial x_1} + x_2 \dfrac{\partial F}{\partial x_2} = 0 \\[2mm] \text{(iv)} \quad x_1 \geqslant 0 \\[1mm] \qquad\quad x_2 \geqslant 0 \end{array}\right\} \tag{7.26}$$

(i) and (ii) state that both first-order *partial derivatives* have to be nonpositive. Condition (iii), taken in conjunction with (i), (ii) and (iv) means that both $x_1(\partial F/\partial x_1)$ and $x_2(\partial F/\partial x_2) = 0$; since neither of these terms can be positive, in order for the sum to be zero each individual term must be zero. For a minimum of F subject to the same sign requirements the directions of the weak inequalities in (i) and (ii) are reversed.

It may be required to find a *saddle point* of a function such as F; a maximum with respect to one variable and a minimum with respect to the other. This is illustrated in Figure 7.4 in which the function $F(x_1, x_2)$ has, at the saddle point S, a maximum in the x_2 direction and a minimum in

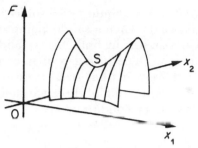

Figure 7.4

the x_1 direction. Necessary conditions are as follows:

$$\left.\begin{aligned}
&\frac{\partial F}{\partial x_1} \geqslant 0 \\[6pt]
&x_1\frac{\partial F}{\partial x_1} = 0 \\[6pt]
&x_1 \geqslant 0 \\[6pt]
&\frac{\partial F}{\partial x_2} \leqslant 0 \\[6pt]
&x_2\frac{\partial F}{\partial x_2} = 0 \\[6pt]
&x_2 \geqslant 0
\end{aligned}\right\} \qquad (7.27)$$

In this case there is no convenient summarizing as with (7.26) (ii) of the requirement that the product of the level of each variable and the corresponding partial derivative by zero.

7.2 Kuhn–Tucker Theory

Consider the case where there are constraints in addition to sign requirements. Suppose that the values of x_1 and x_2 chosen must satisfy the requirement that $g(x_1,x_2) \leqslant b$, where $g(x_1,x_2)$ has continuous first-order partial derivatives and b is a constant. The full problem with sign requirements is

$$\left.\begin{aligned}
&\text{maximize } F = F(x_1,x_2) \\
&\text{subject to } g(x_1,x_2) \leqslant b \\
&\text{and} \qquad x_1 \geqslant 0, x_2 \geqslant 0
\end{aligned}\right\} \qquad (7.28)$$

necessary conditions are obtained by formulating the *Lagrangian function*, L:

$$L = F(x_1,x_2) + y(b - g(x_1,x_2)) \qquad (7.29)$$

y is the *Lagrange multiplier*. A maximum of F subject to the constraint and the sign requirements occurs when a saddle point of L is found such that the value of L is a maximum in both the x_1 and x_2 directions and a *minimum* in the y direction. The problem of maximizing F subject to a constraint and sign requirements has been transformed into one of finding a saddle point of L, a function of three variables subject only to sign requirements. The first-order conditions are

$$
\left.
\begin{aligned}
\frac{\partial L}{\partial x_1} = \frac{\partial F}{\partial x_1} &- y \frac{\partial g}{\partial x_1} \leqslant 0 \\[2mm]
\frac{\partial L}{\partial x_2} = \frac{\partial F}{\partial x_2} &- y \frac{\partial g}{\partial x_2} \leqslant 0 \\[2mm]
x_1 \frac{\partial L}{\partial x_1} + x_2 \frac{\partial L}{\partial x_2} &= 0 \\[2mm]
x_1 &\geqslant 0 \\[2mm]
x_2 &\geqslant 0 \\[2mm]
\frac{\partial L}{\partial y} = b - g(x_1, x_2) &\geqslant 0 \\[2mm]
y \frac{\partial L}{\partial y} &= 0 \\[2mm]
y &\geqslant 0
\end{aligned}
\right\}
\tag{7.30}
$$

The derivative with respect to the Lagrange multiplier is the statement of the constraint itself, so that provided the constraint is incorporated as in (7.29) and the function is minimized with respect to the multiplier, then (7.30) the *Kuhn–Tucker conditions*, guarantee that the values of x_1 and x_2 will satisfy the constraint. The Kuhn–Tucker conditions characterize local maxima of F subject to the constraint and the sign requirements. If the objective function satisfies a condition (is concave) and the constraint is convex and provided that a *constraint qualification* condition is met (a feasible solution exists with all positive x's) the Kuhn–Tucker conditions are both necessary and sufficient for local maximum of F. For a function of n variables subject to m constraints, each constraint is included in the Lagrangian as in (7.19) so that there will be m multipliers required.

Consider the application of the Kuhn–Tucker conditions in the linear programming case. For the problem:

$$
\text{maximize } \pi = \pi_1 x_1 + \pi_2 x_2
$$

$$
\text{subject to} \quad a_{11} x_1 + a_{12} x_2 \leqslant b_1
$$

$$
a_{21} x_1 + a_{22} x_2 \leqslant b_2
$$

$$
x_1 \geqslant 0, x_2 \geqslant 0
$$

The Lagrangian is

$$L = \pi_1 x_1 + \pi_2 x_2 + y_1(b_1 - a_{11}x_1 - a_{12}x_2) + y_2(b_2 - a_{21}x_1 - a_{22}x_2)$$

and the Kuhn–Tucker conditions are as follows:

$$\frac{\partial L}{\partial x_1} = \pi_1 - a_{11}y_1 - a_{21}y_2 \leqslant 0$$

$$\frac{\partial L}{\partial x_2} = \pi_2 - a_{12}y_1 - a_{22}y_2 \leqslant 0$$

$$x_1 \frac{\partial L}{\partial x_1} + x_2 \frac{\partial L}{\partial x_2} = 0$$

$$x_1 \geqslant 0$$

$$x_2 \geqslant 0$$

$$\frac{\partial L}{\partial y_1} = b_1 - a_{11}x_1 - a_{12}x_2 \geqslant 0$$

$$\frac{\partial L}{\partial y_2} = b_2 - a_{21}x_1 - a_{22}x_2 \geqslant 0$$

$$y_1 \frac{\partial L}{\partial y_1} + y_2 \frac{\partial L}{\partial y_2} = 0$$

$$y_1 \geqslant 0$$

$$y_2 \geqslant 0$$

(7.31)

The derivatives of the Lagrangian with respect to the multipliers are the primal constraints. The derivatives with respect to the primal variables are the dual constraints; from which it is evident that the multipliers are the dual structural variables—the shadow prices. In the conditions

$$x_1 \frac{\partial L}{\partial x_1} + x_2 \frac{\partial L}{\partial x_2} = 0$$

and

$$y_1 \frac{\partial L}{\partial y_1} + y_2 \frac{\partial L}{\partial y_2} = 0$$

it is implied that each component is zero. Consider

$$y_1 \cdot \frac{\partial L}{\partial y_1} = 0$$

It is clear that y_1 can be positive only if $\partial L / \partial y_1 = 0$, that is to say: $a_{11}x_1 + a_{12}x_2 = b_1$ and the first constraint is binding, i.e. $s_1 = 0$. A resource can only have a positive shadow price if there are no unused units of that resource. This condition could be written as

$$y_1 s_1 = 0$$

By the same argument

$$y_2 s_2 = 0$$

$$x_1 t_1 = 0$$

$$x_2 t_2 = 0$$

where t_1 and t_2 are the slack variables in the dual constraints. From the penultimate condition it emerges that x_1 can only be positive if there is no opportunity loss involved in its 'production'. Similarly for x_2. These conditions, $y_i x_j = 0$ for $i = j$ and $x_j t_i = 0$ for $i = j$ are the *complementary slackness* conditions. The Kuhn–Tucker conditions could be written in complementary slackness form as

$$
\left.
\begin{aligned}
&\frac{\partial L}{\partial x_1} = \pi_1 - a_{11} y_1 - a_{21} y_2 + t_1 = 0 \\[2mm]
&\frac{\partial L}{\partial x_2} + \pi_2 - a_{12} y_1 - a_{22} y_2 + t_2 = 0 \\[2mm]
&\frac{\partial L}{\partial y_1} = b_1 - a_{11} x_1 - a_{12} x_2 - s_1 = 0 \\[2mm]
&\frac{\partial L}{\partial y_2} = b_2 - a_{21} x_1 - a_{22} x_2 - s_2 = 0 \\[2mm]
&x_1 \geqslant 0 \qquad s_2 \geqslant 0 \\
&x_2 \geqslant 0 \qquad s_2 \geqslant 0 \\
&y_1 \geqslant 0 \qquad t_1 \geqslant 0 \\
&y_2 \geqslant 0 \qquad t_2 \geqslant 0 \\
&y_1 s_1 + y_2 s_2 + x_1 t_1 + x_2 t_2 = 0
\end{aligned}
\right\} \qquad (7.32)
$$

If the dual problem is formulated as a Lagrangian and the Kuhn–Tucker conditions are derived it will be seen that these are identical to (7.31) meaning that a pair of feasible solutions to both problems implies optimality for both problems.

The general non-linear programming problem can be stated as

$$\text{maximize } F(x_1, \ldots x_n)$$

$$
\left.
\begin{aligned}
\text{subject to} \qquad & g_1(x, \ldots x_n) \leqslant b_1 \\
& \quad\vdots \qquad\qquad \vdots \\
& g_m(x_1, \ldots x_n) \leqslant b_m \\
& x_1 \geqslant 0, \ldots, x_n \geqslant 0
\end{aligned}
\right\} \qquad (7.33)
$$

Where $n = 2$ the problem may appear as in Figure 7.5. The feasible region is the shaded convex set. Contours of the objective function are shown by dashed curves and the optimum solution is (in this case) the boundary point P. An interior optimum is possible, in which case all the constraints (including the sign requirements) are satisfied as strict inequalities. If $n = 2$ it may be helpful to think of the problem as one of finding the highest point in an area of ground corresponding to the feasible region. No generality is lost in formulating the problem as in (7.33) which is one of maximization subject to $\leqslant$ inequalities with all x_j required to be non-negative. If minimization of a function is required the function is negated and maximized. Similarly, $\geqslant$ inequalities can be converted to $\leqslant$ inequalities by negation. Variables constrained to be other than non-negative can be transformed to non-negative variables. If x_j is unrestricted it can be expressed as the difference between two non-negative variables $x_j^* - \hat{x}_j$.

An equality constraint

$$g_i(x_1, \ldots, x_n) = b_i \tag{7.34}$$

can be replaced by the two constraints

$$g_i(x_i, \ldots, x_n) \leqslant b_i \quad \text{and} \quad -g_i(x_1, \ldots, x_n) \leqslant -b_i$$

which can only be satisfied simultaneously if (7.34) holds

In the general non-linear case the Lagrangian function is

$$L = F(x_1, \ldots, x_n) + \sum_{i=1}^{m} y_i(b_i - g_i(x_1, \ldots x_n)) \tag{7.35}$$

and the Kuhn–Tucker conditions are as follows:

$$
\left.
\begin{aligned}
&\frac{\partial L}{\partial x_j} = \frac{\partial F}{\partial x_j} - \sum_{i=1}^{m} y_i \frac{\partial g}{\partial x_j} \leqslant 0 \qquad (j = 1, 2, \ldots n) \\[2ex]
&\sum_{j=1}^{n} x_j \frac{\partial L}{\partial x_j} = 0 \\[2ex]
&x_j \geqslant 0 \qquad (j = 1, 2, \ldots n) \\[2ex]
&\frac{\partial L}{\partial y_i} = b_i - g_i(x_i, \ldots x_n) \geqslant 0 \qquad (i = 1, 2, \ldots m) \\[2ex]
&\sum_{i=1}^{m} y_i \frac{\partial L}{\partial y_i} = 0 \\[2ex]
&y_i \geqslant 0 \qquad (i = 1, 2, \ldots m)
\end{aligned}
\right\} \tag{7.36}
$$

In non-linear programming the economic interpretation of the Lagrange multipliers is not so useful as in the linear programming case. Balinski and Baumol (1967, p. 237) express the position well: 'The

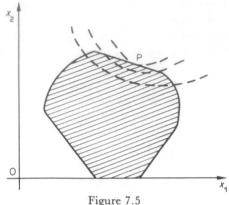

Figure 7.5

specification, interpretation and uses of the dual problem corresponding to any linear programme are well known and well documented in the literature. Amongst economists it is, however, not widely known that duals can be paired with *non-linear* programming problems and that many of the duality relationships which hold in linear programming continue to hold for certain classes of non-linear programmes. Specifically, if the entire primal problem is characterized by diminishing returns then many of the standard duality properties retain their validity, though certain symmetries of the linear case are lost.' Later in the chapter we shall examine a problem in which a quadratic objective function is minimized subject to linear constraints. The objective function employed will be concave—thus exhibiting diminishing returns—and useful sensitivity analysis is carried out.

Whilst the Kuhn–Tucker conditions *characterize* optimal solutions, it does not follow that once these conditions have been set out the solution is at hand. This fact can be seen even in the linear case where the Kuhn–Tucker conditions are the primal and dual constraints plus complementary slackness conditions and sign requirements. A solution to these conditions has still to be found by the Simplex method or otherwise. This is the state of affairs *a fortiori* in non-linear problems. In this chapter we shall detail one of several quadratic programming algorithms that are available, otherwise confining the discussion to descriptive form. But first consider some simpler cases in which non-linearities arise in investment problems.

7.3 Non-constant Returns to Scale

There will be occasions when it is possible to invest in several units of the same project. The problem of choosing the optimum number of units is not trivial if the initial outlay and receipts in each period are not linear functions of the number of units obtained, even if there is no constraint on total expenditure.

Consider a continuously divisible project X which yields returns at the end of each of two years. Let x represent the number of units of X and let $R_1(x)$, $R_2(x)$, $K(x)$ represent the receipts and the initial outlay as functions of x. Thus, with a uniform discount rate of $100i\%$, NTV for any value of x is given by

$$\text{NTV} = (1 + i)R_1(x) + R_2(x) - (1 + i)^2 K(x) \tag{7.37}$$

which is to be maximized. Assuming $R_1(x)$, $R_2(x)$, and $K(x)$ to be differentiable functions, we require the first derivative of NTV with respect to x to be zero. That is

$$(1 + i)R_1'(x) + R_2'(x) = (1 + i)^2 K'(x) \tag{7.38}$$

where $R_1'(x)$, $R_2'(x)$, and $K'(x)$ are the derivatives of $R_1(x)$, $R(x)$, and $K(x)$ with respect to x. Here, (7.38) represents the equation of *marginal terminal revenue* (MTR) with *marginal terminal cost* (MTC). MTR is the left-hand side of (7.38) and is (approximately) the addition to revenue at the end of the project caused by the purchase of an extra unit of X now. MTC, the right-hand side of (7.38), is (approximately) the terminal value of the cost of an extra unit of X.

The first-order condition (7.38) applies to any stationary value of (7.37). To ensure a maximum it is further required that MTC be increasing faster (or decreasing less rapidly) than MTR:

$$(1 + i)^2 K''(x) > (1 + i)R_1''(x) + R_2''(x) \tag{7.39}$$

where $K''(x)$, $R_1''(x)$ and $R_2''(x)$ are the second derivatives of $K(x)$, $R_1(x)$, and $R_2(x)$ with respect to x. In general, several values of x may satisfy both the first- and the second-order conditions, and from among these the best value giving the global optimum may usually be determined by enumeration.

7.4 Product Pricing and Terminal Values

In some circumstances terminal value methods can give useful information to help solve the problem of product pricing. Consider the case of a firm interested in the possible introduction of new capital equipment. Suppose that the project has no external effects and that it would be financed entirely from the firm's own funds which otherwise would have been invested at $100i\%$. If the available funds are L and the cost of the equipment which lasts for n years is K, then the NTV of the investment is given by

$$\text{NTV} = \sum_{h=0}^{n} R_h(1 + i)^{n-h} - L(1 + i)^n \tag{7.40}$$

where $R_0 = L - K$. The remaining returns

$$R_1, \ldots, R_n$$

are after-tax profits. Tax is at a flat rate of $100t\%$. Expressing revenue each year as pq_h (price times quantity sold in the hth year) and costs each year as c_h, then the post-tax return in the hth year is given by

$$R_h = (1 - t)(p_h q_h - c_h) \tag{7.41}$$

The quantity sold in any year is a function of price and costs of production are a function of quantity produced in that year (equals quantity sold) which is in turn a function of price. Consequently, if the relation between price and quantity (the product demand curve) is known, the only unknown in (7.40) is price, so that NTV can be maximized with respect to price, or, in a satisfying context set to some particular value and solved for price. This latter approach could be useful in respect of the problem of the pricing of certain public utilities—with 'profit' margins predetermined and demand estimates already made.

For a numerical example, consider a machine with a two-year lifetime to be used to produce a single product in quantities q_1 and q_2 in each of the two years and sold at prices of p_1 and p_2 respectively. The demand conditions in each year are given by

$$q_1 = 100 - p_1 \quad \text{and} \quad q_2 = 300 - 4p_2 \tag{7.42}$$

Cost of production in each year are

$$c_1 = 20 + 2q_1 \quad \text{and} \quad c_2 = 10 + 3q_2 \tag{7.43}$$

Profits are taxed at the flat rate of 40% each year, and the purchase price of the machine is £2,800. An interest rate of 10% is appropriate for the calculations throughout, and the investor wishes to determine the prices to charge in each period so as to maximize the NTV of the investment. Substitution of (7.41) into (7.40) for $t = 0.4$ and $i = 0.1$ gives

$$\text{NTV} = -2,800(1.1)^2 + (1 - 0.4)(p_1 q_1 - c_1)(1.1) \tag{7.44}$$
$$+ (1 - 0.4)(p_2 q_2 - c_2)$$

in which the terms in L have cancelled out due to the uniform interest rate. Here, (7.44) can be written in terms of the prices alone as

$$\text{NTV} = -2,800(1.1)^2 + 0.6(1.1)(102p_1 - p_1^2 - 220) \tag{7.45}$$
$$+ 0.6(312p_2 - 4p_2^2 - 910)$$

since (7.42) gives the relationships between prices and quantities and substitution of the expressions into (7.34) gives $c_1 = 220 - 2p_1$ and $c_2 = 910 - 12p_2$. Necessary conditions for a maximum of NTV with respect to the prices p_1 and p_2 are by differentiation of (7.45).

$$0.66(102 - 2p_1) = \frac{\partial \text{NTV}}{\partial p_1} = 0$$

and

$$0.6(312 - 8p_2) = \frac{\partial \text{NTV}}{\partial p_2} = 0$$

(7.46)

The only turning point (which can be shown to be a maximum) is at

$$p_1 - 51, \qquad p_2 - 39$$

thus

$$q_1 = 49, \qquad q_2 = 144 \quad \text{and} \quad \text{NTV} = 1,287.86$$

Since NTV is positive the project is worth while, and appropriate prices and corresponding quantities are determined.

In general, where the demand conditions in any one period depend on prices charged and quantities sold in other periods, if forecasts are revised and interest rates and cost structures change over time, then at any moment corrections are possible to the calculated optimum prices and quantities for future periods. That is, calculations of optimal prices and quantities from time t onwards can be 'updated' in the light of the changed interest rates and cost conditions that might apply beyond t.

7.5 Quadratic Programming Investment Model

Suppose that a firm faces the following investment problem

maximize $N = N_1(x_1) + N_2(x_2)$

subject to $\quad a_{11}x_1 + a_{12}x_2 \leqslant b_1$

$\qquad\qquad a_{21}x_1 + a_{22}x_2 \leqslant b_2 \quad x_1 \geqslant 0, x_2 \geqslant 0$

(7.47)

In (7.47) x_1 and x_2 represent the amounts taken of two investments. The constraints are linear and correspond to the consumption of physical resources. The objective function is, however, non-linear. The term $N_1(x_1)$ represents the NPV resulting from accepting x_1 units of the first investment, and similarly $N_2(x_2)$ implies that present value from the second investment is a function of the amount taken of that investment alone. Thus there is assumed to be no interdependence between the investments so far as the objective function is concerned. The function N is said to be *separable and additive*. The x's being related only by the consumption of scarce resources.

The net present values from the two investments can be written in familiar form as

$$N_1 = \sum_t R_{1t}(1 + i)^{-t} - K_1 \quad \text{and} \quad N_2 = \sum_t R_{2t}(1 + i)^{-t} - K_2 \quad (7.48)$$

Consider project one. Returns are given by:

$$R_{1t} = I_{1t} - c_{1t} \tag{7.49}$$

where I_{1t} is income period t and c_{1t} is variable costs in period t; x_1 represents machinery and b_1 and b_2 represent manpower and materials all being combined to produce an output q_1. Now $I_{1t} = p_1 q_{1t}$ and $c_{1t} = c_1(q_{1t})$. Selling price of q_1 is linearly related to volume:

$$p_{1t} = a_{1t} - b_{1t} q_{1t} \tag{7.50}$$

where the parameters of the relationship may differ from year to year. Variable costs are given by

$$c_{1t} = g_{1t} q_{1t} + h_{1t} q_{1t}^2 \tag{7.51}$$

where g_{1t} and h_{1t} are positive constants. Substitution of (7.51) into (7.49) and since $I_{1t} = p_{1t} q_{1t}$ where p_{1t} is defined by (7.50) the expression for R_{1t} becomes

$$(a_{1t} - g_{1t})q_{1t} - (b_{1t} + h_{1t})q_{1t}^2 \tag{7.52}$$

Now let output in each year, q_{1t}, be proportional to the number of units of investment taken, where the factor of proportionality, m_{1t} may vary from year to year thus

$$q_{1t} = m_{1t} x_1 \tag{7.53}$$

If the initial outlay is given by

$$K_1 = e_1 x_1 + f_1 x_2 \tag{7.54}$$

where e_1 and f_1 are constants we can now write $N_1(x_1)$ as

$$N_1(x_1) = A_1 x_1 - B_1 x_1^2 \tag{7.55}$$

where

$$A_1 = \sum_t (a_{1t} - g_{1t})m_{1t}(1 + i)^{-t} - e_1$$

and

$$B_1 = \sum_t (b_{1t} + h_{1t})m_{1t}^2(1 + i)^{-t} + f_1$$

It is assumed that both A_1 and B_1 are positive numbers. If production, demand, cost and outlay conditions are similar for investment x_2 the objective function becomes

$$N = A_1 x_1 - B_1 x_1^2 + A_2 x_2 - B_2 x_2^2 \tag{7.56}$$

Equation (7.56) is to be maximized subject to the constraints and sign requirements. The Lagrangian is

$$L = A_1 x_1 - B_1 x_1^2 + A_2 x_2 - B_2 x_2^2 + y_1(b_1 - a_{11}x_1 - a_{12}x_2)$$
$$+ y_2(b_2 - a_{21}x_1 - a_{22}x_2) \tag{7.57}$$

and the Kuhn–Tucker conditions are as follows

$$\frac{\partial L}{\partial x_1} = A_1 - 2B_1 x_1 - a_{11}y_1 - a_{21}y_2 + t_1 = 0$$

$$\frac{\partial L}{\partial x_2} = A_2 - 2B_2 x_2 - a_{12}y_1 - a_{22}y_2 + t_2 = 0$$

$$x_1 t_1 = 0$$

$$x_2 t_2 = 0$$

$$x_1 \geqslant 0 \quad t_1 \geqslant 0$$

$$x_2 \geqslant 0 \quad t_2 \geqslant 0 \tag{7.58}$$

$$\frac{\partial L}{\partial y_1} = b_1 - a_{11}x_1 - a_{12}x_2 - s_1 = 0$$

$$\frac{\partial L}{\partial y_2} = b_2 - a_{21}x_1 - a_{22}x_2 - s_2 = 0$$

$$y_1 s_1 = 0$$

$$y_2 s_2 = 0$$

$$y_1 \geqslant 0 \quad s_1 \geqslant 0$$

$$y_2 \geqslant 0 \quad s_2 \geqslant 0$$

The Kuhn–Tucker conditions have been expressed in complementary slackness form since this will prove to be more convenient. The crucial point about conditions (7.58) is that, apart from the complementary slackness requirements, they are *linear*. The constraint set is convex and the objective function is strictly concave so that a feasible solution to (7.58) will produce the global maximum value of N; indeed there will be only one set of values of the x's, s's and y's that satisfy (7.58) and this will be optimal.

A feasible solution to (7.58) is found by a variation of the Simplex method. The original objective function (7.56) is not employed. Instead, a substitute objective function (or, as we shall see two substitute objective functions) is employed such that the optimal solution to the new problem gives a feasible solution to (7.58) and hence an optimal solution to the original problem. The algorithm described here is a modified version of Wolfe's Simplex method for quadratic programming.

Consider the problem:

$$\left.\begin{array}{ll} \text{maximize } N = 40x_1 + 60x_2 - x_1^2 - 2x_2^2 \\ \text{subject to} \qquad 5x_1 + \quad 4x_2 \leqslant 120 \\ \qquad\qquad 10x_1 + \quad x_2 \leqslant 140 \\ \qquad\qquad x_1 \geqslant 0, \quad x_2 \geqslant 0 \end{array}\right\} \tag{7.59}$$

This problem is of the form above with $A_1 = 40$, $A_2 = 60$, $B_1 = 1$ and $B_2 = 2$. The objective function is strictly concave and the constraints form a convex set. The Kuhn–Tucker conditions are necessary and sufficient for an optimal solution. The Lagrangian function and the Kuhn–Tucker conditions are as follows:

$$L = 40x_1 + 60x_2 - x_1^2 - 2x_2^2 + y_1(120 - 5x_1 - 4x_2) + y_2(140 - 10x_1 - x_2)$$

$$\left.\begin{array}{l} \dfrac{\partial L}{\partial x_1} = \quad 40 - 2x_1 - 5y_1 - 10y_2 + t_1 = 0 \\[2mm] \dfrac{\partial L}{\partial x_2} = \quad 60 - 4x_2 - 4y_1 - y_2 + t_2 = 0 \\[2mm] \qquad\qquad x_1 t_1 + x_2 t_2 = 0 \\[1mm] \qquad\qquad x_1 \geqslant 0 \quad x_2 \geqslant 0 \\[2mm] \dfrac{\partial L}{\partial y_1} = 120 - 5x_1 - 4x_2 - s_1 = 0 \\[2mm] \dfrac{\partial L}{\partial y_2} = 140 - 10x_1 - x_2 - s_2 = 0 \\[2mm] \qquad\qquad y_1 s_1 + y_2 s_2 = 0 \\[1mm] \qquad\qquad y \geqslant 0 \quad y_2 \geqslant 0 \end{array}\right\} \tag{7.60}$$

The procedure begins by re-expressing the constraints corresponding to the partial derivatives in (7.60) so that the constant terms are on the right and adding in artificial variables:

$$\begin{array}{ll} 2x_1 + 5y_1 + 10y_2 - t_1 + u_1 = 40 \\ 4x_2 + 4y_1 + \quad y_2 - t_2 + u_2 = 60 \\ 5x_1 + 4x_2 + s_1 + u_3 \qquad = 120 \\ 10x_1 + \quad x_2 + s_2 + u_4 \qquad = 140 \end{array} \tag{7.61}$$

For the substitute objective function, coefficients of -1 are attached to the artificial variables and zero for all other variables. This function is then maximized. The maximum value will be zero which will be taken when the artificial variables have been removed from the basis—in other words when a feasible solution has been found to (7.60) provided that the complementary slackness conditions are observed. This solution will, of necessity, be the optimal solution to the original problem. The complementary slackness conditions are observed by making sure that the x's and t's and also the y's and s's do not enter a solution simultaneously. Thus if x_2 was to remain in the solution at some stage, t_2 would not be introduced even if it had the 'most negative' index row number.

It is convenient to tackle the calculation in two stages. In stage one only u_3 and u_4 are given -1 coefficients and only the x's are permitted to replace u's in the basis. In stage two, in which u_3 and u_4 have been driven out of the basis -1 coefficients are attached to u_1 and u_2 and the y's and the s's may now enter—subject to the complementary slackness provisions. It should be noted that if it was not possible for the x's alone to replace u_3 and u_4 there would be no feasible solution to the original constraints in which both x's were positive. Such a circumstance would violate the constraint qualification condition. The calculations of stage one are shown in Figure 7.6. No index row numbers are shown under the variables that are not permitted to enter the basis in this phase. Otherwise the usual simplex procedure is applied and pivotal elements are circled. The stage two calculations are shown in Figure 7.7 in which the u_3 and u_4 columns are deleted. The optimal solution is $x_1 = 88/7$, $x_2 = 100/7$, $s_1 = 0$ and $s_2 = 0$ giving $N = 38,896/49$.

Now consider sensitivity analysis. In the last array of Figure 7.7 the inverse of the basis can be obtained from the last four columns of rates of exchange. In the original tableau (Figure 7.6) the four columns under the artificial variables in the first array form an identity matrix. Now u_3 and u_4 were deleted in phase two of the calculation, but it will be noted that the columns of coefficients under s_1 and s_2 are identical to those under u_3 and u_4. Therefore the columns of rates of exchange under u_1, u_2, s_1, s_2 respectively, form the inverse of the basis. The optimal solution can be expressed as

$$
\begin{pmatrix} y_2 \\ y_1 \\ x_2 \\ x_1 \end{pmatrix} = \frac{1}{49} \begin{pmatrix} 5.6 & -7 & 8.32 & -5.28 \\ -1.4 & 14 & -16.08 & 8.32 \\ 0 & 0 & 14 & -7 \\ 0 & 0 & -1.4 & 5.6 \end{pmatrix} \begin{pmatrix} 40 \\ 60 \\ 120 \\ 140 \end{pmatrix}
$$

$$
= \frac{1}{49} \begin{pmatrix} 63.2 \\ 19.2 \\ 700 \\ 616 \end{pmatrix} \tag{7.62}
$$

c_B	Basis		x_1	x_2	y_1	y_2	t_1	t_2	s_1	s_2	u_1	u_2	u_3	u_4
			0	0	0	0	0	0	0	0	0	0	-1	-1
0	u_1	40	2	0	5	10	-1	0	0	0	1	0	0	0
0	u_2	60	0	4	4	1	0	-1	1	0	0	1	0	0
-1	u_3	120	5	4	0	0	0	0	0	0	0	0	1	0
-1	u_4	140	(10)	1	0	0	0	0	0	1	0	0	0	1
		-260	-15	-5										
0	u_1	12	0	-0.2	5	10	-1	0	0	-0.2	1	0	0	-0.2
0	u_2	60	0	4	4	1	0	-1	1	0	0	1	0	0
-1	u_3	50	0	(3.5)	0	0	0	0	0	-0.5	0	0	1	-0.5
0	x_1	14	1	0.1	0	0	0	0	0	0.1	0	0	0	0.1
		-50	0	-3.5										
0	u_1	104/7	0	0	5	10	-1	0	0.4/7	$-1.6/7$	1	0	0.4/7	$-1.6/7$
0	u_2	20/7	0	0	4	1	0	-1	$-8/7$	4/7	0	1	$-8/7$	4/7
0	x_2	100/7	0	1	0	0	0	0	2/7	$-1/7$	0	0	2/7	$-1/7$
0	x_1	88/7	1	0	0	0	0	0	$-0.2/7$	0.8/7	0	0	$-0.2/7$	0.8/7
		0	0	0	0	0	0	0	0	0	0	0	1	1

Figure 7.6

			0	0	0	0	0	0	0	0	-1	-1
			x_1	x_2	y_1	y_2	t_1	t_2	s_1	s_2	u_1	u_2
-1	u_1	104/7	0	0	5	(10)	-1	0	0.4/7	-1.6/7	1	0
-1	u_2	20/7	0	0	4	1	0	-1	-8/7	4/7	0	1
0	x_2	100/7	0	1	0	0	0	0	2/7	-1/7	0	0
0	x_1	88/7	1	0	0	0	0	0	-0.2/7	+0.8/7	0	0
		-124/7	0	0	-9	-11	1	1	7.6/7	-2.4/7	0	0
0	y_2	10.4/7	0	0	0.5	1	-0.1	0	0.04/7	-0.16/7	0.1	0
-1	u_2	9.6/7	0	0	(3.5)	0	0.1	-1	-8.04/7	4.16/7	-0.1	1
0	x_2	100/7	0	1	0	0	0	0	2/7	-1/7	0	0
0	x_1	88/7	1	0	0	0	0	0	-0.2/7	0.8/7	0	0
		-9.6/7	0	0	-3.5	0	-0.1	1	8.04/7	-4.16/7	0.9	0
0	y_2	63.2/49	0	0	0	1	-0.8/7	1/7	8.32/49	-5.28/49	0.8/7	-1/7
0	y_1	19.2/49	0	0	1	0	0.2/7	-2/7	-16.08/49	8.32/49	-0.2/7	2/7
0	x_2	100/7	0	1	0	0	0	0	2/7	-1/7	0	0
0	x_1	88/7	1	0	0	0	0	0	-0.2/7	0.8/7	0	0
		0	0	0	0	0	0	0	0	0	1	1

Figure 7.7

Consequently the effects of variations in A_1, A_2, b_1 and b_2 (currently at levels 40, 60, 120 and 140 respectively) can be readily determined. The analysis is conducted as for variations in resource levels in linear programming. Note that the optimal values of the x's are functions only of b_1 and b_2. So long as A_1 and A_2 change in such a manner as to leave y_1 and y_2 non-negative the levels of the x's will be unaffected.

What of changes in the resource levels b_1 and b_2? If the objective function had been linear, y_1 and y_2 would have been the shadow prices of the resources and would have shown how much the objective function would change, per unit of change in the resource levels. Our objective function is strictly concave, however. The result of this is that y_1 and y_2 represent *upper bounds* on the change in N. The value of y_2 is the rate of change of the constrained maximum of N as b_2 is changed, but this rate of change is itself variable (unlike the linear case 'within' a basis) and is in fact diminishing. This can be seen from the coefficients of b_1 and b_2 for y_1 and y_2 in (7.62). The coefficients are -16.08 and -5.28 respectively. Consequently, for any finite increase Δb_2 in b_2 the increase in N, $\Delta N \leqslant \Delta b_2 \cdot y_2$. For instance if 141 units of the second resource were available from (7.62) it will be seen that the new optimal values of the x's are 621.6/49, and 99/7 for x_1 and x_2 respectively; consequently the new optimal value of N is 38,956.56/49 an increase of 60.56/49 which is less than the value of y_2 of 63.2/49. The new value of y_2 corresponding to 141 units of the second resource is seen to be $(63.2/49) - (5.28/49) = 57.92/49$ which is less than the increase in N, as we should expect.

A unit increase in the first resource causes N to increase by $11.16/49 < 19.2/49$. In this case the actual change in N is further away from the value of y_1 than was the case for ΔN and y_2 when b_2 increased. This is due to the fact that it is x_2 that increases with increasing b_1, and x_2 has the absolutely larger negative coefficient of the quadratic term in N and the quadratic term becomes more important as x_2 is increased.

Note that y_2 is an increasing function of b_1, and y_1 is also an increasing function of b_2, i.e. the marginal value of each resource increases as the amount of the other resource increases, the rate of change being the same (8.32/49) in each case. This results from the fact that for 'well-behaved' functions second-order cross-partial derivatives (which is what the number 8.32/49 is) are equal. A second order cross-partial derivative of a function is obtained by differentiating the function partially first with respect to one variable then with respect to another. In our case

$$y_1 = \frac{\partial L}{\partial b_1} \quad \text{and} \quad y_2 = \frac{\partial L}{\partial y_2}$$

Differentiate y_1 partially with respect to b_2:

$$\frac{\partial y_1}{\partial b_2} \equiv \frac{\partial^2 L}{\partial b_2 \partial b_1} \tag{7.63}$$

and y_2 partially with respect to b_1:

$$\frac{\partial y_2}{\partial b_1} \equiv \frac{\partial^2 L}{\partial b_1 \partial b_2} \tag{7.64}$$

(7.63) and (7.64) will be equal if they are continuous.

How may the values of y_1 and y_2 be used? Given any finite increase in the amount of an individual resource, the product of the increase in resource level and the corresponding Lagrange multiplier gives an *upper bound* on the change in N. If this is exceeded by the additional cost of the resource increment the resource increase possibility would be rejected. It is necessary for the acceptance of a resource increment for the cost of the increment to be strictly less than the upper bound on the increase in N.

The effects of variations in the parameters B_1 and B_2 in the objective function are less readily evaluated. A change in B_j affects the 'technical coefficient' in the Kuhn–Tucker constraint corresponding to the partial derivative with respect to x_j. Sensitivity analysis for changes in technical coefficients is a long-winded business involving the introduction of an extra column into the tableau and the determination of new rates of exchange for this column. Changes in the B's are, of course, changes in objective function coefficients of the problem as *originally formulated* in (7.59). The slopes of the objective function contours change, and in the case of an optimum at a point of tangency between a contour of the objective function and a constraint, the point of tangency will change. The situation is unlike the linear case in which changes meant either remaining at the original basis or moving to a new one.

The coefficients A_1, A_2, B_1 and B_2 are arrived at after present value calculations have been made. Changes in the discount rate, length of horizon, future prices and so on will normally cause simultaneous changes in both the A and B coefficients. Consequently, sensitivity analysis on (say) the discount rate would be cumbersome. In most cases it would be preferable to solve separate problems for alternative values of the discount rate rather than attempt post optimality analysis in the usual manner.

7.6 A Quadratic Constraint

Occasionally investment projects entered into simultaneously may be technically interdependent in terms of resource consumption. In this section we consider the problem of maximizing a linear objective function subject to a set of linear constraints and one quadratic constraint. In general the problem can be expressed as

$$\text{maximize } F = \sum_{j=1}^{n} R_j x_j$$

$$\text{subject to: } \sum_{j=1}^{n} a_j x_{ij} \leqslant b_i \quad (i = 1, 2, \ldots, m)$$

$$\text{and } \sum_{j=1}^{n} d_j x_j + \sum_{h=1}^{n} \sum_{j=1}^{n} d_{hj} x_h x_j \leqslant b_0$$

(7.65)

In (7.65) the R_j, a_{ij}, d_j, d_j, d_{hj}, b_i and b_0 are constants and where at least one of the d_{hj} is non-zero. If $d_{ij} \neq 0$ then the requirements for the zeroth resource by the jth activity is a non-linear function of activity level and if $d_{hj} \neq 0$ there exists interdependency between the zeroth resource consumption by the hth and jth activities. Consider an example. A company wishes to choose the amounts to take of two investments subject to a linear initial outlay constraint and a quadratic constraint on consumption of some fixed resource. The coefficients of the problem are as in (7.66):

$$\text{maximize } F = 7x_1 + 8x_2$$

$$\text{subject to } x_1 + 3x_2 \leqslant 15$$

$$\text{and } 10x_1 + 12x_2 + 0.2x_1^2 + 0.5x_2^2 + 0.6x_1x_2 \leqslant 100$$

$$x_1 \geqslant 0 \quad x_2 \geqslant 0$$

(7.66)

The Lagrangian function and the Kuhn–Tucker conditions would then be as follows:

$$L = 7x_1 + 8x_2 + y_1(15 - x_1 - 3x_2) + y_2(100 - 10x_1$$
$$- 12x_2 - 0.2x_1^2 - 0.5x_2^2 - 0.6x_1x_2)$$

$$\frac{\partial L}{\partial x_1} = 7 - y_1 - y_2(10 + 0.4x_1 + 0.6x_2) \leqslant 0$$

$$\frac{\partial L}{\partial x_2} = 8 - 3y_1 - y_2(12 + x_2 + 0.6x_1) \leqslant 0$$

$$x_1 \frac{\partial L}{\partial x_1} + x_2 \frac{\partial L}{\partial x_2} = 0$$

$$x_1 \geqslant 0, \quad x_2 \geqslant 0$$

$$\frac{\partial L}{\partial y_1} = 15 - x_1 - 3x_2 \geqslant 0$$

$$\frac{\partial L}{\partial y_2} = 100 - 10x_1 - 12x_2 - 0.2x_1^2 - 0.5x_2^2 - 0.6x_1x_2 \geqslant 0$$

$$y_1 \frac{\partial L}{\partial y_1} + y_2 \frac{\partial L}{\partial y_2} = 0$$

$$y_1 \geqslant 0, \quad y_2 \geqslant 0.$$

(7.67)

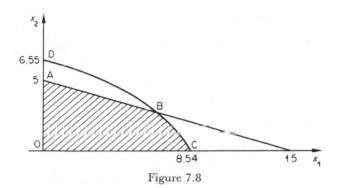

Figure 7.8

As in all programming problems, the Kuhn–Tucker conditions characterize an optimum but finding solutions to (7.67) is by no means easy. The constraint set in the current problem is graphed in Figure 7.8 where the feasible region is shaded. It will be noted that the feasible region is convex. A sufficient condition for this is that the d_{hj} in the constraints (7.65) form a positive semi-definite matrix. This being so, it follows that since the objective function is linear the optimal solution will be *either* at one of the points OABC *or* a point of tangency between points B and C. The values of x_2 and x_1 at points B and C are obtained by setting x_1 and x_2 (respectively) equal to zero in the quadratic constraint. The objective function contours have a slope of -0.875 and are thus steeper (in absolute terms) than the linear constraint. Thus point A will not be optimal. As x_1 increases, the slope (in absolute terms) of the quadratic constraint also increases, so that if the slope of the quadratic constraint at point C is less than the slope of the objective function contours then point C will be optimal. If the slope of the quadratic constraint at point C is greater (again in absolute terms) than the objective function contours, then the optimum will be either at point B or at a point of tangency between B and C.

The slope of the objective function contours is given by the ratio of the coefficients of x_1 and x_2 in the objective function. These coefficients are the partial derivatives of F with respect to x_1 and x_2. The same applies in the case of the quadratic constraint. If the RHS is at the level b_0, then:

$$db_0 = \frac{\partial b_0}{\partial x_1} dx_1 + \frac{\partial b_0}{\partial x_2} db_2$$

Along the constraint there must be no change in b_0; therefore $db_0 = 0$ and so

$$\frac{dx_2}{dx_1} = -\frac{\dfrac{\partial b_0}{\partial x_1}}{\dfrac{\partial b_0}{\partial x_2}}$$

thus in the present example

$$\frac{dx_2}{dx_1} = -\frac{(10 + 0.4x_1 + 0.6x_2)}{(12 + x_2 + 0.6x_1)}$$

and at point C, where $x_2 = 0$ and $x_1 = 8.54$

$$\frac{dx_2}{dx_1} = -\frac{(10 + 0.4x_1)}{(12 + 0.6x_1)} = -\frac{13.42}{17.12} = -0.78$$

The objective function is steeper than the quadratic constraint at point C so point C is optimal giving a value of F of 59.78.

In theory the optimality of a point obtained by means other than solution of the Kuhn–Tucker conditions can be verified by substitution into the conditions (and solving for the Lagrange multipliers). However, the problem of rounding errors arises. The value of x_1 at C is only *approximately* 8.54. The Kuhn–Tucker conditions can be usefully employed to find (in this case approximately) the values of the Lagrange multipliers. Here we have found $x_1 = 8.54$, $x_2 = 0$ and since the first constraint is not binding $y_1 = 0$. Also since $x_1 \geqslant 0$ then $\partial L/\partial x_1 = 0$ thus

$$7 - y_2(10 + 0.4(8.54)) = 0$$

therefore

$$y_2 \simeq 0.52$$

The value of y_2 is the rate of change of the optimal value of F as the RHS of the quadratic constraint is altered, but since the constraint is non-linear the value of y_2 is not constant for a finite change in b. Thus it can be used only to place an upper bound on the change in F. For example, if 110 units of the second resource were available the upper bound on the increase in F given by use of the Lagrange multiplier y_2 is 5.2. The new value of x_1 is approximately 9.28 and the corresponding value of F is 64.96, an increase of 5.18. Thus the use of y_2 in this instance for a 10% increase in resource 2 availability is accurate to one decimal place.

Van de Panne (1966) has developed a solution procedure for these problems which represents 'an application of the simplex and dual methods for quadratic programming to parametric quadratic programming problems'. Although the algorithm will terminate in a finite number of iterations the calculations involved may be lengthy although the method lends itself well to computer application. Unfortunately the method cannot cope with more than one quadratic constraint. If the feasible area for the quadratic constraint is non-convex Van de Panne's method cannot be employed and an approximation method is indicated.

7.7 Approximation and Gradient Methods

There will be occasions when the constrained maximization of present values produces a non-linear problem structure which is of a more complex character than those so far considered. Some observations on computation in non-linear programming problems in general are worth adding here.

There is a class of procedures known as *gradient methods* in which the principle used is that of changing the x vector in such a way as to move in the 'direction' in which the objective function is increasing most rapidly. There are various ways in which this principle is employed in the presence of constraints, depending upon the way in which it is modified to take account of the constraints. Even though gradient methods are not of the same ilk as the Simplex method (they are not 'adjacent extreme point' methods) the Simplex algorithm is frequently of use in determining the direction in which to move, if moving in the direction of the gradient vector (the direction of steepest ascent) is ruled out by constraints or sign requirements. However, gradient methods, as Hadley (1964) points out '. . . will normally converge at best to a local optimum, and perhaps not even a local optimum. It is only when the problem possesses the appropriate convexity or concavity properties that we can be sure that the process will converge to the global optimum. Generally, an infinit number of iterations may be required for convergence, although for certain special cases such as linear programming problems, convergence can always be made to take place in a finite number of steps.' This is not to condemn the methods. It is frequently out of the question to determine the global optimum (or to know that it has been found). Gradient methods are among the best available and it should be recalled that a technique is justified if it improves on what otherwise would have been done.

In those problems in which the objective function and constraints are separable and can therefore be written as

$$
\left.
\begin{array}{ll}
\text{maximize } F = \sum_{j=1}^{n} f_j(x_j) & \\[2mm]
\text{subject to} \quad \sum_{j=1}^{n} g_{ij}(x_j) \leqslant b & (i = 1, 2, \ldots, m) \\[2mm]
\text{and} \quad\quad\quad\quad x_j \geqslant 0 & (j = 1, 2, \ldots, n)
\end{array}
\right\}
\quad (7.68)
$$

the functions $g_{ij}(x_j)$ and $f_j(x_j)$ in (7.68) can be replaced by polygonal approximations. Such an approximation is shown in Figure (7.9) where $f_j(x_j)$ is rather crudely approximated by the series of dashed lines. The approximation can be made as good as is desired (at the price of computational effort) by appropriate selection of the x_{kj} (above, $k = 1, \ldots 4$) and fine enough division of the interval over which x_j is permitted to vary. Having made such approximations a local maximum for the approximating problem is found. Only when the appropriate convexity/concavity conditions are satisfied will there be an assurance of finding the

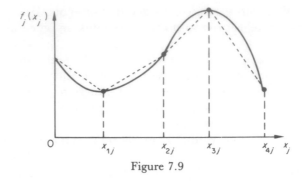

Figure 7.9

global optimum to the approximating problem. However, apparently innocuous approximations can have dramatic effects in terms of the original problem.

In those problems in which only the objective function is non-linear, extensions of the Simplex method can be applied. The problem becomes less tractable when the partial derivatives of the objective function with respect to the x_j are not linear. A quadratic programming approach to such problems has been developed by Fletcher (1970) and extended by Murray (1969) and Biggs (1971) to problems with non-linear constraints. When the objective function is linear but the constraint set is not, Kelley (1960) suggested that a cutting plane approach may be employed. In this approach a set of linear constraints is generated that contain the original feasible region (which must be convex). This LP problem is then solved by the Simplex method. The solution produced will not in general be feasible in terms of the original constraints and a cutting plane is introduced rendering the LP solution infeasible but not cutting off any of the original feasible region. The new LP problem is then solved and a new cut generated. Convergence, however, may require an infinite number of steps so that in practical terms there appears to be little advantage over other approximating techniques.

7.8 Dynamic Programming and Investment Decisions

The programming methods described so far are *static economizing models*. The problem was the allocation of scarce resources between alternative competing uses. In a capital-rationing context the scarce resources obviously include finance at one or more points in time, physical resources such as equipment, materials and labour and also less tangible 'resources' such as upper bounds and allowable limits on financial ratios. The alternative competing uses are the capital projects. While the typical budgeting problem involves cash inputs at several points in time it nevertheless allows of formulation within the static economizing framework. There is only one decision point and, formally, it is quite allowable to represent next year's financial inputs as the use of just another resource—the mathematics after all cannot tell the difference.

However, many capital-budgeting problems allow of a *dynamic* formulation. There may actually be several decision points, but even if this is not so if the decision problem can be divided up into *stages* then a discrete dynamic expression is possible. Many problems (for example, Lorie–Savage problems) allow of either static or dynamic expression. The choice of form would be up to the problem solver. Characteristically, a dynamic economizing model allocates scarce resources between alternative uses between initial and terminal times. Optimal time paths are required for control variables which are linked to state variables descriptive of the system under study. The time path may be that of a missile or an economy; the state of the system may be a trajectory or total capital expenditure. Classical types of control problem are approachable via the calculus of variations. Along with the *maximum principle*, dynamic programming arose as a modern approach to *control theory*. Developing out of the work of Bellman in the late 1950s and early 1960s, due to the structural relation to control theory, many engineering applications were found. In relation to the context of this book, there have been applications to capital-rationing problems, network flows and integer programming.

In this section and section 7.9 we shall examine certain types of investment problem—those that can be formulated as multistage problems. This may mean either that there are, in fact, several times at which action is required in an investment programme, or it may mean that the decision procedure itself can be divided into stages—all the real action itself being at $t = 0$. This would be the case where a number of investments were being taken into consideration with a single capital constraint at $t = 0$. The objective of this section is to display a simple tabular method that is suitable for discrete problems of a form commonly taken by capital-rationing problems—for example the Lorie–Savage class of problems for which two solution procedures have already been suggested. The following section will expound an interesting case of sequential investments under a rationing constraint. This represents an unusual dynamic problem for which analytical results are possible.

We shall start by examining a Lorie–Savage-type capital-rationing problem. The objective will be to select those investments which maximize present value overall. There is one financial constraint but, unlike the Lorie–Savage problem proper, various discretely separate levels are possible for each type of investment. We shall decompose the problem into *stages*. The first stage will represent consideration of the levels of *any* one of the investments. The second stage will consider a second investment. This second stage is linked to the first through the *state of the system*. We shall see in the tabular layout the importance of recording the state of the system at state t. In dynamic programming problems it is not always obvious how this should be defined, but it is essential to define

	Type 1				Type 2				Type 3				
Initial outlay	10	15	20	30	10	15	20	30	10	15	20	25	30
Net present value	25	35	40	48	25	28	30	48	30	35	38	40	48

Figure 7.10

'state' so as to provide linkage between stages so that it is possible to obtain feasible solutions at one stage without having to confirm feasibility in terms of other stages. In our capital-budgeting context, the state of the system at stage t will be total capital expended at all stages up to and including stage t. We shall be examining problems which are *additively* decomposible—where the objective function will be the sum of net present values added between stages.

Consider a numerical example. Three types of investment are available. Initial capital outlays and net present values (units of £1,000) are as detailed in Figure 7.10. Note that the alternative of zero investment in any one type is not available. The total budget is £45,000. There are no other constraints.

An obvious simplification is that the most expensive alternative (30) can be ruled out in each case, since even if the cheapest option was used in the other cases (10) the budget limit would be exceeded.

System state will be measured by total outlay up to and including any stage. Stage one will involve one product only (Type 3 here), stage two will introduce a second product and stage three the third product. A simple layout for the tabular workings is shown in Figure 7.11. For the moment nothing more is done other than to record possibilities. Later on, we shall come back through the stages and the appropriate stage one state and outlay will be indicated. Stage two introduces the type 2 investment. Details are laid out in Figure 7.12. The state of 20 (at stage two) can only be made up of an outlay on type 2 of 10 following on from a stage one state of 10. The present value achieved up to this point would be 55. The state of 25 at stage two can be arrived at in two ways—as shown. Only the *higher* value of the objective is relevant. Bracketed figures in the present value column correspond to arrangements that could never be optimal. All we are concerned with here is producing a list of the efficient ways that the various states at stage two may be made up. Stage three is shown in Figure 7.13. The solution can now be 'unrolled'. The maximum present value is 100, resulting from the state of the system 45 arriv-

Stage one (type 3 outlays)		
State	Outlay	Present value
10	10	30
15	15	35
20	20	38
25	25	40

Figure 7.11

Stage two			
State	Type 2 outlay	Stage one state	Present value
20	10	10	55
25	15	10	(58)
	10	15	60
30	20	10	(60)
	15	15	63
	10	20	63
35	20	15	(65)
	15	20	66
	10	25	65

Figure 7.12

Stage three			
State	Type 1 outlay	Stage two state	Present value
30	10	20	80
35	15	20	90
	10	25	(85)
40	20	20	95
	15	25	95
	10	30	(88)
45	20	25	100
	15	30	(98)
	10	35	(91)

Figure 7.13

ed at by an outlay of 20 on type 1 investment *and* a stage two state of 25. Reference back to Figure 7.12 shows that the state of 25 at stage two should consist of an investment of 10 in type 2 and a stage one state of 15. In turn a state of 15 at stage one can only mean investment of 15 in type 3. Thus the ideal states at pre-final stages will not necessarily (or usually) correspond to the maximum value that can be achieved at that stage. Rather it is an *appropriate* state that is being sought. This becomes evident only at unrolling.

Some aspects of sensitivity analysis are facilitated by the tableau layout. For instance, on the RHS of the constraint. If capital available is reduced from 45 to 40 then, from Figure 7.13, it is clear that total present value goes down to 95 and the optimum is non-unique. One arrangement would reduce type 1 outlay to 15, thus pointing to a stage two state of 25 and unchanged values for the other outlays. Alternatively, it could be the type 3 outlay that is reduced.

Sensitivity analysis on the objective function coefficients is not dissimilar to that under zero–one programming by the pseudo-Boolean method. The maximum downward variation in the present value figure for a variable in the optimum is the difference between the current optimal value of the objective function and the next best value of the

Stage one (type 1)		
State	Outlay	Present value
10	10	25
15	15	35
20	**20**	**40**

	Stage two		
State	Type 3 outlay	Stage one state	Present value
20	10	10	55
25	15	10	(60)
	10	15	65
30	20	10	(63)
	15	15	70
	10	20	70
35	25	10	(65)
	20	15	(73)
	15	**20**	**75**

	Stage three		
State	Type 2 outlay	Stage two state	Present value
30	10	20	80
35	15	20	(83)
	10	25	90
40	20	20	(85)
	15	25	(93)
	10	30	95
45	20	25	(95)
	15	30	(98)
	10	**35**	**100**

Figure 7.14

objective function for a solution that does not contain the variable in question. For example, if the NPV on the 20-unit investment on type 1 fell by more than two units then the solution would change (to one of the two arrangements giving the PV = 98 result).

Figure 7.14 shows the problem solved with a different choice of investment type to be considered at each stage. The optimal position at each stage is boxed. Note that (naturally) the optimum solution is unchanged and that there is no significance in the fact that the best stage two state is here 35 in contrast to the best stage two state of 25 obtained previously. Sensitivity analysis would also give the same results, as the final stage must include the optimal arrangement corresponding to each state. In general there will be $n!$ different ways in which the final stage can be arrived at.

The tableau presentation should have given a clear intuitive idea of the basic principles of dynamic programming. The recursive relationship can be simply stated:

maximum total value = maximum of [value added at last stage

+ value from all previous stages]

Nothing could be much simpler or more obvious than this statement. Once the maximum overall value has been found, this will point to the appropriate value to be obtained from the $(n-1)$th stage which itself, by recursion, points to the appropriate value at the $n-2$)th stage and so on. Whilst it is true that not all dynamic investment problems will be so simply expressed and tabulated, the general principles of approach remain the same. The recursive relationship will be formalized for a more general context later.

It is interesting to compare the speed of solution by the method just outlined with an alternative approach. If the various levels of type 1 investment are represented by x_1 to x_4, type 2 investment by x_5 to x_8 and type 3 investment by x_9 to x_{13}, then the problem can be expressed as in (7.69). In (7.69) a zero–one programming formulation is given in which there are four explicit constraints.

Maximize $F = 25x_1 + 35x_2 + 40x_3 + 48x_4 + 25x_5 + 28x_6 + 30x_7 + 48x_8$
$$+ 30x_9 + 35x_{10} + 38x_{11} + 40x_{12} + 48x_{13}$$

subject to
$$x_1 + x_2 + x_3 + x_4 \quad\quad = 1$$
$$x_5 + x_6 + x_7 + x_8 \quad\quad = 1$$
$$x_9 + x_{10} + x_{11} + x_{12} + x_{13} = 1 \quad\quad\quad\quad (7.69)$$
$$10x_1 + 15x_2 + 20x_3 + 30x_4 + 10x_5 + 15x_6 + 20x_7 + 30x_8$$
$$+ 10x_9 + 15x_{10} + 20x_{11} + 25x_{12} + 30x_{13} \leqslant 45$$
$$x_j = 0 \quad \text{or} \quad 1, \quad\quad j = 1, \ldots, 13$$

Clearly, dynamic programming will represent one of the more efficient approaches for this class of problem. But how efficient is the procedure in comparison with complete enumeration?

In both sets of workings (as it happens) we have evaluated 22 combinations of three, two or one levels of outlay on each type. Excluding the levels of 30 there are 36 ($= 3 \times 3 \times 4$) combinations of the remaining possibilities (three at a time). The work done was thus $[100 \times (22/36)]\%$ = 61% of the work involved in enumeration calculations. This is a higher percentage—but would rapidly drop as problem size becomes more realistic. It could easily turn out that dynamic programming workings occupy less than 1%, or less than one-tenth of 1% or less than one-hundreth part of 1%, of the time needed for complete enumeration.

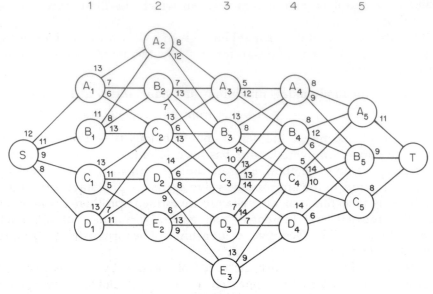

Figure 7.15

Some types of dynamic problem allow of a convenient graphical solution. Pipeline construction is a typical utility venture involving substantial capital expenditures. In this context there is a physical stage-by-stage segregation. In the example to follow it will be assumed that the revenues from the project are independent of choice of route. The problem is, in fact, known as the *routing problem*.

From a storage reservoir S a pipeline is to be routed through five intermediate stations to a terminal T. There are a number of alternative locations for each station. Costs of constructing links between possible stations are shown in Figure 7.15. The feasible linkages are as illustrated. What is the cheapest route for the pipeline? Consider first the choice of location for station 5. There are three possibilities: A_5, B_5 or C_5. In each of the circles enter the *least cost* of getting to the terminus, T, from that location. In fact there is no choice. It costs 11 from A_5, 9 from B_5 and 8 from C_5. Entries would be as shown in Figure 7.16.

Now consider the choice of location for station 4. There are four possibilities: A_4, B_4, C_4 and D_4. For each of these stations we want to

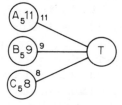

Figure 7.16

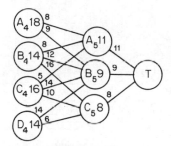

Figure 7.17

determine the least cost of completing the journey to T. Consider A_4. From here we can go, at a cost of 8, to A_5 and from there it costs 11 to get to T. Thus the cost would be 19. But there is another possibility. We can go from A_4 to B_5 and thence to T. This means of completing the journey from A_4 would cost 9 (from A_4 to B_5) + 9 (from B_5 to T), a total of 18. These are the only possibilities. Enter the *lower* figure in the circle for A_4 and do the same for B_4, C_4 and D_4. From B_4 there are three choices: via A_5 costing 8 + 11 = 19; via B_5 costing 12 + 9 = 21; or via C_5 costing 6 + 8 = 14. So in the B_4 circle enter 14. Applying the same simple procedure to C_4 and D_4 gives the picture as shown in Figure 7.17.

Now apply the same ideas to the station three locations. The results are shown in Figure 7.18. Similar procedures are applied to stations two and one. The complete picture is shown in Figure 7.19. The first thing that is found is that the cheapest pipeline would cost 44. The actual route is then 'unrolled' quite simply since it was D_1 that gave rise to the 44 at S, it was D_2 that gave rise to the 36 at D_1 and so on. It will be seen that there are *two* optimal routes marked ——||—— They diverge at D_3 and consist of

D_1, D_2, D_3, B_4, C_5

and

D_1, D_2, D_3, D_4, C_5

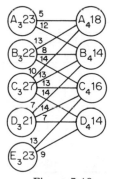

Figure 7.18

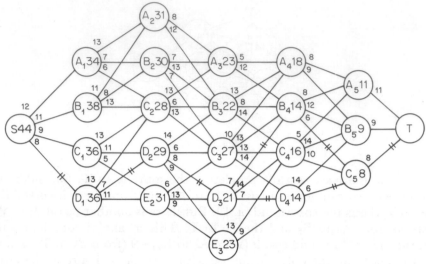

Figure 7.19

This *non-uniqueness* is usually welcomed in practice as some flexibility is introduced—although it is minimal here. The procedure used a *backwards* pass. Confirmation that the solution is correct can be obtained by repeating the exercise going *forwards* from S.

The problem involved five stages. At each of these stages the system may be on any one of a number of states which correspond to choice of location. For instance, at the *first* stage we are concerned with the choice of location for the fifth station. The states possible here are 'being at A_5', 'being at B_5' and 'being at C_5' The *second* stage in the problem solution relates to the location of station four. The possible states here are being at A_4, at B_4, at C_4 or at D_4. For each of the states we need a *state description*—a presentation of all relevant information for future decision. Here, we are concerned with costs. The state description at A_4, for in-

Month (t)	Ex factory price (c_t	Wholesale price (p^t)
January ($t=1$)	70	90
February ($t=2$)	64	82
March ($t=3$)	72	70
April ($t=4$)	70	85
May ($t=5$)	65	90
June ($t=6$)	65	85

Figure 7.20

stance, is the cost of 18. Working back from T we have seen that 18 is the lowest cost that can be arrived at. Put another way, 18 is the least cost of completing the journey from A_4. The sequence of states that gave rise to the optimal cost of 19 was A_4, A_5, T. This sequence of states constitutes an optimal *sub-policy*. In the system as a whole we look for the optimal *policy* which is a sequence of states from start to finish. Now the fundamental concept in dynamic programming is the *principle of optimality*. This can be stated in numerous ways. In respect of a least-cost routing problem:

Principle of optimality: The overall least cost route from origin to destination (i.e. from S to T) contains the least cost route between any two stations on the overall least cost route.

By 'station' here we intend to include both S and T. So that the overall least-cost route gives, for example, the cheapest route between B_4 and T, or between S and D_3, or between D_1 and C_5.

As a final example consider the classical *warehousing* problem. A wholesaler stocks a single item. The ex factory price (c_t) at which he buys and the wholesale price (p_t) at which he sells varies from month to month. *Lead time* on his purchases is 14 days, i.e. an order placed on 18 March arrives in stock on 1 April. Each month he buys an amount, q_t, around mid-month so that it arrives in stock on the first day of the following month. Sales volume in any month, v_t, will not exceed the stock available at the start of that month. Total storage capacity is K. Ignore storage and transactions costs. The prices are expected to be as shown in Figure 7.20. The wholesaler holds an initial stock of 300 units on 1 January. What should be the pattern of purchases and sales to maximize profit over the six-month period? A backward working method will be employed. Consider the situation in June. Let this be stage one. Profit in this stage, Π_1, is revenue from sales less cost of purchases. Viz.

$$\Pi_1 = p_6 v_6 - c_6 q_6$$

which we wish to maximize with respect to v_6 and q_6; the June sales and purchases. Clearly:

$$v_6 \leqslant I_6$$

since by the specification of the problem sales in any month cannot exceed the inventory at the start of the month. Now purchases in June are limited by storage capacity:

$$q_6 \leqslant K - I_6 + v_6$$

i.e. storage capacity is K; there was already I_6 in stock to start with but v_6 have already been sold. Naturally, v_6 and q_6 cannot be negative. So a linear programming problem is to be solved:

$$\left.\begin{array}{l} \text{maximize } \Pi_1 = p_6 v_6 - c_6 q_6 \\[1mm] \text{subject to} \qquad v_6 \leqslant I_6 \\[3mm] \qquad\qquad q_6 \leqslant K - I_6 + v_6 \\[1mm] \text{where} \qquad\qquad q_6 \geqslant 0, \qquad v_6 \geqslant 0. \end{array}\right\} \qquad (7.70)$$

Now the problem (7.70) is trivial. We shall assume that no terminal stocks are required (these could be incorporated) and June is the last month being considered—thus it is pointless making purchases—so $q_6 = 0$. Also, v_6 is made as large as possible (all stock is sold) so $v_6 = I_6$. Thus maximum $\Pi_1 = p_6 I_6$ and we should note that

$$I_6 = I_5 + q_5 - v_5 \qquad (7.71)$$

Now consider transactions in May. This is stage two. In keeping with the principle of optimality we want the profit *from here on* (i.e. May *plus* June's) to be as large as possible. So we write the profit function at stage two as

$$\Pi_2 = p_5 v_5 - c_5 q_5 + \Pi_1 \qquad (7.72)$$

in which the *maximum* value of Π_1 would be used, i.e. $p_6 I_6$. But if we now substitute for I_6 from (7.71):

$$\text{maximum} \quad \Pi_1 = p_6 I_6 = p_6 I_5 + p_6 q_5 - p_6 v_5 \qquad (7.73)$$

and substituting (7.73) into (7.72) gives

$$\Pi_2 = p_5 v_5 - c_5 q_5 + p_6 I_5 + p_6 q_5 - p_6 v_5$$

$$\therefore \quad \Pi_2 = (p_5 - p_6)v_5 + (p_6 - c_5)q_5 + p_6 I_5$$

which is the expression to be maximized with respect to the two variables v_5 and q_5. The constraints are

$$v_5 \leqslant I_5$$

$$q_5 \leqslant K - I_5 + v_5$$

so that the linear programming problem is

$$\left.\begin{array}{l} \text{maximize } \Pi_2 = (p_5 - p_6)v_5 + (p_6 - c_5)q_5 + p_6 I_5 \\[2mm] \text{subject to} \qquad v_5 \leqslant I_5 \\[3mm] \qquad\qquad q_5 \leqslant K - I_5 + v_5 \\[2mm] \qquad\qquad v_5 \geqslant 0, \qquad q_5 \geqslant 0. \end{array}\right\} \qquad (7.74)$$

Figure 7.21 graphs the feasible region (shaded) for the non-trivial problem (7.74). The optimum will be at one of the corners OABC depending on the slope of the objective function contours.

This whole procedure is repeated for each month until January (stage

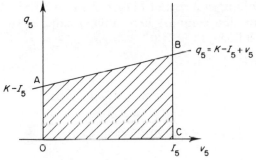

Figure 7.21

six). The solution is then unrolled. With the data of Figure 7.20. For stage one we can straightaway write

maximum $\quad \Pi_1 = p_6 I_6 - \boxed{85 I_6}$

Now the LP problem for stage two is

maximize $\quad \Pi_2 = (90 - 85)v_5 + (85 - 65)q_5 + 85 I_5$

subject to $\qquad v_5 \leqslant I_5$

$\qquad\qquad q_5 \leqslant K - I_5 + v_5$

In terms of Figure 7.21 the objective function contours have negative slope (= − 5/20) so B will be the optimal point. Thus $v_5 = I_5$ and $q_5 - K$. So that

maximum $\quad \Pi_2 = \quad 5v_5 + 20q_5 + 85 I_5$

$\qquad\qquad = \quad 5 I_5 + 20K + 85 I_5$

$\qquad\qquad = \boxed{90 I_5 + 20K}$

Now for April (stage three, $t = 4$) we must maximize Π_3, that is

maximize $\quad \Pi_3 = p_4 v_4 - c_4 q_4 + \text{maximum } \Pi_2$

$\qquad\qquad = 85 v_4 - 70 q_4 + 90 I_5 + 20K$

but $I_5 = I_4 + q_4 - v_4$ so that

$\Pi_3 = 85 v_4 - 70 q_4 + 90(I_4 + q_4 - v_4) + 20K$

$\qquad = -5v_4 + 20q_4 + 90 I_4 + 20K$

and the linear programming problem is to

maximize $\quad \Pi_3 = -5v_4 + 20q_4 + 90 I_4 + 20K$

subject to: $\qquad v_4 \leqslant I_4$

$\qquad\qquad q_4 \leqslant K - I_4 + v_4$

$\qquad\qquad v_4 \geqslant 0, \qquad q_4 \geqslant 0.$

Now, again thinking in terms of Figure 7.21, AB has a slope of $+1$ and the objective function contours here have a slope of $+1/4$. So that B is again optimal. Thus:

$$v_4 = I_4$$

$$q_4 = K$$

and

$$\text{maximum} \quad \Pi_3 = -5I_4 + 20K + 90I_4 + 20K$$

so

$$\text{maximum} \quad \Pi_3 = \boxed{85I_4 + 40K}$$

Now for the fourth stage (March):

$$\Pi_4 = p_3 v_3 - c_3 q_3 + \max \Pi_3$$

So

$$\Pi_4 = 70v_3 - 72q_3 + 85I_4 + 40K$$

$$= -15v_3 + 13q_3 + 85I_3 + 40K$$

and in this case the objective function contours (slope = 15/13) are steeper than the constraint line AB so that point A is optimal. At this point $v_3 = 0$ and $q_3 = K - I_3$. This results in

$$\text{maximum} \quad \Pi_4 = 72I_3 + 53K$$

So $v_1 = 300$
$q_1 = 1,000$
So $I_2 = 1,000$
$\therefore$ $v_2 = 1,000$
$q_2 = 1,000$
$I_3 = 1,000$
$v_3 = 0$
$q_3 = 0$
$I_4 = 1,000$
$v_4 = 1,000$
$q_4 = 1,000$
$I_5 = 1,000$
$v_5 = 1,000$
$q_5 = 1,000$
$I_6 = 1,000$
$v_6 = 1,000$
$q_6 = 0$

and the total profit made is:

$$\Pi_6 = 90I_1 + 73K = 27,000 + 73,000 = 100,000$$

Figure 7.22

By similar processes we obtain

$$\text{maximum} \quad \Pi_5 = 82I_2 + 61K \qquad (v_2 = I_2, \; q_2 = K)$$

and

$$\text{maximum} \quad \Pi_6 = 90I_1 + 73K \qquad (v_1 = I_1, \; q_1 = K)$$

and the fully unrolled results sequence (recalling that $I_1 = 300$) and setting $K = 1,000$) is shown in Figure 7.22.

The optimal level of profit (the 100,000 is a *linear* function of initial stock and warehouse capacity (the coefficients 90 and 73 depend upon the pattern of prices) and the whole problem was a sequence of linear programming problems. Note that the dynamic programming process did not tell us how the LP problem at each state was to be solved.

We have illustrated problems which allowed of a very convenient tabular expression. More complex examples will require a more precise notation, and the relation of objective function value to a decision variable, which, in the most compact notation, is a subscript. In this context, the equations (7.75) and (7.76) capture the essential pattern of the dynamic programming approach in a capital-rationing context:

$$V_t(b_t) = \max_{x_t} \left[W_{tx_t} + V_{t-1}(b_t - k_{tx_t}) \right] k_{tx_t} \leqslant b_t \qquad (7.75)$$

$$V_1(b_1) = \max_{x_t} \left[W_{1x_t} \right] k_{1x_t} \leqslant b_1 \qquad (7.76)$$

V_t = amount of net *present* value achieved by all stages up to and including stage t;

x_t = the *decision variable* at stage t. It is itself a subscript of other variables and identifies the alternatives available at that stage; $x_t = 1, 2, \ldots, n_t$;

n_t = number of alternatives available at stage t;

w_{tx_t} = the increment in net present value resulting from the selection of alternative x_t at stage t;

k_{tx_t} = the capital cost (at the *present*, for which the one constraint is defined) of alternative x_t at stage t;

b_t = the amount of capital allocated to stage t. This is not itself the *decision* variable although it is indeed variable; the best level emerging when the solution is unrolled.

Equation (7.75) states that the net present value achievable in total by all stages up to and including the tth is the best *combination* of NPV achieved by stages up to and including the $t - 1$th *and* the increment added in the tth stage. Note that neither the net present value up to stage $t - 1$ (V_{t-1}) nor the increment of the tth stage (w_{tx_t}) need necessarily be at maximum possible levels. The 'best' level of V_{t-1} is not necessarily its maximum. By implication, when (7.75) is formulated for $t + 1$, it follows that the best level of V_t is not necessarily *its* maximum. What is going to matter is the level of V_N net present value—all stages considered. The value of V_{N-1}

that leads to this is the best value of V_{N-1} and the best value of V_{N-2} is the value that leads to the best value of V_{N-1} and so on. This is the idea of recursion—'coming back'—that we have frequently made use of. Equation (7.75) is the *general recursive equation*.

It is important to recall that dynamic programming gives the unifying recursive relationship but does not provide a solution procedure at each stage. The problems vary in many ways, and from the computational point of view one of the most important differences between problems is the complexity of each stage. Another important factor is the *number* of state variables required. In such *multiple-state* problems, great computational gains may follow if the number of state variables does not exceed three. In general, dynamic programming problems do not have analytical solutions (although the maximum principle has advantages in this respect). We now turn, however, to a dynamic investment problem that does allow of analytical solution.

7.9 Dynamic Investment Sequences

In this section we consider a rather special form of capital-rationing problem. The case is that of an investment which requires net inputs of capital in each of a number of years before any positive returns start to come in. In a once-only case, the project would be assessed by NPV or NTV in the usual manner. Where repetition is possible, that is, where several sequences of the same investment can be undertaken, commencing at different points in time and where initial capital is limited, the problem is somewhat more difficult. The conventional rationing framework of Chapter 4 can indeed accommodate such a problem, but to leave things at that point would fail to exploit the special characteristics of the problem. The example and discussion to follow is based upon pathbreaking work by Gale (1964).

A project requires cash inputs in each of a number of years and gives a single positive return thereafter. Certain insurance policies are examples of this type of investment which can be thought of as the converse case of a one-period outlay, several-return project. The problem will be to determine the points at which to start such investments and the scale of each so as to maximize terminal value at a specified date. Consider the investment sequence -1, -2, 4, in other words, inputs required at £1 initially and £2 after one year, yielding a return of £4 a further year thereafter. It is envisaged that several such sequences can be started; the number limited only by available funds of £4 initially. The objective is to maximize terminal value four years hence. Taking fractions of the project to be meaningful, it might be thought that the best policy would be given by Figure 7.23.

It is convenient to refer to the initial year as *one* and the sequence started in that year as sequence one, so that 'year five' means 'at the

Year	1	2	3	4	5
Savings	4	8/3	0	32/9	0
Sequence one	−4/3	−8/3	+16/3		
Sequence two			−16/9	−32/9	+64/9

Figure 7.23

beginning of the fifth year'—four years after sequence one was begun. The row labelled 'savings' shows funds available for investment in a year. The policy described by Figure 7.23 is to invest 4/3 in year one, 8/3 in year two, giving a return of 16/3 in year three, 16/9 of which is used to start a second sequence which then results in savings of 32/9 in the fourth year, being just the amount required to complete the second sequence. The result is a terminal value of 64/9. This policy is not optimal. The optimum policy is that shown in Figure 7.24. Three sequences should be completed (clearly there is no time for a fourth) as detailed and an improvement of $12\frac{1}{2}$% in NTV over that of the naïve pattern is achieved.

To ensure optimality it is only necessary that the sequences are such that there are no savings arising in any year after the first sequence has been completed. The problem is in fact, one of dynamic linear programming, but is uncharacteristic of such problems in that a relatively simple formula can be derived for its solution.

Let $\mathbf{Y}_t$ be the vector of the first inputs in the n sequences in the optimal programme beginning with the tth sequence. Then we can write

$$\mathbf{Y}_t = \frac{\mathbf{K}^{T-t}\mathbf{r}_r}{\mathbf{k}\mathbf{K}^{T-1}\mathbf{c}_1} \tag{7.77}$$

where, in (7.77) t is the subscript of the first element of the vector. For example if $t = 4$

$$\mathbf{Y}_4 = \begin{bmatrix} Y_4 \\ Y_5 \\ \vdots \\ Y_{4+n-1} \end{bmatrix}$$

and, for the example above, if $t = 1$

$$\mathbf{Y}_1 = \begin{pmatrix} Y_1 \\ Y_2 \end{pmatrix} = \begin{pmatrix} 1 \\ 1 \end{pmatrix}$$

Year	1	2	3	4	5
Savings	4	3	0	0	0
Sequence one	−1	−2	+4		
Sequence two		−1	−2	+4	
Sequence three			−2	−4	8

Figure 7.24

T is the number of periods to the horizon after the first sequence has been completed. There are n successive inputs in a sequence, $k_1, k_2, \ldots, k_n$ leading to a return of R. Initial funds available are L. In the example above, therefore, $T = 3$, $n = 2$, $k_1 = 1$, $k_2 = 2$, $R = 4$, $L = 4$. In general the matrix $\mathbf{K}$ has n rows and n columns. The only non-zero elements are the first row consisting of the k_h/R (in reverse order) and the diagonal below the principal diagonal, which consists of ones. It is written as

$$\mathbf{K} = \begin{bmatrix} \dfrac{k_n}{R} & \dfrac{k_{n-1}}{R} & \cdots & \dfrac{k_1}{R} \\ 1 & 0 & \cdots & 0 \\ 0 & 1 & \cdots & 0 \\ \vdots & \vdots & & \vdots \\ 0 & 0 & & 1 \end{bmatrix}$$

$\mathbf{e}_r$ is an n element column vector, only the first element being non-zero and equal to Lk_1/R. It is therefore written as

$$\mathbf{e}_r = \begin{bmatrix} \dfrac{Lk_1}{R} \\ 0 \\ \vdots \\ 0 \end{bmatrix}$$

$\mathbf{e}_1$ is an n element column vector. The first element is unity and the remainder are zero. We write

$$\mathbf{e}_1 = \begin{bmatrix} 1 \\ 0 \\ 0 \\ \vdots \\ 0 \\ 0 \end{bmatrix}$$

$\mathbf{k}$ is a row vector with n elements. The first element is

$$\sum_{h=1}^{n} k_h/R$$

the second is

$$\sum_{h=1}^{n-1} k_h/R$$

and so on. The $(i + 1)$th term therefore is

$$\sum_{h=1}^{n-i} k_h/r$$

and we write the vector $\mathbf{k}$ as a whole as

$$\mathbf{k} = \left(\sum_{h-1}^{n} k_h/R, \sum_{h-1}^{n-1} k_h/R, \ldots, \sum_{h-1}^{n-(n-2)} k_h/R, k_1/R \right)$$

In order to obtain the vector of first inputs beginning with the tth, the $(T - t)$th and the $(T - 1)$th power of the matrix $\mathbf{K}$ are required. This can be tedious for large values of T and n, but for the data above the solution is simple. For example:

$$\mathbf{Y}_2 = \begin{pmatrix} Y_2 \\ Y_3 \end{pmatrix} \quad \frac{\begin{pmatrix} \frac{1}{2} & \frac{1}{4} \\ 1 & 0 \end{pmatrix} \begin{pmatrix} 1 \\ 0 \end{pmatrix}}{\begin{pmatrix} \frac{3}{4} & \frac{1}{4} \end{pmatrix} \begin{pmatrix} \frac{1}{2} & \frac{1}{4} \\ 1 & 0 \end{pmatrix}^2 \begin{pmatrix} 1 \\ 0 \end{pmatrix}} = \begin{pmatrix} 1 \\ 2 \end{pmatrix}$$

That is, the second sequence should should be started with an input of 1 (shown as -1 in Figure 7.24) and the third sequence should be begun with an input of 2 (shown as -2 in Figure 7.24) with these initial inputs and the resulting second inputs, savings are at zero level at the beginning of years three and four. Initial capital is exhausted at the start of the second year and subsequent inputs to existing and new sequences are provided out of returns from completed sequences. An ideal matching of the inflows from old sequences and the outflows due to new ones has been achieved.

References

Balinski, M. L., and Baumol, W. J. (1967), 'The dual in non-linear programming and its economic interpretation', *Review of Economic Studies*, Vol. 34.
Biggs, M. C. (1971), *A New Method of Constrained Minimisation Using Recursive Equality Quadratic Programming*, Technical Report No. 24, The Numerical Optimisation Centre, The Hatfield Polytechnic.
Fletcher, R. (1970), 'An efficient, globally convergent, algorithm for unconstrained and linearly constrained optimisation problems', Paper at Seventh International Mathematical Programming Symposium, The Hague.
Hadley, G. (1964), *Non-linear and Dynamic Programming*, Addison-Wesley, Reading, Mass.
Kelley, J. E. (1960), 'The cutting plane method for solving convex programs', *Journal of the Society for Industrial and Applied Mathematics*, **8**.
Murray, W. (1969), 'An algorithm for constrained minimisation', in Fletcher, R. (ed.), *Optimisation*, Academic Press, New York.
Van de Panne, C. (1966), 'Programming with a quadratic constraint', *Management Science*, **12**.

Further reading

Abadie, J. (ed.), *Non-linear Programming*, North-Holland, Amsterdam, 1967.

Allen, R. G. D., *Mathematical Analysis for Economists*, Macmillan, London, 1960.

Bellman, R. E., *Dynamic Programming*, Princeton University Press, 1957.

Bradley, S. P., and Crane, D. B., 'A dynamic model for bond portfolio management', *Management Science*, **19**, 1972.

Braitsch, R. J., 'A computer comparison of four quadratic programming algorithms', *Management Science*, **19 (A)**, 1972.

Candler, W., and Townsley, R. J., 'The maximisation of a quadratic function of variables subject to linear inequalities', *Management Science*, **10**, 1964.

Cooper, L., and Cooper, M. W., *Introduction to Dynamic Porgramming*, Pergamon, 1981.

Cozzolino, J. M., 'Optimal scheduling for investment of excess cash', *Decision Sciences*, **2**, 1971.

Davidson, I., 'An optimal control theory framework for dividend determination and the implications for intertemporal dividend change', *Journal of Business Finance and Accounting*, **7**, No. 4, Winter, 1980.

Denardo, E. V., and Mitten, L. G., 'Elements of sequential decision processes', *Journal of Industrial Engineering*, **18**, 1967.

Dixit, A. K., *Optimisation in Economic Theory*, Oxford University Press, 1976.

Dixon, L. C. W., *Non-linear Optimisation*, The English Universities Press, London, 1972.

Dore, M. H. I., *Dynamic Investment Planning*, Croom Helm, London, 1977.

Dorn, W. S., 'Duality in quadratic programming', *Quarterly of Applied Mathematics*, **18**, 1960.

Dorn, W. S., 'Non-linear programming—a survey', *Management Science*, **9**, 1963.

Dorn, W. S., 'On Lagrangian multipliers', *Operations Research*, **9** 1963.

Fama, E. F., 'Multiperiod consumption—investment decisions', *American Economic Review*, **60**, 1970.

Flavell, R. B., 'Mathematical programming and the robustness of solutions to sequential investment problems', Ph.D. thesis, University of London, 1972.

Fletcher, R. (ed.), *Optimisation*, Academic Press, London, 1969.

Gale, D. (1964), 'Optimal programs for sequential investments', *Technical Report No. 1*, Department of Mathematics, Brown University, Providence, Rhode Island,.

Groves, R. L., and Wolfe, P. (eds.), *Recent Advances in Mathematical Programming*, McGraw-Hill, New York, 1963.

Hartley, H. O., 'Non-linear programming by the simplex method', *Econometrica*, **29**, 1961.

Intriligator, M. D., *Mathematical Optimisation and Economic Theory*, Prentice-Hall, Englewood Cliffs, NJ, 1971.

Kuhn, H. W., and Tucker, A., 'Non-linear programming', in Neyman, J. (ed.), *Proceedings of the Second Berkeley Symposium on Mathematical Statistics and Probability*, University of California Press, Berkeley, 1951.

Marglin, S. A., *Approaches to Dynamic Investment Planning*, North-Holland, Amsterdam, 1963.

Naylor, T. H., and Vernon, R. M., *Microeconomics and Decision Models of the Firm*, Harcourt, Brace and World, New York, 1969.

Puterman, M. L., *Dynamic Programming and its Applications*, Academic Press, New York, 1978.

Rockefeller, R. T., 'Duality in nonlinear programming', in Dantzig, G. B. and Veinott, A. F. (eds.), *Mathematics of the Decision Sciences*, Part I, American Mathematical Society, 1968.

Taha, H. A., *Operations Research: An Introduction* (2nd edn.), Collier-Macmillan, New York, 1976.

Terborgh, G., *Dynamic Equipment Policy*, McGraw-Hill, New York, 1949.

Van de Panne, C., and Whinston, A., 'Simplical methods for quadratic programming', *Naval Research Logistic Quarterly*, 11, 1964.

Van de Panne, C., and Whinston, A., 'A comparison of two methods of quadratic programming', *Operations Research*, 14, 1966.

Wagner, H. M., *Principles of Operations Research with Applications to Managerial Decisions*, Prentice-Hall, Englewood Cliffs, NJ, 1969.

Wilkes, F. M., *Elements of Operational Research*, McGraw-Hill, New York, 1980.

Wolfe, P., 'A duality theorem for non-linear programming', *Quarterly of Applied Mathematics*, 14, 1961.

Wolfe, P., 'Methods of non-linear programming', in Abadie, J. (ed.), *Nonlinear Programming*, North-Holland, Amsterdam, 1967

Zangwill, W. I., *Nonlinear Programming: A Unified Approach*, Prentice-Hall, Englewood Cliffs, NJ, 1969.

Zionts, S., 'Programming with linear fractional functionals', *Naval Research Logistics Quarterly*, 15, 1968.

Zoutendijk, G., 'Nonlinear programming: a numerical survey', *SIAM J. on Control*, 4, 1966.

CHAPTER 8

Mean—Variance Analysis and Project Risk

Overview
Following the introductory remarks various statistical descriptions of investments are presented. Section 8.3 continues the probabilistic description, taking account of interactions between projects. In section 8.4 judgemental issues are taken up while the following section illustrates some further points in the context of numerical examples. Section 8.6 presents a unifying framework for mean—variance analysis. The chapter concludes with a presentation of stochastic dominance.

8.1 Introduction

In the preceding chapters, except where it was unavoidable in context, the parameters of investment projects have been treated as if they were determinate. There are sound didactic reasons for this. More importantly, there are numerous occasions—especially for the small investor, when deterministic or near-deterministic investment opportunities arise. Departing from exactitude there are also pragmatic reasons for the presumption of 'effective certainty'. Outside of the area of portfolio selection few practitioners use formal frameworks which include explicit representation of risks. Simple devices and expedients predominate—such as payback period, return on capital or the classification of projects into risk categories. While excessive sophistry is eschewed, where the quality and quantity of information allows, explicit representation of risk should be considered. For the larger capital projects it is positively indicated.

For much of this chapter the analysis of risk is presented within what has come to be known as the 'single project framework'. This unflattering title has a simplistic ring which is unwarranted as the whole activities of the company can be treated as a single project. The alternative pole to this standpoint is represented by the 'asset pricing' approach of Chapter 10. On the whole we shall *not* automatically assume that the investor holds, or is seeking to hold, a 'balanced' portfolio of assets. Some do, and some patently do not. The typical small businessman is the classic example of the latter. If a balanced portfolio *is* held then the asset-pricing approach has much to commend it. If a properly diversified portfolio is *not* held then the single project framework can conveniently accommodate limited diversification.

In technical terms we shall draw a distinction between 'uncertainty' and 'risk'. *Risk* is taken to mean a situation in which various outcomes to a decision are possible but where the probabilities of the alternative outcomes are known. *Uncertainty* describes a situation in which there is no such probabilistic knowledge or where the information is fragmentary. Techniques for dealing with uncertainty are the principal subject of Chapter 9.

8.2 Probabilistic Description of the Single Project

In this section we describe means by which the probabilistic data on an investment may be summarized for the decision-maker. Some practicable decision rules are suggested along the way, but it will be recalled that there is no universally applicable rule which will identify the 'correct' single investment for all investors in all cases.

Suppose that there are no assured returns to an investment, but that the probability distributions of returns in each year are known. How can this information be used? Consider year t. Suppose that there are three possible returns R_{t1}, R_{t2}, and R_{t3} that can occur with probabilities p_{t1}, p_{t2}, p_{t3}. The mathematical 'expected' return for the year $\bar{R}_t$ is given by

$$\bar{R}_t = p_{t1}R_{t1} + p_{t2}R_{t2} + p_{t3}R_{t3}$$

or in general if there are m discrete outcomes then:

$$\bar{R}_t = \sum_{i=1}^{m} p_{ti}R_{ti} \tag{8.1}$$

If (8.1) describes the situation in each of $n+1$ years then the mathematically *expected net present value* ENPV is

$$\text{ENPV} = \sum_{t=1}^{n} \bar{R}_t(1+r)^{-t} \tag{8.2}$$

where in (8.2) $\bar{R}_0$ is the expected value of the outlay on the project and $100r\%$ is the appropriate discount rate. Possible decision rules involving

Year one		Year two		Year three	
Return	Probability	Return	Probability	Return	Probability
10,000	0.1	20,000	0.4	10,000	0.3
12,000	0.6	30,000	0.6	16,000	0.5
16,000	0.3			20,000	0.2

Figure 8.1

ENPV are discussed later. For the moment let us see how the arithmetic works out. Consider an example. A project runs for three years with the distributions of returns in each year as shown in Figure 8.1

Let the outlay for the project be established with certainty at £42,000 (i.e. $\bar{R}_0 = -42,000$) and let the discount rate be 10%. First find the expected return in each year. These are the arithmetic mean returns with the probabilities as weights. Thus for year one the workings are

R_{1i}	p_{1i}	$p_{1i}R_{1i}$
10,000	0.1	1,000
12,000	0.6	7,200
16,000	0.3	4,800

$$13,000 = \sum_{i=1}^{3} p_{1i}R_{1i} = \bar{R}_1$$

Similar calculations for years two and three give expected returns of 26,000 and 15,000 for those years. The present value of the expected returns, the *expected gross present value*, is 44,576 producing an ENPV of + 2,576. What about the range of possible outcomes? The example is a small-scale one and the possibilities can be enumerated: details are presented in Figure 8.2.

In Figure 8.2 the column headed 'cash flow pattern' shows the possible combinations of returns in each year (£1,000s) and the second column gives the chance that each particular pattern will arise *assuming that the returns in any year are independent of returns in any other year*. In this connection it should be noted that the ENPV formula (8.2) applies whether or not the returns are independent. The third column gives the NPV of each

Cash flow pattern			Probability (p)	NPV (10%)	$p \times$ NPV
10	20	10	0.012	− 8.867	− 0.106
10	20	16	0.020	− 4.359	− 0.087
10	20	20	0.008	− 1.354	− 0.011
10	30	10	0.018	− 0.603	− 0.011
10	30	16	0.030	+ 3.905	+ 0.117
10	30	20	0.012	+ 6.911	+ 0.083
12	20	10	0.072	− 7.049	− 0.508
12	20	16	0.120	− 2.541	− 0.305
12	20	20	0.048	+ 0.464	+ 0.022
12	30	10	0.108	+ 1.216	+ 0.131
12	30	16	0.180	+ 5.724	+ 1.030
12	30	20	0.072	+ 8.729	+ 0.628
16	20	10	0.036	− 3.412	− 0.123
16	20	16	0.060	+ 1.095	+ 0.066
16	20	20	0.024	+ 4.101	+ 0.098
16	30	10	0.054	+ 4.852	+ 0.262
16	30	16	0.090	+ 9.360	+ 0.842
16	30	20	0.036	+ 12.365	+ 0.445
			1.000		+ 2.576

Figure 8.2

cash flow pattern (recall that there is an outlaying of £42,000) and the arithmetic mean NPV is shown at the foot of column four.

Summing the probabilities associated with positive NPV values given the overall probability of achieving a positive NPV. This is 0.714. Of course 0.714 is also the chance that the yield on the investment exceeds 10%. Conversely, there is a 28.6% chance of making a loss in present value terms or equivalently of the project's yield being below 10%. The probability that NPV exceeds some value other than zero can be worked out in a similar fashion: for example the probability that NPV exceeds £2,000 is 0.498.

It may be very useful to know the *variance or standard deviation* of NPV. These are statistical measures of dispersion—measures of the spread about the mean value. The standard deviation of NPV, σ_{NPV}, is given by the formula:

$$\sigma_{NPV} = \sqrt{\Sigma p(NPV - ENPV)^2} \qquad (8.3)$$

variance, the square of standard deviation, represented by σ_{NPV}^2 is the average *squared* departure of NPV from its mean value. Squared deviations are used to avoid cancelling out of pluses and minuses and in the standard deviation the square root is taken to return to the original units of measure. Thus in the present context variance is in units of $(£)^2$ while standard deviation is, more conveniently, in units of £. The reader may care to extend Figure 8.2 to calculate σ_{NPV} using (8.3). Three extra columns would be needed headed: $NPV - ENPV$; $(NPV - ENPV)^2$ and $P(NPV - ENPV)^2$; the sum of the last column's entries being variance of present value for the project. The result of this exercise should be $\sigma_{NPV} = £5,216$.

Standard deviation of NPV is a *proxy* measure of risk on the investment. It is a measure of *total* risk for the investment and of course takes no account of possible offsetting variations in other projects that may be undertaken by the same investor. It is a 'proxy' measure of risk since perceived risk is a psychological entity that, so far as we know, is not directly measurable. Standard deviation is by no means a perfect measure of risk: for example it might reasonably be argued that only the 'downside' variation—NPV values below the mean—constitutes risk. Such a 'semi-standard deviation' is awkward mathematically and it is usually the case that s.d. and semi-s.d. move together. Thus standard deviation is normally employed.

What does a value of standard deviation of NPV of £5,216 tell us? Of itself, very little in fact. In relation to the mean figure, ENPV, however it is more revealing. The relation to a mean of £2,576 a standard deviation of £5,216 is 'large' (in a sense that will be detailed shortly) in relation to a mean of £50,000 the same figure would be 'small'. The ratio of standard deviation to mean makes allowance for scale. It is known as the *coefficient of variation* (which will here be labelled c) so that

$$c = \frac{\sigma_{NPV}}{ENPV} \tag{8.4}$$

coefficient of variation is a measure of *relative* dispersion (standard deviation is absolute). The coefficient of variation can be a more suitable measure of risk in that scale is taken into account. Possible use of the coefficient of variation as a risk measure is not a new idea, being suggested by Marschak (1938). However, there are problems if ENPV is close to zero or is negative. Apart from such cases the lower the value of c the less risky the project. In the present case we have

$$c = \frac{5,216}{2,576} = 2.02$$

Is 2.02 large or small? There are good reasons for describing this value as large. Suppose that the distribution of NPV was, in fact, normal. The normal density function is shown in Figure 8.3.

Areas under the curve correspond to probabilities and no matter what the context, 95% of the observations of the x variable (NPV here) lie within 1.96 standard deviations of the mean value. The shaded tails in the figure each account for $2\frac{1}{2}\%$ of the total area under the curve and there is a probability of 0.025 of finding an observation in one of these regions.

Now consider the data from the numerical example. Here the value of zero for NPV is only $(2,576/5,216) = 0.494$ standard deviations below the mean. Reference to a table of areas under the normal density function (Table 7) shows that 68.93% of observations of NPV are above this value and thus 31.07% are below it. These precise figures are obtained by interpolation viz: $0.6893 = 0.6879 + 0.4(0.6915 - 0.6879)$. Thus if we made the assumption that NPV was normally distributed about a mean of £2,576 with a standard deviation of £5,216 there would be a 31.07% chance of the investment making a loss. Note that the value 0.3107 compares well with the true probability of 0.286 as previously determined. Most investors would regard a 30% or so chance of making a loss as 'high'. It is arbitrary where a line is drawn, but let us say that a 10% chance of making a loss is acceptable. Reference to Table 7 shows that to achieve this figure (or better) the mean value must be no less than 1.28 times the standard deviation. This implies a coefficient of variation of $(1/1.28) = 0.78$. Thus in this context a value of c of 2.02 is 'high'.

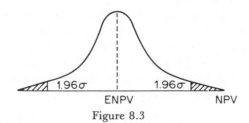

Figure 8.3

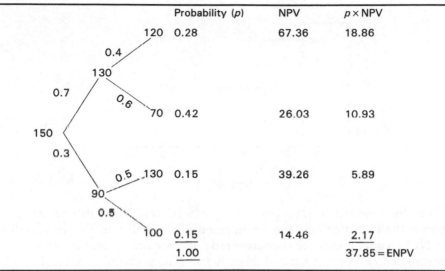

	Probability (p)	NPV	$p \times$ NPV
120	0.28	67.36	18.86
70	0.42	26.03	10.93
130	0.15	39.26	5.89
100	0.15	14.46	2.17
	1.00		37.85 = ENPV

Figure 8.4

Now consider an example in which returns in one year influence returns in another. A project costs 150 to initiate—let us assume that is known with certainly—but after one year could return 130 with probability 0.7 or 90 with probability 0.3. Provided that the 130 return materializes, there is then a 0.4 chance of a return of 120 and a 0.6 chance of a return of 70 after two years. If the return of 90 occurred in the first year then the probability distribution of returns in year two is 130 with a probability of 0.5 and 100 also with probability 0.5. The 'tree' of Figure 8.4 presents the information concisely. From the tree it can be seen that there is a 0.28 ($= 0.4 \times 0.7$) chance of the project giving a return of 130 in the first year and 120 in the second, so that assuming that a 10% rate of discount is employed there is a 0.28 chance of NPV being 67.4 ($= 130/(1.1) + 120/(1.1)^2 - 150$). The other possible values of NPV are shown in Figure 8.4.

The ENPV of the investment emerges as 37.85, being the sum of products of each possible value of NPV and its chance of arising. Note that in the NPV column there are no negative entries: this project will not make a loss in its own right. The investor may nevertheless be concerned about the distribution of returns. Workings for the calculation of standard deviation of NPV are:

Probability	(NPV − ENPV)	(NPV − ENPV)^2	p(NPV − ENPV)^2
0.28	29.51	870.84	243.84
0.42	− 11.55	133.40	56.03
0.15	1.41	1.99	0.30
0.15	− 23.39	547.09	82.06
			$\sigma^2_{NPV} = 382.23$

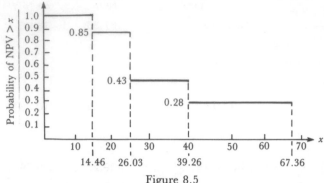

Figure 8.5

Thus the standard deviation of NPV is £19.55 and the coefficient of variation is 0.52. In this case the assumption of normality of the distribution of NPV would clearly be unwarranted. A 'probability profile' for the investment could be constructed directly from the probability and NPV columns of Figure 8.4. Two ways of presenting such results graphically are shown in Figures 8.5 and 8.6.

Figure 8.5 is the optimist's diagram, while the user of 8.6 sees his cup of tea as half empty rather than half full. Both diagrams use cumulated probabilities and step-function character arises because of the discrete probability distribution employed in the example. The diagrams may represent effective ways of presenting the probabilistic information at senior management level.

Now let us consider matters in general (where there may or may not be dependence between the returns). Consider an n year project with returns

$$R_0 R_1 R_2 \ldots R_t \ldots R_{n-1} R_n$$

where the returns R_t are random variables and where R_t has a mean value of $\bar{R}_t$ and variance σ_t^2. The expected net present value is given by

$$\text{ENPV} = \sum_{t=0}^{n} \bar{R}_t (1 + r)^{-t} \tag{8.5}$$

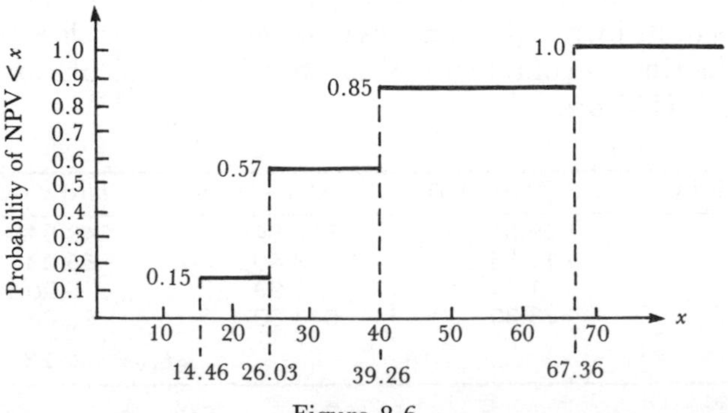

Figure 8.6

That is, the ENPV of the whole project (R_0 represents the outlay) is the present value of the means. Equation (8.5) applies no matter what are the interdependencies between returns in the various years. So in the case of a two-year project

$$\text{ENPV} = \bar{R}_0 + \frac{\bar{R}_1}{(1+r)} + \frac{\bar{R}_2}{(1+r)^2} \tag{8.6}$$

Now, what of the variance of NPV? The variance of the year t return is written as:

$$\text{E}(R_t - \bar{R}_t)^2 = \sigma_t^2 \tag{8.7}$$

where (8.7) is read as 'the expectation of the squared departure from the mean, is the variance'. In the case of a discrete probability distribution the expectation would be found by weighting each squared deviation by its chance of arising and summing up. In the case of a continuous distribution integration would be required. The variance of the present value of the year t return will be

$$\text{E}\left[\frac{R_t - \bar{R}_t}{(1+r)^t}\right]^2 = \left[\frac{1}{(1+r)^t}\right]^2 \text{E}(R_t - \bar{R}_t)^2 = \frac{\sigma_t^2}{(1+r)^{2t}} \tag{8.8}$$

Thus the variance of the present value of the year t return is the variance of the return discounted using as exponent of $(1+r)$ *twice* the value of t. More of this presently. For the moment ignore the necessity of discounting and consider the variance of the undiscounted sum of returns $\Sigma_{t=0}^n R_t$. This will be the sum of the variances plus the sum of the *covariances*, viz.

$$\text{Var}\left(\sum_{t=0}^n R_t\right) = \sum_{t=0}^n \sigma_t^2 + \sum_{\substack{s=0}}^n \sum_{\substack{t=0 \\ s \neq t}}^n \text{Cov}(R_s, R_t) \tag{8.9}$$

The covariance between two variables is a measure of the extent to which the variables move in step with each other. In general terms

$$\text{Cov}(R_s R_t) = \text{E}[(R_s - \bar{R}_s)(R_t - \bar{R}_t)] \tag{8.10}$$

Note that covariance could be positive (if the returns in years s and t tend to increase or decrease together) or negative (if the returns are inversely related) or zero (if the returns are unrelated). Note also in (8.9) that there will typically be very many more terms in the covariance summation $((n+1)n/2$ distinct values) than in the variance summation $(n+1$ terms). Now bring the ideas of (8.9) and (8.8) together. The result is the desired expression for variance of NPV. It is

$$\sigma_{\text{NPV}}^2 = \text{Var}\left[\sum_{t=0}^n \frac{R_t}{(1+r)^t}\right]$$

$$= \sum_{t=0}^n \frac{\sigma_t^2}{(1+r)^{2t}} + \sum_{\substack{s=0}}^n \sum_{\substack{t=0 \\ s \neq t}}^n \frac{\text{Cov}(R_s, R_t)}{(1+r)^{s+t}} \tag{8.11}$$

Equation (8.11) is the most general formula that we shall use and from it a number of special cases emerge. Before examining special cases spell out the $n = 2$ version of (8.11). For $n = 2$:

$$\sigma_{\text{NPV}}^2 = \sigma_0^2 + \frac{\sigma_1^2}{(1 + r)^2} + \frac{\sigma_2^2}{(1 + r)^4} + \frac{2\text{Cov}(R_0, R_1)}{(1 + r)}$$

$$+ \frac{2\text{Cov}(R_0 R_2)}{(1 + r)^2} + \frac{2\text{Cov}(R_1 R_2)}{(1 + r)^3} \tag{8.12}$$

In (8.12) note the powers to which $(1 + r)$ is raised in each denominator. Each distinct covariance term appears twice since $\text{Cov}(R_0, R_2)$ is identical to $\text{Cov}(R_2, R_0)$. The term $\text{Cov}(R_0, R_2)$ is the covariance of the initial outlay and the year two return.

Two simplified cases present themselves from (8.11). The first is that of returns independently distributed in each year. In this event the covariance terms are all zero (a necessary condition for independence) and the variance of NPV reduces to

$$\sigma_{\text{NPV}}^2 = \sum_{t=0}^{n} \frac{\sigma_t^2}{(1 + r)^{2t}} \tag{8.13}$$

in general; or in the $n = 2$ case

$$\sigma_{\text{NPV}}^2 = \sigma_0^2 + \frac{\sigma_1^2}{(1 + r)^2} + \frac{\sigma_2^2}{(1 + r)^4}$$

The second special case in that of *perfectly correlated returns* between the years. The coefficient of correlation, r, is given by

$$r = \frac{\text{Cov}(R_s, R_t)}{\sigma_s \sigma_t} \tag{8.14}$$

and must lie between extremes of -1 and $+1$. A value of $+1$ indicates perfect positive correlation. The returns move in lockstep with each other. Thus if $r = +1$ the $\text{Cov}(R_s, R_t) = \sigma_s \sigma_t$ and the formula (8.11) can in this case be written more concisely as

$$\sigma_{\text{NPV}}^2 = \left[\sum_{t=0}^{n} \frac{\sigma_t}{(1 + r)^t} \right]^2 \tag{8.15}$$

which in the $n = 2$ case would be

$$\sigma_{\text{NPV}}^2 = \left[\sigma_0 + \frac{\sigma_1}{(1 + r)} + \frac{\sigma_2}{(1 + r)^2} \right]^2$$

It is evident that in both of the special cases the calculation of σ_{NPV}^2 is greatly simplified.

Consider again the first example given in this section: that of independent returns. Mean returns had already been established. The value of $\bar{R}_1$ was £13,000. The calculation of σ_1^2 is quite straightforward. Workings are shown in Figure 8.7. Thus variance of return in year one, σ_1^2 is

		(£000s)		
Probability (p)	R_t	$R_t - \bar{R}_t$	$(R_t - \bar{R}_t)^2$	$p(R_t - \bar{R}_t)^2$
0.1	10	3	0	0.9
0.6	12	−1	1	0.6
0.3	16	+3	9	2.7
				4.2

Figure 8.7

4,200,000. Similar calculations produce $\sigma_2^2 = 24,000,000$ and $\sigma_3^2 = 13,000,000$. Recalling that the initial outlay was fixed (so that $\sigma_0^2 = 0$) and inserting the results into (8.13) gives

$$\sigma_{NPV}^2 = 0 + \frac{4,200,000}{(1.1)^2} + \frac{24,000,000}{(1.1)^4} + \frac{13,000,000}{(1.1)^6}$$

$$= 27,201,559$$

and so

$$\sigma_{NPV} = \sqrt{27,201,559} = £5,216$$

The result checks with the answer obtained by the lengthier means mentioned at the start of the section.

Now let us use the most general formula. Consider the second example, that of Figure 8.4. Here the returns in year two depend upon what happened in year one. But first the mean returns. Outlay is certain so that $\bar{R}_0 = 150$. In year one we rapidly obtain

$$\bar{R}_1 = 130(0.7) + 90(0.3) = 118$$

and in year two

$$\bar{R}_2 = 120(0.28) + 70(0.42) + 130(0.15) + 100(0.15)$$
$$= 97.5$$

Now for the variances. In the first year:

P	R_1	$R_1 - \bar{R}_1$	$(R_1 - \bar{R}_1)^2$	$P(R_1 - \bar{R}_1)^2$
0.7	130	+12	144	100.8
0.3	90	−28	784	235.2
				$336 = \sigma_1^2$

and in the second year:

P	R_2	$R_2 - \bar{R}_2$	$(R_2 - \bar{R}_2)^2$	$P(R_2 - \bar{R}_2)^2$
0.28	120	22.5	506.25	141.7500
0.42	70	−27.5	756.25	317.6250
0.15	130	32.5	1056.25	158.4375
0.15	100	2.5	6.25	0.9375
				$618.75 = \sigma_2^2$

Now in this example, since the outlay is fixed the terms $\text{Cov}(R_0, R_1)$ and $\text{Cov}(R_0, R_2)$ are both zero. The only non-zero covariance term is $\text{Cov}(R_1 R_2)$ which we must now determine. The workings are as follows:

P	$(R_1 - \bar{R}_1)$	$(R_2 - \bar{R}_2)$	$(R_1 - \bar{R}_1)$ $(R_2 - R_2)$	$P(R_1 - \bar{R}_1)$ $(R_2 - \bar{R}_2)$
0.28	(130 – 118)	(120 – 97.5)	270	75.6
0.42	(130 – 118)	(70 – 97.5)	– 330	– 138.6
0.15	(90 – 118)	(130 – 97.5)	– 910	– 136.5
0.15	(90 – 118)	(100 – 97.5)	– 70	– 10.5
			$\text{Cov}(R_1, R_2) =$	– 210.0

In this layout the deviations from the mean values in the respective years have been left in their original form. Thus associated with a deviation of $+12(= 130 - 118)$ in the first year are two possible deviations in the second: $22.5(= 120 - 97.5)$ and $-27.5(= 70 - 97.5)$. These deviations can only arise in conjunction with the return of 130 and hence the deviation of $+12$ in the first year.

Finally applying the general formula

$$\sigma^2_{\text{NPV}} = \frac{\sigma_1^2}{(1+r)^2} + \frac{\sigma_2^2}{(1+r)^4} + \frac{2\text{Cov}(R_1, R_2)}{(1+r)^3}$$

$$= \frac{336}{(1.1)^2} + \frac{618.25}{(1.1)^4} + \frac{-420}{(1.1)^3}$$

$$= 384.75$$

So that

$$\sigma_{\text{NPV}} = \sqrt{384.75} = 19.62$$

The slight difference in results being due to rounding errors, the figure of 19.62 being more accurate. Of course the ENPV is a simple calculation here with

$$\text{ENPV} = -150 + \frac{118}{(1.1)} + \frac{97.5}{(1.21)} = 37.85$$

and the coefficient of variation of $c = 0.52$ being the same value as previously calculated to two decimal places. Whichever layout for the workings is used in such a case (Figures 8.4 and 8.5) format and the use of the formula (8.11) is a matter of convenience.

Now consider the special case of perfectly correlated returns and the use of formula (8.3). The simplest possible instance would be where there is just the outlay and one return. Specifically let the data be

Probability	R_0	R_1
0.4	– 100	125
0.6	– 80	150

that is, there is a 0.4 probability of the pair of values (– 100, – 25) and a 0.6 chance of the pair of values (-80, 150). It might be thought more likely that outlay and return increase together; this is no doubt the case but this would represent *negative* correlation. In the present instance again with a 10% discount rate, the relevant formula is

$$\sigma^2_{NPV} = \left[\sigma_0 + \frac{\sigma_1}{(1.1)}\right]^2$$

and the workings for the standard deviations are

P	$R_0 - \bar{R}_0$	$(R_0 - \bar{R}_0)^2$	$P(R_0 - \bar{R}_0)^2$
0.4	-12	144	57.6
0.6	$+8$	64	38.4

$$\sigma^2_0 = 96.0 \therefore \sigma_0 = 9.7980$$

where $\bar{R}_0 = -100(0.4) - 80(0.6) = -88$ and where the deviation of -12 is given by $-100 - (-88) = -12$. For σ_1 we have

P	$R_1 - \bar{R}_1$	$(R_1 - \bar{R}_1)^2$	$P(R_1 - \bar{R}_1)^2$
0.4	-15	225	90
0.6	$+10$	100	60

$$\sigma^2_1 = 150 \therefore \sigma_1 = 12.2474$$

So that

$$\sigma^2_{VPV} = \left[9.7980 + \frac{12.2474}{(1.1)}\right]^2 = 438.15$$

$\therefore \sigma_{NPV} = 20.93$

Note in passing that the correlation coefficient is indeed $+1$ since $CovR_0R_1 = +120$ given by

P	$R_0 - \bar{R}_0$	$R_1 - \bar{R}_1$	$(R_0 - \bar{R}_0)$ $(R_1 - \bar{R}_1)$	$P(R_0 - \bar{R}_0)$ $(R_1 - \bar{R}_1)$
0.4	-12	-15	180	72
0.6	$+8$	$+10$	80	48

$$CovR_0R_1 = 120$$

and

$$r = \frac{CovR_0R_1}{\sigma_0\sigma_1} = \frac{+120}{\sqrt{(96)(150)}} = +1$$

The covariance value can be used to check the result by substitution into the general formula. A rather more independent check would be found by recalling that

$$\sigma^2_{NPV} = \Sigma p(NPV - ENPV)^2$$

which is usable in this instance as there are only two possible values of NPV.

The more plausible data

P	R_0	R_1
0.4	-100	125
0.6	-120	150

represents perfect negative correlation between outlay and return. This could result from a straightforward 20% increase in scale. Both σ_0^2 and σ_1^2 are unaltered but the covariance figure is changed in sign: $\text{Cov}(R_0 R_1) = -120$ and use of the general formula produces $\sigma_{\text{NPV}}^2 = 1.7851$. In this special case of outlay and one return perfectly negatively correlated we can write

$$\sigma_{\text{NPV}}^2 = \left[\sigma_0 - \frac{\sigma_1}{(1.1)}\right]^2 \tag{8.16}$$

Substitution of σ_0 and σ_1 values into (8.16) also produces $\sigma_{\text{NPV}}^2 = 1.7851$. While it may be argued that (8.16) is so special a case as to be hardly worth mentioning, it would be useful in single time period analysis in which much of portfolio theory is expressed.

There are, in fact, numerous other special cases for which simplified formulae can be calculated. For instance the ultra special case where $R_{ti} = k_t R_{0i}$ where k_t is a constant and the R_{ti} and R_{0i} are typical paired values of R_t and R_0. A more likely special case would be where all the returns are perfectly correlated (positively) with each other and perfectly negatively correlated with the outlay R_0 (assumed negative here). In this case we can consider the present value of the returns R_1 to R_n *as a whole* and write

$$\text{NPV} = R_0 + \text{GPV}$$

from which it follows that:

$$\sigma_{\text{NPV}}^2 = \sigma_0^2 + \sigma_{\text{GPV}}^2 + 2\ \text{Cov}(R_0,\ \text{GPV}) \tag{8.17}$$

but since all returns are perfectly positively correlated:

$$\sigma_{\text{GPV}}^2 = \frac{1}{(1+r)^2}\left[\sum_{t=1}^{n}\frac{\sigma_t}{(1+r)^{t-1}}\right]^2 \tag{8.18}$$

Furthermore, since in the present case

$$\text{Cov}(R_0,\ \text{GPV}) = -\sigma_0\sigma_{\text{GPV}} \tag{8.19}$$

the calculation of σ_{NPV} is greatly simplified requiring only substitution of (8.9) into (8.17) and calculation of σ_0^2 and σ_{GPV}^2.

8.3 Probabilistic Description of Multiple Investments

When an investment proposal does not represent the only source of cash flow from the investor then possible interactions with existing or with other proposed investments must be taken into account. These 'interactions' can be of two kinds. There may be cases where one project alters the cash flows of another through being complementary to, or in competition with, the other project. But even when these effects are not present the *joint* cash flows of two projects may present a very different picture from that produced by each project in isolation. This latter circumstance is the one that will occupy our attention.

The setting for the discussion is a firm already committed to some investments which generate (in a probabilistic fashion) its *existing* cash flow. The firm is in the position of considering further investment projects. The examples which follow are of absolutely minimal arithmetic complexity, and are not themselves supposed to be realistic, but are intended to illustrate principles of approach.

First of all consider one of the commonest possibilities—that of a firm contemplating *expansion of its existing range of activities*. Let us characterize the situation thus

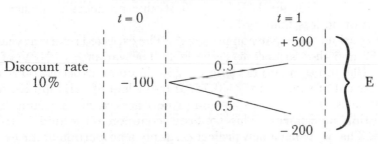

Existing cash flow pattern

This cash flow pattern: 100 out with certainty at $t = 0$ followed at $t = 1$ by equally likely outcomes of $+500$ or -200 is labelled E. To this the firm is considering adding an idealized expansion project A. Details are:

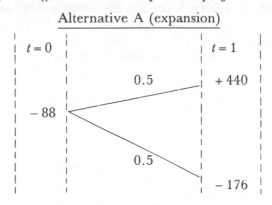

Alternative A (expansion)

The cash flow pattern for A is simply eighty-eight hundredths of the pattern for E and in concrete terms might represent the establishment of a similar plant in another location on a slightly smaller scale. The two diagrams are to be understood in the following fashion. If the $+500$ materializes for E then if A has been undertaken the $+440$ return will accrue. Similarly, the losses of -200 and -176 would coincide. This would be the case if the two projects are affected in the same way by the same underlying economic or other forces. Other possibilities will be examined shortly. For the moment consider the data for E by itself.

The variance of return at $t = 1$, σ^2_{1E} is given by

P	$R_E - R_E$	$(R_E - \bar{R}_E)^2$	$P(R_E - \bar{R}_E)^2$
0.5	350	122,500	61,250
0.5	-350	122,500	61,250
			$\sigma^2_{1E} = 122,500$

Where the mean return figure, $\bar{R}_E$ is 150. With a 10% rate of discount the variance of NPV for E is

$$(\sigma^2_{NPV})_E = \frac{122,500}{1.21} = 101,239.67$$

thus the standard deviation of NPV for the existing cash flow is $318.\overline{18}$. In conjunction with the ENPV of $36.\overline{36}$ this produces a coefficient of variation of no less than $c = 8.75$.

Now consider the expansion project A. The expected return at year one $\bar{R}_A = 132$ and the variance $\sigma^2_{1A} = 94,864$. The variance of NPV of A is thus 78,400 and standard deviation is 280. With an expected NPV of 32 the coefficient of variation is $c = 8.75$. If coefficient of variation is used as the risk measure then the expansion project has exactly the same risk as the existing investment. This confirms common sense and is true in general. That is, when a new project is simply a proportion of the existing cash flows it will have an identical coefficient of variation.

The reader may wish to verify two other, rather obvious facts. The returns at time $t = 1$ for the two projects are perfectly positively correlated as are the net present values. Secondly, the coefficient of variation of NPV of the two projects together (E + A) is also 8.75. Of course variance or standard deviation of NPV will be higher for E + A simply due to the increased scale but most would consider the riskiness to be unchanged.

Now consider an alternative further investment B. Data are

Alternative B (diversification)

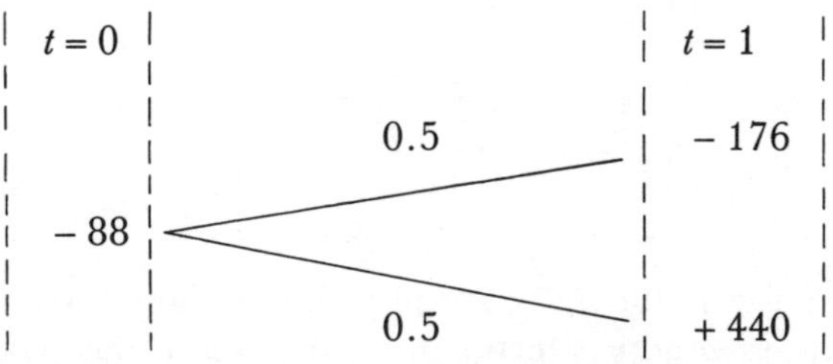

Where the diagram is to be interpreted to mean that should the return of 500 materialize for E then at the same time B would lose 176.

However, if E does badly, producing -200, then B will return $+440$. Thus E and B are oppositely affected by underlying forces. Investment B would represent an ideal kind of diversification. For B alone all summary data: ENPV, variance of return and of NPV and coefficient of variation are identical to investment A. But now consider E and B taken together. The result would be

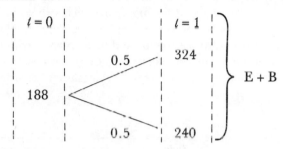

For which ENPV is of course $68.\overline{36}$, being simply the sum of the separate ENPVs but the standard deviation of NPV $(\sigma_{NPV})_{E+B} = 38.\overline{18}$ is dramatically small: in fact since E and B are perfectly *negatively* correlated the standard deviation of the two together is the difference between the individual standard deviations i.e. $38.\overline{18} = 318.\overline{18} - 280$. This is easily shown to be true in general for any pair of perfectly negatively correlated variables X and Y. Let

$$Z = X + Y$$

then:

$$\sigma_Z^2 = \sigma_X^2 + \sigma_Y^2 + 2 \operatorname{Cov} XY \tag{8.20}$$

but:

$$\operatorname{Cov} XY = \sigma_X \sigma_Y$$

So

$$\sigma_Z^2 = \sigma_X^2 + \sigma_Y^2 - 2\sigma_X \sigma_Y$$
$$= (\sigma_X - \sigma_Y)^2$$

thus

$$\sigma_Z = \sigma_X - \sigma_Y \tag{8.21}$$

From (8.21) it is apparent that if X and Y have the same value of standard deviation then their sum is constant. In the language of physics, if each investment project had an 'anti-project' then risk arising from variability of return could be completely eliminated. The project–anti-project pair E and $\bar{E}$ would be an attractive investment costing 200 and returning 300 with certainty after one year. But return now to the choice between A and B. These projects are, by themselves, identical so far as cash flows are concerned, but they combine very differently with E. Clearly, given E,

B is preferable to A. The main point being made is this: A and B cannot be accurately assessed in isolation from the existing cash flows. If A and B are alternatives then the investor can choose between three possible cash flow patterns (E; E + A; E + B) which can be viewed as three mutually exclusive single projects. However many additional investments may be being contemplated, the choice can be expressed as being between mutually exclusive 'packages' differing from each other by at least one investment.

It follows from this grouping together that a project which by itself is completely unattractive may be acceptable in conjunction with another project with complementary cash flows. For instance consider project C:

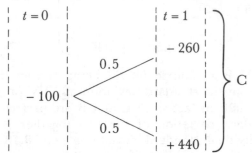

This project would have negative ENPV even at a zero discount rate and has 'high' variance. Most people would reject C out of hand, but taken in conjunction with E it produces

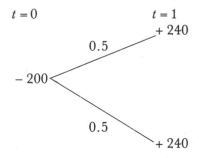

which some investors might prefer to E alone because of the guaranteed return. Of course E + C has a lower ENPV (= + 18.$\overline{18}$) than E, but still the yield is 20% and return is assured. In capital-rationing situations it is the case that projects cannot be assessed independently of the asset set to which they are to be adjoined even under complete certainty. Viewing an asset in conjunction with existing investments is doubly important when returns are risky.

Perfect negative correlation between the cash flows of investments is unlikely. However, equation 8.20 shows that benefit can be obtained so long as covariance is negative. We shall now consider some instances where the correlation is less than perfect. Suppose the existing project to

be

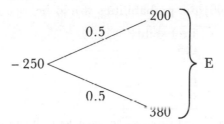

and consider a possible additional project:

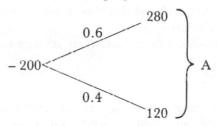

Clearly, there cannot be perfect correlation (either negative or positive) between E and A. In intuitive terms, the return of 280 for A must have some chance of coinciding with both 220 and 380 in E. In a repeated experiment there will be occasions when 280 is bracketed with 220 and others when 380 and 280 occur simultaneously.

In order to determine the covariance of returns between E and A we need to know the probabilities of joint occurrence of pairs of returns (one from each project). This is an additional information requirement, the data not being deducible from the diagrams. Note that in our earlier examples we have been saying that the probabilities of coincidence of pairs of returns are either one or zero. The present case is less extreme. First find the expected return in each case. These turn out to be $\bar{R}_E = 300$ and $\bar{R}_A = 216$, so that products of pairs of deviations are

$$(220 - 300)(280 - 216) = -5120$$
$$(220 - 300)(120 - 216) = +7680$$
$$(380 - 300)(280 - 216) = +5120$$
$$(380 - 300)(120 - 216) = -7680$$

Now probabilities need to be assigned to each of these cases. There is a good degree of discretion here. It turns out that for maximum positive covariance the probabilities are

Product	Probability
− 5120	0.1
+ 7680	0.4
+ 5120	0.5
− 7680	0

The resulting covariance value is $+5,200$. For maximum *negative* covariance $(-5,200)$ the probabilities would be

Product	Probability
-5120	0.5
$+7680$	0
$+5120$	0.1
-7680	0.4

The probabilities selected have to be such as to be in agreement with the data for E and A individually. The reader may verify that the problem of finding the extreme probabilities shown above has the structure of a 'transportation' problem!

Now the correlation coefficient between returns is given by

$$r = \frac{\text{Cov}(R_E R_A)}{\sigma_E \sigma_A}$$

and we can quickly establish that σ_A, the standard deviation of returns in project A, is $\sqrt{6144}$ and that $\sigma_E = 80$. Thus the extreme values of covariance produce the range of values

$$-0.829254 \leqslant r \leqslant +0.829254$$

In the limit if A and E are, as far as possible, negatively correlated then for the joint project $A + E$ the variance of return is

$$
\begin{aligned}
\text{Var}(R_E + R_A) &= \sigma_E^2 + \sigma_A^2 + 2\ \text{Cov}\ R_E R_A \\
&= 6,400 + 6,144 - 10,400 \\
&= 2,144
\end{aligned}
$$

thus in this case

$$\sigma_{NPV}^2(E + A) = \frac{2,144}{(1.1)^2} = 1771.90$$

$$\therefore \ \sigma_{NPV} = \boxed{42.09}$$

Now suppose that there is zero correlation between E and A, that is $r = 0$. Then

$$
\begin{aligned}
\text{Var}(R_E + R_A) &= 6400 + 6144 + 0 \\
&= 12,544
\end{aligned}
$$
$$\therefore \ \sigma_{NPV}^2(E + A) = 10,366.94$$

$$\text{and } \sigma_{NPV} = \boxed{101.82}$$

Now consider extreme positive correlation. In this case

$$
\begin{aligned}
\text{Var}(R_E + R_A) &= 6400 + 6144 + 10,400 \\
&= 22,944
\end{aligned}
$$

So $\sigma_{NPV}^2 = 18{,}961.98$

and $\sigma_{NPV} = \boxed{137.70}$

The boxed figures illustrate graphically the effect of increasing correlation between the investments.

The workings above could have been put in terms of the value of the correlation coefficient itself. Sometimes this will be more convenient—for instance if information is given in this form. To illustrate, suppose that $r = +0.6$. We can use the formula

$$\text{Var}(R_E + R_A) = \sigma_E^2 + \sigma_A^2 + 2r\sigma_E\sigma_A$$
$$= 6{,}400 + 6{,}144 + 1.2(80)(78.38)$$
$$= 20{,}068.48$$
$$\therefore \quad \sigma_{NPV}(A + E) = 128.78$$

Return for a moment to the maximum covariance cases earlier on. If we are given the probability of each possible pair of deviations then we can easily work out the probability distribution of returns for the joint project. Consider the maximum negative covariance data. These were:

Joint returns	Probability
220,280	0.5
220,120	0.0
380,280	0.1
380,120	0.4

which can be represented as

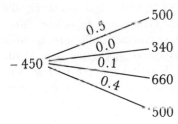

which simplifies to

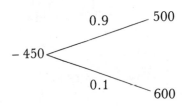

which means that there is a 90% chance of an NPV of $+4.54$ and a 10% chance of an NPV of 150.

Even if we were merely given the correlation coefficient the cash flow probability distribution could still be obtained since each covariance figure can be shown to be produced by a unique set of probabilities. Since the standard deviations of return on each project are already known, once r is given this determines the covariance which in turn determines the probabilities.

Throughout this section the numerical exercises have been restricted to simple cases. This has been most marked in the latter part of the section when we have used ultra simple one-time-period examples—very much as in portfolio and asset-pricing theory. It is not difficult to envisage much more involved cases with wholesale interconnection between returns over several years and many projects. A general framework is provided in Section 8.6, from which the cases discussed have emerged as special.

8.4 Comparison of Mean/Variance Combinations

The calculation of ENPV and variance of NPV can be done *objectively*; by anyone (or by machine) and the same results will emerge. Making choices between pairs of values is a *subjective* exercise. Different people/investors will come forward with differing answers. There is no getting away from this; only a few obvious cases are clear cut.

It could be argued that the fact that we have singled out mean and variance for special consideration represents an *a priori* value judgement. Hence if *only* means and variances are calculated and a feasible set constructed from mean–variance combinations, then a subjective element has already entered.

If we now assume that investors are 'variance averse' then if alternative A offers both higher ENPV and lower variance than does B then everyone will rank A above B. This only separates the wood from the chaff, eliminating the mean–variance inefficient combinations.

The situation is illustrated in Figure 8.8. With standard deviation on the horizontal scale each circle represents the combination of ENPV and σ_{ENPV} produced by a combination of E and an investment possibility. The

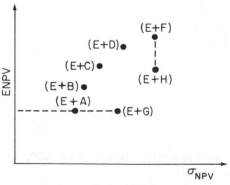

Figure 8.8

cases (E + G) and (E + H) are inefficient. For the same return (E + G) produces more variability than (E + A). On the other hand (E + H) has a lower return than (E + F) for the same variability. These can be eliminated. The remaining possibilities form a *frontier* of opportunities: greater return coinciding with greater variability. This is where the buck gets passed. The investor must choose between the remaining alternatives.

From a theoretical standpoint the process of subjective choice can be formalized by supposing that an index of utility can be constructed given by

$$U = f(\text{ENPV}, \sigma_{\text{NPV}}) \tag{8.22}$$

where, in (8.22) U is the level of *expected utility*. It is supposed satisfaction *ex ante*. Things may well turn out badly, but one could be comforted by the thought of having made the best *a priori* decision. Approaches making explicit use of utility functions are for the most part non-operational; at least at the moment. However, utility theory does allow important general statements to be made and provides theoretical underscoring for the techniques.

In relation to the problem of Figure 8.8, *indifference curves* could be added in. These are *contours* of U in (8.22) each curve showing combinations of ENPV and σ_{NPV} which yield equal satisfaction. Figure 8.9 includes indifference curves against the same broken frontier of non-inefficient projects. The maximum of utility that can be generated by the choices available is $U = U_3$ obtained from selection of the (E + C) combination. It is evident from the diagram that an investor with the indifference curves shown would rank (E + B) and (E + D) equally since they both produce $U = U_2$. The other alternatives; (E + A) and (E + F) lie on even lower curves and are relatively unattractive to the investor. Indifference curves are not suggested as a practical aid. There are serious difficulties to be overcome in constructing a utility index even for a willing and impoverished student selecting between hypothetical or trivial alternatives. It is all the more difficult for the individual entrepreneur making *real* decisions and practically hopeless in the case of a company shared by

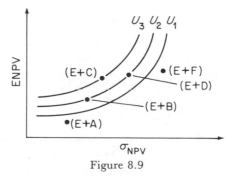

Figure 8.9

many diverse persons. Hypothetically, if (a) the alternatives (E + A to E + F here) were grouped fairly close together (b) over a small range of values of σ, linearity of the indifference curves could be assumed, we could write

$$U = \text{ENPV} - w \cdot \sigma_{\text{NPV}} \qquad (8.23)$$

where w is a positive constant to be selected by the investor: the bigger the value of w the more averse to risk (as measured by σ) is the investor, but this aversion does not rise with increase in σ (unlike the curves of Figure 8.9). Having selected w, and determined ENPV and σ as previously shown the utility rating for the alternative follows readily. Another simplified possibility would be to suppose that the indifference curves were straight lines emanating from the origin like rays, as shown in Figure 8.10 in which $U_3 > U_2 > U_1$. Such would be the case if

$$U = \frac{\text{ENPV}}{\sigma_{\text{NPV}}} = \frac{1}{c}$$

i.e. if utility was the reciprocal of the coefficient of variation. The lower the coefficient of variation the greater the value of U. This is the simple *coefficient of variation decision rule*. In other words, while c can be viewed as a measure of risk only, it, or its reciprocal can be seen as a measure of overall desirability too.

There is some dispute concerning the discount rate to be used in the ENPV and σ calculations. Many writers suggest that the *risk-free* rate be used: the rate of interest that would be appropriate were everything about the project certain. The justification being that if the cost of capital is used then *risk has already been allowed for*. It would be 'double counting' to discount at the cost of capital and then use σ_{NPV} as a further statistic on risk. These will certainly be cases in which the use of the rate of return on 30-day Treasury bills should be employed. But this will not always be so. If I take a small loan on overdraft the rate that I pay expresses the *bank's* view of what *its* risks are on average. Nevertheless, it is my over-the-counter cost of capital. Suppose this rate is 20%. Suppose that the risk-free rate of interest is estimated as 12%. I can choose between two pro-

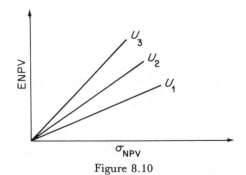

Figure 8.10

jects which have risk profiles such that neither has a yield of less than 13% nor more than 19%. Use of the risk-free rate cannot possibly result in a correct decision. Perhaps if all capital markets were perfect this sort of situation could not arise. But there are massive imperfections and the case *does* arise. Once again, the investor must decide. Probabilistic information may be presented in whatever summary form is most convenient, but frequently the mean–variance format will be most useful. The mean–variance approach is not without its shortcomings, however—some of these are pointed up in the discussion of stochastic dominance. In objective terms it stops at the efficiency frontier, leaving the investor to make a subjective choice between the remaining alternatives. Section 8.5 presents three illustrative examples.

8.5 Three Cases in Mean–Variance Analysis

In this first example we consider what happens to expected NPV and its variances as the discounting interest rate changes. The subject of interest-rate variability is discussed in more detail in Chapter 9. Given the data for an investment project:

P	R_0	R_1
0.7	-80	$+100$
0.3	-64	$+120$

It is evident that R_0 and R_1 are perfectly positively correlated; a 20% increase in R_0 coincides with a 20% increase in R_1. The relevant formula would be

$$\sigma_{NPV}^2 = \left[\sigma_0 + \frac{\sigma_1}{(1.1)} \right]^2$$

where σ_0 and σ_1 are the standard deviations of R_0 and R_1 respectively. Thus for σ_0 the workings are

P	R_0	pR_0	$R_0 - \bar{R}_0$	$(R_0 - \bar{R}_0)^2$	$p(R_0 - \bar{R}_0)^2$
0.7	-80	-56	-4.8	23.04	16.128
0.3	-64	-19.2	11.2	125.44	37.632
		$\bar{R}_0 = -75.2$		Var $R_0 = 53.76$	

So that $\sigma_0 = \sqrt{\text{Var } R_0} = \sqrt{53.76} = 7.3321$.
For σ_1 the workings are

P	R_1	pR_1	$R_1 - \bar{R}_1$	$(R_1 - \bar{R}_1)^2$	$p(R_1 - \bar{R}_1)^2$
0.7	100	70	-6	36	25.2
0.3	200	36	$+14$	196	58.8
		106		Var $R_1 = 84$	

So that $\sigma_1 = \sqrt{84} = 9.1652$.

Consequently, applying the simplified formula above we obtain

$$\sigma^2_{NPV} = \left[7.3321 + \frac{9.1652}{(1.1)}\right]^2$$

$$= \underline{245.36}$$

Let us now check the result by using the longer formula

$$\sigma^2_{NPV} = Var(R_0) + \frac{Var(R_1)}{(1.21)} + \frac{2\ Cov(R_0 R_1)}{(1.1)}$$

We have already found the variances. For the covariance the working are

P	$(R_0 - \bar{R}_0)$	$(R_1 - \bar{R}_1)$	$(R_0 - \bar{R}_0)(R_1 - \bar{R}_1)$	$p(R_0 - \bar{R}_0)(R_1 - \bar{R}_1)$
0.7	− 4.8	− 6	28.8	20.16
0.3	+ 11.2	+ 14	156.8	47.04
			$Cov(R_0 R_1) =$	67.20

Thus

$$\sigma^2_{NPV} = 53.76 + \frac{84}{(1.21)} + \frac{134.4}{(1.1)}$$

$$= \underline{245.36}$$

Having obtained the covariance we can now check on the correlation coefficient, r. The formula for r is

$$r = \frac{Cov(R_0, R_1)}{\sigma_0 \sigma_1}$$

$$= \frac{67.2}{(7.3321)(9.1652)}$$

$$= 1$$

Now consider the effect on the variance of NPV as the interest rate changes. Reference to either of the formulae shows that variance will be at a maximum when the discount rate is negative; it will fall asymptotically to 53.76 (which is the variance of R_0) as the discount rate increases indefinitely. However, the variation for small changes in the discount rate is slight. The situation is graphed in Figure 8.11.

ENPV (expected net present value) is affected in a similar fashion, although there is no squared term involving the discount factor. With a discount rate of $100r\%$ the ENPV can be written as

$$ENPV = \bar{R}_0 + \frac{\bar{R}_1}{(1 + r)}$$

$$= -75.2 + \frac{106}{(1 + r)}$$

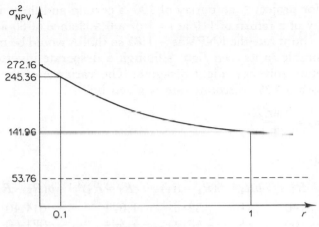

Figure 8.11

So that, obviously, ENPV starts at 30.8 and asymptotes to -75.2. Tabular information on σ^2_{NPV} and ENPV is given in Figure 8.12

In the second of the cases we highlight the importance of allowing for covariant cash flows between projects when more than one project may be selected. The joint cash flows of several projects may present a very different picture from that produced by the cash flow pattern of each investment taken in isolation. When the returns to projects are negatively correlated there will be beneficial reductions in variance overall. The cash flow of a project in isolation may not be at all attractive to the decision-maker. However, if this project is strongly negatively correlated with existing investments then it may prove to be a desirable acquisition.

For example, suppose that the project that is being considered is project A where

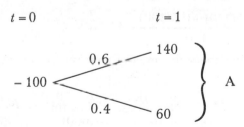

Discount rate (%)	σ^2_{NPV}	ENPV
0	272.16	+30.80
5	257.95	+25.75
10	245.36	+21.16
20	224.09	+13.13
50	180.69	−4.53
100	141.96	−22.20
500	78.49	−57.53
1,000	66.67	−65.56
10,000	55.10	−74.15

Figure 8.12

That is, for project A an outlay of 100 is certain and there is then a 0.6 probability of a return of 140 at $t = 1$ or a 0.4 chance of 60 at $t = 1$. With a 10% discount rate the ENPV is -1.82 so that A would be most unlikely to be desirable in its own right although a desperate investor requiring 140 to retain solvency might disagree! The variance of the NPV of A, σ^2_{NPVA}, with a 10% discount rate is given by

$$\sigma^2_{\text{NPVA}} = \frac{\text{Var}(R_1)}{(1.1)^2}$$

The workings are

p	R_1	pR_1	$(R_1 - \bar{R}_1)$	$(R_1 - \bar{R}_1)^2$	$p(R_1 - \bar{R}_1)^2$
0.6	140	84	32	1,024	614.40
0.4	60	24	-48	2,304	921.60
		$\bar{R}_1 = 108$		$\text{Var}(R_1) = 1,536.00$	

$$\therefore\ \sigma^2_{\text{NPVA}} = \frac{1536}{1.21} = 1,269.42$$

Now suppose that the existing investment is E where

So that as things stand without the new investment there is an ENPV value of 11.36 where

$$-125 + \frac{0.5(110) + 0.5(190)}{1.1} = 11.36$$

and the dispersion about this mean figure is σ^2_{NPVE} for which the workings are

p	R_1	pR_1	$R_1 - \bar{R}_1$	$(R_1 - \bar{R}_1)^2$	$p(R_1 - \bar{R}_1)^2$
0.5	110	55	-40	1,600	800
0.5	190	95	40	1,600	800
		$\bar{R}_1 = 150$		$\text{Var}(R_1) = 1600$	

So that

$$\sigma^2_{\text{NPVE}} = \frac{1600}{1.21} = 1,322.31$$

In order to ascertain the outcome if the two projects are taken together we need to know either the probabilities of joint occurrence of each possible pair of year one returns or the correlation coefficient. Let the probabilities of each pair of returns be labelled as follows:

Pair of returns	Probability
110, 140	p_{11}
110, 60	p_{12}
190, 140	p_{21}
190, 60	p_{22}

So that, for example, p_{12} will be the chance that the existing project, E, returns 110 *and* project A returns 60. Now for consistency with the probability data given initially, p_{11}, p_{12}, p_{21} and p_{22} will have to satisfy certain conditions. For instance, there must be a probability of 0.5 that E returns 110; thus the probabilities for the two pairs that include the return 110 must sum to 0.5. That is

$$p_{11} + p_{12} = 0.5$$

Similarly, the 190 return of E must have a 0.5 chance of arising. Thus

$$p_{21} + p_{22} = 0.5$$

The probabilities for project A's returns must also be correct:

$$p_{11} + p_{21} = 0.6$$

and

$$p_{12} + p_{22} = 0.4$$

Given these conditions, there is still plenty of latitude. Suppose that the probabilities are:

$$p_{11} = 0.48$$
$$p_{12} = 0.02$$
$$p_{21} = 0.12$$
$$p_{22} = 0.38$$

Then the covariance between the year one returns of the two projects can be calculated. Recalling that the covariance is given by

$$Cov(R_1(A), R_1(E)) = \Sigma p(R_1(A) - \bar{R}_1(A))(R_1(E) - \bar{R}_1(E))$$

the workings are

(1) p	(2) $(R_1(A) - \bar{R}_1(A))(R_1(E) - \bar{R}_1(E))$	(1) × (2)
0.48	$(140 - 108)(110 - 150)$	$- 614.40$
0.02	$(60 - 108)(110 - 150)$	38.40
0.12	$(140 - 108)(190 - 150)$	153.60
0.38	$(60 - 108)(190 - 150)$	$- 729.60$
	$Cov(R_1(A), R_1(E)) =$	$- 1,152.00$

So that the variance of the composite $(E + A)$ year one return is

$$\begin{aligned}
\text{Var}(R_1(E) + R_1(A)) &= \text{Var } R_1(E) + \text{Var } R_1(A) + 2 \text{ Cov}(R_1(A)R_1(E)) \\
&= 1,600 + 1,536 - 2(1,152) \\
&= 832
\end{aligned}$$

and the variance of the NPV of $E + A$ is

$$\sigma^2_{\text{NPV}}(E + A) = \frac{832}{1.21} = 687.60$$

These variance figures should be compared with the original variance for E alone, which was 1,322.1. Now what happens when the decision-maker takes project A is that he, in effect, purchases a 48% reduction in variance of his overall NPV (687.6 compared to 1,322.1) for the price of a 16% reduction in ENPV (11.36 becomes 11.36 − 1.82).

In the third example we shall suppose that a firm's existing cash flow is given by

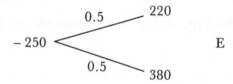

and where a possible additional project is given by

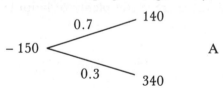

The discount rate is 10%. We shall calculate the variance of NPV of $E + A$ for $r = -0.65$, $r = 0$, $r = +0.65$ (r being the correlation between returns on E and A).

The variance of return on $E + A$, $\text{Var}(R(E) + R(A))$ is given by

$$\begin{aligned}
\text{Var}(R(E) + R(A)) = \text{Var}(R(E)) + \text{Var}(R(A)) \\
+ 2r\sqrt{\text{Var}(R(E))\text{Var}(R(A))}
\end{aligned}$$

where r is the correlation coefficient. The variance of NPV, $\sigma^2_{\text{NPV}(E + A)}$, will then be given by

$$\sigma^2_{\text{NPV}(E + A)} = \frac{\text{Var}(R(E) + R(A))}{1.21}$$

So far the variance of return on project E the workings are

p	$R(E)$	$pR(E)$	$R(E) - \bar{R}(E)$	$[R(E) - \bar{R}(E)]^2$	$p[R(E) - \bar{R}(E)]^2$
0.5	220	110	-80	6,400	3,200
0.5	380	190	$+80$	6,400	3,200
	$\bar{R}(E) = 300$			$Var(R(E)) = 6,400$	

And for project A

p	$R(A)$	$pR(A)$	$R(A) - \bar{R}(A)$	$[R(A) - \bar{R}(A)]^2$	$p[R(A) - \bar{R}(A)]^2$
0.7	140	98	-60	3,600	2,520
0.3	340	102	140	19,600	5,880
	$\bar{R}(A) = 200$				8,400

So that when $r = -0.65$, substitution into the formula for variance of return on E + A gives

$$Var(R(E) + R(A)) = 6,400 + 8,400 - 1.3\sqrt{(6,400)(8,400)}$$
$$= 5,268.24$$

So that the variance of NPV for the two projects taken together is given by

$$\sigma^2_{NPV(E + A)} = \frac{5,268.24}{1.21} = 4,353.92$$

In contrast, when the correlation coefficient is of the same absolute magnitude but positive, we obtain

$$Var(R(E) + R(A)) = 6,400 + 8,400 + 1.3\sqrt{(6,400)(8,400)}$$
$$= 24,331.76$$

So that

$$\sigma^2_{NPV(E + A)} = 20,108.89$$

which represents an almost fivefold increase in variance.

Now assume that E represents an investment possibility and is not the existing cash flow. Assume that the correlation between E and A is $r = -0.3$. We shall now construct the set of mean/standard deviation combinations for E, A, E + A, and the null project.

For project E the expected NPV is given by

$$ENPV(E) = -250 + \frac{300}{(1.1)} = 22.73$$

and, using the information in the previous answer,

$$\sigma^2_{NPV(E)} = \frac{Var(R(E))}{1.21}$$

So that

$$\sigma^2_{\text{NPV(E)}} = \sqrt{\frac{6400}{1.21}} = 72.73$$

Now for project A

$$\text{ENPV(A)} = -150 + \frac{200}{(1.1)} = 31.82$$

and

$$\sigma^2_{\text{NPV(A)}} = \sqrt{\frac{8400}{1.21}} = 83.32$$

For (E + A) the expected NPV will be the sum of the separate ENPV's so that

$$\text{ENPV(E + A)} = 22.73 + 31.82 = 54.55$$

Now,

$$\text{Var}(R(\text{E}) + R(\text{A})) = 6,400 + 8,400 - 0.6\sqrt{(6,400)(8,400)}$$
$$= 10,400.73$$

So that

$$\sigma^2_{\text{NPV(E + A)}} = \sqrt{\frac{10,400.73}{1.21}} = 92.71$$

While, of course, for the null project both ENPV and its variance are zero. The alternatives are graphed in Figure 8.13. We observe that increased expected NPV can only be obtained at the cost of increased standard deviation. Thus all the projects are efficient in their own right.

Suppose now that investor utility is given by $U = 10(\text{ENPV}) - 0.03$

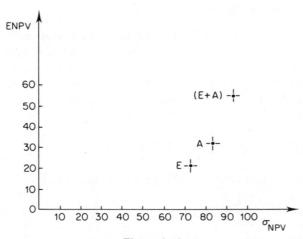

Figure 8.13

Alternative	ENPV	σ^2_{NPV}	Utility
O	0	0	0
E	22.73	5,289	68.6
A	31.82	6,942	109.9
(E + A)	54.55	8,596	287.6

Figure 8.14

σ^2_{NPV}. Which of the alternatives should be selected? When the decision is to be one in terms of the best discrete alternative, it will be a matter simply of selecting the project that gives the highest value of the utility index. The results are given in Figure 8.14.

Thus the preferred alternative is to take E + A.

As we have seen, in the case where the projects are indivisible the efficiency frontier consists of the set of discrete points given by the mean and standard deviation combinations of the individual investments. However, when *divisibility* is allowed the efficiency frontier will comprise the line segment representing linear combinations of O and E + A. A somewhat simplified picture is shown in Figure 8.15. This will render the individual projects E and A inefficient. For instance in the figure, the blend of O and E + A (i.e. a fraction of E + A) indicated by A' will give the same standard deviation as A but greater ENPV; while at A" ENPV is the same as at A but standard deviation is lower. The picture is 'slightly simplified' since it is not necessarily optimal to combine E and A in equal proportions. However, the diagram should illustrate the fact that E and A by themselves are now certainly inefficient.

If, for the sake of simplicity, we retain the restriction that E and A are equally weighted in what is now a 'portfolio', the optimal arrangement will be *either* a point of tangency between a contour of U—an indifference curve—and the line segment; *or* the optimum will remain at E + A.

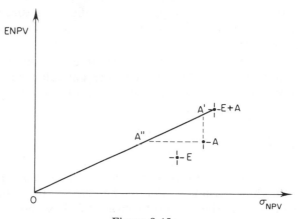

Figure 8.15

The equation of the line segment is

$$\text{ENPV} = \frac{54.55}{92.71} \sigma_{\text{NPV}}$$

Substitution into the expression for U gives

$$U = 5.884\sigma_{\text{NPV}} = -0.03\sigma_{\text{NPV}}^2$$

which when maximized with respect to σ_{NPV} gives the preferred value of $\sigma_{\text{NPV}} \simeq 98$. This is larger than can, in fact, be achieved (tangency would occur to the *right* of $E + A$) so that $E + A$ remains optimal. The actual tangency position would be achieved if more than one unit of an investment could be taken.

However, consider the problem of the best blend between E and A. Suppose we consider $k_1 E + k_2 A$. We should then have

$$\text{ENPV} = 22.73k_1 + 31.82k_2$$

Now the values of k_1 and k_2 will not affect the correlation coefficient and the variance of $k_2 A$ will be the variance of A multiplied by k_2^2. Thus the variance of NPV for the combination will be

$$\sigma_{\text{NPV}(k_1 E + k_2 A)}^2 = \frac{6{,}400k_1^2 + 8{,}400k_2^2 - 0.6 \sqrt{(6{,}400)(8{,}400)}k_1 k_2}{1.21}$$

and substitution into the utility function gives U in terms of k_1 and k_2

$$U = 227.3k_1 + 318.2k_2 - 158.7k_1^2 - 208.3k_2^2 + 109.1k_1 k_2$$

for which calculus maximization produces the values of $k_1 = 1.05$ and $k_2 = 1.08$. Thus our original view that E and A be in approximate balance, and that the ideal point is a little beyond $E + A$, is confirmed.

8.6 A General Framework for Mean–variance Analysis

In this section the objective is to provide a unified structure for the foregoing work and to show that the portfolio material of Chapter 10 also has the same background.

Suppose that a group of m projects is under consideration and it is desired to find the mean and variance of present values of this group. Let the present value of the investments be represented by the random variables $x_1 \ldots x_i \ldots x_m$, where

$$x_i = \sum_{t=0}^{n} k_t R_{it}$$

in which R_{it} represents the return on the ith investment in the tth year. The R_{it} are random variables. The coefficients k_t (the same in any year for all investments) are the discount factors. We have not written $(1 + r)^{-t}$ since the k_t form allows for different (but known a priori) rates between years, so that in general

$$k_t = \prod_{s=0}^{t} (1 + i_s)$$

in which $100 i_s \%$ is the rate of interest obtaining between the $(s-1)$th and sth years $(s_0 = 0)$.

For the group of m investments as a whole, the expected NPV is the sum of the ENPVs on the individual x's. For the variance of NPV on the whole group we can start by writing:

$$\text{Var}\left(\sum_{i=1}^{m} x_i\right) = \sum_{i=1}^{m} \text{Var}(x_i) + \sum_{\substack{i=1 \\ i \neq j}}^{m} \sum_{i=1}^{m} \text{Cov}(x_i, x_j) \tag{8.24}$$

That is: the variance of the sum is the sum of the individual variances plus the covariances. Now consider the separate terms in (8.24). We can write

$$\sum_{i=1}^{m} \text{Var}(x_i) = \sum_{i=1}^{m} \left[\sum_{t=0}^{n} k_t^2 \text{Var}(R_{it}) + \sum_{\substack{s=0 \\ s \neq t}}^{n} \sum_{t=1}^{n} k_s k_t \text{Cov}(R_{is} R_{it}) \right] \tag{8.25}$$

In (8.25) it is seen that the variance of an individual x_i is weighted sum of the variances and covariances of the returns. The covariance part of (8.24) can also be written in terms of the covariances of returns. In fact

$$\sum_{\substack{i=1 \\ i \neq j}}^{m} \sum_{j=1}^{m} \text{Cov}(x_i, x_j) = \sum_{\substack{i=1 \\ i \neq j}}^{m} \sum_{j=1}^{m} \sum_{s=0}^{n} \sum_{t=0}^{n} k_s k_t \text{Cov}(R_{is}, R_{jt}) \tag{8.26}$$

We shall now think of the variance of the sum of the x's as the sum of the right hand sides of (8.25) and (8.26). Clearly the information and computational requirements can assume daunting proportions. If the universe of investments contains M projects then there are

$\begin{bmatrix} M \\ m \end{bmatrix}$ groups of size m to consider and there will be a grand total of

2^M groups of all possible sizes. The total information required (means, variances, covariances only, ignoring discount factors) is

$$\frac{3M(n+1) + M^2(n+1)^2}{2}$$

but can be much reduced in special cases, of which we now consider four.

(i) Independent Projects

Here we assume that there is no correlation between the returns of different projects. In this case the quadruple sum of (8.26) disappears. At a stroke this reduces the information required by $M(M-1)(n+1)^2$ pieces. Within any group of size m the group variance is found by summing m

individual project variances obtained after the fashion of (8.11). Indeed (8.11) is a special case of (8.25) for $m = 1$ and $k_t = (1 + r)^{-t}$.

(ii) Independent Years

In this case the returns of any one year are assumed to have no bearing on returns in any other year, although there *can* be influence between projects within the same year. So in this case

$$\text{Cov}(R_{is}, R_{jt}) = 0 \quad \text{for all } s \neq t$$

This provision eliminates the covariance term in (8.25) entirely and reduces (8.26) to a triple sum. The result is that

$$\text{Var}\left(\sum_{i=1}^{m} x_i\right) = \sum_{i=1}^{m} \sum_{t=0}^{n} k_t^2 \text{Var}(R_{it}) + \sum_{t=0}^{n} \sum_{\substack{i=1 \\ i \neq j}}^{m} \sum_{j=1}^{m} k_t^2 \text{Cov}(R_{it}, R_{jt}) \quad (8.27)$$

which, in the case of $m = M$, contains $M^2(n + 1)$ terms.

(iii) Independent Years and Projects

Here all that matters is the variance of individual cash flow items. All covariances are zero and the whole picture is given by

$$\text{Var}\left(\sum_{i=1}^{m} x_i\right) = \sum_{i=1}^{m} \sum_{t=0}^{n} k_t^2 \text{Var}(R_{it}) \quad (8.28)$$

of which (8.13) is the special case for $m = 1$ and $k_t = (1 + r)^{-t}$.

(iv) The case of $n = 1$, $\text{Var}(R_{i0}) = 0$

This is the m project generalization of examples used in section 8.3. This is really a special special case since it drops out of (8.27). The variance overall is given by

$$\text{Var}\left(\sum_{i=1}^{m} x_i\right) = \sum_{i=1}^{m} k_1^2 \text{Var}(R_{i1}) + \sum_{\substack{i=1 \\ i \neq j}}^{m} \sum_{j=1}^{m} k_1^2 \text{Cov}(R_{i1}, R_{j1}) \quad (8.29)$$

and for $m = 2$ (8.29) reduces to

$$\text{Var}(x_1 + x_2) = k_1^2(\text{Var}(R_{11}) + \text{Var}(R_{21}) + 2 \, \text{Cov}(R_{11}, R_{21}))$$

which for $k_1 = (1 + r)^{-1}$ is a familiar expression from the latter part of Section 8.3.

Finally it is not impossible to provide a further generalization, albeit rather contrived, which includes the foregoing, general case and all, and also the Markowitz portfolio model. Consider

$$\text{Var}\left(\sum_{i=1}^{m} w_i x_i\right) \quad (8.30)$$

where $0 \leqslant w_i \leqslant 1$. Thus (8.30) is the variance of a weighted sum of x's. It simply follows that (8.30) can be written as

$$\sum_{t=1}^{m} w_i^2 \mathrm{Var}(x_i) + \sum_{\substack{i=1 \\ i \neq j}}^{m} \sum_{j=1}^{m} w_i w_j \mathrm{Cov}(x_i, x_j) \tag{8.31}$$

Now redefine present values more generally as

$$x_i = \sum_{t=0}^{n} k_{it} R_{it} \tag{8.32}$$

that is, with k's specific to x's. But now consider the expression of (8.30) in terms of the covariances of the R's. By way of (8.31) and (8.32) we obtain

$$\mathrm{Var}\left(\sum_{i=1}^{m} w_i x_i\right) = \sum_{i=1}^{m} w_i^2 \left[\sum_{t=0}^{n} k_{jt}^2 \mathrm{Var}(R_{it}) \right.$$

$$\left. + \sum_{\substack{s=0 \\ s \neq t}}^{n} \sum_{t=0}^{n} k_{is} k_{it} \mathrm{Cov}(R_{is} R_{it}) \right] \tag{8.33}$$

$$+ \sum_{\substack{i=1 \\ i \neq j}}^{m} \sum_{j=1}^{m} \sum_{s=0}^{n} \sum_{t=0}^{n} w_i w_j k_{is} k_{jt} \mathrm{Cov}(R_{is}, R_{jt})$$

Clearly our work so far is a special case in which $w_i = 1$ and $k_{it} = k_t$ for all i. Now set $n = 1$ and let Var $(R_{i0}) = 0$ for all i. Set $k_{i0} = -R_{i0}^{-1}$ and $k_{t1} = +R_{i0}^{-1}$. Then in (8.32) we have

$$x_i = k_{i0} R_{i0} + k_{i1} R_{i1}$$

$$= -1 + \frac{R_{i1}}{R_{i0}} = \frac{R_{i1} - R_{i0}}{R_{i0}}$$

which is the yield, or internal rate of return on an investment. Clearly R_{i0} could be the price of a share and R_{i1} could be end of period price plus dividend. Thus the x_i's are now yields on securities and (8.33); more clearly seen in the guise (8.31), represents portfolio variance.

8.7 Stochastic Dominance

In section 8.4 it was stated that the mean–variance efficiency criterion could be improved upon. Specifically, it may be possible to eliminate some of the combinations on a particular frontier by use of the criteria of *stochastic dominance*. An investment A is said to *dominate* an investment B by some criterion if *all* investors using that criterion would prefer A to B. We have, in fact, already considered dominance by the mean–variance criterion. By this, investment A dominates investment B provided that

$$\text{ENPV}_A \geqslant \text{ENPV}_B$$

and   (8.34)

$$\sigma^2_{\text{NPVA}} \leqslant \sigma^2_{\text{NPVB}}$$

with the strict inequality holding in at least one of the cases. 'Investment' here may mean existing plus new investments, and in portfolio theory we employed expected yield rather than ENPV but the principle is the same. The mean–variance efficiency frontier is the set of investments between which there is no dominance relation as defined by (8.34). However, it turns out that even among those investments on such a frontier there may be some which are 'obviously' preferable to others. Consider a numerical example.

An investor must choose one of the alternative investments A and B which have the distributions of returns given in Figure 8.16. The reader may verify that $\text{ENPV}_A = 112$, $\text{ENPV}_B = 104.5$, $\sigma^2_{\text{NPVA}} = 513.50$ and $\sigma^2_{\text{NPVB}} = 467.25$. Thus, in a mean variance analysis both investments would appear on the efficiency frontier since the investment with greater expected return also has the greater variance. But let us take a closer look at the two investments. For each let us find the probability that NPV will exceed certain values. For example with investment A there is no chance at all that NPV will be below 65, so that it is *certain* that NPV will exceed any value less than 65. We can write this as follows: for all x such that $x < 65$, $p(\text{NPV} > x) = 1$. Now for x given by $65 \leqslant x < 85$ there is a 0.9 probability that $\text{NPV} > x$. We can obtain this figure either by summing the probabilities that NPV is 85, 90, 105, etc. or by subtracting from unity the chance that NPV is 65.

The full results of continuing these calculations are shown in Figure 8.17. These results are reproduced in Figure 8.18—the optimist's diagram first encountered in Figure 8.5. Reference to the diagram reveals that no matter what the value of x selected the chance tht NPV_A will exceed this value is greater than or equal to the chance that NPV_B will exceed it. For some values of x, investment A provides a strictly greater chance of producing an NPV exceeding these values. Thus, provided that an investor prefers

Investment A		Investment B	
Probability	NPV	Probability	NPV
0.10	65	0.10	65
0.05	85	0.15	80
0.05	90	0.25	100
0.20	105	0.20	110
0.30	115	0.20	125
0.15	130	0.10	140
0.05	135		
0.10	150		

Figure 8.16

Investment A			
Probability	NPV	x	p(NPV > x)
0.10	65	x < 65	1.00
0.05	85	65 ≤ x < 85	0.90
0.05	90	85 ≤ x ≤ 90	0.85
0.20	105	90 ≤ x < 105	0.80
0.30	115	105 ≤ x < 115	0.60
0.15	130	115 ≤ x < 130	0.30
0.05	135	130 ≤ x < 135	0.15
0.10	150	135 ≤ x < 150	0.10
		150 ≤ x	0.00

Investment B			
Probability	NPV	x	p(NPV > x)
0.10	65	x < 65	1.00
0.15	80	65 ≤ x < 80	0.90
0.25	100	80 ≤ x < 100	0.75
0.20	110	100 ≤ x < 110	0.50
0.20	125	110 ≤ x < 125	0.30
0.10	140	125 ≤ x < 140	0.10
		140 ≤ x	0.00

Figure 8.17

more return to less, these seem few possible grounds for choosing B. In fact, given that for all investors utility is expressible as non-decreasing functions of wealth at some time, and that existing wealth is non-stochastic (or uncorrelated with either investment) then A will be preferred to B by *all* investors regardless of their attitude to risk. This is *first-degree stochastic dominance*.

Now consider *second-degree* stochastic dominance. Here we make the

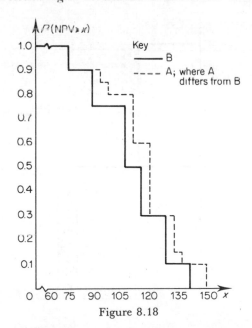

Figure 8.18

Investment A			
Probability	NPV	x	$p(NPV > x)$
0.60	125	$x < 125$	1.00
0.40	230	$125 \leqslant x < 230$	0.40
		$230 \leqslant x$	0.00
Investment B			
Probability	NPV	x	$p(NPV > x)$
0.50	100	$x < 100$	1.00
0.50	200	$100 \leqslant x < 200$	0.50
		$200 \leqslant x$	0.00

Figure 8.19

additional assumption that all investors have declining marginal utility of wealth—a condition frequently used as the definition of *risk aversion*; and we shall so use it here. Consider the problem of choice between the two projects shown in Figure 8.19, the data of which is graphed in Figure 8.20. The deciding factor here is the areas A_1, A_2 and A_3. The areas represent 'excesses' of A over B, hence A_2 is given a negative sign. It can be shown that all risk averters will prefer A to B provided that for any value of x the total 'excess' of A over B is never negative and, for some values of x, is positive. Note that $ENPV_A = A_0 + A_1 + A_3$ and $ENPV_B = A_1 + |A_2|$ where A_0 is the unshaded region beneath both distributions. Since the total areas correspond to the ENPVs it follows that it is a *necessary* condition for second-degree stochastic dominance that $ENPV_A \geqslant ENPV_B$ although this condition is not *sufficient* of course.

In the example given here it turns out that the variance of the present

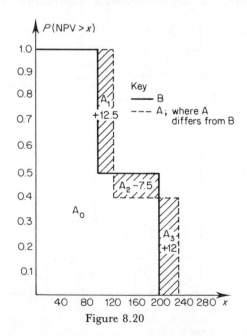

Figure 8.20

value of A exceeds that of B (sometimes the dominated project can have greater variance) so that both projects would appear on the mean–variance efficiency frontier. However, no risk averter would prefer B to A so that it could be removed from the frontier. But what harm would it do to leave B in the frontier and save the trouble of checking for stochastic dominance? The answer is that stochastic dominance—of even the first degree—is not obvious. Unless the exercise is undertaken the investor *may not know where dominance exists.*

The computational burden of checking for dominance may be considerable. For instance suppose that there are just four possible investments, A, B, C, D, of which none, some or all may be undertaken. This problem may be viewed in a single project framework by relabelling combinations as individual projects as in Figure 8.21 the choice now being between the 'single projects' 0 P. Where any combination of investments can be made there will be 2^n possible choices (we have $2^4 = 16$ above) where n is the number of projects. If not all possible combinations are feasible then the number of choices may be much less than 2^n. Given a list such as that of Figure 8.21, the means and variances are first ascertained and dominated combinations by the MV criterion are eliminated. The remainder can then be checked for stochastic dominance. If 8 of the 16 possibilities remain there will be 28 pairs to check. In general, if m projects remain there will be $\frac{1}{2}(m^2 - m)$ pairs to check. It is easy to assert that computation should proceed to the point where its marginal cost equals the marginal improvement made in NPV, but it is not easy to turn this admirable paper precept even into a rule of thumb.

As a further example, consider the case of a company that can invest in a new facility to the alternative levels of £2m. and £3m. Estimates of probable cash flows are given in Figure 8.22. The rate of discount is 10%. Which project should be selected?

New 'project'	Old projects
0	—
A	A
B	B
C	C
D	D
E	AB
F	AC
G	AD
H	BC
I	BD
J	CD
K	ABC
L	ABD
M	ACD
N	BCD
P	ABCD

Figure 8.21

	A (£3m.)			B (£2m.)	
Years	Cash flow	Prob.	Years	Cash flow	Prob.
1–4	1.0	⎫ 0.3	1–4	0.6	⎫ 0.4
5–10	0.7	⎭	5–10	0.5	⎭
1–4	0.8	⎫ 0.5	1–4	0.6	⎫ 0.4
5–10	0.4	⎭	5–10	0.2	⎭
1–10	0.1	0.2	1–10	0.2	0.2

Figure 8.22

	$t=1$	$t=2$	$t=3$	$t=4$	$t=5$	$t=6$	$t=7$	$t=8$	$t=9$	$t=10$
A_1	1	1	1	1	0.7	0.7	0.7	0.7	0.7	0.7
A_2	0.8	0.8	0.8	0.8	0.4	0.4	0.4	0.4	0.4	0.4
A_3	0.1	0.1	0.1	0.1	0.1	0.1	0.1	0.1	0.1	0.1

Figure 8.23

First consider the possible cash flow patterns for project A. These are shown in Figure 8.23. The stream of returns A_1 consists of an immediate annuity of 1 for four years followed by a six-year annuity of 0.7 deferred for four years. Thus using the annuity table the gross present value (GPV) will be given by

$$GPV(A_1) = 3.1699 + \frac{0.7(4.3553)}{(1.1)^4} = 5.2522$$

So that NVP for this stream is 2.2522. The second stream is similarly a combination of an immediate and a deferred annuity and GPV is given by

$$GPV(A_2) = 0.8(3.1699) + \frac{0.4(4.3553)}{(1.1)^4} = 3.7258$$

So that NPV in this case will be 0.7258. For the third stream:

$$GPV(A_3) = 0.1(6.1446) = 0.6145.$$

So that NPV here is -2.3855. These three possible present values and their associated probabilities are given in the first two columns of Figure 8.24. The expected NPV is positive at 0.5615 and we note that the probability of achieving a positive NPV is 0.8.

	Project A	
Probability(p)	NPV	pNPV
0.3	2.2522	0.6757
0.5	0.7258	0.3629
0.2	-2.3855	-0.4771
	ENPV(A) =	0.5615

Figure 8.24

	$t=1$	$t=2$	$t=3$	$t=4$	$t=5$	$t=6$	$t=7$	$t=8$	$t=9$	$t=10$
B_1	0.6	0.6	0.6	0.6	0.5	0.5	0.5	0.5	0.5	0.5
B_2	0.6	0.6	0.6	0.6	0.2	0.2	0.2	0.2	0.2	0.2
B_3	0.2	0.2	0.2	0.2	0.2	0.2	0.2	0.2	0.2	0.2

Figure 8.25

For project B the three alternative cash flow patterns are as shown in Figure 8.25. The GPV for stream B_1 is given by

$$GPV(B_1) = 0.6(3.1699) + \frac{0.5(4.3553)}{(1.1)^4} = 3.3893$$

So that NPV in this case is 1.3893. For stream B_2:

$$GPV(B_2) = 0.6(3.1699) + \frac{0.2(4.3553)}{(1.1)^4} = 2.4969$$

Thus NPV in this case is 0.4969. For stream B_3:

$$GPV(B_3) = 0.2(6.1446) = 1.2289$$

So that NPV here is -0.7711. Workings for the ENPV of project B are as shown in Figure 8.26. So that project B has the higher ENPV. As with project A there is a 0.8 probability of yield exceeding 10%. The distribution of NPV values for the two projects shows that B, which has the higher mean return, also has less variability. There is a more telling way to make the point, however.

There is no first-degree dominance, as the project (A) with the lowest possible NPV value also has the highest possible value so that profiles based on cumulative distributions must intersect. If one project dominates another in the second degree then it will be preferred by all risk averters. Thus, provided that the company attitudes satisfy the modest provisions underlying the definition of risk aversion, if B dominates A it will be preferred regardless of the detailed attitude to risk. For project A, the NPV outcomes are collated in Figure 8.27 and for project B, the rele-

	Project B	
Probability(p)	NPV	pNPV
0.4	1.3893	0.5557
0.4	0.4969	0.1988
0.2	-0.7711	-0.1542
	ENPV(B) =	0.6003

Figure 8.26

p	NPV	x	$p(\text{NPV} > x)$
0.2	-2.3855	$x < -2.3855$	1.0
0.5	0.7258	$-2.3855 \leqslant x < 0.7258$	0.8
0.3	2.2522	$0.7258 \leqslant x < 2.2522$	0.3
		$2.2522 \leqslant x$	0

Figure 8.27

p	NPV	x	p(NPV > x)
0.2	− 0.771	x < − 0.7711	1.0
0.4	0.4969	− 0.7711 ⩽ x < 0.4969	0.8
0.4	1.3893	0.4969 ⩽ x < 1.3893	0.4
		1.3893 ⩽ x	0

Figure 8.28

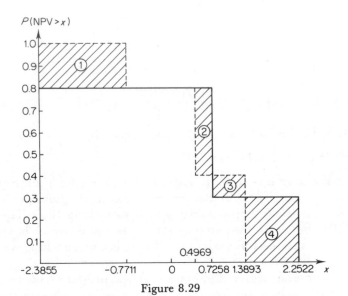

Figure 8.29

Region	Area	Cumulative area
(1)	+0.3229	+0.3229
(2)	−0.0916	+0.2313 (=(1)+(2))
(3)	+0.0664	+0.2977 (=(1)+(2)+(3))
(4)	−0.2589	+0.0388 (=(1)+(2)+(3)+(4))

Figure 8.30

vant table is shown in Figure 8.28. The situation is graphed in Figure 8.29 where the dimensions of area (1) (which will be given a positive sign as we shall consider B over A) are 0.2 in the probability dimension and 2.3855 – 0.7711 in the NPV dimension. The resulting area is + 0.3229. The remaining areas, appropriately signed are shown along with the running total in Figure 8.30. Thus the total is never negative so that project B dominates A in the second degree, i.e. it will be preferred by all risk averters. The final recommendation is unambiguous. Project B calls for less in the way of committed funds, it gives a higher expected return and has less variability than A. Any risk averter would prefer B to A. Therefore project B is selected.

8.8 Further Topics

A mean–variance approach underlies the discussion in this chapter. In common with any other approach simple enough to pretend to practicality, it is not without drawbacks. For instance there is some evidence to suggest that the third 'moment' of the probability distribution of returns is important to investors. The first moment, the mean, gives location on the horizontal axis; the second moment, variance, represents dispersion; the third moment, 'skewness' measures asymmetry. Investors in American mutual funds seem to prefer *positive* skewness as shown in Figure 8.31. This is plausible since positive skewness is characterized by a relative scarcity of large numbers to the left (low or negative returns).

The possible importance of skewness is not a new idea, being suggested by Hicks in 1939. The fourth moment, kurtosis, does not appear to be of much significance and is in any case difficult to interpret. Levy and Sarnat (1972) examined all the first *twenty* moments. Not surprisingly moments 5 to 20 never showed up as being significant. The fact that skewness was of some account means that the distribution of returns in the study cannot have been precisely normal (which has zero skewness) although normality is frequently a reasonable approximation. The use of a criterion based on mean and variance alone means that we implicitly assume one of two things—either investors do not care about skewness, kurtosis, etc. or the moments higher than the second are zero.

As regards the utilitarian support on which the mean–variance approach is supposed to depend, the situation is this. *If* it is reasonable to think of utility in terms of expected utility of wealth at some point in time and *provided* that problems resulting from the essentially stochastic nature of wealth can be surmounted, then if rationality and risk aversion only are assumed, it follows that the returns must belong to the same family of *independent two-parameter distributions*. The two parameters must be independent functions of the mean and variance respectively. The normal distribution is a special case of such a distribution; the mean can be varied without altering the variance and the variance can be altered without changing the mean. On the other hand, if a quadratic form is assumed for the utility functions of investors (a stronger, i.e. more restrictive, assumption than mere concavity) then the mean–variance approach applies for any type of distribution of return. But the assumption of

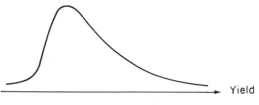

Figure 8.31

quadratic utility of wealth brings some serious shortcomings—viz. that contrary to observation, ever increasing absolute risk aversion is implied and the function must become *downward* sloping eventually. This prohibits the use of the function for some investments offering a very high return with (presumably) low probability. So the function can be used for some investments but not others! In the modern view it is the utility functions that are determined by individual behaviour and *not* vice versa. Let us take this view to its logical conclusion and say that *if* the investor finds mean–variance analysis appropriate and useful and *if* assuming some particular shape for indifference curves helps to select a point on the efficiency frontier—all well and good. If not, some other approach is indicated.

In keeping the use of utility concepts to a minimum we have forgone detailed discussion of *certainty equivalent* procedures and utility-based notions of *cash risk premia*. The *notion* of certainty equivalence is simple enough. It is an assured return (or stream of returns) between which and a risky project the investor is indifferent. Risk premia, either in the form of lump sums or adjustments to discount rates can follow from this approach. While specific use is made of the linear certainty equivalence theorem in the context of a stochastic capital rationing problem in the following chapter, in general there are real difficulties with the character of utility functions used and with the treatment of time. This brings us to a mention of the *state-preference* approach. Sometimes this is known as time-state-preference. Suppose there are two time periods. It is assumed that a finite number of alternative *states of the world* are possible for next year. The utility obtainable by an individual from £1 received next year is seen as depending on the state that obtains then (high inflation or low inflation, recession or boom, war or peace). Investment appraisal techniques using this theory require knowledge of the utilities of money in different states and, possibly subjective, knowledge of the probabilities of occurrence of the alternative states.

References

Hicks, J. R. (1975), *Value and Capital, Inquiry into some Fundamental Principles of Economic Theory*, Oxford University Press.
Levy, H., and Sarnat, M., *Investment and Portfolio Analysis*, Wiley, 1972.

Further Reading

Aharony, J., and Loeb, M., 'Mean variance vs. stochastic dominance: some empirical findings on efficient sets', *Journal of Banking and Finance*, **1977** (June).
Bierwag, G. O., 'The rationale of mean-standard deviation analysis: comment', *American Economic Review*, **64**, No. 3, June 1974.

Borch, K. H., 'The rationale of mean-standard deviation analysis: comment', *American Economic Review*, **64**, No. 3, June 1974.

Brumelle, S. L., and Vickson, R. G., 'A unified approach to stochastic dominance', in Ziemba, W. T. and Vickson, R. G. (eds), *Stochastic Optimisation Models in Finance*, Academic Press, New York, 1975.

Copeland, T. E., and Weston, J. F., *Financial Theory and Corporate Policy*, Addison-Wesley, Reading, Mass., 1979.

Fishburn, P. C., 'Convex stochastic dominance with continuous distribution functions', *Journal of Economic Theory*, **7**, 1974.

Gandhi, D. K., and Saunders, A., 'The superiority of stochastic dominance over mean–variance efficiency criteria: some clarifications', *Journal of Business Finance and Accounting*, **8**, No. 1, Spring 1981.

Gould, J. P., 'Risk, stochastic preference and the value of information', *Journal of Economic Theory*, **8**, 1974.

Hadar, J., and Russell, W. R., 'Stochastic dominance and diversification', *Journal of Economic Theory*, **3**, 1971.

Hadar, J., and Russell, W. R., 'Diversification of interdependent prospects', *Journal of Economic Theory*, **7**, 1974.

Hillier, F. S., *The Evaluation of Risky Interrelated Investments*, North-Holland, Amsterdam, 1969.

Hirschleifer, J., 'Investment decisions under uncertainty: application of the state preference approach', *Quarterly Journal of Economics*, **1966**.

Hirschleifer, J., *Investment, Interest, and Capital*, Prentice-Hall, Englewood Cliffs, NJ, 1970.

Jean, W. H., 'Comparison of moment and stochastic dominance ranking methods', *Journal of Financial and Quantitative Analysis*, March **1975**.

Levy, H., 'The rationale of mean-standard deviation analysis: comment', *American Economic Review*, **64**, No. 3, June 1974.

Levy, H., and Sarnat, M., *Capital Investment and Financial Decisions*, Prentice-Hall, Englewood Cliffs, NJ, 1978.

Marshak, J., 'Money and the theory of assets', *Econometrica*, No. 6, 1938.

Porter, R. B., 'A comparison of stochastic dominance and mean–variance portfolio models', Paper to Financial Management Association (US), October 1971.

Porter, R. B., 'Semivariance and stochastic dominance: a comparison', *American Economic Review*, **64**, No. 1, March 1974.

Rubinstein, M. E., 'A mean–variance synthesis of corporate financial theory', *Journal of Finance*, **1973** (March).

Tsiang, S. C., 'The rationale of the mean–standard deviation analysis, skewness preference, and the demand for money', *American Economic Review*, **62**, June 1972.

Tsiang, S. C., 'The rationale of mean–standard deviation analysis: reply and errata for original article', *American Economic Review*, **64**, No. 3, June 1974.

Whitmore, G. A., 'Third-degree stochastic dominance', *American Economic Review*, **60**, 1970.

Ziemba, W. T., and Vickson, R. G., *Stochastic Optimisation Models in Finance*, Academic Press, New York, 1975.

CHAPTER 9

Further Topics in Risk, Uncertainty and Investment Appraisal

Overview
One of the most widely useful approaches to decision-making under uncertainty is sensitivity analysis. The chapter begins with this topic, set in the capital budgeting context. This topic blends naturally into simulation, which is the subject of section 9.2. Section 9.3 considers stochastic capital-rationing problems using the linear certainty equivalence theorem and outlining chance constrained programming. Section 9.4 considers the effects on investment decisions when the discount rates are stochastic.

9.1 Sensitivity Analysis

The discussion of Chapter 8 applied to a situation where probabilistic information is available. But what of uncertainty, where the data is much less luxuriant? Here sensitivity analysis can be helpful. The investor may have a set of point estimates of returns, outlay, discount rate and project lifetime, but may be aware that uncertainty surrounds some or all of these figures. In *single parameter analysis* the NPV is first calculated using the original data and then a particular parameter—for instance the discount rate—is singled out and the value found for this parameter that would produce zero NPV. If this latter figure is little different to the original point estimate then we should say that the viability of the project is sensitive to the value of the discount rate. This would point up the desirability of further consideration of the cost of capital problem. The analysis is repeated for some or all of the other parameters and the results are tabulated. It should then be apparent what the critical factors are and where management effort (either in estimation *ex ante* or control *ex post*) should be concentrated.

Consider an example. A manufacturing project requires an initial outlay of £40,000 and would run for six years. Returns, R, result from the sales of a product and it is estimated that sales volume, q, would be 2,000 units per year in each of the first two years, 3,000 units per year in each of the next two years and 1,500 units per year in each of the final years. Selling price, p, is estimated at £20 per unit throughout the lifetime of the project and unit costs, c, are expected to be £15. The appropriate discount rate is estimated to be 10%.

The return on the investment in any year t, is given by $R_t = (p - c)q_t$ so that anticipated cash flows over the six-year life are: $- 40,000$, $+ 10,000$, $+ 10,000$, $+ 15,000$, $+ 15,000$, $+ 7,500$, $+ 7,500$. At the discount rate of 10% it emerges that GPV = £47,761 and therefore NPV = £7,761 so that the project would be worth while if the original estimates obtained. The question to be answered now is: for what range of variation in each of the estimated figures will the NPV of the project remain non-negative?

First consider the unit profit on the product. This is $p - c$ and is currently £5. Any variation in this figure would have equal proportionate effect on each return and hence on GPV as a whole, so that so long as unit profit is not less than $(40,000/47,761)(£5) = £4.19$ with the other data unchanged NPV will not become negative. Thus with unchanged unit costs, so long as selling price is not less than £19.19, the project will still be viable. In other words price must not drop by more than 4.05%. On the other hand if unit costs remain below £15.81 then NPV will be positive, so that any increase must not exceed 5.40%. If unit profits are unchanged but sales are 83.75% = $(40,000/47,761) \cdot (100)$ of the original estimates in each year (i.e. do not fall by more than 16.25%) the project is viable.

For the remaining parameters, again considered individually, NPV will become zero for an initial outlay for £47,761 that is, 19.40% above the original figure. As regards the discount rate the yield of the project turns out to be 16.57% so that a 65.7% increase over the original value for discount rate is tolerable.

Variation in project lifetime is somewhat more difficult to allow for, for two reasons. If lifetime was increased we should have to have estimates of returns beyond year six and if reductions are being considered we must recall the implicit assumption that returns occur at year end so that some approximating assumption will be necessary if reductions in life involving a fraction of a year are involved. If the project's life was four years, that is, if the last two returns of £7,500 are ignored the GPV would be £38,870, a decrease of £8,891. To make GPV £40,000 the contribution to present value of returns in the fifth year needs to be £1,130.

Suppose that if the project runs for some fraction, f, of the fifth year then the return that arises is $7,500f$ to be received at $t = 4 + f$. Thus if the truncated fifth year is to produce a return giving present value 1,130 then f must be such as to satisfy the equation

$$\frac{7,500f}{(1.1)^{4+f}} = 1,130 \tag{9.1}$$

or:

$$750f = 113(1.1)^{4+f} \tag{9.2}$$

Numerical workings are shown in Figure 9.1. The object is to choose

f	$750f$	$113(1.1)^{4+f}$
0.2	150.00	168.63
0.23	172.50	169.11
0.225	168.75	169.03
0.226	169.50	169.05
0.2254	169.05	169.04
0.2253	168.98	169.03

Figure 9.1

a value of f so as to equate the left- and right-hand sides of the equation (9.2). This is accomplished for $f = 0.2254$. Thus the breakeven lifetime is 4.2254 years, a reduction of 1.7746 years or 29.58%.

The full results of the one-parameter break-even exercise are shown in Figure 9.2. Entries in the % change column are the unfavourable change (decreases or increases as the case may be) which, if occurring individually, would reduce NPV to zero. It is evident that the present value is much more sensitive to sales price and unit costs than any other datum. What is indicated by this is that management efforts should be concentrated in these areas either before the event in obtaining more precise estimates of the figures, or, if it is decided to go ahead with the project, in controlling any unfavourable variations that may arise.

Consider a further example. For an investment project, the following point estimates have been made:

Outlay	£100,000	*Sales volumes*	
Sales price	£30	Year one	4,000 units
Unit cost	£20	Year two	6,000 units
Discount rate	10% p.a.	Year three	3,000 units
Life	3 years		

The £100,000 purchases equipment which will manufacture a product produced, it is intended, at the above unit cost and selling at the estimated sales price and in the volumes indicated. A sensitivity analysis is required for the individual years' sales volumes. Further, if Government anti-inflation policy allowed sales prices to rise by only 10% p.a. compound but unit costs are expected to rise at an annual rate of 20% compound (both starting at $t = 0$), what initial cash subsidy would be necessary to retain financial viability for the project?

Datum	% change
Selling price	4.05
Unit cost	5.40
Sales volume	16.25
Initial outlay	19.40
Discount rate	65.70
Project lifetime	29.58

Figure 9.2

Assuming all other parameters to be as originally estimated, if sales volume in year one is v_1 then v_1 must be such as to produce zero NPV. Thus

$$\frac{10v_1}{(1.1)} + \frac{60,000}{(1.21)} + \frac{30,000}{(1.331)} = 100,000$$

This equation solves for $v_1 = 3,066$, a reduction of 23.35%. For year two the equation is

$$\frac{40,000}{(1.1)} + \frac{10v_2}{(1.21)} + \frac{30,000}{(1.331)} = 100,000$$

which solves for $v_2 = 4,973$, a reduction of 17.12%. Finally, for year three:

$$\frac{40,000}{(1.1)} + \frac{60,000}{(1.21)} + \frac{10v_3}{(1.331)} = 100,000$$

solves for $v_3 = 1,870$, a reduction of 37.67%. The project is most sensitive to sales performance in the second year, and least sensitive to third-year volume.

Now consider the question of possible subsidy. The calculations necessary to ascertain present value are shown in Figure 9.3. It will be seen that margin starts to decline at once and in increasing absolute amounts. The GPV plunges to 82,021. Therefore, a subsidy sufficient to bring this figure up to 100,000 would be needed for economic viability. Thus the subsidy required would be 17,979. Problems raised by inflation are discussed in more detail later in the section.

It should be noted that there are no purely theoretical grounds for saying that one factor always has a more dramatic effect (on yield or on NPV) than another. In other words, it cannot be said *in general* that projects' desirability (measured in some way) will be more sensitive to the selling price than to—say—the rate of corporation tax. It all depends on how the cash flow is made up in any particular case. Consider a project, the returns to which are made up as follows:

$$R = (1 - t)(p - u)v$$

where t is the rate of tax, p the selling price, u the unit cost and v the sales volume. The proportionate effect on returns, of variation in any one of these parameters depends heavily on their initial values. For instance,

t	p	c	$p-c$	R	PV
1	33.00	24.00	9.00	36,000	32,727.27
2	36.30	28.80	7.50	45,000	37,190.08
3	39.93	34.56	5.37	16,110	12,103.68
					82,021.03

Figure 9.3

suppose the return is 1,000 with the details

$$1{,}000 = (1 - 0.9)(250 - 50)50$$

Thus the after-tax return is 1,000; with tax rate of 90% (to point up the results—not a prediction!) sales price at 250, unit cost at 50 and with 50 as sales volume. Now a 10% variation in the tax *rate* would produce the return

$$R = (1 - 0.99)(250 - 50)50 = 100$$

i.e. a 10% increase in tax rate has produced a 90% fall in R—and a similar percentage fall in GPV if this is the situation in each year. Of course, the tax *take* has not increased by only 10%—but that is another matter. Now consider a 10% cut in sales price—to 225 (with the original tax rate). Revenue would be

$$R = (1 - 0.9)(225 - 50)50 = 875$$

which is a drop of 'only' 12.5%. The reader may verify that (again with other data at the original values) a 10% increase in unit cost produces only a $2\frac{1}{2}$% fall in revenue. Conclusion? For this project the tax rate is vital—price is much, much less important and unit cost hardly matters at all.

Now consider the same revenue of 1,000 with different original values for the data:

$$1{,}000 = (1 - 0.2)(250 - 225)50$$

Now, with an original tax rate of 20%, an increase of 10% in this value gives $t = 0.22$ and the return is

$$R = (1 - 0.22)(250 - 225)50 = 975.$$

Thus the 10% increase in tax rate gives a 2.5% reduction in annual return. However, if now sales price fell by 10%, the returns would be eliminated entirely—a 100% reduction! A 10% increase in unit cost—to 247.5 would have given a 90% reduction in return.

However, should empirical work reveal that in the UK as a whole large projects *tend on the average* to be most sensitive to prices and costs then this would give an indication of the importance of the way that government anti-inflationary policy is framed.

For a given NPV the time distribution of returns can be important—especially when project lifetime is being considered. If the returns are increasing towards the end of the project it will be the biggest nominal returns that are lost if the project fails to run its full course. To illustrate, the cash flow:

$t = 1$	$t = 2$	$t = 3$	$t = 4$	$t = 5$
100	200	300	400	500

has present value of 1,065 at 10%. If the lifetime is cut by 20% (from five years to four) the present value drops to 755. Now a five-year annuity for 281 also has a present value of 1,065 but reducing this to 4 years only reduces present value to 891. This is a much lesser effect, as would be expected.

Multiparameter analysis considers groups of changes that are thought possible. In particular, it would be reasonable to suppose that there will be simultaneous movement of prices. In the exercise that follows we shall consider the consequences that would result from various inflation *scenarios*. In this version of sensitivity analysis all that is done is that a group of changes of parameters (in this case prices) is specified and then the present value consequences are deduced. Then a different group of changes is specified and the consequences of that 'state' are ascertained—and so on. Whether any subjective probabilities are attached to the various states or scenarios is a matter for the individual investor. Here we simply deduce the consequences in a formalized version of the 'what would happen if . . .' approach.

As inflation scenario one, suppose that it is expected that future government policy will limit product price rises to 10% per annum but that less control is proposed for resource prices so that unit costs are expected to rise at 15% per annum. Assume that both sets of rises begin right away at $t = 0$. The first thing to do is to find out what selling price and unit costs will be at the end of each year; then unit profit is obtained as the difference of the two. Unit profit is then multiplied by sales volume and discounted in the usual way. The results (with p_t given by $p_t = 20(1.1)^t$ and c_t given by $c_t = 15(1.15)^t$) are shown in Figure 9.4. The end result of the different rates of inflation has been to turn a positive present value of £7,761 into a loss of £6,822.30 in present value terms. Note that the major impact of the different rates of inflation is in the later years. In years one and two there are relatively minor reductions in unit profit; but this figure is rapidly approaching zero by $t = 6$.

The above results are hardly surprising, but now consider inflation scenario two. In this case there are dire prognostications of 23% inflation of selling price and 28% of unit cost. With a similar layout the results are displaced in Figure 9.5.

t	p_t	c_t	$p_t - c_t$	q_t	R_t		PV
1	22.00	17.25	4.75	2,000	9,500		8,636.36
2	24.20	19.84	4.36	2,000	8,720		7,206.61
3	26.62	22.81	3.81	3,000	11,430		8,587.53
4	29.28	26.24	3.04	3,000	9,120		6,229.08
5	32.21	30.17	2.04	1,500	3,060		1,900.02
6	35.43	34.70	0.73	1,500	1,095		618.10
						GPV =	33,177.70
					∴	NPV =	6,822.30

Figure 9.4

t	p_t	c_t	$p_t - c_t$	q_t	R_t	PV
1	24.60	19.20	5.40	2,000	10,800	9,818.18
2	30.26	24.58	5.68	2,000	11,360	9,388.43
3	37.22	31.46	5.76	3,000	17,280	12,280.72
4	45.78	40.27	5.51	3,000	16,530	11,290.21
5	56.31	51.54	4.77	1,500	7.155	4,442.69
6	69.26	65.97	3.29	1,500	4,935	2,785.68

					GPV =	50,707.91
				$\therefore$	NPV =	10,707.91

Figure 9.5

In this case the end result is an *increase* of 38% in NPV. This is due to the increase in nominal unit profit in the earlier years of the project. This illusion of prosperity is due to the fact that although the escalation of selling price is slower than that of unit cost, it works from a larger base. This is sufficient at first to more than counteract the difference of five percentage points. However, as is evidenced in Figure 9.5, the chickens are coming home to roost in the later years of the project with unit profit falling rapidly (it would have become negative by year eight). The example suggests that differences in inflation rates between prices and costs can possibly be 'gotten away with' for a while, if there is profitability to begin with, before the damage becomes manifest.

Thus far we have worked with the original discount rate of 10%. However, where other prices are moving upwards the price of money will not remain constant for long. Under rapid inflation the rise in interest rates may not produce a non-negative 'real' rate of interest—but some movement will occur. Under deflation, real interest rates may be well into the positive range. Inflation scenario three might represent the situation where some authority is exercised by Government and compliance of labour unions purchased by allowing costs to rise at 8%, while product prices increase at 5% and where interest rates rise such that the discount rate becomes 12.5%. The results are shown in Figure 9.6. Here the apparently modest difference between the cost and price inflation rates— three percentage points—eats into unit profits at once. The important fact is that is it 60% greater. The rise in discount rate adds to the damage and the investment would no longer be undertaken if this scenario were

t	p_t	c_t	$p_t - c_t$	q_t	R_t	PV
1	21.00	16.20	4.80	2,000	9,600	8,533.33
2	22.05	17.50	4.55	2,000	9,100	7,190.12
3	23.15	18.90	4.25	3,000	12,750	8,954.73
4	24.31	20.41	3.90	3,000	11.700	7,304.25
5	25.53	22.04	3.49	1,500	5,235	2,905.05
6	26.80	23.80	3.00	1,500	4,500	2,219.72

					GPV =	37,107.20
				$\therefore$	NPV =	− £2,892.8

Figure 9.6

assured. Of course, there are many other possible futures that could be projected, for example with periods of rising inflation then falling inflation, varying interest rates and with effects on sales volume considered.

In an early empirical study in the United States, W. C. House (1968) remarked:

> By concentrating its resources on improving techniques of estimating sales prices, sales volume and project life for proposals with increasing patterns of estimated annual cash flows, management can make the greatest potential improvement in capital investment decision making with the least expenditure of time, effort and money.

House continued:

> For example, the accuracy of estimates of sales prices, sales volume and project life can be improved by conducting more intensive market research studies for current investment proposals and by analysing differences in estimates and actual figures for these three elements for past investment proposals similar to those currently being considered. In addition, the use of such forecasting techniques as multiple correlation analysis and exponential smoothing may be helpful in improving the accuracy of these estimates.

Put another way, the point is that research into data is itself likely to be a very good investment.

For further research, House suggested examination of individual elements in the firm's capital structure—the cost of equity, preferred dividend rates, loan stock interest and the gearing ratio. Also, for the larger projects more detailed examination of certain tax parameters might be worth while. A longstanding complaint in the UK has been that a prolonged environment of changes in Government tax rates and allowances has reduced the level of corporate investment. This (presuming that the response is not merely petulant) is an assertion that investment decisions (in the way that they are currently made) are sensitive to tax parameters.

In the concluding paragraphs of the monograph House mentions the limitations that he believes sensitivity analysis has: 'The technique itself is not very precise, the effects of combinations of errors on project profit ability (more precisely upon measures of return) are ignored, and little attention is given to the possibility that errors in some estimates are more likely to occur than errors in other estimates.' The writer is not sure what 'precision' means in this context, and House does not spell this out. If the lack of precision is merely an admission that we are working with vague data—agreed! If it means that we do not really understand the technique or use it sloppily—not agreed! The second point concerning combinations of errors is just not true. The writer has seen this fallacious assertion made on a number of occasions. Combinations of errors *can* be examined—we did so when considering the effects of different rates of inflation for prices and unit costs. In an environment of inflation, while the physical inputs to the project remain constant, *all* prices are likely to be changing—at different rates. The problem is to specify how the changes are related—to spell out the structure of the simultaneous changes. If this can be done, the analysis can be applied just as before. What *cannot* be made are general statements about the consequences of group changes *regardless* of the functional relationships within the group. This is not a limitation of the method, but merely a statement that it has been provided with insufficient information. Of course, sensitivity analysis could then follow on the parameters of the supposed structural relationships. . . .

As regards the *likelihood* of the errors there are two points here. If we *do* have some probabilistic information—for example that the distribution of fifth year returns is R_{51} with probability p or R_{52} with probability $(1 - p)$, then, of course, sensitivity analysis can be conducted on the value of p. If there is *no* probabilistic information—in quantified form—we get to the main *raison d'être* of sensitivity analysis—it does not require any. Of course, management will have ideas as to what are likely to be the volatile parameters. The procedure would normally be that the investigator *suspects* what is important—conducts the analysis and considers the results. Management may then see that the project is sensitive to sales price (say) and it knows (in a non-quantitative fashion) that prices are volatile—thus more management resources would be channelled into this area of investigation (*ex ante*) or control (*ex post*). If a project turned out to be highly sensitive to a parameter (say outlay) that management knew to be virtually fixed then, of course, the sensitivity is much less important. It is a mistake to attempt to quantify everything and it is equally mistaken to quantify nothing. In sensitivity analysis (while there may of course be feedbacks and further analysis) the judgemental problem is not removed but, importantly, it is *separated out* and conducted after the workings. In not fully quantified areas it is vital to distinguish the value judgements and the number crunching. Both are essential ingredients in scientific decision-making but, like Box and Cox, they should work separately to the common objective.

9.2 Simulation

Simulation enables complex systems and subsystems (e.g. financial) to be studied and influenced that are not approachable analytically or via experimental intervention in the real situation. The effects of parameter changes (e.g. sales promotion expenditure level) and variations in structure can be explored *within the mathematical model*. Compressed or real-time studies of dynamic models are rendered possible and the exercise of constructing the model can itself be a valuable learning experience. Known originally as *Monte-Carlo simulation* and currently also as *simulated sampling*, the technique has found wide usage in management science generally and in such diverse areas as cosmogony and historical demography. It is so highly malleable an instrument that the temptation may be to over-use it—for example in attempting to model systems where variables are related in complex ways that cannot find convenient expression in mathematical form.

There is no clear dividing line where sensitivity analysis ends and where simulation may be said to begin. For example, sensitivity analysis of the 'inflation scenario' variety has been called *deterministic simulation*. Balance sheet projections—highlighting the values of certain crucial financial statistics if particular investment projects were undertaken—are an example of deterministic simulation/projective sensitivity analysis. However, simulation proper is confined to the realm of the stochastic.

Some investment projects may depend on so many stochastic variables that analytical results are unobtainable. In simulation a mathematical model is constructed and artificial, appropriately selected data is fed in. The desired parameters of the system are then determined from the output of the model. For instance the exercise may produce the empirical probability distribution of NPV, from which mean and variance may be calculated.

Simulation is not in itself usually employed as an optimizing technique. It provides a highly convenient representation of reality and, in some cases, can be used to improve NPV by adjusting certain variables under the decision-maker's control. The art of the process is at two levels—the construction of the model and the judgement of changes to be made to controllable variables.

Consider a comparatively simple exercise. Suppose that it is known with certainty that the outlay on a project would be £50,000, the discount rate 10%, and the project would run for four years. Risk is attached only to the returns in each year. Suppose that these are given by the probability distribution of Figure 9.7 (the same for each year, independence between years).

Of course, this situation is simple enough to handle analytically and indeed we shall do so later to check the results. The first step in the exercise is to allocate blocks of two-digit numbers to each value of return. The size of each block in relation to the total must be such as to correspond to the probabilities above. The numbers used will be: 00, 01, 02, 03, . . . 97, 98, 99. For the 9,000 return (which has probability 0.1) we assign 10% of the 100, two-digit numbers 00 to 99. In principle *any* ten of the numbers would suffice, but for convenience sake we shall select 00 to 09 inclusive. Now the 12,000 return has probability 0.25 of arising so that 25% of the

Probability	Return
0.10	9,000
0.25	12,000
0.35	18,000
0.25	24,000
0.05	36,000

Figure 9.7

Return	Nos. allocated
9,000	00–09
12,000	10–34
18,000	35–69
24,000	70–94
36,000	95–99

Figure 9.8

two-digit numbers are assigned to this eventuality. Again these 25 could be any of the remaining 90 numbers but we shall employ 10 to 34 inclusive. The procedure is applied in a similar fashion to the remaining returns with the results shown in Figure 9.8. Next, random digits are obtained from a calculator or a pre-prepared table. Suppose the sequence of digits is:

0358579353819388232296790614946

A pair of digits is selected from the given string—for convenience let this be the first pair, 03. This number is used to give the hypothetical first-year return in run one. The number 03 falls in the range 00–09 so that the first return is 9,000. The second return is then given by the next pair of digits in the string. This is 58 and being in the range 35–69 signifies a return of 18,000 in year two. In similar fashion the third- and fourth-year returns are 18,000 and 24,000, as pointed to by the numbers 57 and 93. This completes the 'drawings' for the first run. So the result is as follows. Run no. 1, cash flow:

$t = 1$	$t = 1$	$t = 2$	$t = 3$	$t = 4$
$-50,000$	9,000	18,000	18,000	24,000

It is important to note that this cash flow pattern is in no sense a prediction of what would happen if the project was accepted. It is merely a simulated sample of possible futures drawn according to the appropriate probabilities. Discounting the run no. 1 cash flow at 10% gives an NPV of $+2,974$. Now run no. 2 is started. The first return here (recall that the outlay is always 50,000 in this example) is 18,000 as given by the next pair of digits in the string; 53. Working along the line of digits the results of the second and subsequently third and fourth runs are as shown in Figure 9.9.

	Run number			
	1	2	3	4
$t = 0$	$-50,000$	$-50,000$	$-50,000$	$-50,000$
$t = 1$	9,000	18,000	12,000	9,000
$t = 2$	18,000	24,000	12,000	12,000
$t = 3$	18,000	24,000	36,000	24,000
$t = 4$	24,000	24,000	24,000	18,000
NPV	$+2,974$	$+20,622$	$+14,266$	$-1,575$

Figure 9.9

In a practical case a much larger number of runs would be required, but for convenience we shall restrict ourselves to four runs here. The important row of Figure 9.9 is the last one—an array of numbers being four observations of NPV. From these numbers we obtain the simulation estimate of expected net present value (ENPV*) as the arithmetic mean of the NPV output thus

$$
\begin{array}{l}
\text{NPV} \\
+ 2,974 \\
+ 20,622 \\
+ 14,266 \qquad \therefore \quad \text{ENPV*} = \dfrac{36,287}{4} = 9,072 \\
- 1,575 \\
\hline
+ 36,287
\end{array}
$$

Next we can obtain an estimate of the standard deviation of NPV from the data generated:

$$
\sigma_{\text{NPV}}^* = \sqrt{\frac{(\text{NPV} - \text{ENPV*})^2}{n-1}}
$$

where n is the number of observations (runs of the simulation). The workings are:

NPV	NPV − ENPV*	(NPV − ENPV*)^2
2,974	− 6,098	37,185,604
20,622	+ 11,550	133,402,500
14,266	+ 5,194	26,977,636
− 1,575	− 10,647	113,358,609
		310,924,349

thus;

$$
\sigma_{\text{NPV}}^* = \sqrt{\frac{310,924,349}{3}} = 10,180
$$

The simulation estimated coefficient of variation, c^*, will be

$$
c^* = \frac{10,180}{9,072} = 1.12
$$

Now check these results by direct calculation. From Figure 9.7 the mean yearly return is found to be 18,000. The variance of return in any year $\sigma_R^2 = \Sigma p(R - 18,000)^2$ where the p and R values are as shown in Figure 9.7. The reader may verify that $\sigma_R^2 = 42,300,000$. Now applying formula (8.13) we find that

$$
\sigma_{\text{NPV}}^2 = 0 + 42,300,000 \left[\frac{1}{(1.1)^2} + \frac{1}{(1.1)^4} + \frac{1}{(1.1)^6} + \frac{1}{(1.1)^8} \right]
$$

$$
= 10,366
$$

so that the value produced by the simulation was quite accurate. Now for ENPV, discounting the expected return in each year gives the result:

$$\text{ENPV} = -50,000 + 18,000 \times 3.1699 = 7,058$$

so that the simulation estimate is somewhat out. The true coefficient of variation is given by

$$c = \frac{10,366}{7,058} = 1.47$$

here again there is rather a difference between the theoretical true value and the simulation result. These differences are neither surprising nor alarming since many more than four runs would be required in practice. The reader may continue the exercise and see how the performance of the simulation improves.

Now consider a slightly different problem. In the forthcoming week's trading a firm will manufacture and sell 100 units of a certain product. Selling price is normally distributed about a mean of £80, with a standard deviation of £10. The only sources of cost are unit variable cost and overhead. Unit variable cost (which is independent of price and overhead) is normally distributed with a mean value of £60 and a standard deviation of £4. Overhead (which is independent of price) is normally distributed with a mean of £1,000 and a standard deviation of £300. Figure 9.10 allocates random digits to the numbers of standard deviations

Random number	No of standard deviations from mean	Random number	No. of standard deviations from mean	Random number	No. of standard deviations from mean
00	−2.5	22−24	−0.7	79−81	0.8
01	−2.3	25−27	−0.6	82−83	0.9
02	−2.0	28−31	−0.5	84−85	1.0
03	−1.9	32−34	−0.4	86−87	1.1
04	−1.8	35−38	−0.3	88−89	1.2
05	−1.7	39−42	−0.2	90−91	1.3
06	−1.6	43−46	−0.1	92	1.4
07	−1.5	47−53	0.0	93	1.5
08	−1.4	54−57	0.1	94	1.6
09−10	−1.3	58−61	0.2	95	1.7
11−12	−1.2	62−65	0.3	96	1.8
13−14	−1.1	66−68	0.4	97	1.9
15−16	−1.0	69−72	0.5	98	2.0
17−18	−0.9	73−75	0.6	99	2.3
19−21	−0.8	76−78	0.7		

Random digits

2798964728107440839656242909852886899431503
74008078518473949

Figure 9.10

that a normally distributed variable is away from its mean. The company would like point and bracketed estimates of profitability.

Again the solution procedure primarily involves simulated sampling of values of the variables using the data of Figure 9.10. Profit is the difference between revenue on the one hand and variable and fixed costs on the other. Revenue will be price × 100 and total variable costs are unit variable costs × 100. Letting 27, the first pair of digits, select the first value of price (p) this corresponds to a value of p which is 0.6 standard deviation below the mean. So the actual value of price indicated is

$$p = 80 - 0.6(10) = 74$$

This will give a revenue of £7,400. Let the next two digits signal a value for unit variable cost (v). Thus the value will be 2.0 standard deviations above the mean, as signalled by the number 98. Thus:

$$v = 60 + 2(4) = 68,$$

and total variable costs will be £6,800. Finally, the first value of fixed costs (F) will be 1.8 standard deviations above its mean as indicated by the digits 96. Thus

$$F = 1,000 + 1.8(300) = 1,540.$$

The remainder of the results, obtained in a similar fashion, are as shown in Figure 9.11. Thus the estimated mean weekly profit ($\overline{\Pi}$) will be

$$\overline{\Pi} = \frac{10,000}{10} = 1.000$$

Simulation estimated weekly variance is given by

$$\sigma^2 = \frac{\Sigma(\Pi - \overline{\Pi})^2}{n - 1}$$

Digit pairs	Revenue	Costs Variable	Fixed	Profit (Π)
27/98/96	7,400	6,800	1,540	− 940
47/28/10	8,000	5,800	610	+ 1,590
74/40/83	8,700	5,920	1,270	+ 1,510
96/56/24	9,800	6,040	790	+ 2,970
29/09/85	7,500	5,480	1,300	+ 720
28/86/89	7,500	6,440	1,360	− 300
94/31/50	9,600	5,800	1,000	+ 2,800
37/40/08	7,700	5,920	580	+ 1,200
07/85/18	6,500	6,400	730	− 630
47/39/49	8,000	5,920	1,000	+ 1,080
				$\Sigma = $ 10,000

Figure 9.11

$\Pi - \overline{\Pi}$	$(\Pi - \overline{\Pi})^2$
$-1,940$	$3,763,600$
$+590$	$348,100$
$+510$	$260,100$
$+1,970$	$3,880,900$
-280	$78,400$
$-1,300$	$1,690,000$
$+1,800$	$3,240,000$
$+200$	$40,000$
$-1,630$	$2,656,900$
$+80$	$6,400$
	$15,964,400$

Figure 9.12

workings for which are shown in Figure 9.12. Thus weekly standard deviation will be

$$\sigma = \sqrt{\frac{15,964,400}{9}} = 1,322$$

and the simulation estimated 95% confidence interval for weekly profit is therefore

$$\overline{\Pi} \pm 1.96\sigma$$

that is

$$-1,611 \quad \text{to} \quad +3,611$$

The whole approach can be much more ambitious, but the procedure would in principle be the same. For instance suppose that a half-dozen factors had been singled out as important and subject to risk. If the model was similar to that used in the sensitivity analysis section these might be selling price(s), unit cost(s), sales volume(s), initial outlay, project life and discount rate. For each of these factors a probability distribution has to be specified (perhaps normal, beta or gamma) and simultaneous drawings are taken from these distributions to give sample values of the parameters, NPV is calculated using this data and the exercise is then repeated many times over. The distribution of yield may be thus obtained as well as that of NPV and risk profiles can be produced. Once again, at the end of the exercise a decision must be taken in the light of the evidence produced.

9.3 Stochastic Capital Rationing Problems

In principle any of the parameters of a capital-rationing problem may be random variables. We have already studied problems in which investments had NPVs which were random variables. Quite clearly, the capital inputs to investments may not be deterministic, nor need the budget levels be known with absolute certainty. Of course, the more random variability a problem contains, the more difficult, in general, it will be to solve. We shall see that there are a number of simplifying assumptions that will, while allowing random variability in one or more groups of parameters, restrict the range of possible outcomes.

We begin with a problem in which all of the per-unit capital inputs are known with certainty and in which the right-hand sides—the budget limits—are also deterministic. Thus random variability will be confined to the objective function coefficients—the per-unit NPVs of the investments. Let the problem be

$$
\left.
\begin{aligned}
\text{maximize} \quad & N = \sum_{j=1}^{n} N_j x_j \\
\text{subject to} \quad & \sum_{j=1}^{n} k_{ij} x_j \leqslant b_i \qquad (i = 1, 2,, \ldots, m) \\
& x_j \geqslant 0 \qquad (j = 1, 2, \ldots, n)
\end{aligned}
\right\} \qquad (9.3)
$$

In (9.3) the x_j are investment levels and the b_i the capital availabilities at each of m points in time; k_{ij} is the outlay required per unit of the jth project at time i and N_j the per-unit NPV on project j.

Clearly, the feasible region of the problem is determined, but we shall suppose that the values of the x_j must be selected *before* the actual values of the N_j become known. If we assume that the appropriate objective is to maximize the expected value of N and that the N_j are random variables independent of all x_j, with the k_{ij} and b_i known with certainty, then a maximum of (9.4) subject to the constraints and sign requirements

$$E(\sum N_j x_j) \qquad (9.4)$$

is obtained for the levels of x_j which maximize (9.5)

$$\sum E(N_j) x_j \qquad (9.5)$$

subject to the constraints and sign requirements. This result is known as the *linear certainty equivalence theorem*, and where if applies the problem is reduced to an ordinary linear programming problem in which the coefficients of the x_j are the expectations of the per-unit NPVs. The problem becomes much more complex if some of the x_j may be set *after* some of the N_j have become known or if there are other random elements.

Consider now a more involved problem. Suppose that in (9.3) the N_j are random variables as before but that in addition some of the per-unit capital outlays k_{ij} are also random variables. We shall make a number of simplifying assumptions namely:

  (i) The value that is taken by each random element is independent of the levels of all of the x_j.
  (ii) The values of x_j for $j = 1, 2, \ldots, b \leqslant n$ must be determined before any exact values of the random elements are known. This will be

called the *first stage* of the problem and x_j for $j \leqslant b$ are *first-stage variables*.

(iii) The constraints $i = 1, 2, \ldots, g \leqslant m$ contain only the first-stage variables, and the technical coefficients in these constraints are known with certainty as are the right-hand side values.

(iv) There always exist feasible levels for the *second-stage* variables. These are the x_j for $j = b + 1, \ldots, n$ and these levels are to be set after all of the values of the random elements have become known.

(v) There is only a finite number, H, of possible sets of values for the random elements and each possible set of values has a known probability of occurrence.

(vi) It is appropriate to maximize the expected value of N.

These assumptions underlie the two-stage linear model in which the levels of the first-stage variables are decided upon initially as are the *decision rules* for the selection of the second-stage variables. Once the first-stage variables are set at particular values the decision rules tell us what levels to choose for the second-stage variables in each and every possible outcome (H possibilities in total) for the random coefficients. Let the sets of possible values of the random N_j, k_{ij}, and b_i be denoted by

$$(N_{hj}, k_{hij}, b_{hi}) \tag{9.6}$$

with probability of occurrence p_h for the hth set where $h = 1, 2, \ldots, H$. An optimal decision rule is now found by solving the linear programme:

$$
\left.
\begin{aligned}
\text{maximize} \quad & \sum_{j=1}^{n} E(N_j)x_j + \sum_{h=1}^{H} p_h \left(\sum_{j=b+1}^{n} N_{hj}x_{hj} \right) \\
\text{subject to} \quad & \sum_{j=1}^{b} k_{ij}x_j = b_i \qquad (i = 1, 2, \ldots, g) \\
\text{and} \quad & \sum_{j=1}^{b} k_{hij}x_j + \sum_{j=b+1}^{n} k_{hij}x_{hj} = b_{hi} \quad \begin{array}{l}(i = g + 1 \ldots m) \\ (h = (1, 2, \ldots H)\end{array} \\
& \qquad\qquad\qquad x_j \geqslant 0, \quad x_{kj} \geqslant 0
\end{aligned}
\right\} \tag{9.7}
$$

Where, in (9.7) the first g constraints relate to the first stage of the problem and the remaining $m - g$ are the second-stage decision rules. Note that the x_j for $j = 1, \ldots b$ appear in the second stage of the problem and once the random coefficients are known all terms in x_j assume constant values. The number of possible values of the N_j for $j = 1, 2, \ldots b$ is not restricted to H. A numerical example will help to understand the use and validity of the model (9.7).

A firm has three investment projects that it may undertake. Let the levels of these investments be represented by x_1, x_3 and x_4. Investment 1 can produce three alternative values for per unit GPV of 8, 13 and 14 with probabilities 0.1, 0.7 and 0.2 respectively. Gross present values per unit from the other investments and initial outlays per unit on all investments are random variables, as is the amount of finance to be made available. Two possible sets of values of these random elements are possible (i.e. $H = 2$). They are

with probability 0.4:   (12, 23, 5, 7, 11, 50)   ($h = 1$)
with probability 0.6:   (17, 23, 6, 8, 12, 60)   ($h = 2$)

where the elements within the parentheses are from left to right: GPV per unit of investment 3, GPV per unit of investment 4, outlay per unit of investment 1, outlay per unit of investment 3, outlay per unit of invest-ment 4 and available funds. In addition, investment 1 has an upper bound of 3 and its level must be decided upon before any of the random elements take known values. The values of x_3 and x_4 are to be set when the actual values of the random elements are known.

In the first summation term of the objective function in (9.7) there is just one element in this example since we shall take it that the objective function coefficient of the slack variable (x_2) in the upper bound on x_1 is zero. The upper bound is written as:

$x_1 + x_2 = 3$

Thus $g = 1$ and $b = 2$ and in the objective function $E(N_1)$ is

$E(N_1) = 0.1(8) + 0.7(13) + 0.2(14) - 0.4(5) - 0.6(6) = 7.1$

The second summation term in the objective function is

$$0.4[(12 - 7)x_{13} + (23 - 11)x_{14} + x_{15}]$$
$$+ 0.6[(17 - 8)x_{23} + (23 - 12)x_{24} + x_{25}]$$

where x_{15} and x_{25} are the slack variables in the 'two' constraints relating to outlay and unused funds are included in the objective function here. These are

$5x_1 + 7x_{13} + 11x_{14} + x_{15} = 50$

and

$6x_1 + 8x_{23} + 12x_{24} + x_{25} = 60$

Note that x_{14} represents the level of x_4 if the first set of values of the ran-dom elements materializes, otherwise x_4 will assume the level x_{24}. The full problem in the form of (9.7) is

$$
\left.
\begin{aligned}
&\text{maximize} \quad F = 7.1x_1 + 2x_{13} + 4.8x_{14} + 0.4x_{15} \\
&\qquad\qquad\quad + 5.4x_{23} + 6.6x_{24} + 0.6x_{25} \\
&\text{subject to} \quad x_1 + x_2 = 3 \\
&\qquad\qquad\quad 5x_1 + 7x_{13} + 11x_{14} + x_{15} = 50 \\
&\qquad\qquad\quad 6x_1 + 8x_{23} + 12x_{24} + x_{25} = 60 \\
&\qquad\qquad\quad x_1 \geqslant 0, \quad x_2 \geqslant 0, \quad x_{13} \geqslant 0, \quad x_{23} \geqslant 0 \\
&\qquad\qquad\quad x_{14} \geqslant 0, \quad x_{24} \geqslant 0, \quad x_{15} \geqslant 0, \quad x_{25} \geqslant 0
\end{aligned}
\right\} \quad (9.8)
$$

Now the procedure is that x_1 must be determined first and the full LP problem (9.8) is solved to give values for x_1 and x_2. Then, once these values have been obtained and the actual values of the random elements have become known the remainder of the x's are determined (which will be a trivial exercise here). The calculations for the first-stage variables are shown in Figure 9.13 from which it is evident that x_1 is set at its maximal level of three units. Now if the first possible set of values of the random elements arises then x_4 should be set equal to 35/11. If the second set of values of the random element arises then x_3 should be set at the level 21/4. These values for x_4 and x_3 can be checked by looking at the second-stage problem in either event. If $h = 1$ then having set $x_1 = 3$ the problem is to

maximize $\quad 5x_{13} + 12x_{14} + x_{15}$

subject to $\quad 7x_{13} + 11x_{14} + x_{15} = 35$

$$x_{13} \geqslant 0, \quad x_{14} \geqslant 0, \quad x_{15} \geqslant 0$$

which is achieved for $x_{14} = 35/11$, $x_{13} = 0$, $x_{15} = 0$. The NPV obtained will thus be 420/11 plus that resulting from three units of x_1 (which will depend on the actual figure for GPV that occurred).

If, on the other hand, the $h = 2$ value arose the second-stage problem would then be to

maximize $\quad 9x_{23} + 11x_{24} + x_{25}$

subject to $\quad 8x_{23} + 12x_{24} + x_{25} = 42$

$$x_{23} \geqslant 0, \quad x_{24} \geqslant 0, \quad x_{25} \geqslant 0$$

which is solved for $x_{23} = 42/8$ (i.e. 21/4), $x_{24} = 0$, $x_{25} = 0$. The reader will recall from earlier work that in these one-constraint problems the one positive variable will be that having the greatest ratio of GPV to outlay.

The solution to (9.7) given in tableau like that of Figure 9.13 will give the optimal values of the second-stage variables since the second-stage constraint set divides into H separate sections once the levels of the first-stage variables have been set and in the original objective function of (9.7) the objective function of each possible second-stage problem is simply multiplied through by a constant (the probability of occurrence).

Now the two-stage procedure that has been outlined here can be generalized to multi-stage problems which can be written as very large ordinary linear programming problems. This factor of size can render the approach impracticable. In a two-stage problem, for example, there will be $H(m - g)$ second-stage constraints, and if $m - g = 100$ and $H = 20$ there will be 2,000 second-stage constraints. While this in itself is not problematical as an alternative, in such cases it is possible to obtain bounds on the optimal value of the objective function without too much difficulty.

There is an alternative approach which at the cost of a few more simplifying assumptions, retains the same number of constraints as in the

			7.1	0	2	4.8	0.4	5.4	6.6	0.6
			x_1	x_2	x_{13}	x_{14}	x_{15}	x_{23}	x_{24}	x_{25}
0	x_2	3	1	1	0	0	0	0	0	0
0.4	x_{15}	50	5	0	7	11	1	0	0	0
0.6	x_{25}	60	6	0	0	0	0	8	12	1
		56	−1.5	0	0.8	−0.4	0	−0.6	0.6	0
7.1	x_1	3	1	1	0	0	0	0	0	0
0.4	x_{15}	35	0	−5	7	11	1	0	0	0
0.6	x_{25}	42	0	−8	0	0	0	8	12	1
		60.5	0	1.5	0.8	−0.4	0	−0.6	0.6	0
7.1	x_1	3	1	1	0	0	0	0	0	0
0.4	x_{13}	35	0	−5	7	11	1	0	0	0
5.4	x_{23}	21/4	0	−3/4	0	0	0	1	3/2	1/8
		63.65	0	3.05	0.8	−0.4	0	0	1.5	0.075
7.1	x_1	3	1	1	0	0	0	0	0	0
4.8	x_{14}	35/11	0	−5/11	7/11	1	1/11	0	0	0
5.4	x_{23}	21/4	0	−3/4	0	0	0	1	3/2	1/8
		64.923	0	0.868	1.055	0	0.036	0	1.5	0.075

Figure 9.13

original stochastic programming problem. As the name would suggest, the constraints of the original problem need be satisfied only with a particular level of probability. This is *chance constrained programming*. That is (with slack variables not explicitly included)

$$P\left(\sum_j k_{ij}x_j \geqslant b_i\right) \geqslant p_i \quad \text{for} \quad i = 1, 2, \ldots, m \tag{9.9}$$

In (9.9) it is assumed that the k_{ij} are known with certainty but the b_i are random variables independent of the x_j. The chance constraints can be shown to imply an equivalent set of m deterministic constraints

$$\sum_j k_{ij}x_j \leqslant B_i \quad i = 1, 2, \ldots, m \tag{9.10}$$

where each B_i in (9.10) is the largest number such that $P[b_i \geqslant B_i] \geqslant p_i$. The objective function $\sum E(N_j)x_j$ is then maximized subject to (9.10).

To see how the numbers B_i are determined suppose that b_1 has the discrete marginal probability distribution

$$P(b_1 = 5) = 0.3$$
$$P(b_1 = 9) = 0.4$$
$$P(b_1 = 12) = 0.2$$
$$P(b_1 = 14) = 0.1$$

324

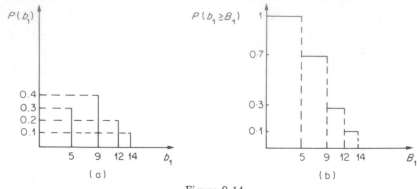

Figure 9.14

This data is shown in Figure 9.14(a) and from this is obtained Figure 9.14(b) the probabilities that b_1 is at least specified amounts (the B_1). Thus for instance if p_1 in (9.9) is 0.6 then the appropriate B_1 figure is 5. for $0.1 \leqslant p_1 \leqslant 0.3$ then $B_1 = 9$.

The chance constrained approach is not without its limitations, however. For example there is no differential penalty attached to the various amounts by which $\Sigma k_{ij}x_j$ may exceed b_i for different x_j. In fact specifying the appropriate values for the p_i should be part of the optimization problem. Furthermore, in a multi-stage situation the conceptual difficulties in a chance constrained approach increase enormously, but the method can be applied to cases where there are several joint chance constraints. In this case the probability that a group of constraints are jointly satisfied at the original values of the b_i must not be less than a particular figure. In addition the chance constrained approach can be used (at the price of non-linearity) in cases where the k_{ij} are stochastic and the problem becomes one of programming with a quadratic constraint or constraints (if there is more than one chance constraint with stochastic coefficients). Thus the quadratic constraint problem discussed in Chapter 7 represents a possibile means of formulating a class of stochastic problems and the method of Van de Panne (1966) would find application in this area.

In stochastic problems with a present value criterion, the problem in general is to determine that feasible set of investments for which the probability distribution of present value maximizes the expected utility of the investor. Only when the investor's utility function satisfies particular axioms will there exist a utility function with the property that the investor may maximize expected utility. As Hadley (1964) points out: 'Procedures for cases where it cannot be assumed that the decision maker has a utility function of the type needed and/or where the probability distributions for the random variables are not known are much less clear cut and also more controversial.' When the problem is of a sequential, dynamic nature, difficulties are magnified in comparison with non-sequential problems.

We asserted that in an investment context problems with non-linear objective functions and linear constraints were more important than those in which the objective was linear but the constraints were not. We would argue a similar point in a stochastic context. That is, problems in which the objective function *alone* is stochastic are of most importance—more frequently occurring. Let us briefly consider some material in this area, which is primarily due to Hillier (1969).

If projects are interrelated, then the return in any year from one of them depends upon the choice of other investments that are made and the actual returns that these investments give. Let $N(I)$ be the NPV of a set, I, of investments giving aggregate cash flows $X_t(I)$ in the years $t = 1, 2, \ldots n$. Aggregate initial outlay K is assumed known with certainty. $N(I)$ is normally distributed whenever the joint distribution of $X_1(I), X_2(I), \ldots, X_n(I)$ is multivariate normal. I is a set of values I_k where $I_k = 1$ if the kth investment is accepted or zero if the kth investment is rejected. In this case (multivariate normal distribution of returns) the ENPV is given by

$$E[N(I)] = -K + \sum_{t=1}^{n} E[X_t(I)] \left[\prod_{s=1}^{t} (1 + i_s(I)) \right]^{-1} \tag{9.11}$$

where the discount factor for each year [the second square-bracketed term in (9.11)] allows for different rates between each adjacent pair of years and the rates themselves may depend upon the set of investments I. Thus the interest rate applying in the sth year for set of investments I is $i_s(I)$. If a uniform rate of discount (over time and sets of investments) prevailed then the discount factor for year t would be the familiar $(1 + i)^{-t}$. So the assumptions made enable us to write in (9.11), the expected NPV of the set of investments, as the sum of the discounted returns in each year minus aggregate outlay.

However, expressions for the individual $E[X_t(I)]$ and the variance of NPV, var$[N(I)]$ are complicated. Here, $X_t(I)\{\prod_{s=1}^{t}[1 + i_s(I)]\}^{-1}$ is a random variable which is itself a sum of random variables and $N(I)$ is the sum of these (less K). Under certain conditions the distribution of a sum of a large, finite number of these random variables is asymptotically normal, so that $N(I)$ should be approximately normal if these conditions hold for the random variables whose sum is $N(I) + K$. The *central limit problem* is the problem of determining these conditions.

Knowledge of the probability distribution of $N(I)$ for all feasible I provides a substantial basis for a subjective selection of I. For computational purposes it is very convenient if we can write:

$$N(I) = \sum_{k=1}^{m} N_k I_k + \sum_{j=1}^{m} \sum_{\substack{k=1 \\ k \neq j}}^{m} u_{jk} I_j I_k \tag{9.12}$$

where in (9.12) the u_{jk} are specified constants and $u_{jk} = u_{kj}$. For this to be so we need to assume a particular model of cash flows; the same cost of capital i_t in the tth year irrespective of I and that interactive effects are pairwise additive or the cumulation of pairwise effects. The problem would then be to maximize the quadratic function:

$$E[N(I)] = \sum_{k=1}^{m} u_k I_k + \sum_{j=1}^{m} \sum_{\substack{k=1 \\ k \neq j}}^{m} u_{jk} I_j I_k \qquad (9.13)$$

subject to constraints. It will be recalled that the I_k are two-state variables so that we are confronted with something more than an ordinary quadratic programming problem. There are various possible exact solution procedures depending on the differing constraint circumstances as detailed below.

If all zero–one investment combinations are feasible then an algorithm by Reiter can be applied. Reiter's procedure can be used to find optimal or near-optimal solutions. The method is a stochastic algorithm (using random starting programs) and can be shown to converge on an optimal program in a finite number of steps. The probability that a global optimum will be found in a relatively small number of steps is large. In addition, the probability of finding a nearly optimal solution in a small number of steps (two or three trials with randomly selected starting programs) is 'substantial'.

If, in addition to the zero–one requirements there are linear constraints and provided rounding off is possible then a non-concave quadratic programming method due to Candler and Townsley (1964) may be employed.

Again assuming linear constraints and a zero–one context, if the matrix of the u_{jk} is negative semi-definite, the objective function will be concave. There is then a choice among several methods of quadratic programming. The problem is a 'conventional' quadratic programming problem and the Simplex based method outlined in section 7.5 could be employed. Finally, if the matrix of the u_{jk} is negative definite then (in principle) an integer solution can be obtained by integer quadratic programming algorithms.

In more general terms Hillier (1969) has discussed the problem of maximizing the expected utility (maximize $E\{u[N(I)]\}$) from investments and gives an approximate linear programming approach in which a sequence of linear programming problems is solved. Firstly, an approximate solution to: maximize $E[N(I)]$ subject to linear programming type requirements with $0 \leqslant I_k \leqslant 1$; is found which enables a good linear approximation of $E\{U[N(I)]\}$ to be obtained and a solution found in a similar approximate manner.

9.4 Investment Appraisal and Stochastic Discount Rates

In Chapter 8 we devoted a good deal of space to the question of random elements in the cash flow. We have discussed interest rate changes in a deterministic term structure sense in Chapter 1 and in terms of sensitivity analysis. In this section we consider certain aspects of discount rate variability in a statistical context. Pioneering work in this field is due to Malkiel (1962) and here we draw out consequences in the area of investment appraisal.

Consider the project with the cash flow:

$t = 0$	$t = 1$	$t = 2$	$t = 3$
$-1,000$	$3,600$	$-4,310$	$1,716$

All elements of the cash flow are assured. The project has multiple yields of 10%, 20% and 30% as shown in Figure 9.15. The NPV never exceeds 6 and is negative for discount rates between 10% and 20% and over 30%. The local minimum at B occurs at 14.23% with NPV = −0.258. The local maximum at C is at 25.77% and gives NPV = +0.193. It will also be found that at point A NPV = +0.193 and A is at 8.93%. If the project is being evaluated when the interest rate is known in advance to be 14.23%, since the project has negative NPV it would be rejected. But suppose that the discount rate follows the discrete distribution:

Probability	Discount rate (%)
0.685	8.93
0.315	25.77

the arithmetic mean of which is 14.23%. This situation is preferred to the fixed rate case so long as greater return is preferred to less. In the first case there is a guaranteed loss of 0.258 and in the second there is an *assured* gain of 0.193. Note that the question of risk aversion or preference does not arise. In both cases the return is assured.

It is not being suggested that there are mysterious economy-wide gains in such a situation; only that it is the case that not all types of interest-rate variability are undesirable in the microcosm. In hypothetical perfect markets in equilibrium such situations are forbidden. But so are the non-

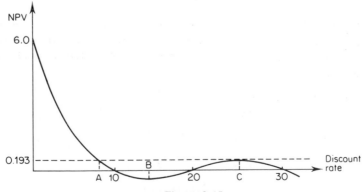

Figure 9.15

zero NPVs in which the real world abounds. To assert that one should consider only hypothetical perfect markets in equilibrium is as foolish as to assert that one should consider only hypothetical perfect driving and make no provision for the care of road accident victims.

Now consider a narrower spread of possibilities. Suppose that the probability distribution for the discount rate is given by:

Probability	Discount rate (%)
0.685	13.0
0.315	16.9

the mean of which is again 14.23%. Which probability distribution for the discount rate would the investor prefer? In the case of the narrower spread of possibilities at 13% NPV $= -0.247$ and at 16.9% NPV $= -0.175$. The 'expected' NPV here is about -0.224 and of course there is now a distribution (of all negative NPV values) about this mean. The wider range of discount rates produces a 'distribution' of NPV which is stochastically dominant in the first degree over the narrow spread alternative and will be preferred even by risk-lovers.

Consider the simplest cash flow pattern—an annuity. Suppose that the project is an immediate perpetuity with an annual sum of £1,000 and with an initial outlay of £10,050. At a fixed 10% discount rate the investment would not be worth while since

$$NPV = \frac{1,000}{0.1} - 10,050 = -50$$

Under mean–variance efficiency A will be preferred to B if

$$\left. \begin{array}{l} ENPV_A \quad \geqslant ENPV_B \\ Var(NPV_A) \leqslant Var(NPV_B) \end{array} \right\} \tag{9.14}$$

with a strict inequality holding in at least one case. Applying (9.14) to the perpetuity, in the original circumstances (subscript o)

$$ENPV_o = -50, \quad Var(NPV_o) = 0$$

Now consider case 1 where the discount rate may be 9, 10 or 11 per cent. Recall that only one of these rates will apply throughout the perpetuity but which is not known before the project commences. Let the distribution be

Interest rate $(i\%)$	Probability (p)	P_i
9	0.4	3.6
10	0.2	2.0
11	0.4	4.4
	$\Sigma pi =$	$\overline{10.0}$

so that the discount rate has an expected value of 10%. Consider now the variance of i. This is $0.8(\%)^2$ the workings are as follows:

i	p	$i - E(i)$	$[i - E(i)]^2$	$p[i - E(i)]^2$
9	0.4	-1	1	0.4
10	0.2	0	0	0
11	0.4	$+1$	1	0.4
			Var $i =$	0.8

Now consider ENPV. We have

NPV	Prob. (p)	$p \times$ NPV
$(9\%) + 1,061.\overline{11}$	0.4	$+424.\overline{44}$
$(10\%) - \quad 50$	0.2	$- \quad 10$
$(11\%) - \quad 959.09$	0.4	$- 383.\overline{63}$
		$+ \quad 30.\overline{80}$

If ENPV alone had been employed as the efficiency criterion the investment would now be desirable since ENPV > 0. One effect of having a *mean* of 10% as against a certain 10% is to transform a certain loss into an expected gain.

Now consider the variance of NPV. This case:

NPV	Prob.	NPV − ENPV	$(NPV - ENPV)^2$	$p(NPV - ENPV)^2$
$+ 1061.\overline{11}$	0.4	$+ 1,030.\overline{30}$	$1,061,524.\overline{33}$	$424,609.73$
$- \quad 50$	0.2	$- \quad 80.\overline{80}$	$6,529.95$	$1,305.99$
$- \quad 959.09$	0.4	$- \quad 989.89$	$979,900.01$	$391,960.00$
			Var NPV =	$817,875.72$

The variance of NPV is now $817,875.72(\pounds)^2$ and an investor would need to make a subjective judgement between case o and case 1. However, *all* investors (risk-lovers or risk-haters) would reject case o but *some* would accept case 1.

Now consider case 2 with the following interest rate distribution:

Interest rate $(i\%)$	Probability (p)	p_i
9.5	0.8	7.6
12.0	0.2	2.4
		10.0

again the expected value of i is 10% but the range is over an interval of 2.5 percentage points. The variance of i in this case is given by

i	p	$i - E(i)$	$[i - E(i)]^2$	$p[i - E(i)]^2$
9.5	0.8	-0.5	0.25	0.2
12.0	0.2	2.0	4.00	0.8
			Var $i =$	1.0

so that the variance of the interest rate has increased by 25% in comparison to case 1.

Now consider the ENPV:

NPV	p	$p \times$ NPV
$(9.5\%) + 476.3\underline{2}$	0.8	$381.\underline{05}$
$(12.0\%) - 1,716.66$	0.2	$-343.\overline{33}$
	ENPV =	$+37.72$

so that the ENPV in this case is higher than in either case o or case 1. The variance of NPV is given by

NPV	p	NPV – ENPV	$(NPV - ENPV)^2$	$p(NPV - ENPV)^2$
$+\quad 476.3\underline{2}$	0.8	438.60	192,366.88	153,893.51
$-1,716.66$	0.2	$-1,754.39$	3,077,870.12	615,574.02
			Var $NPV_2 =$	769,467.53

The expected value of the interest rate is the same in both case 2 and case 1. The variance of the *interest rate* in case 2 is 25% greater than in case 1; ENPV is higher in case 2 than in case 1, but VarNPV in case 2 is 5.92% *lower* than in case 1. Thus by the criterior of mean–variance effiiency case 2 is preferable to case 1. *The increased variance in the interest rate is unambiguously desirable for all investors using the criterion of mean–variance efficiency.*

Thus essentially due to the curvature properties of the present value function, increased dispersion of the discount rate may not always be undesirable. In general terms increased dispersion in the argument of a function—for a given mean—may produce reduced dispersion in the value of the function and an increased mean.

A similar effect is found in terms of year-to-year variability of the discount rate. Suppose that in each year of a two-year annuity the discount rate is determined by a random process. Suppose further that the annuity is for £100 and that for *each* year (independently) there is the probability distribution

Inerest rate (i_k)	Probability (p_k)
8%	0.6
13%	0.4

the arithmetic mean interest rate is 10%. If the rate was *fixed* at 10% then the present value of the annuity would be £173.55. In the stochastic case there are four possible combinations of discount rates, giving the following results:

Year one	Year two	Probability	NPV	p(NPV)
8%	8%	0.36	178.33	64.20
8%	13%	0.24	174.53	41.89
13%	8%	0.24	170.44	40.90
13%	13%	0.16	166.81	26.69

$$\text{ENPV} = 173.68$$

Thus ENPV is greater than in the 10% case amd *may* be preferred by some investors.

In such cases the ENPV can be obtained by discounting the harmonic mean of the values $(1 + 0.01i_k)$ using the given probabilities. The harmonic mean, H, is given by

$$\frac{1}{H} = \Sigma \frac{p_k}{(1 + 0.01i_k)} \tag{9.15}$$

In the numerical example

$$\frac{1}{H} = \frac{0.6}{1.08} + \frac{0.4}{1.13}$$

$$\therefore \quad H = 1.099,459$$

so

$$\frac{100}{(1.099,459)} + \frac{100}{(1.099,459)^2} = 173.68$$

Now suppose that the £100 becomes an immediate perpetuity. The harmonic mean result enables us to write the present value of the perpetuity as

$$\text{PV} = \frac{100}{H - 1} \tag{9.16}$$

Now examine the value of (9.16) as the dispersion of the interest rates increases. Retain an arithmetic mean value of 10% for the interest rate and use the data

Probability	i_k	i_k	i_k	
0.5	9	8	5	etc.
0.5	11	12	15	

The results emerge as shown in Figure 9.16.

The expected present value of the perpetuity becomes *infinite* from the two equally probable interest rates:

$$(0.1 - \sqrt{0.11})100\% \quad \text{and} \quad (0.1 + \sqrt{0.11})100\%$$

which have an arithmetic mean of 10%. While the fact that the expected

	i_k	$100(H-1)^{-1}$
10	10	1,000.00
9	11	1,000.91
8	12	1,003.65
5	15	1,023.26
0	20	1,100.00
-10	30	1,571.43
-20	40	5,500.00
-23	43	100,000
-23.1	43.1	250,569
-23.16	43.16	2,654,421

Figure 9.16

present value of a perpetuity can become infinite for an entirely finite range of interest rates with positive arithmetic mean is counter-intuitive, it should be noted that one of the rates must be negative. It is on more practical significance to see that when the interest rate is equally likely to be 0% or 20% in any year there is a 10% increase in ENPV compared to the situation when the interest rate is set at 10%. Thus the uncertainty surrounding the interest rate *might* be found desirable by some investors.

Suppose that the perpetuity is growing at a constant geometric rate, $100g\%$. The sums received annually would be

$$100, \ 100(1+g), \ 100(1+g)^2, \ \ldots$$

If the discount rate is $100r\%$ then the present value of the infinite stream is given by

$$PV = \frac{100}{r-g} \tag{9.17}$$

provided that $r > g$. If the rate of growth is equal to or greater than the discount rate, the present value is infinite. An infinite present value can arise in the stochastic case even if every possible value of the interest rate is positive. This can arise since the harmonic mean of the interest-rate values will be strictly less than the arithmetic mean, provided that there are two or more distinct values. We can write the expected value of the growth of perpetuity as

$$EPV = \frac{100}{H-g} \tag{9.18}$$

and we can clearly choose g such that $g = H < r$, so that (9.17) is finite but (9.18) is infinite. Also, in this case since H is strictly positive for $g > 0$ we can construct the probability distribution of interest rates so that there are no negative values therein. For instance, let the probability distribution be

i_k	p
5	0.5
15	0.5

then

$$H^{-1} = \frac{0.5}{1.05} + \frac{0.5}{1.15} \qquad \therefore \quad H = 1.097727$$

so that we have only to choose $g = 9.7727\%$ to produce an infinite expected value in the stochastic case while the present value at a fixed 10% is

$$\frac{100}{0.1 - 0.09727} = 43{,}995$$

In practice infinite prices of securities are not observed. But an infinite price need *not* be consequent upon an infinite expected NPV—in this respect the situation is similar to the St Petersburg paradox.

References

Candler, W., and Townsley, R. J. (1964). 'The maximisation of a quadratic function of variables subject to linear inequalities', *Management Science*, **10**.

Hadley, G. (1964), *Nonlinear and Dynamic Programming*, Addison Wesley, Reading, Mass.

Hillier, F. S. (1969), *The Evaluation of Risky, Interrelated Investments*, North-Holland, Amsterdam.

House, W. C. (1968), *Sensitivity Analysis in Making Capital Investment Decisions*, National Association of Accountants, New York.

Malkiel, B. K., 'Expectations, Bond Prices and the Term Structure of Interest Rates', *Quarterly Journal of Economics*, May 1962.

Reiter, S. (1963), 'Choosing an investment programme among interdependent projects', *Review of Economic Studies*, **30**, No. 2.

van de Panne, C. (1966:), 'Programming with a quadratic constraint', *Management Science*, **12**.

Further Reading

Ahimud, Y., 'Uncertainty in Future Interest Rates and the Term Structure,' *Journal of Business Finance and Accounting*, 5, 1978.

Ahsan, S. M., *Chance Constraints, Safety First and Portfolio Seleciton*, McMaster University Economics Department Working Paper 7322, 1973.

Charnes, A., and Cooper, W. W., 'Chance Constrained Programming', *Management Science*, 5, 1969.

Crane, D. B., 'A stochastic programming model for commercial bank bond portfolio management', *Journal of Financial and Quantitative Analysis*, 6, 1971.

Faisley, W., and Jacoby, H., 'Investment Analysis using the Probability Distribution of the Internal Rate of Return', *Management Science*, 22, August 1975.

Freund, R. J., 'The introduction of risk into a programming model', *Econometrica*, **24**, 1956.

Haegert, L., 'An analysis of the Kuhn–Tucker conditions of stochastic programming with reference to the estimation of discount rates and risk premia', *Journal of Business Finance and Accounting*, 1, No. 3, Autumn 1974.

Hertz, D. B., 'Risk analysis in capital budgeting', *Harvard Business Review*, **1964**.

Hertz, D. B., 'Investment policies that pay off', *Harvard Business Review*, **1968** (Jan–Feb).

Keown, A. J., 'A chance constrained Goal programming model for bank liquidity management', *Decision Science*, 9, 1978.

Lewellen, W. G., and Long, M. S., 'Simulation versus single value estimates in capital expenditure analysis', *Decision Sciences*, **3**, 1972.

Madansky, A., 'Methods of solution of linear programs under uncertainty', *Operations Research*, **10**, 1962.

Myers, S. C., 'Procedures for capital budgeting under uncertainty', *Industrial Management Review*, **9**, Spring 1968.

Myers, S. C. (ed.), *Modern Developments in Financial Management*, Praeger, New York, 1976.

Olsen, P. L., *Multistage Stochastic Programming: The Deterministic Equivalent Problem*, Cornell University, Department of Operational Research, Technical Report No. 191, 1973.

Porter, R. B., *A Comparison of Stochastic Dominance and Stochastic Programming as Corporate Financial Decision Models Under Uncertainty*, University of Kansas School of Business (Working Paper), 1972.

Pyle, D. H., and Turnovsky, S. J., 'Risk aversion in chance constrained portfolio selection', *Management Science*, **18**, 1971.

Samuels, J. M., and Wilkes, F. M., *Management of Company Finance* (3rd edn.), Nelson, London, 1980.

Samuels, J. M., and Wilkes, F M., *Management of Company Finance, Students Manual*, Nelson, London, 1981.

Szego, G., and Shell, K. (eds.), *Mathematical Methods in Investment and Finance*, North-Holland, Amsterdam, 1972.

Townsend, E. C., *Investment and Uncertainty—A Practical Guide*, Oliver and Boyd, Edinburgh, 1969.

Wagner, H. M., *Principles of Operational Research with Applications to Managerial Decisions*, Prentice-Hall, Englewood Cliffs, NJ, 1969.

Wets, R., 'Programming under uncertainty: the solution set', *SIAM*, **14**, 1966.

Wilkes, F. M., 'Stochastic Interest Rates and Investment Appraisal', *Journal of Business Finance and Accounting*, 6, 1979.

Wilkes, F. M., *Elements of Operations Research*, McGraw-Hill, New York, 1980.

Wilson, R., 'Investment analysis under uncertainty', *Management Science*, **15**, Series B, 1969.

Ziemba, W. T., and Vickson, R. G., *Stochastic Optimisation Models in Finance*, Academic Press, New York, 1975.

CHAPTER 10

Investment Portfolios, Asset Prices and Capital Budgeting

Overview
Section 10.1 provides general background for portfolio theory and graphical analysis is presented in section 10.2. A Lagrange multiplier approach is the subject of section 10.3 which leads into the application of quadratic programming methods in section 10.4. Index models are discussed in section 10.5 while capital market theory and the capital asset pricing model are introduced in section 10.6. The final section of the chapter draws out the capital budgeting implications of the capital asset pricing model and compares the asset pricing and cost of capital approaches to investment appraisal.

10.1 Introduction

Portfolio theory is concerned with the problem of selecting, building and revising an optimal set of investments—the portfolio—bearing in mind the anticipated returns to these investments, the risk associated with them and the utility of the investor. There is considerable overlap between the material of this chapter and the quadratic programming and stochastic problems of Chapters 7 and 9. This work will be drawn upon in section four. Portfolio theory is a vast subject and we shall principally be concerned here with the problem of the *selection* of one optimal portfolio. We are to be involved with diversification on a large scale. The scene is that in which an investor, rather than concentrating his activities and assets mainly in one line of business—as many firms seem to do—wishes to take advantage of the large number of diverse securities traded on the stock market. After introducing the problem in general terms we shall present a semi-graphical solution procedure before proceeding to more technical work.

Modern approaches to the problem of portfolio selection began with Markowitz (1952). The principal advance that Markowitz made was in the *manner* in which the risks associated with investments were taken into account—using variance (or standard deviation) of the return on an investment as a measure of risk. As we have seen, variance is not a perfect

335

measure of risk, but on the whole the idea of using statistical measures of dispersion as measures of risk was a significant advance. Investors were assumed to be *rational* in so far as they would prefer greater returns to lesser ones given equal or smaller risk, and *risk averse*. Risk aversion in this context means merely that as between two investments with equal expected returns, the investment with the smaller risk would be preferred. 'Return' could be any suitable measure of monetary inflows such as NPV, but yield has been the most commonly used measure of return in this context; so that when the standard deviation of returns is referred to we shall mean the standard deviation of yield about its expected value.

The portfolio selection problem can be divided into two stages: first finding the mean–variance efficient portfolios, and secondly one such portfolio. We have seen a similar two-stage procedure in earlier work on risky investments. Here it will be convenient to make rather more liberal use of utility functions and indifference curve analysis.

Let the investor's level of *expected utility* be written as:

$$E(U) = f(\bar{R}, \sigma) \tag{10.1}$$

where $E(U)$, expected utility, is a single index of performance, $\bar{R}$ is the expected return on the portfolio as a whole and σ is the associated standard deviation of return. The function (10.1) relates to a single time period, but this is the entire planning horizon. Note that in maximizing $E(U)$ in (10.1) the investor is maximizing what he expects 'utility' to be and not what it will actually turn out to be, since this is unknown at the time the decision has to be taken. Henceforward for convenience, we shall write simply U for 'expected utility'.

It is worth noting what the function (10.1) would imply in the absence of risk (where $\sigma = 0$ for all portfolios and $\bar{R}$ is the actual return). In this situation of certainty this would mean choosing a portfolio of investments to maximize NPV or yield (subject to scale considerations). If the world is linear and continuously divisible as well as certain, this would mean selecting one investment alone, that is no diversification whatever. Since, however, diminishing returns and an insistence on being integral are quite natural, a limited amount of diversification would be suggested even by a deterministic theory. This degree of diversification, however, falls short of that which is commonly observed—a compelling explanation of which is that risk exists, is undesirable, and that diversification can reduce risk. However, not all rules that give rise to diversification of investment *do* reduce risk. In fact some naive diversification rules can actually cause the level of risk to increase. The assumptions of rationality and risk aversion mean that U will change in the same direction as a change in $\bar{R}$ alone (written $\partial U/\partial \bar{R} > 0$) and that U will change in the opposite direction to a change in σ alone (written $\partial U/\partial \sigma < 0$). The objective then is to choose a portfolio of investments that maximizes subject to whatever financial and other constraints may apply. It is clear that such a portfolio must

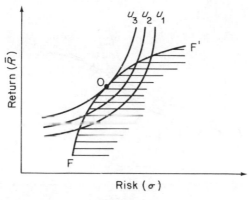

Figure 10.1

satisfy the following condition: it must have maximum expected return for all risk levels not exceeding its own, and it must have minimum risk for all levels of return not lower than its own. The portfolios which satisfy this conditon are the *mean–variance efficient portfolios*. The investor must now make a choice between these efficient portfolios.

Graphically the mean–variance efficient portfolios lie on a line such as FF'—the efficiency frontier—in Figure 10.1. All portfolios in the shaded area are mean–variance inefficient—that is to say there are other port-folios (nearer to FF') which have greater expected returns for the same or smaller risk or smaller risk for the same or greater returns. Points to the left of FF' represent unobtainable risk–return combinations.

The lines labelled $u_1u_2u_3$ in the figure are indifference curves. All points on any one such curve are combinations of risk and return which are equally satisfactory for the investor. Higher numbered curves correspond to greater levels of utility, that is, $u_3 > u_2 > u_1$. They possess the curvature as drawn, if investors have a diminishing marginal rate of substitution between expected return and risk. This would mean that investors were decreasingly willing to accept higher returns to compensate for greater risk. If all assets are risky, the optimal portfolio is portfolio 0, at a point of tangency between an indifference curve and the efficiency frontier.

If there is a 'riskless' investment, however, the investor may be able to improve on 0. For instance, very short dated Government securities are usually taken to be risk free. Once the security has been purchased the return is known and assured. Figure 10.2 graphs the situation. The risk-free interest rate is R_f and, by investing partly in the riskless asset and partly in portfolio M, the investor could obtain risk/return combinations along the line R_fM.

If $\bar{R}_M$ is the expected rate of return on portfolio M and σ_M, the standard deviation of this return, then for $0 \leqslant \alpha \leqslant 1$ by investing in the proportions in the riskless asset and $1 - \alpha$ in portfolio M the investor can achieve an

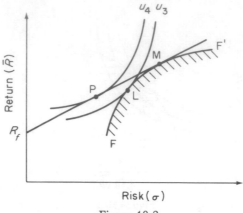

Figure 10.2

expected return of $\bar{R}_{f,M}$ where

$$\bar{R}_{f,M} = \alpha R_f + (1 - \alpha)\bar{R}_M \tag{10.2}$$

with an associated level of risk given by

$$\sigma_{f,M} = (1 - \alpha)\sigma_M \tag{10.3}$$

The optimum position is now P. If borrowing was possible at the pure interest rate then risk/return combinations above M on the extension of the line R_fM would be attainable. The investor with the indifference curves above, however, would not choose to borrow; clearly, P could not be improved upon by borrowing.

Consider the problem of determining the efficient set of portfolios for a problem in two securities. The investor has £b at his disposal. If the prices of the two securities are, respectively, S_1 and S_2 per unit and n_1 and n_2 units respectively of each security are purchased, then the budget constraint can be written as

$$n_1S_1 + n_2S_2 \leqslant b \tag{10.4}$$

or alternatively as:

$$\frac{n_1S_1}{b} + \frac{n_2S_2}{b} \leqslant 1 \tag{10.5}$$

Now define $x_1 = n_1S_1/b$ and $x_2 = n_2S_2/b$ and impose the restrictions that the entire budget be spent. The constraint can now be written as:

$$x_1 + x_2 = 1 \tag{10.6}$$

No generality is lost in (10.6) since one of the securities can be cash. Now let $\bar{R}_1$ and $\bar{R}_2$ be the expected values of the yields from each security. The expected value of yield on the portfolio, written as $\bar{R}$, will then be given by:

$$\bar{R} = x_1\bar{R}_1 + x_2\bar{R}_2 \tag{10.7}$$

R_{1h}	R_{2h}	p_h
R_{11}	R_{21}	p_1
R_{12}	R_{22}	p_2
R_{13}	R_{23}	p_3

Figure 10.3

Suppose that there are just three pairs of values of yield figures which may emerge. Write these as (R_{1h}, R_{2h}) where $h = 1,2,3$, with probabilities of occurrence p_h where $\Sigma_{h=1}^{3} p_h = 1$. Figure 10.3 presents this information in tabular form.

From this we can readily calculate the expected returns on the portfolio for proportions x_1 and x_2 of the budget spent on the two securities respectively. We obtain

$$\bar{R} = p_1(x_1R_{11} + x_2R_{21}) + p_2(x_1R_{12} + x_2R_{22})$$
$$+ p_3(x_1R_{13} + x_2R_{23})$$
$$= x_1(R_{11}p_1 + R_{12}p_2 + R_{13}p_3) + x_2(R_{21}p_1 + R_{22}p_2 + R_{23}p_3)$$
$$= x_1\bar{R}_1 + x_2\bar{R}_2$$

Portfolio variance, V, is given by

$$V = \sum_{h=1}^{3} p_h d_h^2 \tag{10.8}$$

where

$$d_h = x_1R_{1h} + x_2R_{2h} - x_1\bar{R}_1 - x_2\bar{R}_2$$
$$= x_1(R_{1h} - \bar{R}_1) + x_2(R_{2h} - \bar{R}_2)$$

Now the first term in (10.8), $p_1 d_1^2$, is given by

$$p_1 d_1^2 = p_1[x_1(R_{11} - \bar{R}_1) + x_2(R_{21} - \bar{R}_2)]^2$$
$$= p_1[x_1^2(R_{11} - \bar{R}_1)^2 + 2x_1x_2(R_{11} - \bar{R}_1)(R_{21} - \bar{R}_2)$$
$$+ x_2^2(R_{21} - \bar{R}_2)^2]$$

thus

$$\sum_{h=1}^{3} p_h d_h^2 = x_1^2 \sum_{h=1}^{3} p_h(R_{1h} - \bar{R}_1)^2$$

$$+ 2x_1x_2 \sum_{h=1}^{3} p_h(R_{1h} - \bar{R}_1)(R_{2h} - \bar{R}_2)$$

$$+ x_2^2 \sum_{h=1}^{3} p_h(R_{2h} - \bar{R}_2)^2 \tag{10.9}$$

from which we observe that the first summation on the right of (10.9) is the variance of return on the first security which we shall write as σ_1^2. The third summation on the right is the variance of return on the second security, σ_2^2. The second summation is the *covariance* of returns on the two securities. We can now rewrite (10.9) more conveniently as

$$V = x_1^2 \sigma_1^2 + x_2^2 \sigma_2^2 + 2x_1 x_2 \sigma_{12} \tag{10.10}$$

The three important equations for determining the efficiency frontier in the two-security case have now been obtained. They are

$$\left.\begin{array}{l} \bar{R} = x_1 \bar{R}_1 + x_2 \bar{R}_2 \\ V = x_1^2 \sigma_1^2 + x_2^2 \sigma_2^2 + 2x_1 x_2 \sigma_{12} \\ 1 = x_1 + x_2 \end{array}\right\} \tag{10.11}$$

The system (10.11) can be solved directly for V as a function of $\bar{R}$. For this reason the two-security problem is sometimes described as 'trivial', although a point on the frontier has still to be selected. The interested reader may try the solution and verify that V is a quadratic function of $\bar{R}$.

In the general case, with n securities rather than two, the equations (10.11) would become

$$\left.\begin{array}{l} \bar{R} = \displaystyle\sum_{i=1}^{n} x_i \bar{R}_i \\[2em] V = \displaystyle\sum_{i=1}^{n} x_i^2 \sigma_i^2 + \sum_{\substack{i=1 \\ }}^{n} \sum_{\substack{j=1 \\ j \neq i}}^{n} x_i x_j \sigma_{ij} \\[2em] 1 = \displaystyle\sum_{i=1}^{n} x_i \end{array}\right\} \tag{10.12}$$

The more important of the two summation terms in V is the covariance summation. For a portfolio consisting of a large number of securities, typically the variances of returns on individual securities are relatively unimportant contributors to the variance of return on the portfolio as a whole. The important factor is how the returns on securities vary together. There are just n terms in the variance summation but $n(n-1)$ in the covariance summation. Note that if one more possible security was to be considered this would add one term to the variance summation but $2n$ further terms would have to be included in the covariance summation.

10.2 Graphical Analysis

Consider the problem in three securities. For graphical analysis the problem can be reduced to one in two variables by substitution. Since $x_3 = 1 - x_1 - x_2$ the expected portfolio return is

$$\begin{aligned} \bar{R} &= x_1 \bar{R}_1 + x_2 \bar{R}_2 + (1 - x_1 - x_2) \bar{R}_3 \\ &= x_1(\bar{R}_1 - \bar{R}_3) + x_2(\bar{R}_2 - \bar{R}_3) + R_3 \end{aligned} \tag{10.13}$$

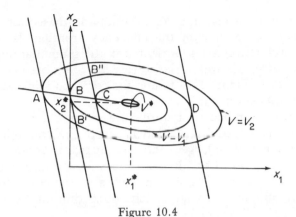

Figure 10.4

and the variance will be

$$V = x_1^2\sigma_1^2 + 2x_1x_2\sigma_{12} + 2x_1(1 - x_1 - x_2)\sigma_{13}$$
$$+ x_2^2\sigma_2^2 + 2x_2(1 - x_1 - x_2)\sigma_{23} + (1 - x_1 - x_2)^2\sigma_3^2$$
$$= x_1^2(\sigma_1^2 + \sigma_3^2 - 2\sigma_{13}) + x_2^2(\sigma_2^2 + \sigma_3^2 - 2\sigma_{23})$$
$$= + 2x_1x_2(\sigma_3^2 + \sigma_{12} - \sigma_{13} - \sigma_{23})$$
$$+ 2x_1(\sigma_{13}\sigma_3^2) + 2x_2(\sigma_{23} - \sigma_3^2) + \sigma_3^2 \qquad (10.14)$$

In Figure 10.4 the ellipses are *isovariance contours* showing combinations of x_2 and x_1 (and by implication x_3) which along any one contour give portfolios of equal variance. Contours nearer to the centre point correspond to lower values of V. The point V^* (given by $x_1 = x_1^*$ and $x_2 = x_2^*$) is the *minimum variance portfolio*.

The parallel straight lines in the figure are *iso-return contours*. Along any one such line the values of x_1 and x_2 give portfolios with equal expected return. With security three representing the highest expected return investment, iso-return contours further to the left correspond to greater values of $\bar{R}$.

The mean–variance efficient portfolios correspond to values of the x's on the locus of points of tangency between isovariance curves and iso-return lines to the left of V^*. This locus is a straight line through points such as A, B and C and is called the *critical line*. A point such as B', off the critical line, is not mean–variance efficient. B', on the same iso-return line as B, is on a higher isovariance curve ($V_2 > V_1$). The point B" corresponds to x's that give the same variance as at B but B" is on a lower iso-return line. It is important to note that points of tangency to the right of V^*, such as point D, correspond to portfolios giving *minimum* return for given variance.

Once the critical line has been found, the efficiency frontier can be plotted. Each point on the critical line corresponds to a value of V (given by the iso-variance line through the critical line) and a value of $\bar{R}$ (given by the iso-return line through the critical line) and these pairs of values are the coordinates of points on the efficiency frontier. If the investor's risk–return preferences are represented in the same diagram the optimal combination of return and variance can then be obtained. The analyst then refers back to Figure 10.4 to find the corresponding values of x_1 and x_2 and, by implication, x_3.

Finally with reference to Figure 10.4 it should be noted that the minimum variance portfolio, V^* may not be one of maximum diversification in that it may consist largely of two securities or perhaps one security. If an investor is obliged to 'diversify' (say by putting one-third of the budget in each security) risk will actually increase. Such activity-spreading investment over a larger than optimum number of securities is an aspect of *naïve diversification*.

In the critical line method eight or nine steps will be needed. These are:

(1) Obtain the slope of the iso-return lines.
(2) Obtain the slope expressions of the iso-variance contours.
(3) Use tangency to produce the critical line.
(4) Substitute the critical line relationship into $\bar{R}$.
(5) Substitute the critical line relationship into V.
(6) Relate V to $\bar{R}$.
(7) Determine the range of values of $\bar{R}$ for which the three-security frontier is legitimate (no negative x's).
(8) See if the use of the presence relationship with the three security frontier gives an optimal portfolio which is legitimate.
(9) If (8) gives a non-legitimate optimal portfolio determine the two security frontier and optimize.

The example to follow will employ a simple, linear utility function of the form

$$u = w\bar{R} - V \qquad (10.15)$$

in which the investor must choose the value of w to suit his particular attitude to risk. The lower the value of w the more sensitive to risk is the investor, although the linearity of the function allows no change in sensitivity as return or variance increases.

Consider an example in which the third security is cash. This will represent a problem in two 'real' securities allowing some of the budget to be unspent if so desired. The return on cash is zero and has zero covariance with returns on the other securities. An investor has £4,000 available; the price of security one is £8 per unit and that of security two £2 per unit. Preferences are given by

$$u = 1.5\bar{R} - V$$

and the return and variance-covariance data are

	$\bar{R}_i(\%)$	σ_i^2	$\sigma_{i,j}$
Security one	10	10	$-20 = \sigma_{12}$
Security two	60	900	$-20 = \sigma_{21}$
Security three (cash)	0	0	0

Thus

$$\bar{R} = 10x_1 + 60x_2$$

and

$$V = 10x_1^2 + 900x_2^2 - 40x_1x_{22}$$

(where, if n_1 and n_2 units of securities one and two are bought then $x_1 \equiv 8n_1/4{,}000$, $x_2 \equiv 2n_2/4{,}000$. Also: $x_3 \equiv n_3/4{,}000$ where n_3 is the number of pounds held as cash). The further requirements are that

$$x_1 + x_2 + x_3 = 1$$

and for legitimacy

$$x_1 \geqslant 0, \quad x_2 \geqslant 0, \quad x_3 \geqslant 0$$

Now, applying the procedure, first find the slope of the iso-return lines.

(1) $\quad \dfrac{dx_2}{dx_1}\bigg|_{\text{iso-return}} = -\dfrac{1}{6}$

(2) $\quad \dfrac{dx_2}{dx_1}\bigg|_{\text{iso-variance}} = -\dfrac{\dfrac{\partial V}{\partial x_1}}{\dfrac{\partial V}{\partial x_2}} = -\left|\dfrac{20x_1 - 40x_2}{1{,}800x_2 - 40x_1}\right|$

(3) Equating slopes:

$$\frac{1}{6} = \frac{20x_1 - 40x_2}{1{,}800x_2 - 40x_1}$$

thus:

$$x_2 = \frac{4}{51}x_1 \tag{10.16}$$

which, it will be noted, is a straight line through the origin where (10.16) is the equation of the critical line.

(4) Thus, substituting into the equation for $\bar{R}$

$$\bar{R} = \frac{750x_1}{51} \tag{10.17}$$

(5) Substituting (10.16) into V gives

$$V = \frac{32,250x_1^2}{2,601} \tag{10.18}$$

(6) Cross-multiplying in (10.17) to give x_1 in terms of $\bar{R}$ and substitution into (10.18) gives the three-security efficiency frontier as:

$$V = 0.0573\bar{R}^2 \tag{10.19}$$

It will be observed that this frontier passes through the origin. This is the case if one of the securities is cash. A zero variance (risk free) 'portfolio' is available at the price of zero return (all funds held as cash).

(7) Now determine the range of values of $\bar{R}$ for which the three-security frontier is legitimate. Since $x_1 + x_2 + x_3 = 1$ from (10.16) and (10.17) we obtain

$$x_1 = \frac{51\bar{R}}{750}, \qquad x_2 = \frac{4\bar{R}}{750}, \qquad x_3 = \frac{750 - 55\bar{R}}{750} \tag{10.20}$$

Thus the portfolio is legitimate provided that

$$0 \leqslant \bar{R} \leqslant \frac{750}{55} \approx 13.64\% \tag{10.21}$$

(8) Now using the preference relationship with (10.19):

$$\begin{aligned} \text{maximize } u &= 1.5\bar{R} - V \\ &= 1.5\bar{R} - 0.0573\bar{R}^2 \end{aligned}$$

$$\frac{du}{d\bar{R}} = 1.5 - 0.1146\bar{R} = 0 \tag{10.22}$$

$$\frac{d^2u}{d\bar{R}^2} = -0.1146 < 0$$

Thus $\bar{R} = 13.09\%$ is the optimal value of expected portfolio return. This figure is within the legitimate range given by (10.21) and substitution into (10.20) gives

$$x_1 = 0.8901, \quad x_2 = 0.0698, \quad x_3 = 0.0401$$

So that: 89.01% of funds should be placed in security one,
6.98% should be placed in security two, and
4.01% should remain as cash.

This gives a best rounded solution in terms of numbers of shares purchased as $n_1 = 445$, $n_2 = 140$, with $n_3 = 160$.

Now with the given value of w of 1.5, step (9) of the procedure was not needed, but from the first-order equilibrium condition (10.22) it can be seen that if $w > 1.5631$ then $\bar{R} > 13.64$ a non-legitimate solution would have resulted. The optimum level of cash would have been negative, implying an interest-free means of expanding the budget.

The figure of $\bar{R} = 13.64$ produces a 'corner portfolio' and for values of $\bar{R}$ in excess of 13.64 the variance that must be accepted is in excess of that figure stated by (10.19) if legitimacy is to be maintained. The value of x_3, having become zero at $\bar{R} = 13.64$, is omitted for higher values of $\bar{R}$ and the two-security frontier is employed. This would be found thus:

$$x_1 + x_2 = 1$$
$$\therefore \quad \bar{R} = 10x_1 + 60(1 - x)$$
$$= 60 - 50x_1$$
$$\therefore \quad x_1 = \frac{6}{5} - \frac{\bar{R}}{50} \tag{10.23}$$

and substitution of this relationship into

$$V = 10x_1^2 + 900(1 - 2x_1 + x_1^2) - 40(1 - x_1)x_1$$

produces

$$V = 0.38\bar{R}^2 - 8.8\bar{R} + 60 \tag{10.24}$$

and (10.24) is the two-security frontier. This will be tangent to the three-security frontier at $\bar{R} = 13.64$, the relationship between the frontiers being shown in Figure 10.5 which, for ease of comparison with the analysis, has drawn V as a function of $\bar{R}$.

As a subsidiary point it will be seen from Figure 10.5 that the least variance that can be obtained if all funds must be invested is 9.05 corresponding to an expected portfolio return of 11.58% (the two-security frontier is legitimate between 10% and 60%). Note that from (10.19) a variance of 9.05 would be associated with an expected return of 12.57%.

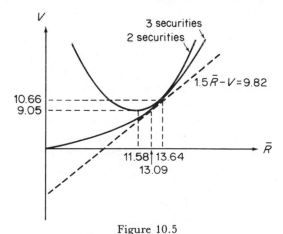

Figure 10.5

Had the original value of w been two then step 9 would have produced:

$$\text{max.} \quad u = 10.8\bar{R} - 0.38\bar{R}^2 - 60$$

$$\therefore \quad \frac{du}{d\bar{R}} = 10.8 - 0.76\bar{R} = 0$$

which solves for $\bar{R} = 14.21$. This value for $\bar{R}$ would produce a non-legitimate portfolio with negative cash holding if the three security relationships are used. Thus the two-security formulae apply. Substitution of $\bar{R} = 14.21$ into (12.48) gives $x_1 = 0.9158$; consequently, since cash is no longer in the picture, $x_2 = 1 - x_1$ we obtain $x_2 = 0.0842$. In rounded terms this would lead to the purchase of 458 units of security one and 168 units of security two with, of course, nothing remaining as cash.

10.3 Lagrange Multiplier Treatment

With sufficiently skilled draftsmanship a portfolio problem in four securities (and hence three dimensions with one x treated implicitly) could be solved graphically. Problems in more than four securities require a non-graphical approach. The problem of finding the set of mean–variance efficient portfolios is one to which the Lagrange multiplier approach seems suited since it is one in constrained minimization. For each given value of portfolio return we require minimum variance. The problem is to

$$\text{minimize} \quad V = \sum_{i=1}^{n} x_i^2 \sigma_i^2 + \sum_{i=1}^{n} \sum_{\substack{i=1 \\ j \neq i}}^{n} x_i x_j \sigma_{ij}$$

$$\text{subject to} \quad \sum_{i=1}^{n} x_i \bar{R}_i = \bar{R} \tag{10.25}$$

$$\text{and} \quad \sum_{i=1}^{n} x_i = 1$$

for each possible value of $\bar{R}$. In this formulation negative values of the x's are not excluded as possibilities. A negative x would represent a leveraged or illegitimate portfolio, the investor would be *issuing* a security. There will be no finite bound on the portfolio return (if the $\bar{R}$s differ) if there are no lower bounds on the x's but in this approach bounds can be introduced at a later stage of the calculations.

In the three-security case the Lagrangian function is written as

$$L = x_1^2 \sigma_1^2 + x_2^2 \sigma_2^2 + x_3^2 \sigma_3^2 + 2x_1 x_2 \sigma_{12} + 2x_1 x_3 \sigma_{13} + 2x_2 x_3 \sigma_{23}$$
$$+ y_1(\bar{R} - x_1 \bar{R}_1 - x_2 \bar{R} - x_3 \bar{R}_3) + y_2(1 - x_1 - x_2 - x_3) \tag{10.26}$$

where y_1 and y_2 are the multipliers. Since the constraints are equalities and there are, as yet, no sign requirements the first-order conditions are as follows

$$\frac{\partial L}{\partial x_1} = 2\sigma_1^2 x_1 + 2\sigma_{12} x_2 + 2\sigma_{13} x_3 - y_1\bar{R}_1 - y_2 = 0$$

$$\frac{\partial L}{\partial x_2} = 2\sigma_2^2 x_2 + 2\sigma_{12} x_1 + 2\sigma_{23} x_3 - y_1\bar{R}_2 - y_2 = 0$$

$$\frac{\partial L}{\partial x_3} = 2\sigma_3^2 x_3 + 2\sigma_{13} x_1 + 2\sigma_{23} x_2 - y_1\bar{R}_3 - y_2 = 0 \qquad (10.27)$$

$$\frac{\partial L}{\partial y_1} = \bar{R} - x_1\bar{R}_1 - x_2\bar{R}_2 - x_3\bar{R}_3 \qquad = 0$$

$$\frac{\partial L}{\partial y_2} = 1 - x_1 - x_2 - x_3 \qquad = 0$$

Since conditions (10.27) are five linear equations in five unknowns; the three x's and two Lagrange multipliers, there will be a unique solution which because of the convexity of the function V, will give the variance minimizing values of the x's. It can be shown that the Lagrange multiplier $y_1 = \mathrm{d}V_{\min}/\mathrm{d}\bar{R}$, the rate of change of the minimum value of variance as required return changes. Therefore y_1 is the slope of the efficiency frontier if variance is represented on the vertical axis.

In the case of the third asset being risk free (zero variance in the security return and zero covariance with the returns from other securities) the matrix of the first derivatives of the Lagrangian will contain zero entries corresponding to the risk-free investment. For example, in a three-security problem with x_3 risk free

$$\begin{pmatrix} 2\sigma_1^2 & 2\sigma_{12} & 0 & -\bar{R}_1-1 \\ 2\sigma_{21} & 2\sigma_2^2 & 0 & -\bar{R}_2-1 \\ 0 & 0 & 0 & -\bar{R}_3-1 \\ 1 & 1 & 1 & 0 & 0 \\ \bar{R}_1 & \bar{R}_2 & \bar{R}_3 & 0 & 0 \end{pmatrix} \begin{pmatrix} x_1 \\ x_2 \\ x_3 \\ y_2 \\ y_1 \end{pmatrix} = \begin{pmatrix} 0 \\ 0 \\ 0 \\ 1 \\ \bar{R} \end{pmatrix}$$

For a numerical example consider the return and variance; covariance data of Figure 10.6.

Security	$\bar{R}_i$	σ_i^2	σ_{ij}
1	6	4	$5(=\sigma_{12})$
2	12	36	$15(=\sigma_{23})$
3	30	625	$2(=\sigma_{13})$

Figure 10.6

For the data of Figure 10.6 the Lagrangian expression and first-order conditions are

$$L = 4x_1^2 + 36x_2^2 + 625x_3^2 + 10x_1x_2 + 4x_1x_3 + 30x_2x_3$$
$$+ y_1(R - 6x_1 - 12x_2 - 30x_3) + y_2(1 - x_1 - x_2 - x_3)$$

$$\frac{\partial L}{\partial x_1} = 8x_1 + 10x_2 + 4x_3 - 6y_1 - y_2 = 0$$

$$\frac{\partial L}{\partial x_2} = 72x_2 + 10x_1 + 30x_3 - 12y_1 - y_2 = 0$$

$$\frac{\partial L}{\partial x_3} = 1250x_3 + 4x_1 + 30x_2 - 30y_1 - y_2 = 0 \qquad (10.28)$$

$$\frac{\partial L}{\partial y_1} = \bar{R} - 6x_1 - 12x_2 - 30x_3 = 0$$

$$\frac{\partial L}{\partial y_2} = 1 - x_1 - x_2 - x_3 = 0$$

The conditions (10.28) solve for

$$x_1 = \frac{10{,}272 - 685\bar{R}}{6{,}054}; \qquad x_2 = \frac{577\bar{R} - 3{,}606}{6{,}054}; \qquad x_3 = \frac{108\bar{R} - 612}{6{,}054}$$

$$y_1 = \frac{6{,}198.\overline{66}\bar{R} - 36{,}490}{6{,}054}; \qquad y_2 = \frac{262{,}608 - 36{,}470\bar{R}}{6{,}054}$$

The solution has several points worthy of note. First, not all of the x's are non-negative for all values of $\bar{R}$. It will be seen that x_1 is positive only if $\bar{R}$ is less than $10{,}272/685$, x_2 is positive only if $\bar{R}$ exceeds $3{,}606/577$ and x_3 will only be positive if $\bar{R}$ exceeds $612/108$. Consequently, variance-minimizing portfolios are only for values of $\bar{R}$ between approximately 6.25% and 15%. If values of $\bar{R}$ outside of this interval are required and the investor may not issue securities then the calculations have to be modified to include the sign requirements. The means by which this provision can be included are described later.

The second point is that the variance-minimizing portfolios for 6%, 12% and 30% do not consist of single investments in x_1, x_2 and x_3 respectively. For instance the variance-minimizing portfolio for $R = 30$ is

$$x_1 = \frac{-10{,}278}{6{,}054}; \qquad x_2 = \frac{13{,}704}{6{,}054}; \qquad x_3 = \frac{2{,}628}{6{,}054}$$

If negative x's are unfeasible, then a return of 30% can only be secured by $x_1 = 0$, $x_2 = 0$, $x_3 = 1$; only x_3 is taken. However the variance-minimizing portfolio for 12% contains all positive x's with

$$x_1 = \frac{2,052}{6,054}; \qquad x_2 = \frac{3,318}{6,054}; \qquad x_3 = \frac{684}{6,054}$$

The corresponding value of V for this portfolio is 23.12, whereas with $x_2 = 1$ the corresponding variance figure is 36.

The third point concerns the optimal value of the Lagrange multiplier y_1 which represents the rate of change of the minimum value of variance as required expected return changes. The value of y_1 becomes zero for $R \sim 5.89$ (corresponding to $x_1 \simeq 1.031$, $x_2 \simeq -0.035$, $x_3 \simeq 0.004$). As required return falls towards 5.89% so variance falls, but as return decreases below 5.89% so the corresponding minimum variance figure rises. That is to say, an attempt to secure lower overall variance by reducing required return below 5.89% would fail; 5.89% is the return on the overall variance-minimizing portfolio. The point is somewhat academic, however, as portfolios with return below 6.25% are not legitimate.

Fourthly it should be noted that there is no limit to the expected return on the portfolio if leveraging is permitted. High values of $\bar{R}$ produce positive values of x_3 and x_2 and negative x_1. The investor is adding to his original funds by issuing securities at 6% and investing the moneys thus raised at 12% (to deep down variance) and 30%.

Fifthly, the Lagrange multiplier y_2, at an optimum, can be shown to be dV_{min}/db, where b, expressed as a decimal is the proportion of the total budget that the investor spends. We have set $b = 1$ in writing $x_1 + x_2 + x_3 = 1$, the investor is constrained to spend the entire budget—there is no cash in this model (though it could be included by introducing x_4 with return and variance zero). In fact, for some low values of portfolio expected return the investor could reduce variance by not spending his entire budget. We see that y_2 is positive for $\bar{R} < 7.20$, meaning that changes in b bring changes of V_{min} in the same direction; a reduction in the proportion of the budget spent brings a reduction in minimum value of variance that can be achieved. However, in order to restrict the problem to three variables we shall ignore the matter of proportion of budget expended.

The equations of the isovariance contours in $x_2 x_1$ space (for a diagram similar to Figure 10.4) can be found by substitution of $x_3 = 1 - x_1 - x_2$ into the formula for variance. The result is

$$V = 625x_1^2 + 631x_2^2 + 1226x_1x_2 - 1246x_1 - 1220x_2 + 625 \qquad (10.29)$$

Setting V equal to a particular value in the above equation generates one isovariance contour. In comparison with Figure 10.4 the contours are rotated clockwise and V^* is positioned just beneath the horizontal axis. The equations of the iso-return lines are obtained by substitution of

$x_3 = 1 - x_1 - x_2$ into $\bar{R} = 6x_1 + 12x_2 + 30x_3$ so that

$$x_2 = \frac{30 - \bar{R}}{18} - \frac{4x_1}{3}$$

Changing $\bar{R}$ simply alters the position of the return line relative to the origin. All iso-return leins have a slope of $-4/3$.

The equation of the critical line can be found by expressing x_2 as a function of x_1 and $\bar{R}$ (from the solutions for x_1 and x_2 given above) and making the substitution $\bar{R} = 6x_1 + 12x_2 + 30(1 - x_1 - x_2)$. The result is (approximate co-efficients)

$$x_2 = 0.834 - 0.842x_1$$

The critical line, the locus of points of tangency of iso-return lines and isovariance contours is a straight line of slope -0.842, the relevant section being above and to the left of V^*.

To obtain the risk–return efficiency frontier first substitute for x_1 and x_2 their solutions as functions of $\bar{R}$ into (10.29). This gives minimum variance as a function of expected return. The result is (approximate coefficients)

$$V = 21.69 - 6.03\bar{R} + 0.512\bar{R}^2 \tag{10.30}$$

We must now tackle the problem of preventing leverage. Clearly, one way of doing this would be to set the problem up in the first instance as a quadratic programming problem and work with the Kuhn–Tucker conditions which contain explicit provisions that the x's be non-negative. But there is another procedure which does not require a QP approach. We have expressed the optimal x_j as functions of $\bar{R}$, and so long as $\bar{R}$ (in the numerical illustration) is not outside of the range $3,606/577$ to $10,272/685$ there are no negative x_j. Consider the upper bound first of all. When $\bar{R}$ reaches this value x_1 becomes zero. At this point x_1 is *removed from the analysis* and the problem is reduced to one in two securities, x_2 and x_3. In general when x_j becomes zero in an n security problem it is dropped from the analysis and the remaining $n - 1$ x_j are solved for afresh as linear functions of the portfolio return. Continuing with the variation in $\bar{R}$, when the next x reaches zero level it, in turn, is deleted and for values of $\bar{R}$ further in the direction of change the problem becomes one in $n - 2$ securities—and so on. Although the procedure is straightforward, the computational efficiency is minimal—a new problem is only one less variable having to be solved at each stage.

However, when a problem is reduced to one in two securities the determination of the efficiency frontier is a trivial problem if all the budget has to be spent. In our example when R exceeds $10,272/685$ the values of x_2 and x_3 in the portfolio can be obtained by reference to the portfolio return equation alone. That is

$$R = 12x_2 + 30x_3 \tag{10.31}$$

but since we require that the budget be spent; $x_3 = 1 - x_2$ so that:

$$x_2 = \frac{30 - \bar{R}}{18} \quad \text{and} \quad x_3 = \frac{\bar{R} - 12}{18}$$

Variance as a function of $\bar{R}$ is obtained as before. That is

$$V = 36x_2^2 - 625x_3^2 + 30x_2x_3 \tag{10.32}$$

Substitution of $(1 - x_2)$ for x_3 in (10.32) produces

$$V = 631x_2^2 - 1220x_2 + 625 \tag{10.33}$$

Substituting $(30 - R)/$ for x_2 in (10.33) gives (approximate coefficients)

$$V = 344.44 - 49.074\bar{R} + 1.9475\bar{R}^2 \tag{10.34}$$

The two expressions for variance, (10.33) and (10.34) give the same figure for V at $\bar{R} = 15$ (any difference due to errors in rounding). The situation is illustrated in Figure 10.7. The lower curve (3) is the three-security efficiency frontier and the upper curve is the efficiency frontier in securities two and three only. The two curves touch at $\bar{R} = 15$, but the two-security curve is steeper as $\bar{R}$ increases above 15. It is this upper curve that is the relevant one for these values of $\bar{R}$ if the leverage is prohibited. Of course the maximum values of $\bar{R}$ that can be achieved in the absence of leverage is 30. The reader may verify the tangency at $R = 15$ and the fact that the two-security frontier is steeper above this value of $\bar{R}$ by reference to the equations for the slopes of the frontiers. These are

(a) $\dfrac{dV}{d\bar{R}} = -6.03 + 1.024\bar{R} \qquad$ (three securities)

(b) $\dfrac{dV}{dR} = -49.074 + 3.895\bar{R} \qquad$ (two securities) $\tag{10.35}$

Setting the RHS of (10.35(b)) to be not less than the RHS of (10.35(a)) gives the result that $\bar{R} \geqslant 15$.

A similar procedure can be applied for low values of $\bar{R}$. When

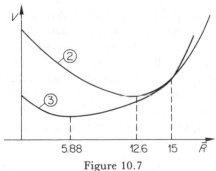

Figure 10.7

$\bar{R} = 3{,}606/577 > x_2 = 0$ and for further reductions in $\bar{R}$, x_2 is omitted. It follows that since

$$\bar{R} = 6x_1 + 30x_3 \quad \text{and} \quad x_1 + x_3 = 1$$

$$x_1 = \frac{30 - \bar{R}}{24} \quad \text{and} \quad x_3 = \frac{\bar{R} - 6}{24}$$

and since V is now given by

$$V = 4x_1^2 + 625x_3^2 + 4x_1x_3$$

we can write

$$V = 625 - 1246x_1 + 625x_1^2$$

and substitution for x_1 produces

$$V = 44.0625 - 13.1875\bar{R} + 1.0851\bar{R}^2 \tag{10.37}$$

Again, the corresponding efficiency frontier given by (10.37) is within the old frontier; variance/return combinations implying negative x_2 being excluded. The range of application of (10.37) and (10.36) is small, however, being $6 \leqslant \bar{R} \leqslant 6.25$ (approx.). It will be seen from (10.36) that x_3 would become negative for $\bar{R} < 6$. Unleveraged portfolios with expected return less than 6% cannot be achieved and portfolios with expected return in excess of 6.25% are more efficient with x_2 included.

The reader may wish to verify that (10.37) gives lower values of V in the range $6 \leqslant \bar{R} \leqslant 6.25$ than does the two-security frontier consisting of x_1 and x_2. This frontier is given by

$$V = 32 - 9.6667\bar{R} + 0.8333\bar{R}^2 \tag{10.38}$$

The unleveraged efficiency frontier is comprised of sections of three and two security frontiers, each of which is a quadratic in $\bar{R}$. This will be the case irrespective of the number of securities involved, since the solution of the n security equivalent of conditions (10.31) will give each x_j as a linear function of $\bar{R}$. Consequently, substitution for the x_j in the expression for V will give a quadratic function of $\bar{R}$. Despite this fact that, in the end, we are dealing with only quadratic expressions in $\bar{R}$ it is evident that the obtaining of the unleveraged efficiency frontier is a considerable task. Also, the investor has yet to decide upon a particular combination of variance and return on the efficiency frontier.

There is a formulation of the efficiency frontier determination problem which allows the incorporation of the investor's risk–return preferences so that the overall optimum portfolio can be identified along with production of the efficiency frontier itself. The objective is to maximize a weighted average of expected return and variance that we first introduced in section 10.2

$$F = w\bar{R} - V \tag{10.39}$$

subject to the expenditure constraint $\Sigma x_j = 1$. The function F can be interpreted as a utility function.

The slope of the indifference curves (the rate at which the investor is prepared to trade security for return, at a point, so as to maintain an unchanged level of satisfaction) is called the *marginal rate of substitution*, which in the case of (10.39) is

$$\frac{\mathrm{d}V}{\mathrm{d}\bar{R}} = \frac{-w}{-1} = w \tag{10.40}$$

so that the weight w expresses the rate at which variance must increase to offset an increase in expected return. Alternatively, $\mathrm{d}\bar{R}/\mathrm{d}V = 1/w$ expresses the rate at which expected return must increase to compensate for increased variance. The lower the value of w the more averse to risk is the investor. For a given value of w the indifference curves are straight lines in V, $\bar{R}$ space.

Now consider the maximization of (10.39). Suppose we fix $\bar{R}$ at some arbitrary value $\bar{R}^0$. In this event for any value of w the difference $w\bar{R}^0 - V$ can be maximal only if V is minimized; that is, if a point on the efficiency frontier is selected. If we now fix V at V^0 for any w the difference can be maximal only if R is maximized—again a point on the efficiency frontier is selected. So, no matter what the value of w is the investor will always choose a point on the efficiency frontier. This means that the optimum will be a point of tangency between an indifference line and the efficiency frontier so that *continuous variation of* w *will produce the efficiency frontier itself*. This fact is illustrated in Figure 10.8 in which point A is selected when the value of w used is greater than that which produces A'. It should be noted that points below A' would correspond to 'negative utility'.

Formally, the problem of maximization of (10.39) can be written in terms of the x's as:

$$\left.\begin{array}{c} \text{maximize } w \sum_{i=1}^{n} x_i \bar{R}_i - \sum_{i=1}^{n} x_i^2 \sigma_i^2 - \sum_{\substack{i=1 \\ }}^{n} \sum_{\substack{j=1 \\ j \neq i}}^{n} x_i x_j \sigma_{ij} \\[2em] \text{subject to } \sum_{i=1}^{n} x_i = 1 \end{array}\right\} \tag{10.41}$$

The problem could be written up as a Lagrangian expression with the constraint explicitly included or, alternatively, the constraint could be included implicitly by substituting

$$x_n = 1 - \sum_{i=1}^{n-1} x_i \tag{10.42}$$

for x_n in the objective function itself. Either way the optimal values of the x's would emerge as linear functions of w producing return/variance combinations on the efficiency frontier. This will be left as an exercise for the interested reader to perform on the numerical data of Figure 10.6.

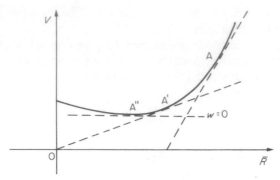

Figure 10.8

Since we have already obtained the efficiency frontier by the minimization approach we have the expression for variance as a function of expected return given by (10.30). Upon substitution, (10.39) for the numerical example becomes:

$$F = (w + 6.03)R - 0.512\bar{R}^2 - 21.69 \tag{10.43}$$

which can now be maximized with respect to $\bar{R}$. The conditions are

$$\frac{dF}{d\bar{R}} = (w + 6.03) - 1.024\bar{R} = 0$$

and

$$\frac{d^2F}{d\bar{R}^2} = -1.024 < 0$$

Thus the optimal value of $\bar{R}$ is given by:

$$\bar{R}(\text{opt}) = \frac{w + 6.03}{1.024} \tag{10.44}$$

and the corresponding value of F is, unsurprisingly, a quadratic in w given by:

$$F_{\text{max}} = 0.488w^2 + 5.888w - 3.936 \tag{10.45}$$

In the special case where $w = 0$ (the investor is concerned only with variance) equation (10.44) gives the return associated with the variance minimizing portfolio, and (10.45) gives (negated) the minimum value of variance itself.

The optimal level of variance as a function of w is found by substituting (10.44) into (10.37). The result is

$$v(\text{opt}) = 0.488w^2 + 3.936$$

If a linear function such as (10.39) provides an adequate representation of the investor's preferences then a one-stage procedure of maximization of this function will be indicated. If a more sophisticated utility function is to be employed then a two-stage solution procedure is preferable. First the efficiency frontier is determined and then the utility function is introduced and maximized with the efficiency frontier as a constraint.

As an example of the latter procedure suppose that the investor's utility function was of the *Cobb–Douglas* type. That is

$$U = A\bar{R}^\alpha (k + V)^{-\beta} \tag{10.46}$$

where $A > 0$, $\alpha > 0$, $\beta > 0$, $k > 0$ and $\alpha < \beta$. The constant k is included so that utility is finite for zero variance. If $\alpha < \beta$ as supposed then the indifference curves are as shown in Figure 10.9, being concave to the $\bar{R}$ axis. It would be reasonable to suppose that $\alpha s < 1$ so that the marginal utility of return $(\partial U/\partial \bar{R})$ is diminishing. The slope of the indifference curves as given by (10.46) is

$$\frac{dV}{d\bar{R}} = \frac{\alpha(k + V)}{\beta R}$$

which can be shown to diminish as $\bar{R}$ increases for given utility so long as $\alpha < \beta$. That is, as variance increases for given utility the investor requires increasing increments in return to compensate. This is more appealing than the linear indifference curve case in which the increments in $\bar{R}$ are constant.

Consider a numerical illustration. Let

$$U = \bar{R}^{0.8}(1 + V)^{-1.5}$$

and with V given by (11.33) the Lagrangian is

$$L = \bar{R}^{0.8}(1 + V)^{-1.5} + \lambda(V - 21.69 + 6.03\bar{R} - 0.512\bar{R}^2)$$

and first-order conditions are

$$\frac{\partial L}{\partial \bar{R}} = 0.8\bar{R}^{-0.2}(1 + V)^{-1.5} + 6.03\lambda - 1.024\bar{R}\lambda = 0$$

$$\frac{\partial L}{\partial V} = -1.5\bar{R}^{0.8}(1 + V)^{-2.5} + \lambda \qquad\qquad = 0$$

$$\frac{\partial L}{\partial \lambda} = V - 21.69 + 6.03\bar{R} - 0.512\bar{R}^2 \qquad\qquad = 0$$

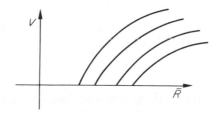

Figure 10.9

Substituting for λ from the second condition into the first gives

$$0.8\bar{R}^{-0.2}(1 + V)^{-1.5} + 9.045\bar{R}^{0.8}(1 + V)^{-2.5} - 1.536\bar{R}^{1.8}(1 + V)^{-2.5} = 0$$

multiplying through by $\bar{R}^{0.2}(1 + V)^{2.5} \neq 0$ and solving for V gives:

$$V = \frac{1.536\bar{R}^2 - 9.045\bar{R} - 0.8}{0.8}$$

Substitution into the third condition produces

$$1.1264\bar{R}^2 - 4.221\bar{R} - 18.152 = 0$$

of which the positive root is $\bar{R} = 6.304$. This is the utility maximizing value of portfolio return.

The purpose of utility functions is to derive a one-dimensional measure of the desirability of a project or portfolio which may have several important characteristics. The form of function used is at the discretion of the investor. In this context the *constant elasticity of substitution* (CES) form is of much interest. Let

$$U = a_0(a_1\bar{R}^{-b} + a_2(k + V)^{-b})^{-c/b} \tag{10.47}$$

where $a_0 > 0$, $a_1 \geq 0$ and $a_2 \leq 0$. In interpretation of (10.47) we note that in a portfolio context the value of a_0 is unimportant and would normally be set at unity, but if U was attached to a *single investment* and the utility of different, mutually exclusive projects was being considered, then a_0 could be interpreted as a 'project-specific' coefficient being different between projects. The coefficients a_1 and a_2 are distribution parameters and the relative magnitudes of these reflect the relative importance attached by the investor to return and risk. The value of b determines the curvature of the indifference curves; b is known as the *substitution parameter* and $b \geq -1$. The parameter c, *degree of homogeneity* of the function, might be thought of as measuring the overall 'sensitivity' of the investor.

The investor selects values of the parameters of (10.47) and solve the portfolio problem by the two-stage procedure. Selection of certain values of the parameters, produces simpler cases. For example as the value of b approaches zero then U approaches the Cobb–Douglas form:

$$U \rightarrow a_0\bar{R}^{a_1 c}(k + V)^{a_2 c} \quad \text{as } b \rightarrow 0$$

If $b = -1$ and $c = 1$ the linear case is produced. That is

$$U = a_0(a_1\bar{R} + a_2(k + V))$$

so that if $a_2 = -a_0^{-1}$ then the linear form (10.39) is produced (set $k = 0$ here and where $w = a_0 a_1$). When $b = -1$ and $c = 2$ (10.47) is a quadratic expression.

10.4 Quadratic Programming and Portfolio Section

Suppose that the investor's preferences regarding return–variance combinations can be described by (10.39). For the problem data of Figure 10.6 we shall now use the quadratic programming procedure of Chapter 7 to solve the portfolio problem for $w = 5$. The objective will be to maximize

$$F = 30x_1 + 60x_2 + 150x_3 - 4x_1^2 - 36x_2^2 - 625x_3^2 - 10x_1x_2 - 4x_1x_3$$
$$- 30x_2x_3 \tag{10.48}$$

Let us suppose, for a change, that not all the budget need be spent, but continue to assume that leveraged portfolios are prohibited. Thus the constraint set is given by

$$\left.\begin{array}{l} x_1 + x_2 + x_3 \leqslant 1 \\[6pt] x_1 \geqslant 0, \quad x_2 \geqslant 0, \quad x_3 \geqslant 0 \end{array}\right\} \tag{10.49}$$

If it should turn out that not all of the budget is spent at an optimum, then the variance of portfolio return that is arrived at, and the return figure itself are still related to the *total* budget. It is as if there were a fourth security (proportion invested being s below) cash, giving zero actual and expected return and zero variance and covariance with other securities. The Lagrangian function will be

$$L = F + y(1 - x_1 - x_2 - x_3) \tag{10.50}$$

and the most convenient form of the Kuhn–Tucker conditions is:

$$\left.\begin{array}{ll} \dfrac{\partial L}{\partial x_1} = 30 - 8x_1 - 10x_2 - 4x_3 - y + t_1 & = 0 \\[14pt] \dfrac{\partial L}{\partial x_2} = 60 - 72x_2 - 10x_1 - 30x_3 - y + t_2 & = 0 \\[14pt] \dfrac{\partial L}{\partial x_3} = 150 - 1250x_3 - 4x_1 - 30x_2 - y + t_3 & = 0 \\[14pt] x_1t_1 = 0 \\[6pt] x_2t_2 = 0 \\[6pt] x_3t_3 = 0 \\[6pt] x_1 \geqslant 0 \qquad t_1 \geqslant 0 \\[6pt] x_2 \geqslant 0 \qquad t_2 \geqslant 0 \\[6pt] x_3 \geqslant 0 \qquad t_3 \geqslant 0 \\[6pt] \dfrac{\partial L}{\partial y} = 1 - x_1 - x_2 - x_3 - s = 0 \\[14pt] ys = 0 \\[6pt] y \geqslant 0 \qquad s \geqslant 0 \end{array}\right\} \tag{10.51}$$

			x_1	x_2	x_3	y	t_1	t_2	t_3	s	u_1	u_2	u_3	u_4
			0	0	0	0	0	0	0	0	0	0	0	−1
0	u_1	30	8	10	4	1	−1	0	0	0	1	0	0	0
0	u_2	60	10	72	30	1	0	−1	0	0	0	1	0	0
0	u_3	150	4	30	1,250	1	0	0	−1	0	0	0	1	0
−1	u_4	1	①	1	1	0	0	0	0	1	0	0	0	1
0	u_1	22	0	2	−4	1	−1	0	0	−8	1	0	0	−8
0	u_2	50	0	62	20	1	0	−1	0	−10	0	1	0	−10
0	u_3	146	0	26	1,246	1	0	0	−1	−4	0	0	1	−4
0	x_1	1	1	1	1	0	0	0	0	1	0	0	0	1

Figure 10.10

Now since F is concave and the constraints (10.49) form a convex set, the Kuhn–Tucker conditions are both necessary and sufficient for a global optimum. Following the procedure of Chapter 7 we now re-express the Kuhn–Tucker conditions corresponding to the partial derivatives in (10.51) so that constant terms are on the right-hand side of the equations. Adding in artificial variables gives:

$$\left. \begin{aligned}
8x_1 + 10x_2 + 4x_3 + y - t_1 + u_1 &= 30 \\
10x_1 + 72x_2 + 30x_3 + y - t_2 + u_2 &= 60 \\
4x_1 + 30x_2 + 1{,}250x_3 + y - t_3 + u_3 &= 150 \\
x_1 + x_2 + x_3 + s + u_4 &= 1
\end{aligned} \right\} \quad (10.52)$$

The phase one calculations are shown in Figure 10.10 and the phase two calculations in Figure 10.11. In phase two, pivotal elements have been chosen with an eye to arithmetic convenience rather than automatic selection of the most negative index row number. Starred zeros are zero to three decimal places. The optimal solution is seen to consist of $x_1 = 0.479$, $x_2 = 0.430$, $x_3 = 0.091$, giving an expected portfolio yield of 10.764%. Reference to equation (10.44) gives, for $w = 5$, a value of $R = 10.771\%$. The difference is attributable to rounding errors.

10.5 Index Models

For operational purposes the amount of information required for the Markowitz model can be a severe disadvantage. If n securities are being considered then n expected returns, n variances and $n(n-1)/2$ covariances would be needed. In total then $(n/2)(n+3)$ bits of data are necessary. Ball and Brown (1969) cite the example that if all of the 1,300 or so stocks traded on the New York Stock Exchange were being considered, then the number of estimates required as data inputs would be approximately

c	Basis	b	x_1	x_2	x_3	y	t_1	t_2	t_3	s	u_1	u_2	u_3
c_j			0	0	0	0	−1	0	0	0	−1	−1	−1
−1	u_1	22	0	2	−4	1	−1	0	0	−8	1	0	0
−1	u_2	50	0	62	20	1	0	−1	0	−10	0	1	0
−1	u_3	146	0	26	1,246	1	0	0	−1	−4	0	0	1
0	x_1	1	1	1	1	0	1	0	0	1	0	0	0
		−218	0	−90	−1,262	−3	−1	1	1	22	0	0	0
0	y	22	0	2	−4	1	1	0	0	−8	1	0	0
−1	u_2	28	0	60	24	0	−1	−1	0	−2	−1	1	0
−1	u_3	124	0	24	1,250	0	1	0	−1	4	−1	0	1
0	x_1	1	1	1	1	0	1	0	0	1	0	0	0
		−152	0	−84	−1,274	0	−2	1	1	−2	3	0	0
0	y	126.4/6	0	0	−28.8/6	1	−1.2/6	0.2/6	0	−47.6/6	1.2/6	−0.2/6	0
0	x_2	2.8/6	0	1	2.4/6	0	0.1/6	−0.1/6	0	−0.2/6	−0.1/6	0.1/6	0
−1	u_3	676.8/6	0	0	7,442.4/6	0	3.6/6	2.4/6	−1	28.8/6	−3.6/6	−2.4/6	1
0	x_1	3.2/6	1	0	3.6/6	0	−0.1/6	0.1/6	0	6.2/6	0.1/6	−0.1/6	0
		−676.8/6	0	0	−7,442.4/6	0	−3.6/6	−2.4/6	1	−28.8/6	9.6/6	8.4/6	0
0	y	21.503	0	0	0	1	−0.177	0.035	−0.005	−7.914	0.177	−0.035	0.005
0	x_2	0.430	0	1	0	0	0.017	−0.017	0*	−0.035	−0.017	0.017	0*
0	x_3	0.091	0	0	1	0	0*	0*	−0.001	0.004	0*	0*	0.001
0	x_1	0.479	1	0	0	0	−0.017	0.016	0.001	1.019	0.017	−0.016	−0.001
		0	0	0	0	0	0	0	0	0	1	1	1

Figure 10.11

850,000. This would be quite impracticable. Markowitz was aware of this limitation of his original model (now referred to as the Markowitz full covariance model, MFC) and suggested a simplification drastically reducing the volume of data that would be required. Subsequently, Sharpe (1965) produced his single-index *diagonal* model.

The single-index model assumes that the returns to individual securities are related only through their own particular relationships with a market index. In particular:

$$R_i = A_i + B_i I + C_i \qquad (i = 1, 2, \ldots, n) \tag{10.53}$$

where R_i is the return (actual) on the ith security, I is the level of a market or economic index, A_i and B_i are parameters and C_i is a random variable with expected value zero and variance Q_j. The error terms for different securities are uncorrelated with each other, i.e. the covariance between C_i and C_j is zero $i \neq j$. The future level of the index is given by

$$I = A_{n+1} + C_{n+1} \tag{10.54}$$

where A_{n+1} is a parameter and C_{n+1} is a random variable with expected value zero and variance Q_{n+1}. The model is pictured in Figure 10.12. The horizontal axis is the level of the index and the value of R_i is measured on the vertical axis above the origin; A_i is the intercept term and the slope of the straight line is B_i. The variance of the C_i is assumed independent of the level of the index. Beneath the horizontal axis the probability distribution of the value of the index is illustrated.

The following relationships may be obtained:

$$\left. \begin{array}{l} \bar{R}_i = A_i + B_i A_{n+1} \\ \sigma_i^2 = B_i^2 Q_{n+1} + Q_i \\ \sigma_{ij} = B_i B_j Q_{n+1} \end{array} \right\} \tag{10.55}$$

Where, in (10.55) the two components of σ_i^2 represent *systematic risk* and *unsystematic risk* respectively.

If it was desired to use the MFC model the covariance data can be

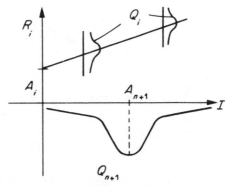

Figure 10.12

obtained from (10.55) having estimated only $2n$ values of the B_i. This alone would go a long way towards making the MFC model practicable for large-scale applications. However, the portfolio problem can be reformulated altogether.

Consider portfolio return. The actual value of this, R is given by

$$R = \sum_{i=1}^{n} x_i R_i$$

$$= \sum_{i=1}^{n} x_i (A_i + B_i I + C_i)$$

$$= \sum_{i=1}^{n} x_i (A_i + C_i) + I \sum_{i=1}^{n} x_i B_i$$

$$= \sum_{i=1}^{n+1} x_i (A_i + C_i) \tag{10.56}$$

where, in (10.56),

$$x_{n+1} = \sum_{i=1}^{n} x_i B_i$$

Sharpe viewed the portfolio as an investment in n *basic securities* and an investment in the index [the $n+1$th term in the summation (10.56)]. The expected value of portfolio return will be given by

$$\bar{R} = \sum_{i=1}^{n+1} x_i A_i \tag{10.57}$$

Now, as regards portfolio variance, this is written in the MFC model as

$$V = \sum_{i=1}^{n} x_i^2 \sigma_i^2 + \sum_{i=1}^{n} \sum_{\substack{j=1 \\ j \neq 1}}^{n} x_i x_j \sigma_{ij} \tag{10.58}$$

which can now be greatly simplified. Substituting for the σ_i^2 and σ_{ij} from (10.55) gives

$$V - \sum_{i=1}^{n} x_i^2 (B_i^2 Q_{n+1} + Q_i) + \sum_{i=1}^{n} \sum_{\substack{j=1 \\ j \neq i}}^{n} x_i x_j B_i B_j Q_{n+1} \tag{10.59}$$

(10.59) can obviously be rewritten as

$$V = \sum_{i=1}^{n} x_i^2 Q_i + \sum_{i=1}^{n} x_i^2 B_i^2 Q_{n+1} + \sum_{i=1}^{n} \sum_{\substack{j=1 \\ j \neq i}}^{n} x_i x_j B_i B_j Q_{n+1}$$

$$= \sum_{i=1}^{n} x_i^2 Q_i + Q_{n+1} \left[\sum_{i=1}^{n} x_i B_i \right]^2 \tag{10.60}$$

$$= \sum_{i=1}^{n+1} x_i^2 Q_i$$

so that the variance equation contains only $n + 1$ terms! The name 'diagonal model' arises from the fact that if (10.60) is expressed in matrix form, only elements in the principal diagonal of the resulting matrix of coefficents are non-zero. Equation (10.60) would appear as

$$(x_1, x_2, \ldots, x_{n+1}) \begin{pmatrix} Q_1 & & & \\ & Q_2 & & 0 \\ & & \ddots & \\ 0 & & & Q_{n+1} \end{pmatrix} \begin{pmatrix} x_1 \\ x_2 \\ \vdots \\ x_{n+1} \end{pmatrix}$$

Viewed as a two-phase procedure the investor's problem is to determine the efficiency frontier from (10.57) and (10.60) and then to choose a point on it. The efficiency frontier thus provided will differ somewhat from the MFC frontier. Theoretically the MFC frontier has maximal efficency and the single-index frontier will be within or, in the extreme, not to the right of the MFC frontier. Further comparisons resulting from empirical work are discussed below.

Before going on to more complex work, consider a simple example in the use of a single-index approach. Following the notation given for Sharpe's diagonal model of portfolio selection, viz.

$$R_i = A_i + B_i I + C_i \quad \text{for } i = 1,2,3$$

where

$$I = A_4 + C_4$$

and given that

$$A_1 = 35, \quad A_2 = -65, \quad A_3 = 0, \quad A_4 = 500$$
$$B_1 = -0.05, \quad B_2 = 0.25, \quad B_3 = 0$$
$$Q_1 = 6, \quad Q_2 = 800, \quad Q_3 = 0, \quad Q_4 = 1,600$$

Let us express expected portfolio return and portfolio variance in terms of the proportions of funds invested in each security. First it should be noted that there are three securities ($n = 3$) and that the subscript 4 ($= n + 1$) therefore refers to the index. For the returns we recall that;

$$\bar{R}_i = A_i + B_i A_{n+1}$$

so that:

$$\bar{R}_1 = A_1 + B_1 A_4 = 35 - 0.05(500) = 10$$
$$\bar{R}_2 = A_2 + B_2 A_4 = -65 + 0.25(500) = 60$$
$$\bar{R}_3 = A_3 + B_3 A_4 = 0 + 0(500) = 0$$

For the variances the relationship is

$$\sigma_i^2 = B_i^2 Q_{n+1} + Q_i$$

So that

$$\sigma_1^2 = B_1^2 Q_4 + Q_1 = (-0.05)^2 \, 1{,}600 + 6 = 10$$
$$\sigma_2^2 = B_2^2 Q_4 + Q_2 = (0.25)^2 \, 1{,}600 + 800 = 900$$
$$\sigma_3^2 = B_3^2 Q_4 + Q_3 \qquad\qquad\qquad = 0$$

For the covariances we have

$$\sigma_{ij} = B_i B_j Q_{n+1}$$

so that

$$\sigma_{12} = B_1 B_2 Q_4 = (-0.05)(0.25)1{,}600 = -20$$

and σ_{13} and σ_{23} are zero since B_3 is zero. Clearly, the third security is (or is equivalent to) cash. The required expressions for portfolio expected return and variance (with x_i representing the proportion of funds in security i) are

$$\bar{R} = 10x_1 + 60x_2$$
$$V = 10x_1^2 + 900x_2^2 - 40x_1x_2$$

where, in the variance expression, note that the covariance term is $-40x_1x_2$ since $\sigma_{12} = \sigma_{21} = -20$. The summation as we have heretofore written it would count σ_{12} and σ_{21} separately.

Consider a two-index model. Suppose the securities are ordered so that the first m are correlated higher with index 1 (I_1) than index 2 (I_2) whilst the remaining $n - m$ are correlated more highly with the second index. The actual returns on the securities will be given by

$$R_i = A_i + B_i I_1 + C_{1i} \qquad (i = 1, 2, \ldots, m)$$
$$R_i = A_i + B_i I_2 + C_{2i} \qquad (i = m+1, \ldots, n) \tag{10.61}$$

where

$$E(C_{1i}) = 0, \qquad E(C_{2i}) = 0, \qquad E(C_{1i}^2) = Q_{1i}, \qquad E(C_{2i}^2) = Q_{2i}$$

and where all pairs of securities have uncorrelated error terms. The levels of the indices are given by

$$I_1 = A_{n+1} + C_{n+1}$$
$$I_2 = A_{n+2} + C_{n+2} \tag{10.62}$$

and where, in (10.62) $E(C_{n+1}) = 0$, $E(C_{n+2}) = 0$, $E(C_{n+1}^2) = Q_{n+1}$,

$E(C_{n+2}^2) = Q_{n+2}$. Actual portfolio return is given by

$$R = \sum_{i=1}^{n} x_i R_i$$

$$= \sum_{i=1}^{m} x_i(A_i + C_{1i}) + \sum_{i=m+1}^{n} x_i(A_i + C_{2i}) + I_1 \sum_{i=1}^{m} x_i B_i \qquad (10.63)$$

$$+ I_2 \sum_{i=m+1}^{n} x_i B_i$$

$$= \sum_{i=1}^{n+2} x_i(A_i + C_i)$$

where, in (10.63), $C_i = C_{1i}$ for $i \leqslant m$; $C_i = C_{2i}$ for $m < i \leqslant n$; $C_i = C_{n+1}$ for $i = n+1$ and $C_i = C_{n+2}$ for $i = n+2$. Also

$$x_{n+1} \equiv \sum_{i=1}^{m} x_i B_i \quad \text{and} \quad x_{n+2} \equiv \sum_{i=m+1}^{n} x_i B_i$$

The expected value of portfolio return will be

$$\bar{R} = \sum_{i=1}^{n+2} x_i A_i \qquad (10.64)$$

Now, as regards variances and covariances we have

$$\left.\begin{array}{ll}
\sigma_i^2 = B_i^2 Q_{n+1} + Q_{1i} & (i = 1, 2, \ldots, m) \\
\sigma_i^2 = B_i^2 Q_{n+2} + Q_{2i} & (i = m+1, \ldots, n) \\
\sigma_{ij} = B_i B_j Q_{n+1} & (i, j \leqslant m) \\
\sigma_{ij} = B_i B_j Q_{n+2} & (i, j > m) \\
\sigma_{ij} = B_i B_j Q_{12} & (i \leqslant m, j > m \quad \text{or} \quad i > m, j \leqslant m)
\end{array}\right\} \qquad (10.65)$$

where, in (10.65) the term Q_{12} is the covariance between C_{n+1} and C_{n+2}. Substitution into (10.58) yields

$$V = \sum_{i=1}^{m} x_i^2 Q_{1i} + \sum_{i=m+1}^{n} x_i^2 Q_{2i} + Q_{n+1} \sum_{i=1}^{m} x_i^2 B_i^2 + Q_{n+2} \sum_{i=m+1}^{n} x_i^2 B_i^2$$

$$+ Q_{n+1} \sum_{\substack{i=1 \\ i \neq j}}^{m} \sum_{j=1}^{m} x_i x_j B_i B_j + Q_{n+2} \sum_{\substack{i=m+1 \\ i \neq j}}^{n} \sum_{j=m+1}^{n} x_i x_j B_i B_j \qquad (10.66)$$

$$+ 2Q_{12} \sum_{i=1}^{m} \sum_{j=m+1}^{n} x_i x_j B_i B_j$$

which can be rewritten as

$$V = \sum_{i=1}^{m} x_i^2 Q_{1i} + x_{n+1}^2 Q_{n+1} + \sum_{i=m+1}^{n} x_i^2 Q_{2i} + x_{n+2}^2 Q_{n+2} \qquad (10.67)$$

$$+ 2Q_{12} \sum_{i=1}^{m} \sum_{j=m+1}^{n} x_i x_j B_i B_j$$

which can be seen to contain no less than $n + 2 + m(n - m)$ terms. Note that if $m = 0$ or $m = n$ the model would be single index and would contain only $n + 1$ terms. While (10.67) contains fewer terms than the MFC equivalent (about 423,000 for a 1,300 security problem if $m = 650$) it too is impracticable *unless the two indices are uncorrelated*. If this was the case then $Q_{12} = 0$ and there are only $n + 2$ terms. Clearly, it is highly desirable to select uncorrelated indices. Finally, note that the approach could be used with three, four or more indices and that the MFC model could be viewed as an n index model with *each security as its own index*.

The comparative performances of the MFC, single-idex and two-index models are most interesting. Clearly the index models have the enormous advantage of requiring much lower information requirements than MFC. However, as Sharpe (1963) himself pointed out in connection with his own single-index model:

> The assumptions of the diagonal model lie near one end of the spectrum of possible assumptions about the relationships among securities. The model's extreme simplicity enables the investigator to perform a portfolio analysis at a very small cost, as we have shown. However, it is entirely possible that this simplicity so restricts the security analyst in making his predictions that the value of the resulting portfolio analysis is also very small.

Investigating this possibility Sharpe conducted a small-scale experiment with 20 securities randomly selected from those traded on the New York Stock Exchange. The performances of these securities over the period 1940–51 was used to obtain two sets of data. Firstly, the mean returns and variances and covariances of returns over the period were obtained directly. Secondly, parameters of the diagonal model were estimated by regression techniques from the performance of the securities over the period. A portfolio analysis was then performed on each set of data. The results indicated that '...the 62 parameters of the diagonal model were able to capture a great deal of the information contained in the complete set of 230 historical relationships. An additional test, using a second set of 20 securities gave similar results.' Sharpe (1965) concluded that:

> These results are, of course, too fragmentary to be considered conclusive but they do suggest that the diagonal model may be able to represent the relationship among securities rather well and thus that the value of the portfolio analyses based on the model will exceed their rather nominal cost. For these reasons it appears to be an excellent choice for the practical applications of the Markowitz procedure.

Subsequently, a considerable amount of further testing has been undertaken. Wallingford (1967), like Sharpe, employed samples containing just 20 securities, but he conducted experiments using actual historical data and as an alternative, simulated data. Within this context two-index models produced more efficient portfolios than single-index models. This is not altogether surprising and indeed must be the case if the increased cost resulting from the use of two indices is to be justified.

However, a study conducted shortly before Wallingford's work (the results of which in fact surprised and motivated Wallingford) by Cohen and Pogue (1967) found that the single-index model outperformed a two-index model. Cohen and Pogue used 150 randomly selected common stocks and found that the MFC model, naturally, generated the dominant efficiency frontier but, in the context of their study, found that Sharpe's single-index model matched or outperformed a two-index model based upon that outlined above. What explanations can be offered for this result? First, as Cohen and Pogue themselves pointed out, their sample, being entirely of common stocks, was fairly homogeneous and thus particularly suitable for single-index treatment. This fact alone, however, is not sufficient to explain away their results. There is, of course, the outside possibility that some peculiarities of the sample or of the indices used could have influenced the results. This seems unlikely, however. A much more likely explanation was provided by Wallingford. While Cohen and Pogue drew from a 'fairly large universe' of common stocks they added institutional constraints (arbitrary diversification rules) limiting the amount invested in any one security. Wallingford's work did not do this. In Wallingford's words: 'This reduction in the size of the universe and the elimination of the investment constraints is a major deviation from the Cohen and Pogue analysis and may help to explain any differences in the results of the studies.' Thus the two studies are not directly comparable.

The quality of information is of great importance. As Francis and Archer (1971) point out: 'The efficient portfolios generated by portfolio analysis are no better than the statistical inputs on which they are based.' Francis and Archer suggest three different approaches for generating the data inputs required: '(a) ex-post data may be tabulated and projected into the future with or without being adjusted; (b) ex-ante probability distributions can be compiled; or (c) a simple econometric relationship may be used to forecast returns'. They further suggest that: 'Ideally, all three approaches should be pursued independently for each of the n assets. These independent forecasts could then be compared and contrasted by a committee of security analysts and a concensus of opinion reached as a final step in security analysis. This final *consensus of opinion* would represent the best attainable statistics and could be given to the portfolio analyst.' There is much to commend a combined approach rather than exclusive reliance on historical data or prior probability distributions.

Approach (a) involves calculating historical values for the security returns, variances and covariances, possibly adjusted on a subjective basis as a result of changed company or economic circumstances. Approach (b) ideally develops subjective probability distributions of returns to each security over all possible business conditions that may obtain—rather a tall order.

Approach (c) generates the required inputs using regression analysis. Blume (1970) carried out an investigation of some simple econometric forecasting models. While concluding that security returns conformed more closely to a non-normal *stable Paretian distribution* than to a normal distribution, he found that the assumptions underlying the least-squares regression model (regarding the error terms) were not significantly violated in the post-war period. In common with approach (a) this third method encounters difficulty in respect of new issues.

The consequences of Blume's stable-Paretian result, and Fama's (1965) subsequent work seem ominous. The particular form of the Paretian distribution that described the *ex-post* returns of many assets has *infinite* variance. If this was also the case for *ex-ante* returns, the Markowitz model would appear to be unusable. In fact there are two possible ways out of the difficulty. Firstly, variance need not be used as the measure of risk. Secondly, if variance was chosen approximations could be made to restrict variances to finite values. Fried (1970) has suggested a method of obtaining *a priori* distributions of asset returns for Markowitz-type models using standard forecasting methods and has provided a rationale for the continued use of these models despite the presence of infinite variance in the *ex-post* distribution of asset returns.

Quality of information—or the lack of it—can be used to provide an excuse for never considering the methods. Firth (1975) reported that: '. . . it is worth noting that many managers say that until analysts' forecasting abilities improve, further development of portfolio theory or its application is not warranted. The contention is that the resources spent on portfolio forecasting techniques and on the formation of probability distributions.'

It must be said that the uptake of the models even by the larger investors has been disappointing to say the least. There is a number of good reasons for this. In addition, however, a number of dubious excuses have been proferred from time to time.

Whilst computational costs for the simplified models need not be excessive in respect of the obtaining of an original portfolio, there is the problem of updating. As time goes on fresh data on prices, returns and variances come in. The updating means further work for the analysts and more computing expenses. Significant changes in parameters can render the original efficient portfolio very inefficient. There are also various legal and administrative constraints that will need to be incorporated. Taxation can give rise to complex problems and ideally we should include all variable costs that are identified with the portfolio. These problems have been considered by various authors.

Mao (1970) Evans and Archer (1968) and Latane and Young (1969) have examined some of the problems caused by non-zero transactions and information costs. While further work by Pogue (1970) has extended the basic Markowitz model to include the possibility of selling short as well as transactions costs, leverage policies and the effects of taxation. Under these circumstances by no means all available securities will be included in a portfolio and the problems arise of how many and which securities to include in a portfolio. A marginal analysis of the sosts and benefits of increased diversification is undoubtedly required to answer the former question but selection criteria are still a source of some debate.

As regards the *dynamics* of portfolio management, clearly over time the information available changes a portfolio that is on the efficiency frontier at time t may not be on the frontier at time $t + 1$. Smith (1967) developed a model for portfolio revision which takes account of both transaction costs and capital gains taxation, and Evans (1970) presented an evaluation of the *buy-and-hold* strategy and a version of the *fixed-proportions* strategy. The buy-and-hold strategy is that the investor should sell securities a predetermined number of periods after their purchase, reinvesting dividends in the securities on which they were paid. The fixed-proportions strategy differs from buy and hold in that reinvestment is such as to maintain the original holdings of the various assets proportionately in monetary terms. Evans assumed equal proportionate holdings and discovered that the choice between the two rules depended upon the amounts of the initial investments and the marginal capital gains tax rate of the investor. There has been a good deal of work done, of an essentially descriptive nature, on the performance of mutual funds and other large public portfolios in the United States. Francis and Archer (1971) cite evidence that the performance of mutual funds is poor and results from poor management practices, principally *naïve diversification*. A study by Farrar (1965) however, comparing mutual fund portfolios to efficient portfolios produced by the Markowitz model, found that the characteristics of the mutual funds portfolios were similar to those of corresponding efficient portfolios. This study shows the mutual funds in the best light. In contrast, Cohen and Pogue (1967) found that even when using as naïve an estimate of expected return as the average of past returns the performance of portfolios that were selected by the Markowitz model was as good as, or better than, the actual performance of the mutual funds.

There have been numerous tests where the performance of a *randomly generated* portfolio of shares has been compared with the performance of a selected portfolio, such as a unit trust or mutual fund. In a detailed study of 115 United States mutual funds over the 10-year period from 1955 to 1964, Jensen (1972) found that the risk–return combination for 58 of the funds was below the market line, they performed less well than the index of general market performance. As would be expected, a number of funds *did* perform better than the index, but Jensen found no evidence that certain funds consistently perform better than the norm. Above-average performance in one period was not associated with above-average performance in other periods. This confirms the findings of other studies. It has been shown with UK unit trusts that during 1964–66 the average unit trust performed no better than random portfolios selected from the same industries in which the trusts themselves invested.

Thus the empirical work gives reason to suppose that the performance of large investors on the stock market could be usefully improved and much progress has now been made in many of the theoretical problems. It is hoped that the methods will be taken up on an increased scale in the future.

10.6 The Capital Market and Asset Prices

If all investors always used portfolio theory what would be the consequences for the capital market? The theory that has come to be called *capital market theory* attempts to answer this question. The capital asset pricing approach to investment decision-making arises from a market populated by Markowitz investors and an examination of capital market theory (CMT) is needed to give context to the asset-pricing approach. A large number of assumptions are made by CMT. The precise number depends on how they are aggregated and how philosophical one chooses to be. To the list below should strictly be added a provision allowing short sales of any asset. However, short sales are not allowed by Sharpe's (1963) original model and in this respect Sharpe's model differs from other general equilibrium models of asset prices deduced from Markowitz's pioneer work. Since we shall be mainly discussing Sharpe's model and modifications of it the assumption is not included in the list.

The assumptions fall into two categories. First there are those underlying the individual portfolio analysis (1–6, 9, 10, 11 and possibly 8 and 12). Then there are further assumptions needed to ensure the operations of a perfect market in capital assets. Here is one version of the list of assumptions:

(1) Investments are judged on the basis of return.
(2) Returns are visualized in stochastic fashion by investors.
(3) Risk is proportional to variance of return.
(4) Investors act as if they maximize expected utility which is expressible as a function of expected return and variance of return.
(5) Investors are 'rational'.
(6) Investors are risk averse.
(7) No monopolistic forces in the market (atomism).
(8) No taxes.
(9) No transaction costs.
(10) Costless information.
(11) Continuously divisible investments.
(12) Unlimited borrowings and lendings ar risk-free rate of interest.
(13) All investors have the same probability distribution of future rates of return ('idealized uncertainty').
(14) All investors have the same one-period time horizon.

(15) All investors are Markowitz efficient.

(16) No unanticipated inflation.

(17) All assets available in fixed quantities.

(18) Capital market equilibrium exists.

Clearly, much courage is required to erect a substantial edifice of theory on the basis of these assumptions. Economists have never lacked such courage. Indeed some have been quite brazen about it. Here are some of the consequences that would follow if the assumptions held.

All investors would face the same return–risk diagram as shown in Figure 10.2. The 'opportunity set' of efficient risk–return combinations would be the whole of the straight line through R_f and M (*not* terminating at M due to the possibility of borrowing). Clearly, such combinations dominate the efficiency frontier (FF') comprised of *all*-risky investments. The straight line is the *capital market line* (CML) and would be identical for all investors. This means that there is just *one* portfolio of risky assets (M) that is combined with the riskless asset. Here, M is called the *market portfolio*. The *separability theorem* states that all investors from the conservative to the cavalier should hold the same mix of stocks (i.e. M) in their portfolio. This result contradicts the 'interior decorator fallacy' in which a 'skilled' analyst is supposed to furnish a client with an individual portfolio to suit the client's psychology. The point is that both the adventurous and the cautious should combine the market portfolio *only*, with the riskless asset. The only difference would be in the point selected on the line. Thus in Figure 10.13 the conservative Mr A selects portfolio P_A, putting a considerable proportion of his funds into the riskless asset, while the happy-go-lucky Mr B *borrowing* at the rate R_f puts more than his original budget into the market portfolio and selects portfolio P_B. The question arises as to the content of the market portfolio. Since no investors will hold risky portfolios other than M and since all securities are held by somebody it follows that M must contain *all* marketable assets.

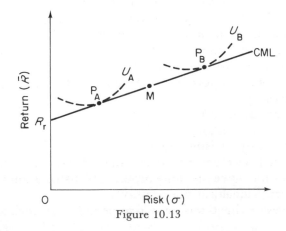

Figure 10.13

Recall that we are assuming no transactions costs or for that matter any other decision-making or implementation costs. It is alright then, for the 'Pru', Granny and Mr Sleeveace to have 1,200 or so securities each in their portfolios. (In reality the average number held is about four or five.)

What of the equation of the CML? This is readily obtained. If $\bar{R}_p$ and σ_p represent expected return and standard deviation on any CML portfolio then since the CML is a straight line we can write

$$\bar{R}_p = a + b\sigma_p \tag{10.68}$$

where a and b are constants. The point $(0, R_f)$ is on the line (a portfolio could consist entirely of the riskless asset) thus

$$R_f = a + b(0) = a$$

Also, the market portfolio is on the line so that

$$\bar{R}_M = a + b_M$$

$$= R_f + b_M$$

$$\therefore \quad b = \frac{R_M - R_f}{\sigma_M}$$

where $\bar{R}_M$ and σ_M are respectively expected return and standard deviation of return on the market portfolio. Thus the equation of the CML is

$$\bar{R}_p = R_f + \left[\frac{\bar{R}_M - R_f}{\sigma_M}\right]\sigma_p \tag{10.69}$$

In (10.69) the bracketed term is the slope of the line and can be thought of as the *price of risk* since in the circumstances assumed it represents the additional expected return required (by everyone) for each extra unit of risk. Knowing the equation of the CML would enable us to decide whether a portfolio was efficient (on the CML), inefficient (below the CML) or unobtainable (above the CML). Suppose that

$$\left.\begin{array}{l} \bar{R}_M = 14\% \\ \sigma_M = 5\% \\ R_f = 6\% \end{array}\right\} \text{CML data}$$

what is the status of the following portfolios?

Portfolio A : $\bar{R}_A = 20\%$ $\qquad \sigma_A = 10\%$

Portfolio B : $\bar{R}_B = 10\%$ $\qquad \sigma_B = 2.5\%$

Portfolio C : $\bar{R}_C = 30\%$ $\qquad \sigma_C = 15\%$

Portfolio D : $\bar{R}_D = 27\%$ $\qquad \sigma_D = 13\%$

To answer the question, first find the numerical equation of the CML, substitute the CML data into (10.69). The result is

$$\bar{R}_p = 6 + 1.6\sigma_p \tag{10.70}$$

Now consider portfolio A. We can ascertain its efficiency status by inserting either σ_A or $\bar{R}_A$ into (10.70). Putting in σ_A we find what $\bar{R}_A$ *should* be for an efficient portfolio. Thus

$$6 + 1.6(10) = 22$$

i.e. return should be 22% not 20%. So portfolio A is inefficient. Alternatively, inserting the return of 20% and solving for the corresponding standard deviation of an efficient portfolio

$$\sigma = \frac{20 - 6}{1.6} = 8.75$$

Thus given the expected return of 20% the standard deviation on portfolio A is too high by 1.25 percentage points. The situation is shown diagrammatically in Figure 10.14. The status of the remaining portfolios are similarly deduced and the reader may verify that B is efficient, C is also efficient, while D is unobtainable (superefficient) being above the CML.

So far we have been discussing portfolios rather than individual (non-portfolio) securities. The CML applies only to efficient portfolios and does not describe the relationship between the expected rate of return on individual assets (or on inefficient portfolios) and their standard deviations. The *capital asset pricing model* (CAPM) of Sharpe states that the expected return on *any* asset or portfolio (efficient or inefficient) is related to the riskless rate of return and the expected return on the market via the expression

$$\bar{R}_i = R_f + \beta_i(\bar{R}_M - R_f) \tag{10.71}$$

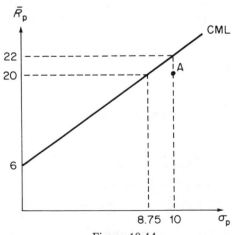

Figure 10.14

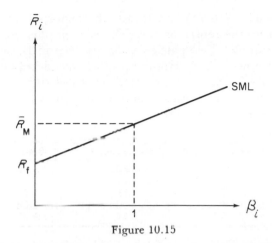

Figure 10.15

where $\bar{R}_i$ is the expected return on security i and where β_i, the *beta* co-efficient, is a measure of the sensitivity of return on an asset to movements in the market. This relationship is graphed in Figure 10.15.

The straight line, SML, is the *security market line*. If the value of β can be obtained for some security then its appropriate rate of return (and hence price) can be determined. For instance, if

$$R_f = 8\%$$
$$\bar{R}_M = 15\%$$

and

$$\beta_i = 0.6$$

then for this ith security or portfolio the expected return should be

$$\bar{R}_i = 8 + 0.6(15 - 8) = 12.2\%$$

If there is temporary disequilibrium in the market such that in fact $\bar{R}_i = 14\%$ then the security would be judged to be underpriced and consequent demand would force up the price until the expected return fell back to 12.2%.

Note that for the market portfolio itself (like all other portfolios, it is on the SML)

$$\bar{R}_M = R_f + \beta_M(\bar{R}_M - R_f)$$

$$\therefore \quad \beta_M = 1$$

i.e. the market portfolio beta is unity.

The excess of return on a security over the riskless return is called the *risk premium* for the security. That is:

$$\bar{R}_i - R_f = \text{risk premium } (i) = \beta_i(\bar{R}_M - R_f)$$

$$= \beta_i \text{ (risk premium on the market)}$$

or, putting equation (10.71) into words: the expected return on an asset should be equal to the return on the riskless asset plus the risk premium. Consider an example. Two particular assets, A and B, are known to lie on the security market line. Here, A, which has a beta of 0.5 carries a risk premium of 4%; B has an expected return of 20% along with a beta of 1.75. In the light of this information, determine whether the following securities are over- or underpriced:

Security No.	Expected return	Beta
1	20	2.00
2	14	0.75
3	15	1.25
4	5	-0.25
5	31	3.25

In terms of the CAPM, being on the SML is being correctly priced. If there is temporary disequilibrium in the market and the return on some asset i is higher than that given by the SML then the security is underpriced. Raising the price—other things being equal— will lower the expected return. If the market mechanism is working ideally the price will continue to rise (because buyers demand the asset as a super-good investment) until the level of return on the asset reaches the SML value. Conversely, if the level of return is too low, given the beta value—and the security is thus below the line—the price should be marked down until the level of return rises to that given by the SML—or there will be no buyers.

Now we must establish the values of $\bar{R}_M$ and R_f. The data given for security A enable us to write

$$4 = 0.5(\bar{R}_M - R_f)$$

so that $\bar{R}_M - R_f = 8$, and for security B:

$$20 = R_f + 1.75(\bar{R}_M - R_f)$$

Thus

$$20 = R_f + 1.75(8) \qquad \therefore \quad R_f = 6$$

So the equation of the SML is

$$\bar{R}_i = 6 + 8\beta_i$$

For equilibrium pricing the values of $\bar{R}$ and β for each security must satisfy this relationship. In the case of security one, given $\beta_1 = 2$ the expected return given by the SML is 22. Thus security one's return is too low. This means that it is at present *over*priced. Security two's return need only be 12% so that it is underpriced. Security three's return is one percentage point too low so that it is overpriced. Security four—a prized specimen with negative β—has an expected rate of return *less* than the riskless rate—a negative risk premium for a security which has, in effect, negative risk. With $\beta_4 = -0.25$ the SML return should be 4%. So that security four is in fact *under*priced. Despite being 31% security five's return is too low—thus it is overpriced.

Since efficient portfolios are on both the CML and the SML, for some efficient portfolio, i, we can write

$$\bar{R}_i = R_f + \left[\frac{\bar{R}_M - R_f}{\sigma_M}\right]\sigma_i \ldots \text{CML}$$

and

$$\bar{R}_i = R_f + \beta_i(\bar{R}_M - R_f) \ldots \text{SML}$$

so that for efficient portfolios only

$$\beta_i = \frac{\sigma_i}{\sigma_M}$$

Either β_i or σ_i is a complete measure or risk for these portfolios. Individual securities and most portfolios do not lie on the CML so that they are not perfectly correlated with the market so that, in turn, not *all* the variation of return on these assets can be attributed to the market. After the market has played its part there is some idiosyncratic variability remaining. This is called *unsystematic risk*. Beta measures *systematic risk*. The unsystematic risk can, theoretically, be completely eliminated by proper diversification whereas systematic risk cannot. So that for a security within a fully diversified portfolio, only the risk that is measured by beta will remain. The implication here is that only the systematic risk should count in determining the risk premium.

There is a specific relationship between the beta for an asset and the correlation of the asset's and the market's returns. The relationship is

$$\beta_i = r_{im} \cdot \frac{\sigma_i}{\sigma_M} \tag{10.72}$$

where r_{im} is the correlation coefficient. If $r_{im} = 1$ the portfolio is on the CML and $\beta_i = \sigma_i/\sigma_M$. Note that if $r_{im} = 0$ then $\beta_i = 0$ no matter what the value of σ_i. In other words if an asset could be found that was completely uncorrelated with the market then no matter how high the variance of its return it should have *no* risk premium; its price would adjust so as to give the same return as the riskless asset.

There is no reason (in theory) why r_{im} should not be negative. An asset that is negatively correlated with the market would attract a *negative* risk premium—its price would adjust so as to give an expected rate of return *less* than on the riskless asset no matter how variable the return may be. It is not surprising to find that securities with negative betas are as hard to trap as the physicists' neutrino.

The negative risk premium result should not be too surprising. We have already seen two ways in which a similar effect could arise in capital budgeting proper. Recall the result that a project with negative ENPV in its own right could be attractive if taken in combination with a more productive investment with which it has negatively correlated returns. Then there is the capital-rationing case where an investment that *provides* funds at the right time could be attractive even if it has negative NPV when discounted at the objective function rate or some external rate.

Clearly the asset pricing model has implications for capital budgeting provided capital market theory is a reasonable model of reality. While in the final analysis this is an *empirical* question, it is instructive to take a second look at the assumptions.

(1) Is uncontentious. Most investors do think in terms of yield.

(2) Highly improbable at face value. But investors are aware, if only vaguely, of possible variations in return so perhaps they behave *as if* they see returns in probabilistic form.

(3) Variance is not perfect as a measure of risk but neither is anything else. Variance is by far the most widely used measure.

(4) A reasonable formalization of the investor's attempt to make the right purchasing decision *ex ante*.

(5) Economists have, rather arrogantly, taken a narrow carrot-to-the-donkey view of 'rationality'. However, few investors stand up at shareholders' meetings and ask for less returns.

(6) This is intuitively reasonable, and the general tendency of stock-market investors to hold portfolios rather than a single asset with the greatest expected return is prima facie evidence of risk aversion.

(7) This is untrue. There are several very big fish that hold significant proportions of some companies' equity and in fact at time of crisis play a decisive role in management.

(8) This clearly does not hold. What are the consequences a priori? After-tax returns will be the relevant considerations. Optimal portfolios for institutions and persons who are tax exempt will differ from those for taxpayers. The optimal portfolios of those paying different marginal rates of tax will also vary. So there will be different CMLs for different investors. Indeed, since the marginal tax position of an investor will vary with the *amount* of return rather than the *rate* this makes an added complication. Since CMLs are now different, an investor operating below some CML would no longer be necessarily inefficient. Investors would also see different SMLs depending on their tax situation. It follows that a static equilibrium set of prices for securities will not emerge in a tax environment that discriminates between investors.

Returns *can* be expressed in after-tax form without undue difficulty. Before tax the actual return on security is given by

$$R_i = \left| \frac{P_{1i} + d_i}{P_{0i}} - 1 \right| 100\% \qquad (10.73)$$

(recall that a one-period horizon is used in the model). Now re-expressing

(10.73) we can write

$$R_i = \left| \frac{(P_{1i} - P_{0i}) + d_i}{P_{0i}} \right| 100\% \tag{10.74}$$

where the excess of end of period price over current price is capital gain and d_i is income. Thus for the jth investor facing a flat gains tax of $100g\%$ and marginal income tax at $100j\%$ we can write

$$R_{itj} = \left| \frac{(P_{1i} - P_{0i})(1 - g) + d_i(1 - j)}{P_{0i}} \right| 100\% \tag{10.75}$$

where it will be noted in (10.75) a subscript for the individual investor is attached to the rate of return.

(9) This assumption certainly does not hold. The consequence is that the CML and the SML now become *banded*. In Figure 10.16 the security market band is shown as the region between the hatched lines. The precise nature of these bands (location, slope, width, parallelism) depends on the nature, in detail, of the transactions costs and how they vary between individuals. At any rate both the CML and SML can be said to be *obscured* since different investors may hold different risky portfolios. In the diagram at point I is located a security which, in the absence of transactions costs would have been underpriced and attractive. However, investors will not buy because of the expenses. Transactions costs can be enormous for certain non-stock market assets (selling a house for example) and indeed some assets can be viewed as having infinite transactions costs. An example would be provided by certain trusts and another by one's own skills. It turns out that the effect of infinite transactions costs is the same as having incomplete information. The model is not destroyed by such phenomena, but needs modification.

Getting back to the CML, the market portfolio now becomes inefficient if the expected return is taken net of transactions costs. However, far fewer than the 1,000 plus securities on the market are needed to ensure

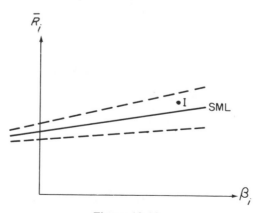

Figure 10.16

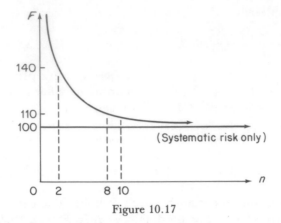

Figure 10.17

almost complete diversification. In this case almost all risk is systematic and *diminishing returns* apply to diversification. The decline in unsystematic risk as the number of securities rises is quite marked as is shown in Figure 10.17.

The total level of risk in a portfolio (as a percentage of that for a fully diversified portfolio) is shown on the vertical scale as F and the number of randomly selected securities in the portfolio, n, is shown on the horizontal scale. With two securities in the portfolio, standard deviation of about 40% above the systematic level could be expected. With 8 or 10 securities it is less than 10% above the minimum level. Thus the marginal gains from diversification rapidly fall (although somewhat less dramatically than this, it would appear, from UK work) to the level where they are cancelled by the transactions costs. So if transactions costs are not too large, limited diversification will produce a portfolio near to the CML. The practical situation, then, may not be quite so bad as at first it appeared. Indeed in some ways it is desirable since it provides relief from

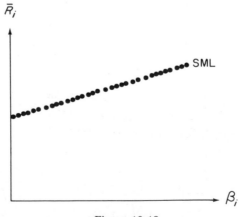

Figure 10.18

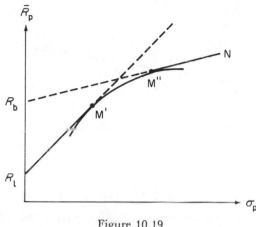

Figure 10.19

the result—so widely at variance with reality—that all investors must hold the market portfolio.

(10) We have already seen that information requirements and the costs associated with them are one of the main drawbacks of portfolio theory. Information commands a price—as many will testify who make their living from it.

(11) Technically this does not hold. Outside of the stock market of course, it does not hold *a fortiori*. Considering shares, however, the effect is minimal—we simply move from continuous straight lines to sets of closely spaced discrete points. This is illustrated for the SML in Figure 10.18. The degree of approximation involved in assuming continuity is negligible.

(12) This is clearly not the case. If we relax this assumption in the simplest fashion, supposing there to be just two interest rates—a uniform rate for borrowing (R_b) and one for lending (R_l) then the CML now appears as in Figure 10.19. The CML falls into *three* segments: R_lM' for investors combining risky portfolio M' with the risk-free lending rate; M'M" which is a segment of the original all-risky frontier (investors finding tangency here would neither borrow nor lend), and M"N (and beyond) for investors supplementing their original funds by borrowing at R_b and putting all into the risky portfolio M". The CML as a whole is then R_l, M', M", N. There remain a number of problems:

(i) R_b may differ between investors depending on their creditworthiness (big companies, 'personal loans').

(ii) For any individual the rate may depend upon the sum borrowed (in which case there would be further segments beyond N).

(iii) The rate may depend upon the investment—recall those chilling words: 'The bank would like to know for what purpose you require the money.'

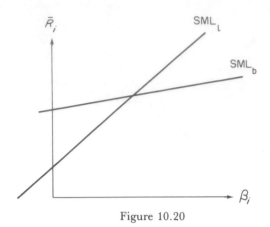

Figure 10.20

Returning to the simple two-rate case, in terms of the SML there would be one SML for lending and one for borrowing, but the relationship between the two is ill defined, although the general appearance would be as in Figure 10.20. Again, there would be no static equilibrium prices for securities.

(13) This is another of the unlikely information requirements of a perfect market (accurate, complete, fully and instantly disseminated, and costless). Performing their calculations on the basis of different expectations investors would arrive at different risky frontiers and so different CMLs. Both the CML and the SML would be blurred and, as in some of the other cases *only major disequilibria would be identifiable* and correctible within limits.

(14) There are undoubtedly significant differences in the time perspectives of investors, even if these are broadly defined as long, medium or short term. The effect of dropping this assumption would be to make estimates of returns and variances different between investors with different horizons and so both the CML and SML will again differ between investors. There is also here the question of multiperiod analysis. Multiperiod models are becoming available in which use is made of the estimated term structure of interest rates. It is possible that significant use will be made of these models in the future and that the obscuring effects of differences in horizon are not too great.

(15) If not all investors were completely efficient Markowitz diversifiers then there would be blurrings of the SML since a given asset would be differently attractive to different investors depending upon how well they were diversified. In a market consisting of naïve diversifiers prices would tend to relate returns to *total* risk in an asset. This would make for a flat efficiency frontier. We should expect a higher correlation coefficient for the estimated CML than for the SML since CML is plotted against total risk. This does seem to be the case. Many investors do hold fewer than 10 securities (how many does the reader have?).

(16) The consequences of dropping this assumption (another of the

information assumptions) are contentious and difficult to ascertain. However, as recent UK experience has shown, sweeping, arbitrary redistributions of income and wealth can occur under inflation. Profitability, returns and prices are all affected. The picture would again be clouded and there is no consensus on the details. It is the *unanticipated* component of inflation that is troublesome here. It might be argued that experience improves foresight in this respect.

(17) This is reasonable enough over not too long a period. There will be, however, some problems concerning entirely new issues from the forecasting point of view (no historical data).

(18) The theory has not hesitated to stretch credibility in other areas and as with the other assumptions it is important *how far* they are from holding. The market is not strictly in equilibrium at some moment if one price is out by one penny, but clearly this is trivial. Trading is a necessary consequence of disequilibrium. The existence of trading is proof that not all investors are satisfied with their holdings and so are not in equilibrium. The excess demand for assets is not zero while trading is going on.

The *joint* consequences of errant assumptions are even more obscuring, but, it should be recalled, the theory, though still evolving, is the only comprehensive theory of capital markets—which must make it attractive. At the end of the day we must ask if a theory is *useful*—specifically does it provide improved predictions? If the market is in disequilibrium does the theory help us to understand how the situation arises and will develop? All models *must* be unrealistic in some respects or they would not be models. Professor Friedman has argued that it is only the predictions of a model that count. At face value this is true, but it is hard to see how a model can *consistently* give good predictions without having many significant, though not necessarily obvious, correspondences with reality. An example would be if we decided to construct a model (in this case physical) to predict the time shown on the dial of a wristwatch. Suppose we specify that our model shall be composed of cast iron and concrete and have *no moving parts*. Ludicrous! But consider the sundial. In climates superior to the UK's our model will give consistently accurate predictions, but as a description of the innards of a watch it leaves something to be desired. Models which are *genuinely* ludicrous in construction will give genuinely ludicrous predictions—otherwise there are parallels which, if properly interpreted, *can* give a description too.

There are a number of difficulties concerned with the testing of capital market theory. The analysis suggests relationships between *ex-ante* returns and expected risk, so that a test of the theory ought to employ prior distributions of returns and not *ex-post* data, although there is no doubt that historical data will considerably influence expectations. There are also technical econometric problems and there has been some persuasive criticism on methodological grounds of the tests conducted so far. The results, then, should not be relied upon for more than general indications.

Work by Sharpe (1965, 1966) testing the CML, showed that some 70%

of differences on the portfolios of mutual funds in returns were attributable to differences in risk as measured by standard deviation. Sharpe surveyed 34 mutual funds over the period 1954–63. Sharpe found that the return–risk relationship was approximately linear—except for the region of high risk. A possible explanation of the non-linearity in the high risk region being that high risk portfolios were less well diversified than others. Jensen (1969) testing the SML, considered 115 mutual funds over the period 1955–65, found that high returns were associated with high systematic risk. Lintner (1965) amd Douglas (1969) both found that the risk premium on assets depended, in part, on unsystematic risk. This result would be expected with less than complete diversification. However, these studies have been subject to criticism (bias in testing procedures, use of ex-post returns). Work by Black, Jensen and Scholes (1972) in a study of all the shares traded on the New York Stock Exchange found good, straight line fits for the SML, but again this study has been shown to have faults. It is therefore an open question as to whether or not the CAPM provides a reasonable approximation to the behaviour of individual securities on stock exchanges.

10.7 CAPM and Capital Budgeting

The capital budgeting implications of the CAPM are interesting. Figure 10.21 contrasts a rigid cost of capital approach with an SML-based approach to investment appraisal. In the figure R_c represents a cost of capital figure which is to be used as a cut-off rate for assessing investments. Using the SML, anything below the SML would be rejected and anything above it would be accepted. The shaded regions are the sets of return/beta combinations that would be judged similarly by the two criteria. Thus both criteria would accept the project giving combination I and both would find J unacceptable. The shaded regions are *regions of agreement*. The two approaches, rigidly applied, would give conflicting recommendations regarding K and L. The cost of capital method would reject L because it gives insufficient return. The CAPM would accept it because the low return is more than offset by the low systematic risk. In

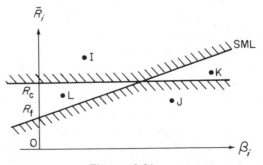

Figure 10.21

contrast, the cost of capital method would accept K but CAPM would reject it because of insufficient return to offset high systematic risk.

Before discussing this conflict, note first of all that there is, in a sense, going to be more agreement than disagreement since the shaded regions are 'larger' than the unshaded ones. Also, the nearer is R_f to R_c, the cost of capital figure, and the smaller the slope of SML then the less will be the disagreement. Thus in the final analysis it is once more an empirical question as to whether there is *substantial* disagreement between SML and cost of capital approach. It also matters, of course, what proportion of projects that come along fall within the unshaded region. It is not impossible that for a particular firm over a number of years hardly any projects fall in the unshaded region. This may not be a chance phenomenon, but could result from the *character* of projects available. Thus it *may* be that in practice it matters little which approach is used—but this is another open empirical question.

Consider such disagreement as there will be. Of course, if *all* the conditions underlying SML hold good then the SML decisions must be correct and the cost of capital decisions are in error, and rigid use of a cost of capital method would tend towards acceptance of higher risk, relatively unprofitable projects and would tend away from sufficiently profitable lower risk projects. However, suppose that the ownership of the company is undiversified. Then the SML decisions could be disastrous. True, L may have low systematic risk, *as part of a fully diversified portfolio*, but at the same time it might have very high total risk. In contrast, K's total risk may be little higher than its systematic component and SML might reject it in favour of some highly speculative proposition. We have already seen reasons why investors may not diversify enough to make CAPM justifiable. Outside of the stock market there may be another, *altogether more compelling reason* for little or no diversification: the ownership does not want to diversify. Entrepreneurs may get considerable utility from running a business they know well, and considerable disutility from attempting to play the market. A man who adopts someone else's utility function is a fool. *De gustibus non est disputandum*—there is *no* arguing about tastes. Individual shareholders may achieve considerable disutility from attempting to manage a portfolio. Tastes are data. It is not possible to sustain a view of individual rationality that implies that it is 'rational' to act *against* one's preferences—whatever these may be.

In an SML-based approach to investment appraisal investments giving expected return/beta combinations below the line would be rejected. Acceptable investments should be on or above the line. The presence of any investment *off* the line at all implies disequilibrium. Outside of the very short term the mere *existence* of large positive NPVs (unless forecast or discount rate errors exist) implies market imperfections in respect of divisibility, fixed charges, opportunities and information. 'The market' *simply is as it is*. To use NPV to advantage individual firms do not need an edifice of economy-wide theory. If there exist substantial rents then there exist substantial rents and that is that. As regards disagreement between SML and cost of capital approaches, the lower the risk premium on the market the more agreement there is between the methods. In this context the measure of 'agreement' is not philosophical but relates to the percentage of projects for which SML and cost of capital give the same answers.

For well-diversified firms the SML approach has much in its favour. However, this would not entail the abandonment of NPV. The important difference would be in the discount rates that were employed. Ideally, each project would have its own discount rate according to its systematic risk as measured by the beta coefficient. The discount rate in any year would then depend on the risk-free rate of interest and the market risk premium in the year. If the risk-free rate can be forecast over the project's lifetime and assuming a constant risk premium on the market the discount rate in any year can be calculated. So, to find the discount rate to apply to a project in a given year, forecast the spot rate (for the risk-free rate) for that year and add a proportion (β) of the market premium. Then discount in the normal way. Various simplifications could be made to this method. Projects could be placed into various, fairly broad *risk classes*. The risk classes would be decided not by total risk—but by systematic risk. An average β value would be used for the whole class. This is the modern variation of the risk permium approach.

Of course, the crucial question is whether or not the investor is well diversified. Many firms and most individuals are nowhere near fully diversified. Many know this and have no intention of further diversification. In the case of individuals this may, in part, be due to transactions and management costs. For firms, the 'line of business' argument is heard. The use of CAPM by inadequately diversified investors would lead to the acceptance of undesirably high total risk projects and the acceptance of unprofitable low return investments.

Both the CAPM and the cost of capital approaches, in actual use, are approximate methods. It would not be surprising to find agreement (the same accept/reject decision) in 90% of cases. An interesting experiment would be to conduct a simulation using Figure 10.21. In crude guise it could proceed as follows. Arbitrarily assign a maximum return figure (this could be varied in sensitivity work) then randomly select 50 (say) points in a rectangle marked out by the axes, the maximum return and some pre-assigned maximum beta value. Select a cost of capital value, then, for various combinations of the SML parameters (intercept and slope) see what proportion of the points fall in the unshaded areas. In such a simple framework analytical results would be possible too. The exercise is left to the willing reader.

It is a consequence of the CAPM that a company itself need not bother about diversification in its own investment programme—the shareholders can, in principle, do this by buying other shares. It has been suggested that such a drastic policy would be ameliorated by separation of ownership and management—the managers gaining considerable utility from the survival of the company. Companies changing their policies in this direction would be well advised to inform the ownership—before the event.

The picture of Figure 10.21 is highly simplified. Sharply drawn lines are misleading—there are many blurred edges. In addition the cost of capital users are not so simple minded; other factors are 'taken into account'. Such an expression may be theoretically unsatisfactory but the question is *how well does it work?* There are other alternatives to the CAPM than the plain cost of capital rule of thumb. We have seen a number earlier on and also have seen how limited diversification could be allowed for by considering the total activities of the company.

There are other reasons why CAPM presents difficulty; one of the main ones being the unsatisfactory and as yet incomplete state of multi-period models. Considerable work has been done in the last few years on more advanced versions of the asset pricing model (including some encouraging results regarding non-marketable assets) with relaxations of some of the less likely assumptions. Some of the analysis involved is rather complex, the attractive simplicity of the original Sharpe–Lintner model falling by the wayside.

It is however with these more involved models that the future of the asset pricing approach lies. In a review article, Jensen (1972) concluded that: 'The currently available empirical evidence seems to indicate that the simple version of the asset pricing model does not provide an adequate description of the structure of expected returns', although, significantly, no non-portfolio risk measure is systematically related to *ex-ante* expected returns. The basic model, though surprisingly robust regarding the relaxation of assumptions in many respects, needs further work. It has certainly, through stimulating both theoretical and empirical research, brought much greater understanding of how asset prices are formed. When the difficulties with multiperiod versions of the CAPM are fully overcome, and when problems of estimating the parameters required by CAPM in project selection are somewhat eased, practical application of the CAPM will be feasible on a much wider scale than at present and the method will cease to be so much more intricate than a sophisticated marginal weighted average approach. We should recall the discussion earlier in the chapter that CAPM and cost of capital need not always be at loggerheads. There may be little difference in practice between groups of projects selected by CAPM and those selected by WACC. Indeed, theoretically—as Partington (1981) points out—in some cases the WACC will be the same as the discount rate derived from the direct application of the CAPM. In general, the measurement of a firm's average cost of capital may require estimates of security returns by use of the CAPM.

Furthermore, future direct applications of the CAPM to project selection may be viewed as an acknowledgement of the importance of the cost of capital at the margin, rather than as discrediting the entire cost of capital concept. As Partington (1981) concludes: 'There is much to recommend the use of CAPM in the selection of investment projects. However, there are practical problems in the implementation of the CAPM approach'. 'Further investigation of the cost of capital concept may provide new insights into financial theory and new roles for the concept itself. Therefore, it is perhaps premature to sever the link provided by the cost of capital between the firm's investment and financing decisions.'

References

Ball, R., and Brown, P. (1969), 'Portfolio theory and accounting', *Journal of Accounting Research*, Autumn.

Black, F., Jensen, M. C., and Scholes, M. (1972), 'The capital asset pricing model: some empirical tests', in Jensen, M. C. (ed.), *Studies in the Theory of Capital Markets*, Praeger, New York.

Blume, M. (1970), 'Portfolio theory: a step towards its practical application', *Journal of Business*, **43**, April.

Cohen, K. J., and Pogue, J. A. (1967), 'An empirical evaluation of alternative portfolio selection models', *Journal of Business*, April.

Douglas, G. W. (1969), 'Risk in the equity markets: an empirical appraisal of market efficiency', *Yale Economic Essays*, **9**, Spring.

Evans, J. L. (1970), 'An analysis of portfolio maintenance strategies', *Journal of Finance*, **25**, June.

Evans, J. L., and Archer, S. H. (1968), 'Diversification and the reduction of dispersion: an empirical analysis', *Journal of Finance*, **23**, December.

Fama, E. (1965a), 'The behaviour of stock market prices', *Journal of Business*, **38**, January.

Fama, E. (1965b), 'Portfolio analysis in a stable paretian market', *Management Science*, **12**, January.

Farrar, D. E. (1965), *The Investment Decision under Uncertainty*, Prentice-Hall, Englewood Cliffs, NJ.

Firth, M. (1975), *Investment Analysis: Techniques of Appraising the British Stock Market*, Harper and Row, New York.

Francis, J. C., and Archer, S. H. (1971), *Portfolio Analysis*, Prentice-Hall, Englewood Cliffs, NJ.

Fried, J. (1970), 'Forecasting and probability distribution for models of portfolio selection', *Journal of Finance*, **25**, June.

Jensen, M. C. (1972), 'Capital markets: theory and evidence', *Bell Journal of Economics and Management Science*, **3**, No. 2, Autumn.

Lintner, J. (1965), 'Security prices, risk and maximal gains from diversification', *Journal of Finance*, **20**, December.

Lintner, J., 'The evaluation of risk assets and the selection of risky investments in stock portfolios and capital budgets', *Review of Economics and Statistics*, **1965** (February).

Mao, J. C. T. (1970), 'Essentials of portfolio diversification strategy', *Journal of Finance*, **25**, December.

Markowitz, H. (1952), 'Portfolio analysis', *Journal of Finance*, **7**.

Partington, G. H. (1981), 'Financial decisions, the cost(s) of capital and the capital asset pricing model', *Journal of Business Finance and Accounting*, **8**, No. 1, Spring.

Pogue, J. A. (1970), 'An extension of the Markowitz portfolio selection model to include variable transaction costs, short sales, leverage policies and taxes', *Journal of Finance*, **25**, December.

Sharpe, W. F. (1963), 'A simplified model for portfolio analysis', *Management Science*, **9**.

Sharpe, W. F. (1965), 'Risk aversion on the stock market: Some empirical evidence', *Journal of Finance*, **20**.

Sharpe, W. F. (1966), 'Mutual fund performance', *Journal of Business*, **39**, (supplement).

Smith, K. V. (1967), 'A transition model for portfolio revision', *Journal of Finance*, **22**, September.

Wallingford, B. A. (1967), 'A survey and comparison of portfolio selection models', *Journal of Financial and Quantitative Analysis*, **2**, June.

Further Reading

Adler, M., 'On the risk–return trade-off in the valuation of assets', *Journal of Financial and Quantitative Analysis*, **4**, 1969.

Bicksler, J. L. (ed.), *Capital Market Equilibrium and Efficiency*, Lexington Books, Mass., 1977.

Bierman, H., and Smidt, S., 'Application of the capital asset pricing model to multi-period investments', *Journal of Business Finance and Accounting*, **2**, No. 3, Autumn 1975.

Blume, M., 'On the assessment of risk', *Journal of Finance*, **26**, March 1971.

Chen, A. H. Y., Jen, F. C., and Zionts, S., 'The optimal portfolio revision policy', *Journal of Business*, **44**, 1971.

Chen, A. H. Y., and Kim, E. H., 'Theories of corporate debt policy: a synthesis', *Journal of Finance*, **34**, May 1979.

Chipman, J. S., 'The ordering of portfolios in terms of mean and variance', *Review of Economic Studies*, **40**, No. 2, April, 1973.

Dickinson, J. P., and Kyuno, K., 'Corporate valuation: a reconciliation of the Miller–Modigliani and traditional views', *Journal of Business Finance and Accounting*, **4**, No. 2, Summer 1977.

Durand, D., 'Growth stocks and the St. Petersburg paradox', *Journal of Finance*, **12**, September 1957.

Faaland, R., 'An integer programming algorithm for portfolio selection', *Management Science*, **20**, Series B, 1973–74.

Fama E. F., 'Risk, return and equilibrium', *Journal of Political Economy*, **79**, Jan.–Feb., 1971.

Fama, E. F., *Foundations of Finance*, Basic Books, 1976.

Fama, E. F., 'Risk adjusted discount rates and capital budgeting under uncertainty', *Journal of Financial Economics*, **1977** (August).

Fama, E. F., and MacBeth, J. D., 'Risk, return and equilibrium: empirical tests', *Journal of Political Economy*, **71**, May–June 1973.

Hakansson, N. H., 'Multi-period mean–variance analysis: toward a general theory of portfolio choice', *Journal of Finance*, **26**, 1971.

Hirschleifer, J., *Investment, Interest and Capital*, Prentice-Hall, Englewood Cliffs, NJ, 1970.

Hodges, S. D., and Brealey, R. A., 'Using the Sharpe model', *Investment Analysis*, **1970** (September).

Jacob, N. L., 'A limited diversification portfolio selection strategy for the small investor', *Journal of Finance*, **29**, June 1974.

Jen, F., *Criteria in Multi-period Portfolio Decisions*, State University of New York, Working Paper No. 131, 1972.

Jensen, M. C., 'Risk, the pricing of capital assets and the evaluation of investment portfolios', *Journal of Business*, **42**, No. 2, April 1969.

Jensen, M. C. (ed.), *Studies in the Theory of Capital Markets*, Praeger, New York, 1972.

Jones-Lee, M., 'Portfolio adjustments and capital budgeting criteria', *Journal of Business Finance*, No. 2, Autumn 1969.

Joy, O. M., and Porter, R. B., 'Stochastic dominance and mutual fund performance', *Journal of Financial and Quantitative Analysis*, **9**, 1974.

Klevorick, A., 'A note on "The ordering of portfolios in terms of mean and variance"', *Review of Economic Studies*, **40**, No. 2, April 1973.

Lee, S. M., and Lerro, A. J., 'Optimising the portfolio selection of mutual funds', *Journal of Finance*, **28**, December 1973.

Levhari, D., and Levy, H., 'The capital asset pricing model and the investment horizon', *Review of Economics and Statistics*, **1977** (February).

Levhari, D., Paroush, J., and Peleg, B., 'Efficiency analysis for multivariate distributions', *Review of Economic Studies*, **62**, No. 1, January 1975.

Levy, H., and Hanoch, G., 'Relative effectiveness of efficiency criteria for portfolio selection', *Journal of Financial and Quantitative Analysis*, **5**, 1970.

Levy, H., and Sarnat, M., *Investment and Portfolio Analysis*, Wiley, New York, 1972.

Merton, R. C., 'An inter-temporal capital asset pricing model', *Econometrica*, **41** September 1973.

Modigliani, F., and Miller, M. H., 'The cost of capital corporation finance and the theory of investment', *American Economic Review*, **48**, June 1958.

Mossin, J., 'Optimal multiperiod portfolio policies', *Journal of Business*, **41**, April 1968.

Myers, S. C. (ed.), *Modern Developments in Financial Management*, Praeger, New York, 1976.

Myers, S. C., and Turnbull, S. M., 'Capital budgeting and the capital asset pricing model: good news and bad news', *Journal of Finance*, **32**, May 1977.

Paine, N. R., 'A case study in mathematical programming of portfolio selections', *Applied Statistics*, **1**, 1966.

Robichek, A. A., and Myers, S. C., 'Conceptual problems in the use of risk adjusted discount rates', *Journal of Finance*, **21**, December 1966.

Roll, R., 'A critique of the asset pricing theory's tests', *Journal of Financial Economics*, **1977** (March).

Ross, S. A., 'The current status of the capital asset pricing model', *Journal of Finance*, **33**, June 1978.

Samuels, J. M., and Wilkes, F. M., *Management of Company Finance* (3rd edn.), Nelson, London, 1980.

Samuelson, P. A., 'Efficient portfolio selection for Pareto–Levy investments', *Journal of Financial and Quantitative Analysis*, **11**, 1967.

Sarnat, M., 'A note on the prediction of portfolio performance from ex-post data', *Journal of Finance*, **27**, September 1972.

Schilbred, C., 'The market price of risk', *Review of Economic Studies*, **40**, No. 2, April 1973.

Schwab, B., 'Conceptual problems in the use of risk adjusted discount rates with disaggregated cash flows', *Journal of Business Finance and Accounting*, **5**, No. 4, Winter 1978.

Scott, J. H., 'A theory of optimal capital structure', *Bell Journal of Economics*, **7**, No. 1, Spring 1976.

Serraino, W. J., Singhvi, J. S., and Soldofsky, R. M. (eds.), *Frontiers of Financial Management* (2nd edn.), South Western Publishing, 1976.

Sharpe, W. F., 'Capital asset prices: a theory of market equilibrium under conditions of risk', *Journal of Finance*, **19**, September 1964.

Sharpe, W. F., *Portfolio Theory and Capital Markets*, McGraw-Hill, New York, 1970.

Sharpe, W. F., *Investments*, Prentice-Hall, Englewood Cliffs, NJ, 1977.

Smith, K. V., *Portfolio Management*, Holt, 1971.

Stapleton, R. C., 'Portfolio analysis, stock valuation and capital budgeting decision rules for risky projects', *Journal of Finance*, **26**, No. 1, March 1971.

Stevens, C. V. G., 'On Tobin's multiperiod portfolio theorem', *Review of Economic Studies*, **39**, 1972.

Tobin, J., 'Liquidity preference as behaviour towards risk', *Review of Economic Studies*, **25**, 1958.

Tobin, J., 'The theory of portfolio selection', in Hahn, F. H., and Brechling, F. P. R., (eds.), *The Theory of Interest Rates*, Macmillan, London, 1965.

Treynor, J. L., and Black, F., 'How to use security analysis to improve portfolio selection', *Journal of Business*, **45**, January 1973.

White, J. R., 'Unit trusts, homogeneous beliefs and the separation property', *Journal of Business Finance and Accounting*, **8**, No. 1, Spring 1981.

Wilkes, F. M., 'Dividend policy and investment appraisal in imperfect capital markets', *Journal of Business Finance and Accounting*, **4**, No. 2, Summer 1977.

Yaari, M. E., 'Some remarks on measures of risk aversion and on their uses', *Journal of Economic Theory*, **1**, 1969.

Zabel, E., 'Consumer choice, portfolio decisions and transaction costs', *Econometrica*, **44**, 1973.

Ziemba, W. T., Parkan, C., and Brooks-Hill, F. J., 'Calculation of investment portfolios with risk free borrowing and lending', *Management Science*, **21**, 1974.

Ziemba, W. T., and Vickson, R. G., *Stochastic Optimisation Models in Finance*, Academic Press, New York, 1975.

Table 1 Terminal value of 1 at compound interest: $(1+r)^n$

Years (n)	Interest rates (r)							
	1	2	3	4	5	6	7	8
1	1.0100	1.0200	1.0300	1.0400	1.0500	1.0600	1.0700	1.0800
2	1.0201	1.0404	1.0609	1.0816	1.1025	1.1236	1.1449	1.1664
3	1.0303	1.0612	1.0927	1.1249	1.1576	1.1910	1.2250	1.2597
4	1.0406	1.0824	1.1255	1.1699	1.2155	1.2625	1.3108	1.3605
5	1.0510	1.1041	1.1593	1.2167	1.2763	1.3382	1.4026	1.4693
6	1.0615	1.1262	1.1941	1.2653	1.3401	1.4185	1.5007	1.5869
7	1.0721	1.1487	1.2299	1.3159	1.4071	1.5036	1.6058	1.7138
8	1.0829	1.1717	1.2668	1.3686	1.4775	1.5938	1.7182	1.8509
9	1.0937	1.1951	1.3048	1.4233	1.5513	1.6895	1.8385	1.9990
10	1.1046	1.2190	1.3439	1.4802	1.6289	1.7908	1.9672	2.1589
11	1.1157	1.2434	1.3842	1.5395	1.7103	1.8983	2.1049	2.3316
12	1.1268	1.2682	1.4258	1.6010	1.7959	2.0122	2.2522	2.5182
13	1.1381	1.2936	1.4685	1.6651	1.8856	2.1329	2.4098	2.7196
14	1.1495	1.3195	1.5126	1.7317	1.9799	2.2609	2.5785	2.9372
15	1.1610	1.3459	1.5580	1.8009	2.0789	2.3966	2.7590	3.1722
16	1.1726	1.3728	1.6047	1.8730	2.1829	2.5404	2.9522	3.4259
17	1.1843	1.4002	1.6528	1.9479	2.2920	2.6928	3.1588	3.7000
18	1.1961	1.4282	1.7024	2.0258	2.4066	2.8543	3.3799	3.9960
19	1.2081	1.4568	1.7535	2.1068	2.5270	3.0256	3.6165	4.3157
20	1.2202	1.4859	1.8061	2.1911	2.6533	3.2071	3.8697	4.6610
25	1.2824	1.6406	2.0938	2.6658	3.3864	4.2919	5.4274	6.8485

	16	17	18	19	20	21	22	23
1	1.1600	1.1700	1.1800	1.1900	1.2000	1.2100	1.2200	1.2300
2	1.3456	1.3689	1.3924	1.4161	1.4400	1.4641	1.4884	1.5129
3	1.5609	1.6016	1.6430	1.6852	1.7280	1.7716	1.8158	1.8609
4	1.8106	1.8739	1.9388	2.0053	2.0736	2.1436	2.2153	2.2889
5	2.1003	2.1924	2.2878	2.3864	2.4883	2.5937	2.7027	2.8153
6	2.4364	2.5652	2.6996	2.8398	2.9860	3.1384	3.2973	3.4628
7	2.8262	3.0012	3.1855	3.3793	3.5832	3.7975	4.0227	4.2593
8	3.2784	3.5115	3.7589	4.0214	4.2998	4.5950	4.9077	5.2389
9	3.8030	4.1084	4.4355	4.7854	5.1598	5.5599	5.9874	6.4439
10	4.4114	4.8068	5.2338	5.6947	6.1917	6.7275	7.3046	7.9259
11	5.1173	5.6240	6.1759	6.7767	7.4301	8.1403	8.9117	9.7489
12	5.9360	6.5801	7.2876	8.0642	8.9161	9.8497	10.8722	11.9912
13	6.8858	7.6987	8.5994	9.5964	10.6993	11.9182	13.2641	14.7491
14	7.9875	9.0075	10.1472	11.4198	12.8392	14.4210	16.1822	18.1414
15	9.2655	10.5387	11.9737	13.5895	15.4070	17.4494	19.7423	22.3140
16	10.7480	12.3303	14.1290	16.1715	18.4884	21.1138	24.0856	27.4462
17	12.4677	14.4265	16.6722	19.2441	22.1861	25.5477	29.3844	33.7588
18	14.4625	16.8790	19.6733	22.9005	26.6233	30.9127	35.8490	41.5233
19	16.7765	19.7484	23.2144	27.2516	31.9480	37.4043	43.7358	51.0737
20	19.4608	23.1056	27.3930	32.4294	38.3376	45.2593	53.3576	62.8206
25	40.8742	50.6578	62.6686	77.3881	95.3962	117.3909	144.2101	176.8593

9	10	11	12	13	14	15	
1.0900	1.1000	1.1100	1.1200	1.1300	1.1400	1.1500	1
1.1881	1.2100	1.2321	1.2544	1.2769	1.2996	1.3225	2
1.2950	1.3310	1.3676	1.4049	1.4429	1.4815	1.5209	3
1.4116	1.4641	1.5181	1.5735	1.6305	1.6890	1.7490	4
1.5386	1.6105	1.6851	1.7623	1.8424	1.9254	2.0114	5
1.6771	1.7716	1.8704	1.9738	2.0820	2.1950	2.3131	6
1.8280	1.9487	2.0762	2.2107	2.3526	2.5023	2.6600	7
1.9926	2.1436	2.3045	2.4760	2.6584	2.8526	3.0590	8
2.1719	2.3579	2.5580	2.7731	3.0040	3.2519	3.5179	9
2.3674	2.5937	2.8394	3.1058	3.3946	3.7072	4.0456	10
2.5804	2.8531	3.1518	3.4785	3.8359	4.2262	4.6524	11
2.8127	3.1384	3.4985	3.8960	4.3345	4.8179	5.3503	12
3.0658	3.4523	3.8833	4.3635	4.8980	5.4924	6.1528	13
3.3417	3.7975	4.3104	4.8871	5.5348	6.2613	7.0757	14
3.6425	4.1772	4.7846	5.4736	6.2543	7.1379	8.1371	15
3.9703	4.5950	5.3109	6.1304	7.0673	8.1372	9.3576	16
4.3276	5.0545	5.8951	6.8660	7.9861	9.2765	10.7613	17
4.7171	5.5599	6.5436	7.6900	9.0243	10.5752	12.3755	18
5.1417	6.1159	7.2633	8.6128	10.1974	12.0557	14.2318	19
5.6044	6.7275	8.0623	9.6463	11.5231	13.7435	16.3665	20
8.6231	10.8347	13.5855	17.0001	21.2305	26.4619	32.9190	25

24	25	26	27	28	29	30	
1.2400	1.2500	1.2600	1.2700	1.2800	1.2900	1.3000	1
1.5376	1.5625	1.5876	1.6129	1.6384	1.6641	1.6900	2
1.9066	1.9531	2.0004	2.0484	2.0972	2.1467	2.1970	3
2.3642	2.4414	2.5205	2.6014	2.6844	2.7692	2.8561	4
2.9316	3.0518	3.1758	3.3038	3.4360	3.5723	3.7129	5
3.6352	3.8147	4.0015	4.1959	4.3980	4.6083	4.8268	6
4.5077	4.7684	5.0419	5.3288	5.6295	5.9447	6.2749	7
5.5895	5.9605	6.3528	6.7675	7.2058	7.6686	8.1573	8
6.9310	7.4506	8.0045	8.5948	9.2234	9.8925	10.6045	9
8.5944	9.3132	10.0857	10.9153	11.8050	12.7614	13.7858	10
10.6571	11.6415	12.7080	13.8625	15.1116	16.4622	17.9216	11
13.2148	14.5519	16.0120	17.6053	19.3428	21.2362	23.2981	12
16.3863	18.1899	20.1752	22.3588	24.7588	27.3947	30.2875	13
20.3191	22.7374	25.4207	28.3957	31.6913	35.3391	39.3738	14
25.1956	28.4217	32.0301	36.0625	40.5648	45.5875	51.1859	15
31.2426	35.5271	40.3579	45.7994	51.9230	58.8079	66.5417	16
38.7408	44.4089	50.8510	58.1652	66.4614	75.8621	86.5042	17
48.0386	55.5112	64.0722	73.8698	85.0706	97.8622	112.4554	18
59.5679	69.3889	80.7310	93.8147	108.8904	126.2422	146.1920	19
73.8641	86.7362	101.7211	119.1446	139.3797	162.8524	190.0496	20
216.5420	264.6978	323.0454	393.6344	478.9049	581.7585	705.6410	25

Table 2 Present value of 1 at compound interest: $(1+r)^{-n}$

Years	Interest rates (r)							
(n)	1	2	3	4	5	6	7	8
1	0.9901	0.9804	0.9709	0.9615	0.9524	0.9434	0.9346	0.9259
2	0.9803	0.9612	0.9426	0.9246	0.9070	0.8900	0.8734	0.8573
3	0.9706	0.9423	0.9151	0.8890	0.8638	0.8396	0.8163	0.7938
4	0.9610	0.9238	0.8885	0.8548	0.8227	0.7921	0.7629	0.7350
5	0.9515	0.9057	0.8626	0.8219	0.7835	0.7473	0.7130	0.6806
6	0.9420	0.8880	0.8375	0.7903	0.7462	0.7050	0.6663	0.6302
7	0.9327	0.8706	0.8131	0.7599	0.7107	0.6651	0.6227	0.5835
8	0.9235	0.8535	0.7894	0.7307	0.6768	0.6274	0.5820	0.5403
9	0.9143	0.8368	0.7664	0.7026	0.6446	0.5919	0.5439	0.5002
10	0.9053	0.8203	0.7441	0.6756	0.6139	0.5584	0.5083	0.4632
11	0.8963	0.8043	0.7224	0.6496	0.5847	0.5268	0.4751	0.4289
12	0.8874	0.7885	0.7014	0.6246	0.5568	0.4970	0.4440	0.3971
13	0.8787	0.7730	0.6810	0.6006	0.5303	0.4688	0.4150	0.3677
14	0.8700	0.7579	0.6611	0.5775	0.5051	0.4423	0.3878	0.3405
15	0.8613	0.7430	0.6419	0.5553	0.4810	0.4173	0.3624	0.3152
16	0.8528	0.7284	0.6232	0.5339	0.4581	0.3936	0.3387	0.2919
17	0.8444	0.7142	0.6050	0.5134	0.4363	0.3714	0.3166	0.2703
18	0.8360	0.7002	0.5874	0.4936	0.4155	0.3503	0.2959	0.2502
19	0.8277	0.6864	0.5703	0.4746	0.3957	0.3305	0.2765	0.2317
20	0.8195	0.6730	0.5537	0.4564	0.3769	0.3118	0.2584	0.2145
25	0.7795	0.6095	0.4776	0.3751	0.2953	0.2330	0.1842	0.1460
30	0.7419	0.5521	0.4120	0.3083	0.2314	0.1741	0.1314	0.0994
35	0.7059	0.5000	0.3554	0.2534	0.1813	0.1301	0.0937	0.0676
40	0.6717	0.4529	0.3066	0.2083	0.1420	0.0972	0.0668	0.0460
45	0.6391	0.4102	0.2644	0.1712	0.1113	0.0727	0.0476	0.0313
50	0.6080	0.3715	0.2281	0.1407	0.0872	0.0543	0.0339	0.0213

	16	17	18	19	20	21	22	23
1	0.8621	0.8547	0.8475	0.8403	0.8333	0.8264	0.8197	0.8130
2	0.7432	0.7305	0.7182	0.7062	0.6944	0.6830	0.6719	0.6610
3	0.6407	0.6244	0.6086	0.5934	0.5787	0.5645	0.5507	0.5374
4	0.5523	0.5337	0.5158	0.4987	0.4823	0.4665	0.4514	0.4369
5	0.4761	0.4561	0.4371	0.4190	0.4019	0.3855	0.3700	0.3552
6	0.4104	0.3898	0.3704	0.3521	0.3349	0.3186	0.3033	0.2888
7	0.3538	0.3332	0.3139	0.2959	0.2791	0.2633	0.2486	0.2348
8	0.3050	0.2848	0.2660	0.2487	0.2326	0.2176	0.2038	0.1909
9	0.2630	0.2434	0.2255	0.2090	0.1938	0.1799	0.1670	0.1552
10	0.2267	0.2080	0.1911	0.1756	0.1615	0.1486	0.1369	0.1262
11	0.1954	0.1778	0.1619	0.1476	0.1346	0.1228	0.1122	0.1026
12	0.1685	0.1520	0.1372	0.1240	0.1122	0.1015	0.0920	0.0834
13	0.1452	0.1299	0.1163	0.1042	0.0935	0.0839	0.0754	0.0678
14	0.1252	0.1110	0.0985	0.0876	0.0779	0.0693	0.0618	0.0551
15	0.1079	0.0949	0.0835	0.0736	0.0649	0.0573	0.0507	0.0448
16	0.0930	0.0811	0.0708	0.0618	0.0541	0.0474	0.0415	0.0364
17	0.0802	0.0693	0.0600	0.0520	0.0451	0.0391	0.0340	0.0296
18	0.0691	0.0592	0.0508	0.0437	0.0376	0.0323	0.0279	0.0241
19	0.0596	0.0506	0.0431	0.0367	0.0313	0.0267	0.0229	0.0196
20	0.0514	0.0433	0.0365	0.0308	0.0261	0.0221	0.0187	0.0159
25	0.0245	0.0197	0.0160	0.0129	0.0105	0.0085	0.0069	0.0057
30	0.0116	0.0090	0.0070	0.0054	0.0042	0.0033	0.0026	0.0020
35	0.0055	0.0041	0.0030	0.0023	0.0017	0.0013	0.0009	0.0007
40	0.0026	0.0019	0.0013	0.0010	0.0007	0.0005	0.0004	0.0003
45	0.0013	0.0009	0.0006	0.0004	0.0003	0.0002	0.0001	0.0001
50	0.0006	0.0004	0.0003	0.0002	0.0001	0.0001	0.0000	0.0000

9	10	11	12	13	14	15	
0.9174	0.9091	0.9009	0.8929	0.8850	0.8772	0.8696	1
0.8417	0.8264	0.8116	0.7972	0.7831	0.7695	0.7561	2
0.7722	0.7513	0.7312	0.7118	0.6931	0.6750	0.6575	3
0.7084	0.6830	0.6587	0.6355	0.6133	0.5921	0.5718	4
0.6499	0.6209	0.5935	0.5674	0.5428	0.5194	0.4972	5
0.5963	0.5645	0.5346	0.5066	0.4803	0.4556	0.4323	6
0.5470	0.5132	0.4817	0.4523	0.4251	0.3996	0.3759	7
0.5019	0.4665	0.4339	0.4039	0.3762	0.3506	0.3269	8
0.4604	0.4241	0.3909	0.3606	0.3329	0.3075	0.2843	9
0.4224	0.3855	0.3522	0.3220	0.2946	0.2697	0.2472	10
0.3875	0.3505	0.3173	0.2875	0.2607	0.2366	0.2149	11
0.3555	0.3186	0.2858	0.2567	0.2307	0.2076	0.1869	12
0.3262	0.2897	0.2575	0.2292	0.2042	0.1821	0.1625	13
0.2992	0.2633	0.2320	0.2046	0.1807	0.1597	0.1413	14
0.2745	0.2394	0.2090	0.1827	0.1599	0.1401	0.1220	15
0.2519	0.2176	0.1883	0.1631	0.1415	0.1229	0.1069	16
0.2311	0.1978	0.1696	0.1456	0.1252	0.1078	0.0929	17
0.2120	0.1799	0.1528	0.1300	0.1108	0.0946	0.0808	18
0.1945	0.1635	0.1377	0.1161	0.0981	0.0829	0.0703	19
0.1784	0.1486	0.1240	0.1037	0.0868	0.0728	0.0611	20
0.1160	0.0923	0.0736	0.0588	0.0471	0.0378	0.0304	25
0.0754	0.0573	0.0437	0.0334	0.0256	0.0196	0.0151	30
0.0490	0.0356	0.0259	0.0189	0.0139	0.0102	0.0075	35
0.0318	0.0221	0.0154	0.0107	0.0075	0.0053	0.0037	40
0.0207	0.0137	0.0091	0.0061	0.0041	0.0027	0.0019	45
0.0134	0.0085	0.0054	0.0035	0.0022	0.0014	0.0009	50

24	25	26	27	28	29	30	
0.8065	0.8000	0.7937	0.7874	0.7812	0.7752	0.7692	1
0.6504	0.6400	0.6299	0.6200	0.6104	0.6009	0.5917	2
0.5245	0.5120	0.4999	0.4882	0.4768	0.4658	0.4552	3
0.4230	0.4096	0.3968	0.3844	0.3725	0.3611	0.3501	4
0.3411	0.3277	0.3149	0.3027	0.2910	0.2799	0.2693	5
0.2751	0.2621	0.2499	0.2383	0.2274	0.2170	0.2072	6
0.2218	0.2097	0.1983	0.1877	0.1776	0.1682	0.1594	7
0.1789	0.1678	0.1574	0.1478	0.1388	0.1304	0.1226	8
0.1443	0.1342	0.1249	0.1164	0.1084	0.1011	0.0943	9
0.1164	0.1074	0.0992	0.0916	0.0847	0.0784	0.0725	10
0.0938	0.0859	0.0787	0.0721	0.0662	0.0607	0.0558	11
0.0757	0.0687	0.0625	0.0568	0.0517	0.0471	0.0429	12
0.0610	0.0550	0.0496	0.0447	0.0404	0.0365	0.0330	13
0.0492	0.0440	0.0393	0.0352	0.0316	0.0283	0.0254	14
0.0397	0.0352	0.0312	0.0277	0.0247	0.0219	0.0195	15
0.0320	0.0281	0.0248	0.0218	0.0193	0.0170	0.0150	16
0.0258	0.0225	0.0197	0.0172	0.0150	0.0132	0.0116	17
0.0208	0.0180	0.0156	0.0135	0.0118	0.0102	0.0089	18
0.0168	0.0144	0.0124	0.0107	0.0092	0.0079	0.0068	19
0.0135	0.0115	0.0098	0.0084	0.0072	0.0061	0.0053	20
0.0046	0.0038	0.0031	0.0025	0.0021	0.0017	0.0014	25
0.0016	0.0012	0.0010	0.0008	0.0006	0.0005	0.0004	30
0.0005	0.0004	0.0003	0.0002	0.0002	0.0001	0.0001	35
0.0002	0.0001	0.0001	0.0001	0.0001	0.0000	0.0000	40
0.0001	0.0000	0.0000	0.0000	0.0000	0.0000	0.0000	45
0.0000	0.0000	0.0000	0.0000	0.0000	0.0000	0.0000	50

Table 3 Present value of an annuity of 1: $\dfrac{1-(1+r)^{-n}}{r}$

Years	Interest rates (r)							
(n)	1	2	3	4	5	6	7	8
1	0.9901	0.9804	0.9709	0.9615	0.9524	0.9434	0.9346	0.9259
2	1.9704	1.9416	1.9135	1.8861	1.8594	1.8334	1.8080	1.7833
3	2.9410	2.8839	2.8286	2.7751	2.7232	2.6730	2.6243	2.5771
4	3.9020	3.8077	3.7171	3.6299	3.5460	3.4651	3.3872	3.3121
5	4.8534	4.7135	4.5797	4.4518	4.3295	4.2124	4.1002	3.9927
6	5.7995	5.6014	5.4172	5.2421	5.0757	4.9173	4.7665	4.6229
7	6.7282	6.4720	6.2303	6.0021	5.7864	5.5824	5.3893	5.2064
8	7.6517	7.3255	7.0197	6.7327	6.4632	6.2098	5.9713	5.7466
9	8.5660	8.1622	7.7861	7.4353	7.1078	6.8017	6.5152	6.2469
10	9.4713	8.9826	8.5302	8.1109	7.7217	7.3601	7.0236	6.7101
11	10.3676	9.7868	9.2526	8.7605	8.3064	7.8869	7.4987	7.1390
12	11.2551	10.5753	9.9540	9.3851	8.8633	8.3838	7.9427	7.5361
13	12.1337	11.3484	10.6350	9.9856	9.3936	8.8527	8.3577	7.9038
14	13.0037	12.1062	11.2961	10.5631	9.8986	9.2950	8.7455	8.2442
15	13.8651	12.8493	11.9379	11.1184	10.3797	9.7122	9.1079	8.5595
16	14.7179	13.5777	12.5611	11.6523	10.8378	10.1059	9.4466	8.8514
17	15.5623	14.2919	13.1661	12.1657	11.2741	10.4773	9.7632	9.1216
18	16.3983	14.9920	13.7535	12.6593	11.6896	10.8276	10.0591	9.3719
19	17.2260	15.6785	14.3238	13.1339	12.0853	11.1581	10.3356	9.6036
20	18.0456	16.3514	14.8775	13.5903	12.4622	11.4699	10.5940	9.8181
25	22.0232	19.5235	17.4131	15.6221	14.0939	12.7834	11.6536	10.6748
30	25.8077	22.3965	19.6004	17.2920	15.3725	13.7648	12.4090	11.2578
35	29.4086	24.9986	21.4872	18.6646	16.3742	14.4982	12.9477	11.6546
40	32.8347	27.3555	23.1148	19.7928	17.1591	15.0463	13.3317	11.9246
45	36.0945	29.4902	24.5187	20.7200	17.7741	15.4558	13.6055	12.1084
50	39.1961	31.4236	25.7298	21.4822	18.2559	15.7619	13.8007	12.2335

	16	17	18	19	20	21	22	23
1	0.8621	0.8547	0.8475	0.8403	0.8333	0.8264	0.8197	0.8130
2	1.6052	1.5852	1.5656	1.5465	1.5278	1.5095	1.4915	1.4740
3	2.2459	2.2096	2.1743	2.1399	2.1065	2.0739	2.0422	2.0114
4	2.7982	2.7432	2.6901	2.6386	2.5887	2.5404	2.4936	2.4483
5	3.2743	3.1993	3.1272	3.0576	2.9906	2.9260	2.8636	2.8035
6	3.6847	3.5892	3.4976	3.4098	3.3255	3.2446	3.1669	3.0923
7	4.0386	3.9224	3.8115	3.7057	3.6046	3.5079	3.4155	3.3270
8	4.3436	4.2072	4.0776	3.9544	3.8372	3.7256	3.6193	3.5179
9	4.6065	4.4506	4.3030	4.1633	4.0310	3.9054	3.7863	3.6731
10	4.8332	4.6586	4.4941	4.3389	4.1925	4.0541	3.9232	3.7993
11	5.0286	4.8364	4.6560	4.4865	4.3271	4.1769	4.0354	3.9018
12	5.1971	4.9884	4.7932	4.6105	4.4392	4.2784	4.1274	3.9852
13	5.3423	5.1183	4.9095	4.7147	4.5327	4.3624	4.2028	4.0530
14	5.4675	5.2293	5.0081	4.8023	4.6106	4.4317	4.2646	4.1082
15	5.5755	5.3242	5.0916	4.8759	4.6755	4.4890	4.3152	4.1530
16	5.6685	5.4053	5.1624	4.9377	4.7296	4.5364	4.3567	4.1894
17	5.7487	5.4746	5.2223	4.9897	4.7746	4.5755	4.3908	4.2190
18	5.8178	5.5339	5.2732	5.0333	4.8122	4.6079	4.4187	4.2431
19	5.8775	5.5845	5.3162	5.0700	4.8435	4.6346	4.4415	4.2627
20	5.9288	5.6278	5.3527	5.1009	4.8696	4.6567	4.4603	4.2786
25	6.0971	5.7662	5.4669	5.1951	4.9476	4.7213	4.5139	4.3232
30	6.1772	5.8294	5.5168	5.2347	4.9789	4.7463	4.5338	4.3391
35	6.2153	5.8582	5.5386	5.2512	4.9915	4.7559	4.5411	4.3447
40	6.2335	5.8713	5.5482	5.2582	4.9966	4.7596	4.5439	4.3467
45	6.2421	5.8773	5.5523	5.2611	4.9986	4.7610	4.5449	4.3474
50	6.2463	5.8801	5.5541	5.2623	4.9995	4.7616	4.5452	4.3477

9	10	11	12	13	14	15	
0.9174	0.9091	0.9009	0.8929	0.8850	0.8772	0.8696	1
1.7591	1.7355	1.7125	1.6901	1.6681	1.6467	1.6257	2
2.5313	2.4869	2.4437	2.4018	2.3612	2.3216	2.2832	3
3.2397	3.1699	3.1024	3.0373	2.9745	2.9137	2.8550	4
3.8897	3.7908	3.6959	3.6048	3.5172	3.4331	3.3522	5
4.4859	4.3553	4.2305	4.1114	3.9975	3.8887	3.7845	6
5.0330	4.8684	4.7122	4.5638	4.4226	4.2883	4.1604	7
5.5348	5.3349	5.1461	4.9676	4.7988	4.6389	4.4873	8
5.9952	5.7590	5.5370	5.3282	5.1317	4.9464	4.7716	9
6.4177	6.1446	5.8892	5.6502	5.4262	5.2161	5.0188	10
6.8052	6.4951	6.2065	5.9377	5.6869	5.4527	5.2337	11
7.1607	6.8137	6.4924	6.1944	5.9176	5.6603	5.4206	12
7.4869	7.1034	6.7499	6.4235	6.1218	5.8424	5.5831	13
7.7862	7.3667	6.9819	6.6282	6.3025	6.0021	5.7245	14
8.0607	7.6061	7.1909	6.8109	6.4624	6.1422	5.8474	15
8.3126	7.8237	7.3792	6.9740	6.6039	6.2651	5.9542	16
8.5436	8.0216	7.5488	7.1196	6.7291	6.3729	6.0472	17
8.7556	8.2014	7.7016	7.2497	6.8399	6.4674	6.1280	18
8.9501	8.3649	7.8393	7.3658	6.9380	6.5504	6.1982	19
9.1285	8.5136	7.9633	7.4694	7.0248	6.6231	6.2593	20
9.8226	9.0770	8.4217	7.8431	7.3300	6.8729	6.4641	25
10.2737	9.4269	8.6938	8.0552	7.4957	7.0027	6.5660	30
10.5668	9.6442	8.8552	8.1755	7.5856	7.0700	6.6166	35
10.7574	9.7791	8.9511	8.2438	7.6344	7.1050	6.6418	40
10.8812	9.8628	9.0079	8.2825	7.6609	7.1232	6.6543	45
10.9617	9.9148	9.0417	8.3045	7.6752	7.1327	6.6605	50

24	25	26	27	28	29	30	
0.8065	0.8000	0.7937	0.7874	0.7812	0.7752	0.7692	1
1.4568	1.4400	1.4235	1.4074	1.3916	1.3761	1.3600	2
1.9813	1.9520	1.9234	1.8956	1.8684	1.8420	1.8161	3
2.4043	2.3616	2.3202	2.2800	2.2410	2.2031	2.1662	4
2.7454	2.6893	2.6351	2.5827	2.5320	2.4830	2.4356	5
3.0205	2.9514	2.8850	2.8210	2.7594	2.7000	2.6427	6
3.2423	3.1611	3.0833	3.0087	2.9370	2.8682	2.8021	7
3.4212	3.3289	3.2407	3.1564	3.0758	2.9986	2.9247	8
3.5655	3.4631	3.3657	3.2728	3.1842	3.0997	3.0190	9
3.6819	3.5705	3.4648	3.3644	3.2689	3.1781	3.0915	10
3.7757	3.6564	3.5435	3.4365	3.3351	3.2388	3.1473	11
3.8514	3.7251	3.6059	3.4933	3.3868	3.2859	3.1903	12
3.9124	3.7801	3.6555	3.5381	3.4272	3.3224	3.2233	13
3.9616	3.8241	3.6949	3.5733	3.4587	3.3507	3.2487	14
4.0013	3.8593	3.7261	3.6010	3.4834	3.3726	3.2682	15
4.0333	3.8874	3.7509	3.6228	3.5026	3.3896	3.2832	16
4.0591	3.9099	3.7705	3.6400	3.5177	3.4028	3.2948	17
4.0799	3.9279	3.7861	3.6536	3.5294	3.4130	3.3037	18
4.0967	3.9424	3.7985	3.6642	3.5386	3.4210	3.3105	19
4.1103	3.9539	3.8083	3.6726	3.5458	3.4271	3.3158	20
4.1474	3.9849	3.8342	3.6943	3.5640	3.4423	3.3286	25
4.1601	3.9950	3.8424	3.7009	3.5693	3.4466	3.3321	30
4.1644	3.9984	3.8450	3.7028	3.5708	3.4478	3.3330	35
4.1659	3.9995	3.8458	3.7034	3.5712	3.4481	3.3332	40
4.1664	3.9998	3.8460	3.7036	3.5714	3.4482	3.3333	45
4.1666	3.9999	3.8461	3.7037	3.5714	3.4483	3.3333	50

Table 4 Terminal value of an annuity of 1: $\dfrac{(1+r)^{-n}-1}{r}$

Years	Interest rates (r)							
(n)	1	2	3	4	5	6	7	8
1	1.0000	1.0000	1.0000	1.0000	1.0000	1.0000	1.0000	1.0000
2	2.0100	2.0200	2.0300	2.0400	2.0500	2.0600	2.0700	2.0800
3	3.0301	3.0604	3.0909	3.1216	3.1525	3.1836	3.2149	3.2464
4	4.0604	4.1216	4.1836	4.2464	4.3101	4.3746	4.4399	4.5061
5	5.1010	5.2040	5.3091	5.4163	5.5256	5.6371	5.7507	5.8666
6	6.1520	6.3081	6.4684	6.6330	6.8019	6.9753	7.1533	7.3359
7	7.2135	7.4343	7.6625	7.8983	8.1420	8.3938	8.6540	8.9228
8	8.2857	8.5830	8.8923	9.2142	9.5491	9.8975	10.2598	10.6366
9	9.3685	9.7546	10.1591	10.5828	11.0266	11.4913	11.9780	12.4876
10	10.4622	10.9497	11.4639	12.0061	12.5779	13.1808	13.8164	14.4866
11	11.5668	12.1687	12.8078	13.4864	14.2068	14.9716	15.7836	16.6455
12	12.6825	13.4121	14.1920	15.0258	15.9171	16.8699	17.8885	18.9771
13	13.8093	14.6803	15.6178	16.6268	17.7130	18.8821	20.1406	21.4953
14	14.9474	15.9739	17.0863	18.2919	19.5986	21.0151	22.5505	24.2149
15	16.0969	17.2934	18.5989	20.0236	21.5786	23.2760	25.1290	27.1521
16	17.2579	18.6393	20.1569	21.8245	23.6575	25.6725	27.8881	30.3243
17	18.4304	20.0121	21.7616	23.6975	25.8404	28.2129	30.8402	33.7502
18	19.6147	21.4123	23.4144	25.6454	28.1324	30.9057	33.9990	37.4502
19	20.8109	22.8406	25.1169	27.6712	30.5390	33.7600	37.3790	41.4463
20	22.0190	24.2974	26.8704	29.7781	33.0660	36.7856	40.9955	45.7620
25	28.2432	32.0303	36.4593	41.6459	47.7271	54.8645	63.2490	73.1059

	16	17	18	19	20	21	22	23
1	1.0000	1.0000	1.0000	1.0000	1.0000	1.0000	1.0000	1.0000
2	2.1600	2.1700	2.1800	2.1900	2.2000	2.2100	2.2200	2.2300
3	3.5056	3.5389	3.5724	3.6061	3.6400	3.6741	3.7084	3.7429
4	5.0665	5.1405	5.2154	5.2913	5.3680	5.4457	5.5242	5.6038
5	6.8771	7.0144	7.1542	7.2966	7.4416	7.5892	7.7396	7.8926
6	8.9775	9.2068	9.4420	9.6830	9.9299	10.1830	10.4423	10.7079
7	11.4139	11.7720	12.1415	12.5227	12.9159	13.3214	13.7396	14.1708
8	14.2401	14.7733	15.3270	15.9020	16.4991	17.1189	17.7623	18.4300
9	17.5185	18.2847	19.0859	19.9234	20.7989	21.7139	22.6700	23.6690
10	21.3215	22.3931	23.5213	24.7089	25.9587	27.2738	28.6574	30.1128
11	25.7329	27.1999	28.7551	30.4035	32.1504	34.0013	35.9620	38.0388
12	30.8502	32.8239	34.9311	37.1802	39.5805	42.1416	44.8737	47.7877
13	36.7862	39.4040	42.2187	45.2445	48.4966	51.9913	55.7459	59.7788
14	43.6720	47.1027	50.8180	54.8409	59.1959	63.9095	69.0100	74.5280
15	51.6595	56.1101	60.9653	66.2607	72.0351	78.3305	85.1922	92.6694
16	60.9250	66.6488	72.9390	79.8502	87.4421	95.7799	104.9345	114.9834
17	71.6730	78.9792	87.0680	96.0218	105.9306	116.8937	129.0201	142.4295
18	84.1407	93.4056	103.7403	115.2659	128.1167	142.4413	158.4045	176.1883
19	98.6032	110.2846	123.4135	138.1664	154.7400	173.3540	194.2535	217.7116
20	115.3797	130.0329	146.6280	165.4180	186.6880	210.7584	237.9893	268.7853
25	249.2140	292.1049	342.6035	402.0425	471.9811	554.2422	650.9551	764.6054

9	10	11	12	13	14	15	
1.0000	1.0000	1.0000	1.0000	1.0000	1.0000	1.0000	1
2.0900	2.1000	2.1100	2.1200	2.1300	2.1400	2.1500	2
3.2781	3.3100	3.3421	3.3744	3.4069	3.4396	3.4725	3
4.5731	4.6410	4.7097	4.7793	4.8498	4.9211	4.9934	4
5.9847	6.1051	6.2278	6.3528	6.4803	6.6101	6.7424	5
7.5233	7.7156	7.9129	8.1152	8.3227	8.5355	8.7537	6
9.2004	9.4872	9.7833	10.0890	10.4047	10.7305	11.0668	7
11.0285	11.4359	11.8594	12.2997	12.7573	13.2328	13.7268	8
13.0210	13.5795	14.1640	14.7757	15.4157	16.0853	16.7858	9
15.1929	15.9374	16.7220	17.5487	18.4197	19.3373	20.3037	10
17.5603	18.5312	19.5614	20.6546	21.8143	23.0445	24.3493	11
20.1407	21.3843	22.7132	24.1331	25.6502	27.2707	29.0017	12
22.9534	24.5227	26.2116	28.0291	29.9847	32.0887	34.3519	13
26.0192	27.9750	30.0949	32.3926	34.8827	37.5811	40.5047	14
29.3609	31.7725	34.4054	37.2797	40.4175	43.8424	47.5804	15
33.0034	35.9497	39.1899	42.7533	46.6717	50.9804	55.7175	16
36.9737	40.5447	44.5008	48.8837	53.7391	59.1176	65.0751	17
41.3013	45.5992	50.3959	55.7497	61.7251	68.3941	75.8364	18
46.0185	51.1591	56.9395	63.4397	70.7494	78.9692	88.2118	19
51.1601	57.2750	64.2028	72.0524	80.9468	91.0249	102.4436	20
84.7009	98.3471	114.4133	133.3339	155.6196	181.8708	212.7930	25

24	25	26	27	28	29	30	
1.0000	1.0000	1.0000	1.0000	1.0000	1.0000	1.0000	1
2.2400	2.2500	2.2600	2.2700	2.2800	2.2900	2.3000	2
3.7776	3.8125	3.8476	3.8829	3.9184	3.9541	3.9900	3
5.6842	5.7656	5.8480	5.9313	6.0156	6.1008	6.1870	4
8.0484	8.2070	8.3684	8.5327	8.6999	8.8700	9.0431	5
10.9801	11.2588	11.5442	11.8366	12.1359	12.4423	12.7560	6
14.6153	15.0735	15.5458	16.0324	16.5339	17.0506	17.5828	7
19.1229	19.8419	20.5876	21.3612	22.1634	22.9953	23.8577	8
24.7125	25.8023	26.9404	28.1287	29.3692	30.6639	32.0150	9
31.6434	33.2529	34.9449	36.7235	38.5926	40.5564	42.6195	10
40.2379	42.5001	45.0306	47.6388	50.3985	53.3178	56.4053	11
50.8950	54.2077	57.7386	61.5013	65.5100	69.7800	74.3270	12
64.1097	68.7596	73.7506	79.1066	84.8529	91.0161	97.6250	13
80.4961	86.9495	93.9258	101.4654	109.6117	118.4108	127.9125	14
100.8151	109.6868	119.3465	129.8611	141.3029	153.7500	167.2863	15
126.0108	138.1085	151.3766	165.9236	181.8677	199.3374	218.4722	16
157.2534	173.6357	191.7345	211.7230	233.7907	258.1453	285.0139	17
195.9942	218.0446	242.5855	269.8882	300.2521	334.0074	371.5180	18
244.0328	273.5558	306.6577	343.7580	385.3227	431.8696	483.9734	19
303.6006	342.9447	387.3887	437.5726	494.2131	558.1118	630.1655	20
898.0916	1054.7912	1238.6363	1454.2014	1706.8031	2002.6156	2348.8033	25

Table 5 Sinking Fund: $\dfrac{r}{(1+r)^n-1}$

Years	Interest rates(r)							
(n)	0.01	0.02	0.03	0.04	0.05	0.06	0.07	0.08
1	1.0000	1.0000	1.0000	1.0000	1.0000	1.0000	1.0000	1.0000
2	0.4975	0.4950	0.4926	0.4902	0.4878	0.4854	0.4831	0.4808
3	0.3300	0.3268	0.3235	0.3203	0.3172	0.3141	0.3111	0.3080
4	0.2463	0.2426	0.2390	0.2355	0.2320	0.2286	0.2252	0.2219
5	0.1960	0.1922	0.1884	0.1846	0.1810	0.1774	0.1739	0.1705
6	0.1625	0.1585	0.1546	0.1508	0.1470	0.1434	0.1398	0.1363
7	0.1386	0.1345	0.1305	0.1266	0.1228	0.1191	0.1156	0.1121
8	0.1207	0.1165	0.1125	0.1085	0.1047	0.1010	0.0975	0.0940
9	0.1067	0.1025	0.0984	0.0945	0.0907	0.0870	0.0835	0.0801
10	0.0956	0.0913	0.0872	0.0833	0.0795	0.0759	0.0724	0.0690
11	0.0865	0.0822	0.0781	0.0741	0.0704	0.0668	0.0634	0.0601
12	0.0788	0.0746	0.0705	0.0666	0.0628	0.0593	0.0559	0.0527
13	0.0724	0.0681	0.0640	0.0601	0.0565	0.0530	0.0497	0.0465
14	0.0669	0.0626	0.0585	0.0547	0.0510	0.0476	0.0443	0.0413
15	0.0621	0.0578	0.0538	0.0499	0.0463	0.0430	0.0398	0.0368
16	0.0579	0.0537	0.0496	0.0458	0.0423	0.0390	0.0359	0.0330
17	0.0543	0.0500	0.0460	0.0422	0.0387	0.0354	0.0324	0.0296
18	0.0510	0.0467	0.0427	0.0390	0.0355	0.0324	0.0294	0.0267
19	0.0481	0.0438	0.0398	0.0361	0.0327	0.0296	0.0268	0.0241
20	0.0454	0.0412	0.0372	0.0336	0.0302	0.0272	0.0244	0.0219
21	0.0430	0.0388	0.0349	0.0313	0.0280	0.0250	0.0223	0.0198
22	0.0409	0.0366	0.0327	0.0292	0.0260	0.0230	0.0204	0.0180
23	0.0389	0.0347	0.0308	0.0273	0.0241	0.0213	0.0187	0.0164
24	0.0371	0.0329	0.0290	0.0256	0.0225	0.0197	0.0172	0.0150
25	0.0354	0.0312	0.0274	0.0240	0.0210	0.0182	0.0158	0.0137

	0.16	0.17	0.18	0.19	0.20	0.21	0.22	0.23
1	1.0000	1.0000	1.0000	1.0000	1.0000	1.0000	1.0000	1.0000
2	0.4630	0.4608	0.4587	0.4566	0.4545	0.4525	0.4505	0.4484
3	0.2853	0.2826	0.2799	0.2773	0.2747	0.2722	0.2697	0.2672
4	0.1974	0.1945	0.1917	0.1890	0.1863	0.1836	0.1810	0.1785
5	0.1454	0.1426	0.1398	0.1371	0.1344	0.1318	0.1292	0.1267
6	0.1114	0.1086	0.1059	0.1033	0.1007	0.0982	0.0958	0.0934
7	0.0876	0.0849	0.0824	0.0799	0.0774	0.0751	0.0728	0.0706
8	0.0702	0.0677	0.0652	0.0629	0.0606	0.0584	0.0563	0.0543
9	0.0571	0.0547	0.0524	0.0502	0.0481	0.0461	0.0441	0.0422
10	0.0469	0.0447	0.0425	0.0405	0.0385	0.0367	0.0349	0.0332
11	0.0389	0.0368	0.0348	0.0329	0.0311	0.0294	0.0278	0.0263
12	0.0324	0.0305	0.0286	0.0269	0.0253	0.0237	0.0223	0.0209
13	0.0272	0.0254	0.0237	0.0221	0.0206	0.0192	0.0179	0.0167
14	0.0229	0.0212	0.0197	0.0182	0.0169	0.0156	0.0145	0.0134
15	0.0194	0.0178	0.0164	0.0151	0.0139	0.0128	0.0117	0.0108
16	0.0164	0.0150	0.0137	0.0125	0.0114	0.0104	0.0095	0.0087
17	0.0140	0.0127	0.0115	0.0104	0.0094	0.0086	0.0078	0.0070
18	0.0119	0.0107	0.0096	0.0087	0.0078	0.0070	0.0063	0.0057
19	0.0101	0.0091	0.0081	0.0072	0.0065	0.0058	0.0051	0.0046
20	0.0087	0.0077	0.0068	0.0060	0.0054	0.0047	0.0042	0.0037
21	0.0074	0.0065	0.0057	0.0051	0.0044	0.0039	0.0034	0.0030
22	0.0064	0.0056	0.0048	0.0042	0.0037	0.0032	0.0028	0.0024
23	0.0054	0.0047	0.0041	0.0035	0.0031	0.0027	0.0023	0.0020
24	0.0047	0.0040	0.0035	0.0030	0.0025	0.0022	0.0019	0.0016
25	0.0040	0.0034	0.0029	0.0025	0.0021	0.0018	0.0015	0.0013

0.09	0.10	0.11	0.12	0.13	0.14	0.15	N
1.0000	1.0000	1.0000	1.0000	1.0000	1.0000	1.0000	1
0.4785	0.4762	0.4739	0.4717	0.4695	0.4673	0.4651	2
0.3051	0.3021	0.2992	0.2963	0.2935	0.2907	0.2880	3
0.2187	0.2155	0.2123	0.2092	0.2062	0.2032	0.2003	4
0.1671	0.1638	0.1606	0.1574	0.1543	0.1513	0.1483	5
0.1329	0.1296	0.1264	0.1232	0.1202	0.1172	0.1142	6
0.1087	0.1054	0.1022	0.0991	0.0961	0.0932	0.0904	7
0.0907	0.0874	0.0843	0.0813	0.0784	0.0756	0.0729	8
0.0768	0.0736	0.0706	0.0677	0.0649	0.0622	0.0596	9
0.0658	0.0627	0.0598	0.0570	0.0543	0.0517	0.0403	10
0.0569	0.0540	0.0511	0.0484	0.0458	0.0434	0.0411	11
0.0497	0.0468	0.0440	0.0414	0.0390	0.0367	0.0345	12
0.0436	0.0408	0.0382	0.0357	0.0334	0.0312	0.0291	13
0.0384	0.0357	0.0332	0.0309	0.0287	0.0266	0.0247	14
0.0341	0.0315	0.0291	0.0268	0.0247	0.0228	0.0210	15
0.0303	0.0278	0.0255	0.0234	0.0214	0.0196	0.0179	16
0.0270	0.0247	0.0225	0.0205	0.0186	0.0169	0.0154	17
0.0242	0.0219	0.0198	0.0179	0.0162	0.0146	0.0132	18
0.0217	0.0195	0.0176	0.0158	0.0141	0.0127	0.0113	19
0.0195	0.0175	0.0156	0.0139	0.0124	0.0110	0.0098	20
0.0176	0.0156	0.0138	0.0122	0.0108	0.0095	0.0084	21
0.0159	0.0140	0.0123	0.0108	0.0095	0.0083	0.0073	22
0.0144	0.0126	0.0110	0.0096	0.0083	0.0072	0.0063	23
0.0130	0.0113	0.0098	0.0085	0.0073	0.0063	0.0054	24
0.0118	0.0102	0.0087	0.0075	0.0064	0.0055	0.0047	25

0.24	0.25	0.26	0.27	0.28	0.19	0.30	
1.0000	1.0000	1.0000	1.0000	1.0000	1.0000	1.0000	1
0.4464	0.4444	0.4425	0.4405	0.4386	0.4367	0.4348	2
0.2647	0.2623	0.2599	0.2575	0.2552	0.2529	0.2506	3
0.1759	0.1734	0.1710	0.1686	0.1662	0.1639	0.1616	4
0.1242	0.1218	0.1195	0.1172	0.1149	0.1127	0.1106	5
0.0911	0.0888	0.0866	0.0845	0.0824	0.0804	0.0784	6
0.0684	0.0663	0.0643	0.0624	0.0605	0.0586	0.0569	7
0.0523	0.0504	0.0486	0.0468	0.0451	0.0435	0.0419	8
0.0405	0.0388	0.0371	0.0356	0.0340	0.0326	0.0312	9
0.0316	0.0301	0.0286	0.0272	0.0259	0.0247	0.0235	10
0.0249	0.0235	0.0222	0.0210	0.0198	0.0188	0.0177	11
0.0196	0.0184	0.0173	0.0163	0.0153	0.0143	0.0135	12
0.0156	0.0145	0.0136	0.0126	0.0118	0.0110	0.0102	13
0.0124	0.0115	0.0106	0.0099	0.0091	0.0084	0.0078	14
0.0099	0.0091	0.0084	0.0077	0.0071	0.0065	0.0060	15
0.0079	0.0072	0.0066	0.0060	0.0055	0.0050	0.0046	16
0.0064	0.0058	0.0052	0.0047	0.0043	0.0039	0.0035	17
0.0051	0.0046	0.0041	0.0037	0.0033	0.0030	0.0027	18
0.0041	0.0037	0.0033	0.0029	0.0026	0.0023	0.0021	19
0.0033	0.0029	0.0026	0.0023	0.0020	0.0018	0.0016	20
0.0026	0.0023	0.0020	0.0018	0.0016	0.0014	0.0012	21
0.0021	0.0019	0.0016	0.0014	0.0012	0.0011	0.0009	22
0.0017	0.0015	0.0013	0.0011	0.0010	0.0008	0.0007	23
0.0014	0.0012	0.0010	0.0009	0.0008	0.0006	0.0006	24
0.0011	0.0009	0.0008	0.0007	0.0006	0.0005	0.0004	25

Table 6 Annual equivalent annuity $\dfrac{r}{1-(1+r)^{-n}}$

Years	Interest rates							
(n)	0.01	0.02	0.03	0.04	0.05	0.06	0.07	0.08
1	1.0100	1.0200	1.0300	1.0400	1.0500	1.0600	1.0700	1.0800
2	0.5075	0.5150	0.5226	0.5302	0.5378	0.5454	0.5531	0.5608
3	0.3400	0.3468	0.3535	0.3603	0.3672	0.3741	0.3811	0.3880
4	0.2563	0.2626	0.2690	0.2755	0.2820	0.2886	0.2952	0.3019
5	0.2060	0.2122	0.2184	0.2246	0.2310	0.2374	0.2439	0.2505
6	0.1725	0.1785	0.1846	0.1908	0.1970	0.2034	0.2098	0.2163
7	0.1486	0.1545	0.1605	0.1666	0.1728	0.1791	0.1856	0.1921
8	0.1307	0.1365	0.1425	0.1485	0.1547	0.1610	0.1675	0.1740
9	0.1167	0.1225	0.1284	0.1345	0.1407	0.1470	0.1535	0.1601
10	0.1056	0.1113	0.1172	0.1233	0.1295	0.1359	0.1424	0.1490
11	0.0965	0.1022	0.1081	0.1141	0.1204	0.1268	0.1334	0.1401
12	0.0888	0.0946	0.1005	0.1066	0.1128	0.1193	0.1259	0.1327
13	0.0824	0.0881	0.0940	0.1001	0.1065	0.1130	0.1197	0.1265
14	0.0769	0.0826	0.0885	0.0947	0.1010	0.1076	0.1143	0.1213
15	0.0721	0.0778	0.0838	0.0899	0.0963	0.1030	0.1098	0.1168
16	0.0679	0.0737	0.0796	0.0858	0.0923	0.0990	0.1059	0.1130
17	0.0643	0.0700	0.0760	0.0822	0.0887	0.0954	0.1024	0.1096
18	0.0610	0.0667	0.0727	0.0790	0.0855	0.0924	0.0994	0.1067
19	0.0581	0.0638	0.0698	0.0761	0.0827	0.0896	0.0968	0.1041
20	0.0554	0.0612	0.0672	0.0736	0.0802	0.0872	0.0944	0.1019
21	0.0530	0.0588	0.0649	0.0713	0.0780	0.0850	0.0923	0.0998
22	0.0509	0.0566	0.0627	0.0692	0.0760	0.0830	0.0904	0.0980
23	0.0489	0.0547	0.0608	0.0673	0.0741	0.0813	0.0887	0.0964
24	0.0471	0.0529	0.0590	0.0656	0.0725	0.0797	0.0872	0.0950
25	0.0454	0.0512	0.0574	0.0640	0.0710	0.0782	0.0858	0.0937

	0.16	0.17	0.18	0.19	0.20	0.21	0.22	0.23
1	1.1600	1.1700	1.1800	1.1900	1.2000	1.2100	1.2200	1.2300
2	0.6230	0.6308	0.6387	0.6466	0.6545	0.6625	0.6705	0.6784
3	0.4453	0.4526	0.4599	0.4673	0.4747	0.4822	0.4897	0.4972
4	0.3574	0.3645	0.3717	0.3790	0.3863	0.3936	0.4010	0.4085
5	0.3054	0.3126	0.3198	0.3271	0.3344	0.3418	0.3492	0.3567
6	0.2714	0.2786	0.2859	0.2933	0.3007	0.3082	0.3158	0.3234
7	0.2476	0.2549	0.2624	0.2699	0.2774	0.2851	0.2928	0.3006
8	0.2302	0.2377	0.2452	0.2529	0.2606	0.2684	0.2763	0.2843
9	0.2171	0.2247	0.2324	0.2402	0.2481	0.2561	0.2641	0.2722
10	0.2069	0.2147	0.2225	0.2305	0.2385	0.2467	0.2549	0.2632
11	0.1989	0.2068	0.2148	0.2229	0.2311	0.2394	0.2478	0.2563
12	0.1924	0.2005	0.2086	0.2169	0.2253	0.2337	0.2423	0.2509
13	0.1872	0.1954	0.2037	0.2121	0.2206	0.2292	0.2379	0.2467
14	0.1829	0.1912	0.1997	0.2082	0.2169	0.2256	0.2345	0.2434
15	0.1794	0.1878	0.1964	0.2051	0.2139	0.2228	0.2317	0.2408
16	0.1764	0.1850	0.1937	0.2025	0.2114	0.2204	0.2295	0.2387
17	0.1740	0.1827	0.1915	0.2004	0.2094	0.2186	0.2278	0.2370
18	0.1719	0.1807	0.1896	0.1987	0.2078	0.2170	0.2263	0.2357
19	0.1701	0.1791	0.1881	0.1972	0.2065	0.2158	0.2251	0.2346
20	0.1687	0.1777	0.1868	0.1960	0.2054	0.2147	0.2242	0.2337
21	0.1674	0.1765	0.1857	0.1951	0.2044	0.2139	0.2234	0.2330
22	0.1664	0.1756	0.1848	0.1942	0.2037	0.2132	0.2228	0.2324
23	0.1654	0.1747	0.1841	0.1935	0.2031	0.2127	0.2223	0.2320
24	0.1647	0.1740	0.1835	0.1930	0.2025	0.2122	0.2219	0.2316
25	0.1640	0.1734	0.1829	0.1925	0.2021	0.2118	0.2215	0.2313

0.09	0.10	0.11	0.12	0.13	0.14	0.15	
1.0900	1.1000	1.1100	1.1200	1.1300	1.1400	1.1500	1
0.5685	0.5762	0.5839	0.5917	0.5995	0.6073	0.6151	2
0.3951	0.4021	0.4092	0.4163	0.4235	0.4307	0.4380	3
0.3087	0.3155	0.3223	0.3292	0.3362	0.3432	0.3503	4
0.2571	0.2638	0.2706	0.2774	0.2843	0.2913	0.2983	5
0.2229	0.2296	0.2364	0.2432	0.2502	0.2572	0.2642	6
0.1987	0.2054	0.2122	0.2191	0.2261	0.2332	0.2404	7
0.1807	0.1874	0.1943	0.2013	0.2084	0.2156	0.2229	8
0.1668	0.1736	0.1806	0.1877	0.1949	0.2022	0.2096	9
0.1558	0.1627	0.1698	0.1770	0.1843	0.1917	0.1993	10
0.1469	0.1540	0.1611	0.1684	0.1758	0.1834	0.1911	11
0.1397	0.1468	0.1540	0.1614	0.1690	0.1767	0.1845	12
0.1336	0.1408	0.1482	0.1557	0.1634	0.1712	0.1791	13
0.1284	0.1357	0.1432	0.1509	0.1587	0.1666	0.1747	14
0.1241	0.1315	0.1391	0.1468	0.1547	0.1628	0.1710	15
0.1203	0.1278	0.1355	0.1434	0.1514	0.1596	0.1679	16
0.1170	0.1247	0.1325	0.1405	0.1486	0.1569	0.1654	17
0.1142	0.1219	0.1298	0.1379	0.1462	0.1546	0.1632	18
0.1117	0.1195	0.1276	0.1358	0.1441	0.1527	0.1613	19
0.1095	0.1175	0.1256	0.1339	0.1424	0.1510	0.1598	20
0.1076	0.1156	0.1238	0.1322	0.1408	0.1495	0.1584	21
0.1059	0.1140	0.1223	0.1308	0.1395	0.1483	0.1573	22
0.1044	0.1126	0.1210	0.1296	0.1383	0.1472	0.1563	23
0.1030	0.1113	0.1198	0.1285	0.1373	0.1463	0.1554	24
0.1018	0.1102	0.1187	0.1275	0.1364	0.1455	0.1547	25

0.24	0.25	0.26	0.27	0.28	0.29	0.30	
1.2400	1.2500	1.2600	1.2700	1.2800	1.2900	1.3000	1
0.6864	0.6944	0.7025	0.7105	0.7185	0.7267	0.7348	2
0.5047	0.5123	0.5199	0.5275	0.5352	0.5429	0.5506	3
0.4159	0.4234	0.4310	0.4386	0.4462	0.4539	0.4616	4
0.3642	0.3718	0.3795	0.3872	0.3949	0.4027	0.4106	5
0.3311	0.3388	0.3466	0.3545	0.3624	0.3704	0.3784	6
0.3084	0.3163	0.3243	0.3324	0.3405	0.3486	0.3569	7
0.2923	0.3004	0.3086	0.3168	0.3251	0.3335	0.3312	8
0.2805	0.2888	0.2971	0.3056	0.3140	0.3226	0.3419	9
0.2716	0.2801	0.2886	0.2972	0.3059	0.3147	0.3235	10
0.2649	0.2736	0.2822	0.2910	0.2998	0.3088	0.3177	11
0.2596	0.2684	0.2773	0.2863	0.2953	0.3043	0.3135	12
0.2556	0.2645	0.2736	0.2826	0.2918	0.3010	0.3102	13
0.2524	0.2615	0.2706	0.2799	0.2891	0.2984	0.3078	14
0.2499	0.2591	0.2684	0.2777	0.2871	0.2965	0.3060	15
0.2479	0.2572	0.2666	0.2760	0.2855	0.2950	0.3046	16
0.2464	0.2558	0.2652	0.2747	0.2843	0.2939	0.3035	17
0.2451	0.2546	0.2641	0.2737	0.2833	0.2930	0.3027	18
0.2441	0.2537	0.2633	0.2729	0.2826	0.2923	0.3021	19
0.2433	0.2529	0.2626	0.2723	0.2820	0.2918	0.3016	20
0.2426	0.2523	0.2620	0.2718	0.2816	0.2914	0.3012	21
0.2421	0.2519	0.2616	0.2714	0.2812	0.2911	0.3009	22
0.2417	0.2515	0.2613	0.2711	0.2810	0.2908	0.3007	23
0.2414	0.2512	0.2610	0.2709	0.2808	0.2906	0.3006	24
0.2411	0.2509	0.2608	0.2707	0.2806	0.2905	0.3004	25

Table 7 Area under the standard normal curve up to z standard units above the mean:

$$\Phi(z) = \frac{1}{\sqrt{2\Pi}} \int_{-\infty}^{z} e^{\frac{-t^2}{2}} \, dt$$

z	0.00	0.01	0.02	0.03	0.04	0.05	0.06	0.07	0.08	0.09
0.0	.5000	.5040	.5080	.5120	.5160	.5199	.5239	.5279	.5319	.5359
0.1	.5398	.5438	.5478	.5517	.5557	.5696	.5636	.5675	.5714	.5753
0.2	.5793	.5832	.5871	.5910	.5948	.5987	.6026	.6064	.6103	.6141
0.3	.6179	.6217	.6255	.6293	.6331	.6368	.6406	.6443	.6480	.6517
0.4	.6554	.6591	.6628	.6664	.6700	.6736	.6772	.6808	.6844	.6879
0.5	.6915	.6950	.6985	.7019	.7054	.7088	.7123	.7157	.7190	.7224
0.6	.7257	.7291	.7324	.7357	.7389	.7422	.7454	.7486	.7517	.7549
0.7	.7580	.7611	.7642	.7673	.7704	.7734	.7764	.7794	.7823	.7852
0.8	.7881	.7910	.7939	.7967	.7995	.8023	.8051	.8078	.8106	.8133
0.9	.8159	.8186	.8212	.8238	.8264	.8289	.8315	.8340	.8365	.8389
1.0	.8413	.8438	.8461	.8485	.8508	.8531	.8554	.8577	.8599	.8621
1.1	.8643	.8665	.8686	.8708	.8729	.8749	.8770	.8790	.8810	.8830
1.2	.8849	.8869	.8888	.8907	.8925	.8944	.8962	.8980	.8997	.9015
1.3	.9032	.9049	.9066	.9082	.9099	.9115	.9131	.9147	.9162	.9177
1.4	.9192	.9207	.9222	.9236	.9251	.9265	.9279	.9292	.9306	.9319
1.5	.9332	.9345	.9357	.9370	.9382	.9394	.9406	.9418	.9429	.9411
1.6	.9452	.9463	.9474	.9484	.9495	.9505	.9515	.9525	.9535	.9545
1.7	.9554	.9564	.9573	.9582	.9591	.9599	.9608	.9616	.9625	.9633
1.8	.9641	.9649	.9656	.9664	.9671	.9678	.9686	.9693	.9699	.9706
1.9	.9713	.9719	.9726	.9732	.9738	.9744	.9750	.9756	.9761	.9767
2.0	.9772	.9778	.9783	.9788	.9793	.9798	.9803	.9808	.9812	.9817
2.1	.9821	.9826	.9830	.9834	.9838	.9842	.9846	.9850	.9854	.9857
2.2	.9861	.9864	.9868	.9871	.9875	.9878	.9881	.9884	.9887	.9890
2.3	.9893	.9896	.9898	.9901	.9904	.9906	.9909	.9911	.9913	.9916
2.4	.9918	.9920	.9922	.9925	.9927	.9929	.9931	.9932	.9934	.9936
2.5	.9938	.9940	.9941	.9943	.9945	.9946	.9948	.9949	.9951	.9952
2.6	.9953	.9955	.9956	.9957	.9959	.9960	.9961	.9962	.9963	.9964
2.7	.9965	.9966	.9967	.9968	.9969	.9970	.9971	.9972	.9973	.9974
2.8	.9974	.9975	.9976	.9977	.9977	.9978	.9979	.9979	.9980	.9981
2.9	.9981	.9982	.9982	.9983	.9984	.9984	.9985	.9985	.9986	.9986
3.0	.9987	.9987	.9987	.9988	.9988	.9989	.9989	.9989	.9990	.9990
3.1	.9990	.9991	.9991	.9991	.9992	.9992	.9992	.9992	.9993	.9993
3.2	.9993	.9993	.9994	.9994	.9994	.9994	.9994	.9995	.9995	.9995
3.3	.9995	.9995	.9995	.9996	.9996	.9996	.9996	.9996	.9996	.9997
3.4	.9997	.9997	.9997	.9997	.9997	.9997	.9997	.9997	.9997	.9998
3.5	.9998	.9998	.9998	.9998	.9998	.9998	.9998	.9998	.9998	.9998
3.6	.9998	.9998	.9999	.9999	.9999	.9999	.9999	.9999	.9999	.9999

Index

405